Fundamentals of Arts Management

EDITORS
PAM KORZA AND MAREN BROWN
WITH CRAIG DREESZEN, PH.D.

College of Humanities and Fine Arts
Arts Extension Service

Fundamentals of Arts Management

Fifth Edition

Arts Extension Service, University of Massachusetts, Amherst

Book design by Tekla McInerney

Library of Congress Cataloging-in-Publication Data
Library of Congress Catalog Card No. 2007921579

ISBN 9780945464143

First published in 1987 as *Fundamentals of Local Arts Management*

Table of Contents

Preface

The fifth edition of *Fundamentals of Arts Management* updates and expands what has become a primary and trusted reference book for arts managers and students of arts administration, as well as cultural programmers in nonarts community organizations. Anchoring the book is a set of tried and true chapters providing principles and best practices for managing community arts organizations and presenting and promoting arts programs. Framing these chapters, respected leaders in the community arts field offer historical and contemporary context regarding the role of the arts in community, as well as insights about arts education and cultural access—two important dimensions of local arts agencies' work. Four new chapters cover fundamentals of personnel management, writing successful funding proposals, advocating effectively for the arts, and providing context and practical approaches to maximizing the arts' role in the economic development of communities.

As *Fundamentals of Arts Management* expands, we have expanded the print format to include online companions to several chapters. An online companion includes some combination of narrative text that offers deeper exploration of subject matter; worksheets and other practical tools that can be downloaded and used or adapted to your purposes; and resource listings that point to organizations, publications, and websites. When an online companion exists for a chapter, it will be noted within that chapter as well as in the Table of Contents. We invite you to check these out for the full benefit of content and tools. Online companions can be accessed by going to the last page of the book for a URL.

This edition of *Fundamentals of Arts Management* is structured in three parts.

Part One—Arts and Culture in Community offers a sense of the role and value of the arts and culture as an integral dimension to community life and ways to effectively plan and advocate for the integration, viability, and health of arts organizations and artists. In Part One, community arts leader, thinker, and chronicler Maryo Gard provides historical context for the work of local cultural organizations and arts organizing. Her chapter, Community Organizing: Building Community Through the Arts, underscores the rootedness, past and present, of arts and cultural organizing in social and civic concerns. Tom Borrup's chapter, Arts and the Economy: Fuel for the Creative Engine, sheds light on current thinking and efforts regarding the economic potential of "creative communities," how art inherently contributes to the identity and economic viability of communities, and ways that the arts and culture can be intentionally engaged as part, or even leaders, of larger economic strategies in communities. Stan Rosenberg's and Dan Hunter's Cultural Advocacy chapter promotes cultural advocacy as a critical function of local cultural organizations to ensure adequate resources to support and grow the arts. It offers valuable principles and practices of developing cultural advocacy campaigns and ongoing efforts.

Part Two—Fundamentals of Managing Arts Organizations offers principles and practices of running effective nonprofit arts organizations. These seven chapters frame the fundamentals of organizational development that guide staff and boards toward fulfilling their institution's mission and internal and external goals. Craig Dreeszen's

Strategic Planning chapter frames the benefits of strategic planning to guide priorities and activities and provides a thorough step-by-step process for developing a strategic plan that will be a usable tool. In Fundamentals of Board Development, Dreeszen aims to help board members of arts organizations understand their governance role and processes while also suggesting ways for staff members to work more effectively with their boards of directors. This chapter offers an approach to developing the board's capacity and effectiveness through building the skills of current board team and recruiting new members.

The Art of Fundraising, by fundraising experts Halsey M. North and Alice H. North, demystifies the fundraising process. Outlining a basic approach that is as effective with the smallest and largest donors, the chapter describes how to identify, contact, and cultivate prospective donors, present a well-considered idea, ask for the contribution, thank, and sustain the relationship. The companion chapter, Essentials of Proposal Writing by the late Norton Kiritz, is reprinted with permission from The Grantsmanship Center. This summary has become the most widely used resource for how to develop a solid proposal to foundation and corporate funders.

Personnel Management, by Amy Brannock, is a primer suited especially to organizations hiring staff for the first time or replacing a sole professional staff person. For organizations that already have professional staff, the chapter concludes with a discussion on planning for leadership succession and the professional and personal qualities of arts leadership. Pam Korza's Volunteers in the Arts chapter focuses on integrating volunteers who can support both ongoing and special activities and covers principles to motivate, manage, and reward volunteers.

Financial Management in the Arts, by Christine Burdett with contributing editors Sally Zinno and Maren Brown, provides a basic overview of the terminology and practices of financial management including: designating responsibility for financial planning and evaluation; developing and using a budget effectively; applying basic accounting principles; preparing and reading financial statements; meeting reporting requirements common to most nonprofits; foreseeing financial problems and opportunities; and analyzing an organization's financial health.

Part Three—Programming and Participation explores ways to engage audiences and the community through effective program design, marketing, accessibility measures, and evaluation.

Program Development, by Pam Korza and contributing editor Denise Boston-Moore, provides a structure for conceiving, planning, and implementing programs. The chapter covers key program planning principles from defining the philosophy underlying an organization's program choices and assessing feasibility of program ideas to considerations concerning responsible programming for cultural specificity and diversity.

Marketing the Arts, by Barbara Schaffer Bacon and contributing editors Maren Brown, Dorothy Chen-Courtin, and Shirley Sneve, introduces contemporary marketing principles and explores their application to promoting the arts. It examines the role of marketing in connecting art and audiences, the marketing mix, marketing research approaches, and developing a marketing plan or campaign using core strategies of public relations, publicity, promotion, and advertising.

The next two chapters take up directions that have become central to the work and advocacy efforts of cultural organizations and that continue to mature. In Cultural Access: Extend the Complete Invitation, authors Gay Hanna and Lisa Kammel discuss the win-win benefits of making arts institutions and their programs accessible to people with differing abilities. This chapter introduces philosophy, terms, best practices, model programs, tools, and resources. Readers will learn ways to adapt existing facilities and programs that will bring the community into the organization and the organization into the community.

Arts Education: Developing a Successful Program, by Marete Wester and contributing editor David O'Fallon, lends invaluable insights to navigating public education systems and the realities of school and arts organization partnerships. The chapter also discusses how to design and implement effective programs that meet learners' needs and help achieve the goals of schools and community organizations, student-centered curriculum development, assessing student learning, the development of afterschool programs, and the role of artist-educators.

In Program Evaluation: Looking for Results, Craig Dreeszen takes an outcome-based approach to evaluation and explains concepts and language, gives a simple six-step process to define hoped-for results, and outlines how to gauge whether these were achieved.

At the end of the book, you'll find a bibliography organized by chapter with authors' selected references for further exploration.

As it has done since its first edition in 1987, we hope *Fundamentals of Arts Management* will continue to serve the learning needs of those who are new to arts administration or are studying for a career in the field, as well as board members and volunteers who play essential roles. We invite veteran administrators to seek it out as a reference that offers a useful refresher to the basics as well as new understanding regarding how to integrate and gain support for the arts in the social, economic, and cultural fabric of our communities.

Acknowledgments

Many people worked hard to bring this publication to fruition. We are exceedingly grateful for everyone whose time and commitment helped to make this publication a reality.

We are indebted to the contributing writers of this book, who share the benefit of their experience in the field with our readers: Mary Altman, Tom Borrup, Denise Boston-Moore, Amy Brannock, Maren Brown, Christine Burdett, Dorothy Chen-Courtin, Craig Dreeszen, Maryo Gard, Gay Hanna, Dan Hunter, Lisa Kammel, Norton Kiritz, Pam Korza, David O'Fallon, Halsey M. North and Alice H. North, Stan Rosenberg, Barbara Schaffer Bacon, Shirley Sneve, Marete Wester, and Sally Zinno.

The editing and design team was truly exceptional. Pam Korza served as lead editor and, drawing upon her substantial writing and editing experience, helped shape the vision of this newest edition and guide the editorial process. Because this book evolved over many years, we also offer a warm collegial nod and enormous thanks to past editors, Craig Dreeszen and Shirley Sneve, for developing and shaping the excellent material for this edition. We thank Anne Canzonetti for her incredible contributions as editor. She has helped to restructure *Fundamentals* to include an online companion, lent a rigorous eye to form and style, and has been an invaluable member of the editing team.

We are also fortunate to have worked with designer Tekla McInerney. Tekla conceived an entirely new design for the book that is outstanding. Her creative talents and conscientious attention to the relationship between form and content make this volume both handsome and functional.

Finally, we wish to thank Alyson Ekblom, AES program assistant, and Cassie Johnson and Victoria Olivera, student office assistants, who painstakingly transcribed elements from previous editions and recreated bibliographies, tables, and diagrams, among other essential tasks that helped to move this edition forward. Thank you all.

We deeply appreciate the ongoing support of the Massachusetts Cultural Council, the National Endowment for the Arts, the UMass Arts Council, and the University of Massachusetts' Division of Outreach, which have all contributed to this latest edition of *Fundamentals of Arts Management.*

Finally, we wish to acknowledge Dr. Sharon Fross, vice provost for outreach at the University of Massachusetts Amherst, for her unflagging support of the Arts Extension Service. Her enthusiasm for and understanding of the community arts field is rare, and we are deeply grateful for her visionary leadership.

Maren Brown, *director, Arts Extension Service*
Pam Korza, *editor*

Introduction

When I first encountered *Fundamentals of Arts Management*, I was working in a performing and visual arts center, struggling with the mechanics of creating an evaluation framework for a school program we offered. When I most needed it, Craig Dreeszen's chapter on evaluation offered step-by-step guidance about how to proceed with the evaluation, including worksheets and other templates to help me to conceptualize the evaluation process. I remember thinking how pragmatic and helpful the book was, and how—as a busy arts professional—I could read the book out of sequence, consulting individual chapters for guidance at critical junctures in my work.

Since joining the UMass Arts Extension Service last year, I now see how others have made use of this invaluable text. As the field matures, we have witnessed substantial growth in arts management programs at colleges and universities throughout the world, including our own Certificate Program in Arts Management. *Fundamentals* serves as the primary textbook in literally hundreds of arts management courses, helping to educate the next generation of community arts leaders. Many state, regional, and local arts agencies use *Fundamentals* in their training programs, as do a growing cadre of consultants, who use this book to complement their work in community arts agencies. And then there are the scores of individuals working in community arts organizations who use this text as an invaluable reference.

Our world is changing rapidly, and like earlier incarnations of *Fundamentals*, this edition has been updated to reflect these changes. The impact of technology on our work, the infusion of arts and culture into community redevelopment efforts, and the increasing need to advocate for our organizations are just a few of the changes that have been integrated into this latest edition. Some of these changes are even reflected in the production of the book, as we utilize print-on-demand technology with a geographically-dispersed editing, writing, and design team that frequently exchanges electronic files over the Internet.

My fondest hope is for this book to become "dog eared, bookmarked, and highlighted," as former Arts Extension Service Director Shirley Sneve said in her introduction to the fourth edition, and that you find this book as helpful to you as I did so many years ago.

Maren Brown, *director, Arts Extension Service*

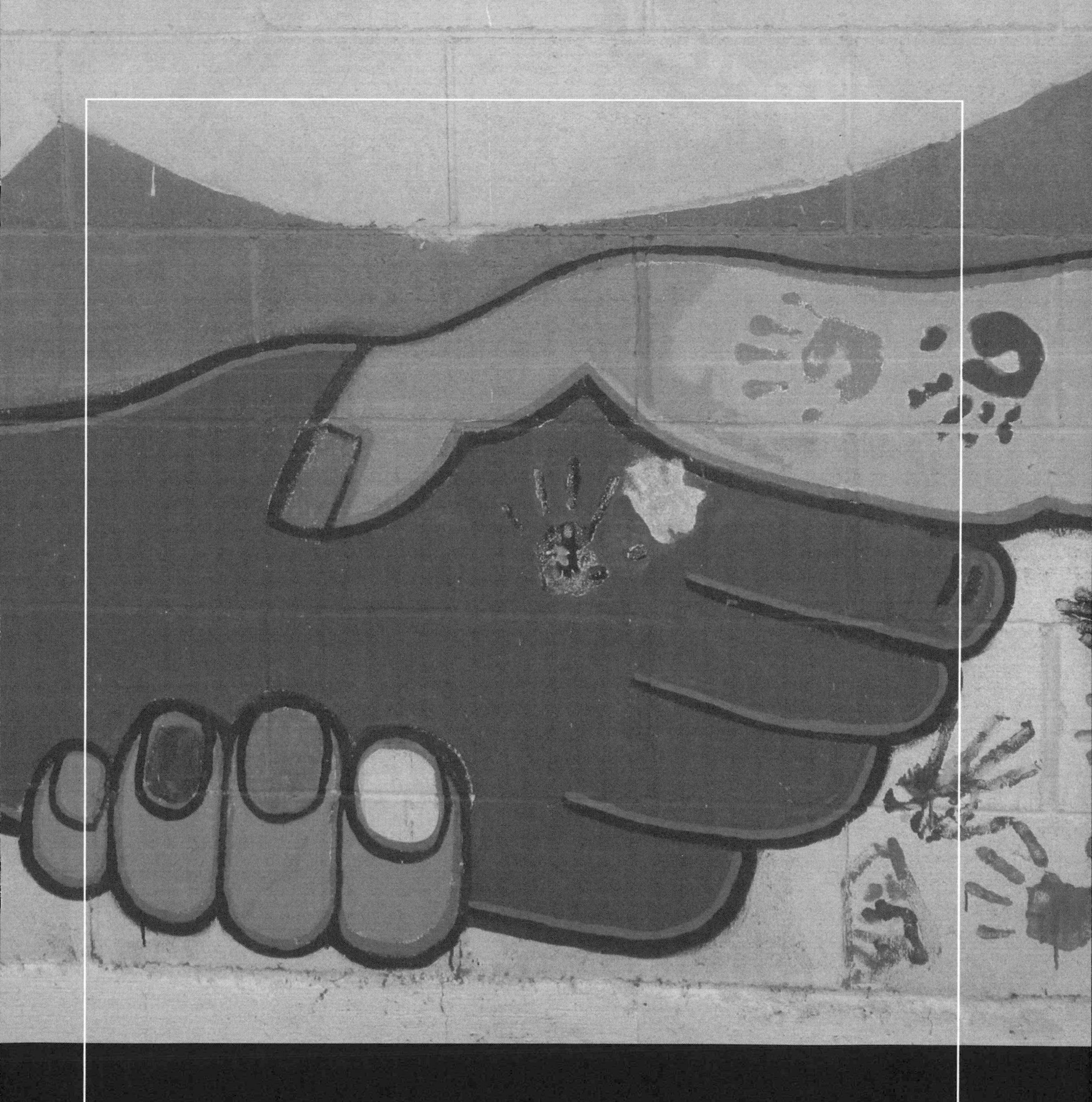

PART ONE

Arts and Culture in Community

CHAPTER 1

Community Organizing: Building Community Through the Arts

1

MARYO GARD

Certain phrases crop up a lot in the mission statements of community arts organizations. One such phrase that is popular is community building. The arts have an important part to play in community building, but let's be clear about what it means.

Community has become one of those much used feel-good words. Political candidates running for office use it in speech after speech. Marketing firms trying to sell anything from cars to Internet access use it in ad after ad. It is clearly a word that people respond to powerfully. If people weren't hungry for "it," politicians and advertisers wouldn't use it so much. In fact, it is used so often it is starting to lose its meaning.

Community defined. For the purposes of this chapter, *community* refers to geography: a neighborhood, a town, a watershed. We are not referring to the "community of Jamaicans in Michigan," the "community of users of America Online," or the "community of gay people." These are groups of people who are demographically similar. Group power is a valid and important process in creating a sense of group identity, but is not within the scope of this chapter. Here, *community* refers to places where people who are different from one another live together and try to carve out a good life together. It is used in the sense that Lewis Thomas, the biologist, did when he said, "...[there are] no independent creatures. The life of any given individual, of any species, is dependent on other individuals, on other species. Moreover, the existence of a given species depends upon the genetic diversity of that species."

Community organizing defined. Within the arts world, the term *community-building* is frequently used as a synonym for audience development—creating groups of people who attend new music events or diversifying the demographics of an audience. Although audience development is covered in the Marketing the Arts chapter, this is not what is addressed here. What is under discussion is the process by which people in geographic communities make use of the arts to create, in Thomas' terms, an "effective interdependency leading to a better life for all." To do that, effective organizing skills are necessary. Accordingly, this chapter on community arts organizing is about building the capacity of the community and its key leaders to use the arts to create an effective interdependency among people in a geographic place. An effective interdependency refers to bettering the community, with better defined by the diversity of people who live there.

There are several points that are critical about this definition of community arts organizing.

- It refers to a geographic place.
- It recognizes the diversity of people who live in that place.

Community arts organizing is about building the capacity of the community and its key leaders to use the arts to create an effective interdependency among people in a geographic place.

- It recognizes that though community members may be very different from one another, they are all interested in creating a good life for themselves and their families.
- It recognizes that a neighbor's idea of a "good life" is as important as your own.
- It recognizes that different people in a community need to work together on common goals and ways of addressing those goals.
- It recognizes that the arts are a key to doing this and so may be most important.
- It makes a "good community" the end, with arts of excellence as the means.

Our intention is community building. This last point is a very important one. For those people who use community building as a synonym for audience development, the arts are still the end goal. Our intention is to get more people, or different people, to arts events. Since increased artistic activity is a hallmark of a livable community, arts people often concentrate on producing more, and better, arts events. While we believe that is the job of many arts organizations, it is outside the scope of this chapter. (See the chapter, Program Development, for guidance on how to create better arts events.)

Here, our intention is a good community, as defined by the diversity of people who live there, not as defined by the art organization. Thus, the organization offers its knowledge and skills as a service to this concept of a *built community*, and works collaboratively with other community groups in order to do so.

Arts excellence matters. Let us put aside once and for all time the common idea that doing this kind of work somehow prostitutes the arts or minimizes their *quality* in the interest of *social service*. This is an old, tired argument. Community-building work is most effectively undertaken when artists or arts organizations with impeccable standards of excellence are involved. This is not "just social work;" rather, the melding of arts knowledge and skills with community ends is creating a new aesthetic, one which may, in time, be considered the cutting edge aesthetic of the early twenty-first century. This kind of work is forging new definitions and standards of what *excellence* means. Initiatives like Americans for the Arts' Animating Democracy program have begun to do just this in the critical writing experiment and resulting book entitled *Critical Perspectives*.[1]

Community-building work is most effectively undertaken when artists or arts organizations with impeccable standards of excellence are involved.

Community change takes time. Change takes time, and truly effecting deep change is the work of generations. You may make some short-term improvements, but larger-scale cultural change isn't going to be effected in your lifetime. We will address this in the part of this chapter on necessary skill sets, but this kind of work requires a person who thinks of him or herself as a player in a game that takes decades to "win," and is prepared not to see any deep results right away—maybe not in their lifetime.

By the end of this chapter, you should know something about your own history and the importance of keeping the "big picture" as your guiding star. Knowing your history will ground and connect you to a lineage of community arts ideas and people. We as community arts organizers need this kind of lineage as much as we need to know who our family forebears were.

HISTORY AND WHAT IT TELLS US

Before we get into the mechanics of this kind of work, it is important to talk a bit about the past, for community arts is not a new idea. These stories will connect you to generations of other community arts organizers. First, your lineage is that of the community "griot," or cultural story-holder. In communities everywhere, the storyteller passes on knowledge to subsequent generations. These are not just good anecdotes; they are ways by which a culture shares its goals and its successes, what it knows, and how to evaluate its progress. Look, for example, at the work of the Roadside Theater in Kentucky (www.roadside.org). They are not just making plays based on stories, but works whose purpose is to articulate wisdom and evaluate cultural progress.

Village Improvement. Consider Anglo cultures in the United States, circa 1853. The Village Improvement movement, started in Massachusetts, addressed issues of ugly billboards and the need for community trees, paved roads, and recreational facilities. By 1900, there were about 3,000 such groups in the United States, trying to develop a sense of place through aesthetics.

City Beautiful. The Village Improvement movement led in turn to the City Beautiful movement, exemplified by the architectural ideas showcased at the Chicago World's Fair at the end of the nineteenth century. City Beautiful emphasized a return to grand, classical architecture for public buildings. The Museum of Science and Industry, the Shedd Aquarium, and the Midway were all World's Fair buildings.

Olmstead and Wright. At about this time, Frederick Law Olmstead was stressing the importance of parks in cities and a few public art commissions were created in urban areas. Two things slowed this civic aesthetics movement down, however. First, there

The Music Man as Example of Community Building

Is this all getting a little too heavy? Take a break and rent the video of Meredith Wilson's *The Music Man!* with Robert Preston. Turn your Saturday night movie-watching experience into a learning experience (with humor, of course). Note that:

- Early on, the people of River City explore what it means to live in Iowa.
- Professor Hill spends a good deal of time considering, and rejecting, possible issues to organize around before he hits on the pool hall idea.
- Professor Hill, the outside organizer, nonetheless collaborates with a local partner, Marian the librarian.
- Marian moves into a position of community leadership, culminating in a very strong stand at the end of the film, and co-leading the final celebration.
- The people (the Mayor) see no reason to change. What about his wife who sees "art" as only about the classics? What can we learn from them?
- The people (the City Council) realize that, through the arts, they have more common ground than they were aware of.
- Change for the youth at risk in the community (the kid with the speech disability; or Tommy, the potential juvenile delinquent) comes in the form of the arts.
- The Think System of preparing for a concert is based on the art of keeping the "big picture" in mind, as well as an unwavering faith that it is the right thing to do.

was the idea that grandeur was classist, just another amenity for the wealthy. Second, efficiency and functionalism were replacing aesthetics as values in the United States. There were a few voices raised in opposition to this. A notable one was Frank Lloyd Wright, who believed that the middle class had the same right to aesthetics that the upper class did; he even designed a line of wallpaper, drapes, and so forth to be marketed through F. Schumaker & Company. In this story are the roots of contemporary public art and design. As we take action to ensure that artists serve on city engineering teams for the design of everything from manhole covers to bridges, as we design public art processes based on public input, as we consider icons at the edge of town to welcome us to the community, we are acting in the tradition begun in the United States 150 years ago.

Lyceum movement. Now return to the early 1800s and follow another thread. In this story, Josiah Holbrook of Massachusetts started inviting neighbors to his home for discussions of books. Gradually, he started inviting professors, and the discussions expanded to encompass new ideas. This led to the founding of the American Lyceum Association in 1831; by 1850 there were about 3,000 of these groups. However, the idea was introduced that discussion leaders should be paid honoraria and the discussions should become lectures. The next logical step was to put lecturers on "the circuit," and James Redpath started a management organization to do exactly that. He valued efficiency, so naturally favored lectures in communities that could afford the fee and that were on the railroad line. The grassroots movement, begun as discussions by ordinary folks in people's homes, began to wither as this more "professional" movement grew.

Chautauquas. Cut to Chautauqua, New York, where Reverend John Vincent was experimenting with the use of the arts to teach the Bible. This approach proved very popular, and pretty soon Reverend Vincent's study packages were being shipped to scores of local Chautauqua Circles. Back at the Redpath agency, now-manager Keith Vawter had a big idea; he had lecturers and the Chautauqua Circles were a network of potential presenters. So he brought the two together; if the lecturer was hot enough and the town was small enough, he even provided tents for the lecture. Do you see our presenting roots in these stories? Furthermore, they reveal the linking of the arts to the introduction of new ideas and new ways of thinking, as well as the notion of learning about a given topic through artistic methodology.

Now think about the growth of the arts themselves. There were theater companies in America in the eighteenth century, especially in the urban areas, though a performance by a so-called professional company was reported in rural Kentucky in 1797. There were performances on showboats and there were Mexican vaudeville companies traveling throughout the southwest. Artists like Edwin Booth and Sarah Bernhardt appeared in many small towns. It was even said that in the Rocky Mountain West, the first building built after the assayer's office and the saloon was the opera house, and in many places that was probably true.

Community concerts. Redpath's idea of traveling lecturers spawned groups like Columbia Artists Management, and suddenly there were community concert series growing throughout the country. Community-based arts were growing too, especially in small towns. Fargo, North Dakota, had an art league well-established by 1911. Quincy, Illinois, had an orchestra with a paid conductor by 1947.

Local arts agencies. In 1944, the Junior League of America took arts management one step further, offering consulting services to communities wanting to expand the number of arts activities and to coordinate existing arts activities. The woman behind this idea, Virginia Lee Comer, was insistent that when she visited a community, she should talk to all groups of people—not just arts groups—about creative activity in the community. She saw churches, union halls, and housing projects as obvious places for arts activity because people already gathered there. (Is this not the forerunner of the "community cultural planning" that our generation believes we invented in the 1980s?) Comer's manual on assessing, coordinating, and stimulating arts activities in small communities, and her work in Winston-Salem, North Carolina, in 1946–1947, probably led directly to the institution of local arts agencies.

Settlement House movement. At the turn of the twentieth century in urban areas, the Settlement House movement begins. Jane Addams founded Hull House in Chicago to provide entry, orientation points, and basic social services for new immigrants to the United States. She was adamant that neither poverty nor language barriers should mean disenfranchisement from one's culture. Her comprehensive social service program included meals and help to locate housing, but it also included a gym, men's and women's clubs, programs in native languages as well as English, a library, art classes, an art gallery, and a drama group.

University extension services. Meanwhile, in rural areas, the extension services of the land grant universities were doing similar work with rural people. They were producing opera in Iowa, encouraging folk arts in Kentucky, inserting the arts into community planning efforts in Ohio—linking arts and recreation, arts and home-making, and arts and the meaningful use of leisure time. Some individuals stand out.

In upstate New York, Alexander Drummond was disgusted by the quality of so-called "rural plays" marketed by Samuel French, which portrayed rural people as hicks. So Drummond called for farmers who might want to write plays, and deployed his graduate students in theater as the dramaturgs to help them do so.

In North Carolina, Frederick Koch believed that because of the nature of the American ideal, America's culture could ONLY be recorded by ordinary Jo(e)s. So he required students in his theater program to start writing "folk plays"—plays about their background, about people in their communities. He insisted that his program be a mix of students rich and poor, sharecropper and landowner, black and white. Literally thousands of these "folk plays" were written in North Carolina during his time on the faculty and in other communities where he was asked to stimulate community playwriting.

Alfred Arvold, in North Dakota, was passionate that a community was an organic whole, and that the arts must not be broken off from the ongoing life of the community. To this end, he promulgated the notion of the community center where there would be a wonderful jumble of activity; it would be a recreation center, science center, arts center, and government center, where the boundaries between activities blurred. In 1917, he wrote:

> A community center is a place, a neighborhood laboratory, so to speak, where people meet in their own way to analyze whatever interests they have in common and participate in such forms of recreation as are healthful and enjoyable. The fundamental principle back of the community center is the democratization of all art so the common people can appreciate it, science so that they can use it, government so that they can take a part in it, and recreation so they can enjoy it. In other words, its highest aim is to make the common interests the great interests. To give a human expression in every locality to the significant meaning of these terms, "come let's reason and play together" is in reality the ultimate object of the community center.[2]

Robert Gard. In Wisconsin, Robert Gard's initial dream was to get every Wisconsinite writing; this ideal grew from the notion of populist government that prevailed in Wisconsin at the time. This "Wisconsin Idea" interrelated civic involvement, public education, access to the newest ideas, and fulfillment of creative potential for all of the citizens of the state. (Indeed, Gard's arts extension program at the University of Wisconsin inspired the founding of the Arts Extension Service at the University of Massachusetts, the publisher of this book!). In 1955, Gard wrote in *Grassroots Theater*[3] about the deep relationship between art and "sense of place." But Gard's dream kept expanding, and in 1967, in *The Arts in the Small Community*,[4] he urged arts groups to work with athletic groups like football teams, churches, ethnic organizations, senior citizens, and others, in the service of a healthy, whole community. These historical projects resonate with the notion of the role of the arts in whole communities, as well as our expressed commitment to empowering the individuals.

Baker Brownell. Another arts activist, working a little earlier than Gard, was Baker Brownell. He was a philosopher from Northwestern University, brought to Montana in the 1940s to help small towns think about their future, especially their economic future. He believed that this process started with a review of the community's economic, religious, creative, ethnic, and educational histories. The self-study process that he designed culminated in the production of a pageant that didn't just recite these histories, but used them as a way of addressing the future. Brownell believed that there are periods when specialists are needed in a society, giving way to periods when generalists are needed. It is tempting, and easier, to remain in a world of specialists, but he saw overspecialization as the path to the death of the soul and of society. Generalists, however, must stride forward and apply their knowledge to issues of the whole, integrated society. Brownell saw artists as people with this special knowledge. He juxtaposed the human community to the culture of specialism. In the human community, a place where the scale is shrunk so that people can know one another as whole persons, he saw the arts as a tool in community planning, but more importantly, as the way to reclaim a society's soul. He believed that art is a verb, that everyone is latently creative and thoughtful but that the art system too often reinforces passivity, and the way of passivity is the way of death.

> Ours is a culture of displaced persons. It is tattered with escape and wandering, and as such is a culture founded on being lost... What the Germans did to millions in the concentration camps, and the Russians to tens of millions in the mass deportations, the western world in general does less dramatically but as

> effectively to hundreds of millions swarming homelessly to centers of vicarious and secondary culture. Their lives die out, love rots, and hope is replaced by avid stimulation. In all this, art may become merely one of the seducers to death. Or it may become the insight of life and survival itself.[5]

Brownell tied artists literally to the life of a society, and this, too, is something to which we are awakening today.

Rachel Davis-Dubois. An educator in New York working in the 1930s to 1950s, Rachel Davis Dubois[6] had a lifelong devotion to multicultural education. But even more than this, she articulated the notion of cultural democracy as the neglected third leg of the American stool, with the other two legs being political and economic democracy. She believed that the American dream could not be realized without equal emphasis on cultural democracy. In 1943, she said:

> The melting pot idea, or "come-let-us-do-something-for-you" attitude on the part of the old-stock American, was wrong. For half the melting pot to rejoice in being made better while the other half rejoiced in being better allowed for neither element to be its true self... The welfare of the group...means [articulating] a creative use of differences. Democracy is the only atmosphere in which this can happen, whether between individuals, within families, among groups in a country, or among countries. This kind of sharing we have [is] called cultural democracy. Political democracy—the right of all to vote—we have inherited. Economic democracy—the right of all to be free from want—we are beginning to envisage. But cultural democracy—a sharing of values among numbers of our various cultural groups—we have scarcely dreamed of. Much less have we devised social techniques for creating it.[7]

Much of her work was about enabling groups to study, understand, and value their own cultures, and to equally value and delight in the cultures of others. Here again, you surely see some of your roots.

Finally, in the first half of the nineteenth century, we see an articulation of the responsibility of the artist to building a stronger civic society. Percy MacKaye, from a long family of theater people, articulated the responsibility of the artist to think explicitly of him or herself as building civic infrastructure, "...This potentiality of the drama could never be realized until the theatre...should be dedicated to public, not private, ends." [8]

Certainly, the artists later in the century, who were put back to work by the Works Progress Administration (WPA), wrote and produced plays and murals that challenged and raised questions while they also beautified and delighted. The film, *The Cradle Will Rock*, offers an important and provocative look at the WPA.[9]

ISOLATION OF THE ARTS

Despite their positive approaches, something happened in each of these stories, and the arts were left isolated. Civic beautification often reaches a point where it is seen as optional, expensive, and something just for the wealthy (How many truly glorious public buildings are being constructed now?), and there is a constant debate about the appropriateness of public funding for artists and arts organizations. The Lyceum-

Chautauqua story, which began as two grassroots, participatory endeavors, evolved into one-way presentations by artists to audiences; true engagement evolved into outreach. The Jane Addams and extension service stories have evolved so that now we separate "real" art from social work or recreation; indeed, the successors to Drummond, Koch, and Arvold were charged by their university with "professionalizing" the art in their departments. As schools struggle, arts education and multicultural education are left behind the "core" subjects of reading, science, and math.

Interestingly, each of these stories began with a deep-seated notion of personal wholeness and community interdependence and acknowledged the role of the arts in helping individuals and communities attain this wholeness and interdependence. Each of the stories ended with the arts being isolated—an amenity, an educational option, a one-way artist-audience relationship.

Let's consider our own organizations. We have done a good job in the past decades becoming institutionalized in the best sense. We do many high-quality shows, we're asked to a lot of community meetings, we've learned how to raise money, we are part of the concept of livable cities, we are becoming skilled in making the political process work for us. Yet as we have become institutionalized, the stakes have also risen. We need more money to keep the doors open. We need more political goodwill to build a facility. As we have struggled to secure more money and political support, it has often been at the expense of other groups in the community against whom we have had to compete for increasingly scarce resources of money, goodwill, and volunteers' time. We are, in fact, segregating ourselves from our communities even, ironically, as the idea of "more arts for all the people" is becomingly an increasingly accepted slogan.

Yet interestingly, in a RAND Corporation study, we learn that "institutions seeing the biggest gains [in diversity and engagement of audiences] are those that are making service to their communities as important as promoting artistic quality." [10]

HEADWATERS GOALS

It is important to be aware of the philosophical origins of the stories we have just told. Yet we must also be aware that they can evolve into relatively simple projects with few philosophical "teeth," which are easily set aside when "times get tough." For example, endeavors whose goals were about relating civic aesthetics to democracy evolved into programs about beautification. The Lyceum, whose goal was to engage neighbors in discussion, evolved into a program about "audience development." As an analogy, consider the Colorado River; it begins as a profoundly important source of life, but it is diverted, used, and dammed so much that by the time it gets to Los Angeles it is but a dusty trickle. In community arts organizing, you must not start with goals analogous to that trickle; rather, start with goals that are analogous to the headwaters. For purposes of community arts organizing, a goal that is about "civic aesthetics and democracy" is a headwaters goal; a goal that is merely about "beautification" is a dusty trickle goal (without the passion to carry you when you are tired, impatient, and feeling as though it's just not worth it). Think about the philosophical "headwaters" of the historical stories recounted above, and see which, if any, relate to your situation.

A better physical community. Beauty and invitations to gather are civic values—because in a democracy, public spaces and public buildings and thoroughfares ought to embody the highest aspirations of human beings. This is the story of the Village Improvement, City Beautiful, and Frank Lloyd Wright movements.

A more thoughtful community. Here people engage in genuine dialogue—questioning, critiquing, leading to more informed personal and collective action—because every individual has a right to improve or change his or her life. This is the story of Josiah Holbrook and his discussion groups, and the Chautauqua clubs.

A multicultured community. People prize the cultures of one another as they value their own—because coexistence is not enough. We cannot move to true globalism without deep understanding. This is the legacy of Frederick Koch and Rachel Davis-Dubois.

A community of empowered individuals. Each person explores his or her own creativity—because each person has a birthright of dignity and a wealth of individual opinions and ideas. This is the story of Alex Drummond, Robert Gard, and extension services.

A human community. People learn to know one another well—because moving forward meaningfully as a community cannot happen until groups move past being special interests and learn to relate as people. This is the story of Alfred Arvold and Baker Brownell.

A just community. Here the norm is decency, dignity, and tolerance for all—because this is the meaning of being an American. This is the legacy of the Settlement House and the Civil Rights movements.

A civic community. Here everyone sees him or herself as responsible to the community and its public processes—because without this individual commitment there can be no true democracy. This is the legacy of Percy MacKaye and the artists who participated in the arts programs of the New Deal.

COMMUNITY ARTS STORIES

Let's look at a few examples where people are thinking about community arts programs with this kind of depth and considering the deep philosophical context that leads to community arts organizing.

Animating Democracy. In the late 1990s, the Ford Foundation and Americans for the Arts undertook a bold new venture called Animating Democracy. Its purpose is to "foster artistic activity that encourages civic dialogue on important contemporary issues." The Land Bridge Project, one of many such projects supported by Animating Democracy, shows how community arts organizing can be approached.

In collaboration with The Children's Theatre Company and the Perpich Center for Arts Education, the Land Bridge Project brought together rural and urban residents of Montevideo and Minneapolis, Minnesota, in dialogue around issues of the expanding farm crisis. The Minnesota farming community is deeply divided between farmers struggling to maintain family farms and those who contract with agribusiness. Related tensions exist between farmers and banks, legislators and rural activists, and between neighbors. The Children's Theatre Company aimed to use the creation of a new play to illuminate the complexity of the issue and to make those further along the food chain aware that this crisis of food, economy, land use, and social well-being is also their crisis.[11]

Pathway to Peace Neighborhood Gateway. A good example of community arts organizing at the local neighborhood level is the Pathway to Peace Gateway in the East Harriet Farmstead neighborhood in south Minneapolis. The Gateway Pathway began as an effort of the local neighborhood association and Lyndale Park, which includes a peace garden, a contemplative place secluded from the rest of the park. Peace garden activists wanted to create a stronger link between the neighborhood and the garden and solicited support from the City of Minneapolis Art in Public Places project for the creation of a gateway. Artists were commissioned to create a series of seven sculptural columns spanning the four-block area from the neighborhood to the garden. Each artwork contains text derived from community dialogues, where people shared their feelings and questions about peace in the community, across the world, and within themselves.

Engaged arts. During a 2001 Grantmakers in the Arts conference panel addressing the topic of meaningful community-building through the arts, Mark Valentine, of The David and Lucile Packard Foundation, said:

> It's about knitting… It's not about expansive kumbaya moments where everybody practices guitar around the campfire... It's about finding places where programs are active concurrently, but in a disaggregated context, and bringing them together. My own bias is that art and culture are a significant part of that conversation. They're woven into the very heart of that community. As you envision what the future might look like, I think it's essential that it be engaged.[12]

He cited projects reviewed by his foundation in which artists are paired with environmentalists to help their community really think about issues of climate change. Similarly, Peter Pennekamp, of the Humboldt Area Foundation, said, "Art outside the context of everyday life, art within a consumption model which is really almost all of what the professional arts world lives in, rather than a participation model, is what makes art not as important as I think all of us would like it to be." [13]

The point is that the arts can both become more important and serve an urgently needed role in our society now, if we shift our thinking back to the original ideas behind each of these historical tales. So whether you are an idealist ("this is the right thing to do") or a pragmatist ("we might not survive if we don't start thinking differently"), consider the idea of committing your arts organization to the community-building process.

WAYS THAT ARTS ORGANIZATIONS LEAD IN COMMUNITY ORGANIZING

Investigate the things we have in common. An example is the work of Roadside Theater. In Appalachia, its home, the dramatic material is drawn directly from community knowledge and stories there.

Investigate our differences. Another of Roadside Theater's artistic thrusts is to collaborate with theater companies from other cultures, exploring what their cultural stories do not have in common as well as what they share.

Further community conversation. Any of the activities in Americans for the Arts' Animating Democracy program fall into this category. Whether the issue is the health of a river on which a town is dependent, youth violence, blighted neighborhoods, or a debate over whose history should be told and how in the local historical museum, examples abound. Go to www.americansforthearts.org/AnimatingDemocracy for case studies and publications.

Educate others about us. In Crested Butte, Colorado, which depends heavily on tourists for its economic life, the buses that transport skiers to the ski area are all painted with something important about the town—its history, current community members, even the dogs that everyone knows. It says, "We live here. Don't just spend money here. Respect our place and people. Get to know us."

Mobilize people. In Los Angeles, the Bus Riders Union collaborated with Cornerstone Theater Company to create a series of mini-plays which were performed on the buses. A small team of players boarded dressed in costume, did their playlet (which had to do with an issue faced by bus riders), distributed leaflets, and got off the bus several stops later.

Prevent issues from developing. In Calgary, Alberta, a neighborhood planner is thinking about a new kind of planning process involving the community theater. Act One might portray the status quo in the community, and groups of citizens would sketch scenarios for Act Two depending on which key decision is made about a particular issue. Visualizing alternatives and their consequences is difficult; this idea could lead to avoidance of poor choices.

Heal. Artists who had been in residence at Columbine High School in Littleton, Colorado, were among the first people that the school turned to after the shooting tragedy in which many students died. Within two days the artists were offering activities to students and teachers, the first of a series of activities that continued for two years. Artists served a similar healing function following the September 11 World Trade Center attacks in 2001 and the devastation wrought upon the Gulf Coast in 2005 by Hurricanes Katrina and Rita.

What is essential in all of these ideas is that the arts organization is not isolated. It must work with a wide variety of nonarts groups in the community—teachers, therapists, "ordinary citizens," planners, union organizers, businesses, farmers. Each group must be equal in bringing what they know, and how they know it, to the table. Together, they devise a new approach to furthering the health of the community that they, as interdependent people, have in common.

The chapter by Mary Altman, Community Arts Organizing Methods, found in the Online Companion, introduces some of the skills that arts organization leaders as well as community organizers will need, or should strive to acquire, in order to stimulate the arts in their community. It offers a step-by-step approach to doing art for community change and where to go for assistance. (See the last page of this book for the URL to access this chapter.)

ENDNOTES

1. Atlas, C., & Korza, P., (Eds.). (2005). *Critical Perspectives: Writings on Art and Civic Dialogue.* Washington, DC: Americans for the Arts.
2. Arvold, A. (1917, May-June). *The Community Center Movement.* College and State, 1(3). North Dakota Agricultural College.
3. Gard, R.(1999). *Grassroots Theater: A Search for Regional Arts in America.* Madison, WI: University of Wisconsin Press.
4. Gard, R., Kohloff, R., & Warlum, M. (1995). *The Arts in the Small Community.* Washington, DC: Americans for the Arts.
5. Baker, B. (1950). *The Human Community*. New York: Harper & Brothers.
6. Rachel Davis-Dubois was no relation to W.E.B. Dubois, though she did work with him.
7. Davis-Dubois, R. (1943). *Get Together Americans: Friendly Approaches to Racial and Cultural Conflicts Through the Neighborhood-Home Festival.* New York: Harper & Brothers.
8. MacKave, P. M. (1909). *The Playhouse and the Play.* New York: MacMillan.
9. Robbins, T. (Producer/Writer/Director). (1999). *The Cradle Will Rock* [Motion picture]. United States: Touchstone Home Video.
10. RAND Corporation. *Examining Why People Participate in the Arts.* Retrieved from www.rand.org/publications/RB/researchprofile/
11. Americans for the Arts. Children's Theatre Company. Retrieved from www.americansforthearts.org/animatingdemocracy/labs/lab_065.asp
12. Pennekamp, P., McPhee, P., Valentine, M., & Zollar, J. W. J. (2001, November 5). *Beyond "Art": A Community Perspective.* Presented at the Grantmakers for the Arts 2001 Conference. Retrieved from www.giarts.org/usr_doc/BeyondArt.pdf

CHAPTER 2

Arts and the Economy: Fuel for the Creative Engine

2

TOM BORRUP

In this chapter, Tom Borrup brings his vast experience as a long-time community art center director and his key research findings on the arts and economic development to examine what is meant by the creative economy. *This chapter explores where and how artists and arts organizations fit in economic development and strategies for impacting economic development through the arts.*

In the AES Online Companion to this chapter (see the last page of the book for the Internet address for related online materials), Borrup charts processes for implementing community development strategies. Check out the online section to learn:

- *how to map and leverage a community's creative assets for economic development;*
- *how to identify and form strategic partnerships; and*
- *the important role of the "intermediary" in arts and economic development work.*

THE ARTS AND THE CREATIVE ECONOMY

Artists and nonprofit arts groups are potent forces in shaping their local communities, whether they know it or not. By recognizing and understanding this capacity—and responsibility—cultural leaders acting with purpose can be larger contributors to the well-being of their communities. In turn, as communities acknowledge the value of the arts and culture, they too will thrive.

In this chapter we'll look at the role culture and the arts play in the economic health of communities. We'll examine the creative economy and six arts-centered economic development strategies typically used by cultural organizations. We'll also review language and tools that help cultural leaders and managers better understand their community's economy and their role in it.

> You can go to any city in America and find an arts organization creating vitality in every neighborhood. And leaders still don't get it. Arts and culture is the genesis of the revitalization of communities.[1]
>
> —Pittsburgh Mayor Tom Murphy

DEFINITION OF TERMS

What is the *Creative Economy*?

The term *creative economy* came into popular use in the 1990s as creative sector industries grew in the so-called post-industrial era. In the for-profit arena, these industries have included advertising, media, entertainment, and the design professions, including product, fashion, and packaging. In the nonprofit sector they include arts producing, presenting, and preservation organizations, big and small. Not only have these industries grown in size at a faster rate than others since the 1990s, but their importance in shaping and propelling other economic sectors has become clearer.

Since 2000, creative communities, creative workforces, and other dimensions of the creative economy have also come into sharper focus. The New England Council, an

A culture persists in time only to the degree it is inventing, creating, and dynamically evolving in a way that promotes the production of ideas across all social classes and groups.[2]

—Shalini Venturelli

association representing major business concerns in that region, issued a report that year examining the nature of this emerging sector and charting its relative size and remarkable growth. The report acknowledged the considerable contribution made by the arts industry to "nurturing innovation, developing a skilled workforce, and helping businesses remain competitive." [3]

This heightened awareness of the importance of creative industries and workforces has caused cities, states, philanthropies, and business organizations to assess and advocate strengthening this sector and its support systems. Key elements of this support system include networks of small, medium, and large cultural organizations, "bohemian" neighborhoods, active artist communities, and social values that appeal to diverse, talented entrepreneurs, and workers. Educational opportunities that stress the use of the imagination are also critical to equip, train, and stimulate creative workers and thinkers.

This is new and productive ground shared by cultural leaders, economic development practitioners, and policymakers alike. It is essential for arts managers to understand their part in it.

The Use of the Word *Community*

For purposes of this chapter, we will use the term *community* to refer to the people and the natural and built environments within a geographically defined area, together with their social, economic, and civic institutions. Not to deny or diminish other definitions of community, such as communities of interest or virtual communities, we will talk only about *place-based* communities. *Community* will be used to include the social, civic, and economic bonds—in addition to the physical connections—between people who reside, work, or otherwise consider themselves part of a geographic place. Whether it is a rural, suburban, small town, or densely urban community, it may be 100 square miles or ten city blocks. What's important is that it has identity as a place, and those in it have reason to coalesce around common interests.

How the Word *Culture* is Used

What makes a community function, in every respect, is its culture. *Culture* can be defined as the "values, attitudes, beliefs, orientations, and underlying assumptions," that exist between people.[4] This contrasts with narrower definitions that have been associated with the practice of highly skilled artists often within the context of institutions that adjudicate and possess artifacts of *culture*. *Culture* comes in forms that include food, language, religion, music, home life, holiday observances, rituals, dance, poetry, visual art, crafts, behaviors, and creative endeavors. They are influenced by the systems of values and aesthetics that evolve and are practiced over a long period of time among people in a particular place. They are dynamic and constantly evolving.

WHERE CULTURE, ECONOMICS, AND COMMUNITIES MEET

While intuitively part of the community building process for centuries, cultural activities have only recently come under serious study as part of economic and human development. Two of the more well-known authors in the fields of economic and social development since the late 1990s include economist Richard Florida and social scientist Robert Putnam. While these thinkers disagree openly on what constitutes a

Mass MoCA: A Case Study in Repositioning Cultural Organizations as Key Contributors to Economic and Overall Community Well-being

The Massachusetts Museum of Contemporary Arts (MassMoCA) has had multiple impacts on its remote western Massachusetts town of North Adams. The museum opened in 1999 in an abandoned 700,000 square foot nineteenth century mill complex. It has been both a magnet and an incubator for dozens of creative industries. Research studies examining the economic and social impacts of arts organizations—conducted by economist Stephen Sheppard, Ph.D., of Williams College, with MassMoCA—have documented the museum's impact on surrounding property values, residential stability, and the success of new and old businesses.

"Local youth see these buildings as symbols of opening the imagination rather than hulking post industrial remnants of exploitation," said Joe Thompson, founder and director.[5] The importance of this change in the community's image of itself and its identity regionally and nationally shouldn't be underestimated. Hundreds of new jobs and millions of dollars in investment can be directly attributed to the museum and have turned around the economy of this small city. At least as importantly, it has begun to restore a sense of self-worth and hope to residents long buffeted by the economics and politics of disinvestment and labor exploitation. And it has done so while staying focused on presenting and commissioning the highest quality contemporary visual, performing, and media arts.

"successful" community, they are on the same page with regards to the overlooked role of culture and art.

Florida postulates that a critical mass of workers who fit his expanded definition of the *creative class* fuels a city's economic engine. He cites characteristics of tolerance, cultural activity, and social climate as key to attracting and retaining these workers. In turn, he argues, their presence results in industries becoming and remaining competitive.[6] Putnam argues that the well-being of a city or region pivots more on the ability of people to act constructively together around mutual interests. He measures this through a community's level of "social capital." [7] This term describes the social connectedness of people across cultures, ages, and other divides (what he labels *bridging social capital*), as well as within groups who are more alike and who organize to advance their well-being (*bonding social capital*).

Florida finds that an active and participatory cultural scene is essential to a strong, creative economy, especially places that are "bohemian" in character and offer diverse, edgy arts, music, film, food, and entertainment. Larger, more passive forms of cultural consumption or entertainment, he says, are of less interest to this group. Putnam makes a similar case for an active cultural environment that includes activities to help people better share their cultures and stories, and to learn, cooperate, and build social and civic connections.[8]

Others are finding that the practical and symbolic significance of creative people, bohemian neighborhoods, and iconic institutions have additional impacts. Economist Ann Markusen draws different connections between the presence and influences of thriving artist communities and successful industries. She argues that standard economic impact studies underestimate the full contribution of an artistic community to a regional economy; that is, they fail to trace the many ways in which creative talent contributes to regional productivity.[9]

Markusen counters the parochial view of the arts as a consequence of, or even parasite on, a successful business community. Using the phrase *the artistic dividend*, she makes the case that productivity in a regional economy rises in correlation to the number of artists within its boundaries. In other words, that an abundance of artists may be more cause than effect of a healthy economy. While Florida's *creative class* is more broadly defined, he and Markusen come to similar conclusions about the importance of creative thinkers—and environments that attract and stimulate them—to economic growth.

Economic Engines Don't Move Without Vehicles

While this chapter is focused on the economic dimensions of communities, there is a larger system at work that must be recognized. For an economic engine to go anywhere the rest of the vehicle has to be in working order. Natural and built environments as well as the social and cultural infrastructures are integrally related. If they are not working together, the community is not moving forward and is not healthy. Cultural leaders are key players in the overall well-being of their communities and bear responsibility for appreciating their key role in a holistic system. Cultural, economic, environmental, and social impacts must all be examined. Some planners have begun to cite these four key elements as equally essential to community health and sustainability.[10]

What draws people to the arts is not the hope that the experience will make them smarter or more self-disciplined. Instead, it is the expectation that encountering a work of art can be a rewarding experience, one that offers them pleasure and emotional stimulation and meaning.

A 2004 report by the RAND Corporation surveys recent literature and research on the social, economic, and human development impacts of the arts, as well as on the more difficult to quantify "intrinsic" values.[11] The findings bring together for the first time the multiple ways arts activities change lives and communities. Importantly, however, they point out that "what draws people to the arts is not the hope that the experience will make them smarter or more self-disciplined. Instead, it is the expectation that encountering a work of art can be a rewarding experience, one that offers them pleasure and emotional stimulation and meaning." RAND researchers conclude that instrumental benefits of the arts are "grounded in compelling arts experiences."

It is in the instrumental impacts of the arts together with their intrinsic power that make them profoundly effective catalysts for personal and community transformation. While choosing to employ the arts' capacity to invigorate an economy, it is impossible to divorce oneself from their multiple meanings and effects.

We shape our cities and then our cities shape us.[12]

—Elizabeth Plater-Zyberk, et al.

Culture and the Creation of Healthy *Places*

Like the arts, the design professions have a bigger impact on communities than we often attribute. In his groundbreaking work, William H. Whyte observed and documented human behaviors in urban settings and how design and policies regulating public spaces, buildings, and cities affect social behaviors.[13] Whyte asserted that crowded, pedestrian-friendly, active spaces are safer, more economically productive, and more conducive to healthy civic communities. "What attracts people most, it would appear, is other people," he wrote.[14]

The art of promoting constructive interaction among people in public spaces is one that's nearly forgotten. Planners, architects, and public administrators have been focused more on the creation of objects and providing for the unimpeded movement and storage of automobiles than on creating good urban spaces that serve people.[15] More recently public officials have been concerned with security and maximizing their ability to observe and control people in public spaces.

Active public space provides opportunities for people to meet and be exposed to the variety and multiple dimensions of their neighbors. These meetings often take place by chance, but also can come through active organizing. Public spaces include streets, sidewalks, parks, waterfronts, and civic buildings. Other important spaces include marketplaces, coffee shops, and restaurants.

"Place is something people do together, it's not just a container," said sociologist David Brain.[16] *Place* refers to a destination or iconic location within a community that has achieved deep and widespread meaning and value to locals and visitors alike. Taking mere *space* and turning it into *place* (or what some call *placemaking*) means creating something collectively valued and used. This is an area to which cultural programmers are uniquely well equipped to contribute—especially when they work together with, or complement the work of, planners, designers, and public officials. Culture contributes to the creation of healthy spaces and meaningful places. Desirable public space, in turn, can translate into economic benefits.

Arts Activities and Community Development

A University of Pennsylvania study led by Mark J. Stern and Susan Siefert[17] found that as the presence of small arts groups in neighborhoods increased, there were multiple positive effects. In areas with higher levels of cultural activity—in both poor and middle class neighborhoods—there was positive impact on school truancy, youth delinquency, civic engagement, teen pregnancy, and a host of other factors. These same researchers also cited positive relationships between arts participation, population stability, and real estate values. They assert that small cultural groups are typically more important to communities and to revitalization of neighborhoods than major institutions.[18]

Cultural activities stimulate community revitalization less through their direct economic impact than by building the social connections between people that in turn stimulate the formation and success of new enterprises. They motivate neighbors and give them increased capacity to see possibility and make changes in their community. They increase connections between neighborhoods of different ethnic and economic groups. Community arts organizations, Stern found, stimulate broader civic engagement, expand residents' sense of collective efficacy, and strengthen the bridges between neighborhoods.

A Chicago-based study by Diane Grams and Michael Warr[19] also looked beyond the art "product" and examined the social and economic activity that goes on around cultural organizations. It found that small community-based arts organizations leveraged a variety of relationships, capacities, and activities in unusually effective ways. The study cited three overarching results of community arts groups: they build social relationships, enable problem solving, and provide access to resources.

Culture in Community Development

The economic, social, and physical dimensions of community building are not only interrelated but inseparable. Over the past 35 years, the newly established field of community development has focused its efforts on construction and management of low and mixed-income housing, job training or workforce development, commercial real estate development, and small business start-up and incubation. It sometimes operates youth development, health, recreation, family counseling, human services, and—in rare instances—cultural programs.

The field of community development includes planners, trainers, housing, real estate and economic development specialists, community organizers, and advocates. They typically function through entities known as community development corporations (CDCs), which are supported locally and nationally by a widespread network of intermediaries such as Local Initiatives Support Corporation (LISC), Enterprise Foundation, and Living Cities: The National Community Development Initiative. These intermediaries depend largely on government, philanthropic, and corporate support and provide operating dollars, training, loans, and loan guarantees, as well as commonly accepted standards of community development practice. Local CDCs that become successful in housing and commercial real estate gradually build their own base of revenues from leasing, rental, sales, and development fees. Over the long term they accrue significant portfolios of real estate assets and become expert at property and small business development.

Neighborhood development strategies have been found to be more successful and equitable when cultural, economic, social, and environmental assets and advocates are acting in concert.

A 2002 report by New York's Center for an Urban Future saw great potential for synergy between CDCs and cultural organizations. It called for integrating cultural and business development and found that the two had the greatest impact side by side but that there's rarely coordination.[20] The report states, "In our survey of over 150 (New York City–based) economic and community development organizations, only six were involved in efforts that directly linked the arts with business." Not only are many arts groups in need of some of the expertise housed within CDCs, but neighborhood development strategies have been found to be more successful and equitable when cultural, economic, social, and environmental assets and advocates are acting in concert.

The Ford Foundation, together with a team of leaders in the culture and community development fields, looked at innovative community building strategies during 2002 and 2003 and report similar findings.[21] It observed that as art and cultural organizations support community involvement and participation, they help increase the potential for people to understand themselves and change how they see the world. This, in turn, bolsters community pride and identity, which bolsters the local economy. The study group also saw that the arts improve derelict buildings; preserve cultural heritage; transmit values and history; bridge cultural, ethnic, and racial boundaries; and stimulate economic development.

The study group found a few cases where community development practitioners in distressed communities successfully partnered with arts and cultural organizations in their community development strategies. However, it observed that community development and arts organizations were typically disparate and isolated from one another. The group found an important synergistic relationship exists but is rarely acknowledged or exploited.

WHEN CULTURE GOES TO WORK

As partners in the larger process of building healthy and economically prosperous communities, arts organizations must ask what they can do for their community rather than what their community can do for them. To do so, they must first take a good look at themselves to understand what assets and core competencies they bring to the table, and what unique qualities exist in the place they call their community.

The ultimate success story is a sustainable and competitive local economy based on a community's distinct assets, particularly cultural assets that enhance the identity and character of that community. Who wouldn't want to attract or nurture enterprises emanating from and reflecting local cultural values, that create jobs, are environmentally friendly, provide satisfying work, and give back to their community's civic and social life?

"Big box" solutions to community economic or social problems tend to become long term problems. Their impacts are less equitable, unbalanced, and not sustainable, whether they're a single manufacturing plant, giant retail outlet, sports or convention center, or giant performing arts complex. Big box developments import and depend on outside capital, labor, goods, culture, and consumers. Typically, they remove profit, damage the environment, overshadow the unique identity of place, and diminish the integrity and value of the people and cultures of that community. Just as a more diverse and balanced natural environment is a healthier one, a more diversified economy—rooted in a community's assets and in tune with the identity of that place—provides a more stable base and returns more to the local economy.

Locally-owned small businesses, including individual artists and small arts organizations, engage in their immediate community and have a unique product that attracts and supplies customers from outside the community. A large number and diverse mix of such enterprises, and an environment that supports their start-up and growth, is ideal. Likewise, a cultural "ecology" inclusive of a mix of ethnic groups, a balance of cultural producers (artists), cultural presenters, and cultural preservationists—a balance that is reflective of the community and draws both from within and from outside its boundaries—is eminently more stable, healthy, and productive.

SIX CULTURALLY-DRIVEN STRATEGIES FOR ECONOMIC DEVELOPMENT

In this section we'll look at six different, although often overlapping, approaches to economic development through arts and culture that readers can examine in relation to their own work. Observation and research has found the following strategies successfully in use by organizations including art centers, community development corporations, business organizations, cities, and other civic agencies or nonprofits. These have been written about in greater length and with additional examples in *Creative Community Builders Handbook*[22] by this same author. Typically, such efforts are successful when carried out in partnerships that straddle different sectors and include individual artists or arts organizations.

It must also be noted that these six approaches rarely function in isolation. They are singled out for purposes of understanding their impact, but rarely is any project so singular in focus or result. The sixth strategy, building trust, if not the central focus, is generally a by-product of all the others.

Creative Community Building Strategies

1. **Create Jobs.** Nurture artists and small cultural organizations as businesses to increase employment.
2. **Stimulate Trade.** Create the right conditions for cultural tourism to bring new resources to the community.
3. **Attract Investment.** Support artists and artist live/work spaces as anchors around which to build local economies.
4. **Diversify Economy.** Cluster arts organizations as retail anchors and activity generators to attract and support other enterprises.
5. **Enhance Value.** Employ the artists' touch to increase property values.
6. **Build Trust.** Create and strengthen the bonds between people of different backgrounds to enable enterprises to grow.

Strategy 1: Create Jobs

Nurture artists and small cultural organizations as businesses to increase employment.

> For too long, creative enterprises have been overlooked by economic developers and public services that have consistently cast their nets for the big fish, rather than the more abundant—and ultimately more self-sustaining—schools of small fish.[23]
>
> —Stuart Rosenfeld

The arts and culture sector has not generally been considered a major contributor to the U.S. economy. However, individual artists and nonprofit cultural organizations account for significant economic activity while bringing other benefits.

A 2002 study by Americans for the Arts estimated that the country's nonprofit arts industry generates $134 billion in annual economic activity.[24] This places nonprofit arts among the top ranks of national industries. They draw more audience participation and expenditures than professional sports, among other industries that are often aggressively courted by states and cities. Significantly, this study covers only formal nonprofit organizations, not individual artists or any of the "informal arts," traditional arts, or craft practices that take place outside institutional settings.

According to the Small Business Administration, small businesses account for more than half of all private sector employees and are growing faster than other types of businesses, creating three-quarters of all new jobs.[25]

In 1970, the Bureau of Labor Statistics estimated 730,000 artists in the United States and by 2001 estimated that number to be more than two million.[26] As many working artists operate "under the radar," and many more supplement their primary income through arts and craft activities, these figures are likely even higher.

As pure entrepreneurs at work in all corners of the country, artists create unique products and services that have considerable value well beyond the raw materials they use. When recognized and nurtured as small business enterprises, artists and small organizations can contribute even more.

There are many examples across the United States where entrepreneurial artists have been essential to the revitalization of neighborhoods, towns, and cities. Legendary urbanist Jane Jacobs said, "New ideas must use old buildings." [27] And old buildings are something many communities have in abundance. Creative entrepreneurs are in no short supply either. Matching the two, and creating a nurturing environment for arts-based enterprises, is the key.

Example: Penn Avenue Arts Initiative
As a neighborhood-based development project, Pittsburgh's Penn Avenue Arts Initiative transformed a nearly abandoned commercial corridor into a thriving multicultural street with artists, arts organizations, arts-related businesses, ethnic restaurants, and new neighborhood businesses. Two CDCs brought to the table their expertise, tools, and resources in real estate development and business incubation. Partnering with several small arts groups and dozens of individual artists—who are now owners, residents, and community activists—the project brought to life old buildings and generated cultural activities resulting in $10 million in investment, two dozen new businesses, and over 75 new jobs in just its first six years.

Strategy 2: Stimulate Trade

Create the conditions for cultural tourism to bring new resources to the community.

The travel and tourism industry is one of the largest in the United States, accounting for estimated economic activity in 2004 of over $600 billion.[29] There is enormous and growing interest among travelers to experience cultural, arts, historic, and heritage activities, especially among people of color.[30] Some 81 percent of adults in this country who traveled in 2002 included historic/cultural sites and activities as part of their travel, an increase of 13 percent from a similar study in 1996. In contrast, about nine percent of travelers included a visit to a theme or amusement park in that same year.[31]

Traditional arts celebrate the heritage, history, landscape, and even politics of places in ways that emphasize the unique features of a community.[28]

—Walker et al., Urban Institute

Travelers visiting historic or cultural sites spend significantly more money ($623 versus $457, excluding the cost of transportation). Four in ten travelers added extra time to their trip specifically to participate in historic or cultural activities. Most travelers indicate that trips where they learn something new are more memorable. Among the fastest growing reasons for leisure travel were biking, festivals and fairs, garden tours, museums, and historic places.

Cultural heritage tourism[32] is generally based on a local theme or landmark and binds multiple small-scale enterprises that complement one another. It creates a ripple effect within the regional economy. Sometimes a community's greatest assets are in plain sight yet invisible to locals. Appreciating and mobilizing local assets requires taking a new look at one's own community and working together across sectors.

Good examples are found in every type of location from inner-city immigrant neighborhoods to small towns in rural regions. They are very much alike in that their activities are rooted in the history and values of the people in the community, and in that their communities invest heavily in themselves. Cultural tourism requires ongoing and interdisciplinary planning. Success comes from cooperation across government, business, and nonprofit sectors, and often leads to even greater collaboration and enhanced capacity for problem-solving on all levels.

Example: Lanesboro, Minnesota
Visitors to remote Lanesboro (population 788) enjoy biking, canoeing, horseback riding, golf, tennis, and walking. They also enjoy theater, art, music, fine cuisine, and cozy accommodations. Lanesboro's leaders—key among them the Lanesboro Art Council, Commonweal Theatre Company, and Cornucopia Art Center—

understand the "brand identity" of their community— the aesthetics of the natural environment, their penchant for hospitality, and a panoply of cultural activities as ingredients for a successful tourism economy. They brought together their frozen-in-time nineteenth century main street, scenic bluffs of the Root River, and energy of local artists to build a remarkable success story.

These arts facilities have distinguished themselves as extremely stable and highly desirable additions to the urban landscape,...generating an immediate and significant positive impact on the surrounding neighborhoods, providing the momentum necessary to further revitalize distressed urban areas.[33]

—John Villani

Strategy 3: Attract Investment

Support artist live/work spaces as anchors around which to build local economies.

Older urban and rural areas have a great deal in common when it comes to suffering disinvestment, poisoned industrial sites, and population loss. Regenerating a more viable, sustainable, and flexible economy can begin with existing assets and result in a place that attracts investment. Some communities have enlisted creative entrepreneurs, chief among them artists, and made use of vacant real estate—such as warehouses, mills, or factory buildings—to jump start their economic development efforts.

"Being able to foster a local arts scene, provide low- and moderate-income housing, preserve historic buildings, and promote downtown and neighborhood economic revitalization—all at the same time—makes these types of projects rewarding far beyond their bottom line," Villani concludes. Typically artist live/work spaces are conceived in tandem with the reuse of historic, commercial, or industrial structures. It's the artists themselves, living and working in the community, who stimulate development of more active street-level environments while they create products of interest to wider markets.

Artist lofts bring a new and different kind of excitement to buildings and their surroundings. "The thing about artists is they're around 24 hours a day," says economist Ann Markusen. "They have unusual hours; they're around coming and going. They have families. These kinds of patterns are really great for reducing crime and stabilizing a community. Galleries, cafes, and other arts-related developments tend to follow, and the revenue from those businesses stays in the community." [34]

Example: City of Peekskill, New York

Marrying vision with various funding sources and municipal tools, Peekskill created artist live/work spaces in its historic but nearly vacant downtown. Planners believed artists could attract visitors and business and be a catalyst to remake the once thriving town center. They were right. Peekskill's Artists' District also built on the momentum of the Paramount Center for the Arts, housed in a vintage 1930s movie palace. The overlapping Business Improvement District now boasts more than 100 artist studio or live/work spaces, 12 galleries and related businesses, a new grocery store, pharmacy, community college branch, restaurants, and increased tourist traffic, especially during numerous annual cultural celebrations and festivals.

Strategy 4: Diversify Economy

Cluster arts organizations as retail anchors and activity generators to attract and support other enterprises.

The more legs an economy has to stand on, the more resistant it is to a downturn in any one sector. Creative economies continually generate new enterprises and reinvent themselves, building new legs and repositioning old ones. Many creative community builders have revived both urban and rural economies by tapping existing assets and applying creative strategies to support a variety of businesses and activities. Building connections between sectors, or legs, is their most creative act.

Cultural organizations and activities are able to attract people and investment and encourage entertainment venues, retail, restaurant, residential, and office development. They tend to increase rental rates, decrease vacancy rates, and increase tax revenues, jobs, and incomes.[35] A critical mass of cultural activities in one district generates enormous interest and a base for building other consumer-driven enterprises. But they cannot stand alone. Large arts complexes or cultural districts planned or created in isolation are not a winning strategy.

Urban redevelopment and historic preservation writer Roberta Brandes Gratz warns against the "big fix" or the "grand plan." She cites successful projects where the key was "thinking small in a big way." [36] Not only did these projects have more equitably distributed economic benefits, but they retained and built upon threads of existing social fabric. Their purpose was to build stronger communities, not entice larger institutions, richer investors, or bigger corporate chains.

Communities that bring together the cultural, business, and civic sectors to create interdependent economic networks do so by combining the unique assets of their residents, natural environment, proximity to other resources, and cultural strengths. The cultures and creative abilities of residents, together with the entrepreneurial drive of small business owners, have served as effective catalysts for the revival of downtrodden and decayed towns and neighborhoods. Culture is the best way to assert or reassert the unique identity of the place, to organize stakeholders, and to attract outside attention and resources.

Example: ACT (Arts, Culture & Trade) Roxbury
The ACT Roxbury Consortium put arts and culture to work for the economic and social revitalization of Boston's Dudley Square Business District and Lower Roxbury neighborhood. The local CDC, Madison Park Development Corporation, used its entrepreneurial skills to help area artists, fledgling arts groups, and nearby institutions. They created cultural events, built a support structure for artists, and developed a new cultural center. They sponsored a film festival, artist open studios, performing arts events, annual literary event, and a holiday shopping catalogue to promote creations of local artists. Coordinated with local businesses, these and other activities draw many people to this reemerging commercial district.

Strategy 5: Enhance Value

Employ the artists' touch to increase property values.

Cities and small towns across the United States are looking for ways to revitalize neglected areas and bolster real estate values and tax rolls. Increasingly, some are courting creative industries and creative class workers, but few see artists as investors and hands-on workers who will enhance property values. Putting artists to work to improve real estate can enhance property values as well as return financial benefit to the artists and help them build artistic careers.

... [T]he arts, increased tourism and community participation, and regional economic redevelopment are mutually reinforcing and inextricably linked... The arts create and bestow community identity. Identity rallies hope, productivity and pride, and economic vibrancy.

—Massachusetts Museum of Contemporary Art website, www.MassMoCA.org

Human cleverness, desires, motivations, imagination, and creativity are replacing location, natural resources, and market access as urban resources. The creativity of those who live in and run cities will determine future success.[37]

—Charles Landry, The Creative City

In taking raw materials and creatively enhancing them or adapting them to other uses, artists enhance value and change meaning. When applying themselves to home construction or rehabilitation, artists create new or increased value. New and historic homes with unique features and quality handmade amenities retain value and embody local history and craftsmanship. They are places with greater meaning that, in turn, move their inhabitants to make greater investment in the place they call home.

It must be noted, however, that in some neighborhoods where real estate values have escalated, artists have been faulted for setting off a process of economic revival that has caused dislocation of poorer people and some small businesses. A 2002 study by the Center for an Urban Future confirmed that such concerns were justified.[38] "In five of the seven neighborhoods we assessed, concerns about displacement were plainly laid at the feet of cultural development," the report stated.

Of course, while artists or arts groups have been blamed for bringing about gentrification, they are more often its victims. The phenomenon of gentrification (the rapid escalation of real estate prices, rents, property taxes, or condominium conversion that results in dislocation of poor and working class residents) does seem to follow on the heels of transient artists. In other cities with much vacant housing and depressed values, artists have become a welcome sight. Neighborhood groups, cities, and small towns are on the hunt for artists or arts organizations or cultural centers that will heat up their tax base.

Example: HandMade in America
Involving artists in rehabbing historic homes and designing new housing is the innovative strategy employed by the West End/Clingman Avenue revitalization project in Asheville, North Carolina. In this downtrodden neighborhood, HandMade in America partnered with Mountain Housing Opportunities, the local residents' association, and others to demonstrate the incorporation of handmade objects in home construction and neighborhood revitalization. Included were local artists working in glass, fiber, metal, ceramics, and stone, as well as liturgical and public art. In less than ten years HandMade exposed a major "new" industry that had been there all along, making the region the "center of the handmade object in America." In applying this approach to homebuilding, they're enhancing the meaning and value of place.

Strategy 6: Build Trust

Create bonds between people that support entrepreneurial projects and new business.

Culture is the "glue," the shared values and meanings that bind us together, that shape our lives and, indeed, shape our attitudes about development and stewardship. Yet it is this intangible dimension of culture that is frequently ignored in public policy discussion, where culture is too often seen as a "soft" topic or an impediment to progress.[39]

—Caroline Marshall

Imagine a community in which a diversity of people regularly mingles, where they build bonds across differences towards a better community and openly and creatively tackle tough and complex issues. Social capital as described by Robert Putnam, and economic capital, both of which are central to the well-being of people and their communities, require people to work together towards common goals.

Francis Fukuyama observes, "The most useful kind of social capital is often not the ability to work under the authority of a traditional community or group, but the capacity to form new associations and to cooperate within the terms of references they establish." [40] Economic success, he finds, depends on the kinds of trust nurtured within different cultures, a capacity he calls spontaneous sociability. That process can begin with neighbors shopping side by side, exchanging goods in the marketplace. It can grow through volunteering with neighbors to produce community theater, participate in a holiday parade, or visit an event at a neighborhood art center, church, or school.

The fabric or social capital that holds communities together and allows them to function is based on relationships that transcend family structures, race, class, religion, ethnicity, etc. Whatever it's called, we know that without social capital, trust, or *collective efficacy*[41] communities' business and civic enterprises would grind to a halt. What is less well known is how these phenomena are produced or where they come from. Many believe that arts and cultural practices both nurture and build on spontaneous sociability, social capital, and the rest. As such, the public practice of the arts, and participation in arts enterprises, is a major factor in a communities' capacity to generate and support the success of new business and social networks.

Example: WaterFire Providence
WaterFire, a recurring public art event, is a key element in the remarkable revitalization of downtown Providence, Rhode Island. As important as its economic impact is its effect on the community's self-esteem. The iconic, ritual-like lighting of fires on downtown waterways has brought international recognition to this once sleepy New England city. It involves hundreds of volunteers working together to create a sense of safety in a once-dreaded downtown. Trust has been built in working together year after year. The symbolic tension between fire and water, well-designed public space, along with crowds eager to enjoy the evening together, draws nearly 100,000 people for each of 25 lightings during a nine-month season. This has propelled new retail, restaurant, commercial, and residential development.

Economic Development Based on Cultural Assets

Looking across these various examples, several best practices begin to emerge, practices that put to work cultural assets toward community and economic development.

Project a distinct and unified identity that focuses on cultural and natural amenities and taps artists and entrepreneurs who reflect and contribute to that identity.

Build and coordinate mutually beneficial relationships and exchanges across sectors and between artists, trades, developers, local business, arts groups, and policymakers from tourism and economic development agencies.

Engage diverse populations, including youth, in the design and realization of cultural activities, learning experiences, projects, and products to both reflect the identity of the community and build a base of ownership and participation.

Utilize familiar public spaces and provide opportunities for social interaction between neighbors, artists, visitors, and other community partners.

Enhance leadership with intermediaries who understand the arts, economic development, and cultural diversity, and who can "translate" skills from one sector or culture to others.

Help artists and entrepreneurs establish ownership, especially of underutilized space that has capacity for mixed used development.

Provide multiple and complementary experiences, products, and services to locals and visitors.

Plan and evaluate activities and policies that promote artists and cultural products and events for their long-term impacts and benefits

Projects described above, and many others that have had similar impacts on their communities, result from the efforts of civic entrepreneurs, artists, philanthropists, visionary mayors, or other leaders. They often grow out of initiatives already at work or are hybrids of things people saw work elsewhere.

Visit the Online Companion for this chapter (see the last page of the book for Internet address) to read author Tom Borrup's outline of a general process that can be adapted in your community to mobilize the human, physical, creative, and economic assets unique to your place toward goals of community and economic development through the arts.

ENDNOTES

1. Speech given at the 2004 National Performing Arts Convention, Pittsburgh, PA. (2004, June 20). *Cincinnati Enquirer.*
2. Venturelli, S. (2001). *From the Information Economy to the Creative Economy.* Washington, DC: Center for Arts and Culture.
3. New England Council. (2000, June). *The Creative Economy Initiative: The Role of the Arts and Culture in New England's Economic Competitiveness.* Retrieved from www.newenglandcouncil.com/initiatives
4. Huntington, S. P., & Harrison, L. E. (Eds.). (2000). *Culture Matters* (Forward, xv). New York: Basic Books.
5. Thompson, J. (2005, February 12). *Post Voodoo Cultural Economics.* Speech given at the Berkshire Conference, Sterling and Francine Clark Art Institute, Williamstown, MA.
6. Florida, R. (2002). *The Rise of the Creative Class.* New York: Basic Books.
7. Putnam, R. (2000). *Bowling Alone.* New York: Touchstone.
8. Putnam, R., & Feldstein, L. (2003). *Better Together.* New York: Simon and Schuster.
9. Markusen, A. (2003). *The Artistic Dividend.* University of Minnesota. Retrieved from www.hhh.umn.edu
10. Hawkes, J. (2004). *The Fourth Pillar of Sustainability: Culture's essential role in public planning.* Victoria, Australia: Humanities.com.
11. McCarthy, K. F., Ondaatje, E. H., Zakaras, L., & Brooks, A. (2004). *Gifts of the Muse: Reframing the Debate About the Benefits of the Arts.* Santa Monica, CA: RAND Corporation.
12. Plater-Zyberk, E., Duany, A., & Speck, J. (2000). *Suburban Nation* (83). New York: North Point Press.
13. Whyte, W. H. (1980). *The Social Life of Small Urban Places.* Washington, DC: Project for Public Places.
14. Ibid.
15. Kent, F. & Madden, K. (2000). *How to Turn A Place Around: A Handbook for Creating Successful Public Places.* New York: Project for Public Spaces.
16. Brain, D. (2004, March). *New College of South Florida, Sarasota.* Speech given at the University of Miami School of Architecture, Placemaking and Community Building.
17. Dr. Mark J. Stern, professor of social welfare and history at the University of Pennsylvania, and urban planner Susan Siefert have studied community-based arts groups for ten years through the Social Impact of the Arts Project (SIAP). www.ssw.upenn.edu/SIAP
18. Stern, M. J. (2003). *Performing Miracles: when it comes to neighborhood revitalization, community arts groups have a thing or two to show business.* Washington, DC: Center for an Urban Future.
19. Grams, D., & Warr, M. (2003). *Leveraging Assets: How Small Budget Arts Activities Benefit Neighborhoods.* Richard H. Driehaus Foundation & John D. and Catherine T. MacArthur Foundation.
20. Kleiman, N.S. (2002). *The Creative Engine.* New York: Center for an Urban Future.
21. Ford Foundation. (2003, April). *Downside Up* [Motion picture]. Listening Tour Project. Asset Building and Community Development Program. New York: Ford Foundation.
22. Borrup, T. (2006). *Creative Community Builders Handbook.* St. Paul, MN: Fieldstone Alliance (formerly Wilder Publishing).
23. Rosenfeld, S. (2004). *Crafting a New Rural Development Strategy.* Economic Development America. Washington, DC, U.S. Department of Commerce Economic Development Administration.
24. Americans for the Arts. (2003). *Arts and Economic Prosperity: The Economic Impact of Nonprofit Arts Organizations and Their Audiences.* Washington, DC. Retrieved from www.artsusa.org
25. According to the Small Business Administration, 2.5 million of the 3.4 million jobs created in 1999–2000 were small businesses. An estimated 16.5 million sole proprietorships were active in 2000. Of all small businesses, 53 percent are home-based, while only three percent are franchises. www.sba.gov
26. Jackson, M., et al. (2003). *Investing in Creativity: A Study of the Support Structure for U.S. Artists.* Washington, DC: The Urban Institute.
27. Jacobs, J. (1961). *The Death and Life and Great American Cities* (188). New York: Vintage Books.
28. Walker, C., Jackson, M., & Rosenstein, C. (2003). *Culture and Commerce, Traditional Arts in Economic Development.* Washington, DC: The Urban Institute & The Fund for Folk Culture.

29. According to a 2003 Travel Industry Association of America and *Smithsonian Magazine* study, these expenditures generated over 7.2 million jobs, $158 billion in payroll income taxes, and $95 billion in local, state, and federal tax revenue.
30. The same travel study also indicated that tourism travel by African Americans grew at a rate of four percent in 2003, double the growth rate of all tourism. Asian American travel grew by ten percent, and Latino travel was up a remarkable 20 percent between 2000 and 2002.
31. Same study as above.
32. Cultural heritage tourism has been defined by Partners for Livable Communities as "travel based on interaction with both human-built and natural environment as a means to learn about and experience the arts, heritage, and the special character of a place." Cultural Heritage Tourism: How Communities Can Reinvent Their Future. (2004). Washington, DC: Partners for Livable Communities.
33. Villani, J. (1999, July). *A Call to Art.* Urban Land Institute.
34. Markusen, Ann as quoted (2005, May 8). *Minneapolis Star Tribune* (D4).
35. Hudnutt, B. (2000). *The Economic Impact of Arts Centers: A Real Estate Perspective.* In Ernst & Young study. Presented at Urban Land Institute conference, Orlando, FL.
36. Gratz has observed community redevelopment strategies for several decades, first in the United States and more recently in Eastern European countries. In her two books, *The Living City*, 1994, and *Cities Back from the Edge*, 1998, she advocates building from within, employing grass-roots and bottom-up strategies.
37. Landry, C. (2000). *The Creative City* (xiii). London: Earthscan.
38. Center for an Urban Future. (2000, November). *The Elephant in the Room: Gentrification and Displacement.* New York.
39. Marshall, C. (2004). *Envisioning Convergence: Cultural Conservation, Environmental Stewardship and Sustainable Livelihoods* (3). Wolf, Keens & Company. Santa Fe, NM: The Fund for Folk Culture.
40. Fukuyama, F. (1995). *Trust: The Social Virtues and the Creation of Prosperity* (27). New York: Free Press Paperbacks.
41. Dr. Felton Earls, Harvard School of Public Health, conducted a 15-year study in Chicago neighborhoods and found the single most important factor differentiating levels of health from one to the next was what he called collective efficacy. It wasn't economic status, access to health care, crime, or some more tangible factor that topped the list. This more elusive ingredient—the capacity of people to act together on matters of common interest—he found was the greatest variable in the health.

RESOURCES

These national organizations have incorporated arts, design, and/or heritage among their interests in community and economic development. Go to the AES Online Companion to this chapter (see the last page of the book for the Internet address) for a comprehensive listing of additional community development and economic development resources and agencies.

Artspace Projects Inc.
250 Third Avenue North, Suite 500
Minneapolis, MN 55401
612-333-9012
www.artspaceprojects.org
Development and management of artist housing and arts organization space

The Center for Rural Strategies
46 East Main Street
Whitesburgh, KY 41858
606-632-3244
www.ruralstrategies.org
Rural economic, environmental, and cultural development and policy

Leveraging Investments in Creativity (LINC)
450 West 37th Street, Suite 502
New York, NY 10018
646-731-3275
www.lincnet.net
Artist support and housing, and arts-based economic development

Mayor's Institute for City Design
1620 Eye Street NW, 3rd Floor
Washington, DC 20006
202-463-1390
www.archfoundation.org/micd
Integrated design policy for economic revitalization

National Trust Main Street Center
National Trust for Historic Preservation
1785 Massachusetts Avenue NW
Washington, DC 20036
202-588-6219
www.mainst.org
Commercial district revitalization

Partners for Livable Communities
1429 21st Street NW
Washington, DC 20036
202-887-5990
www.livable.com
Integrated cultural, economic, and placemaking strategies

Project for Public Spaces
700 Broadway, 4th Floor
New York, NY 10003
212-620-5660
www.pps.org
Public markets and public space design

CHAPTER 3

Cultural Advocacy

3

STAN ROSENBERG AND DAN HUNTER

What is the value of arts and culture to our society? You might answer that question by arguing that arts and cultural organizations are essential to building strong, healthy, and vital communities, and that cultural nonprofits are integral to education and public learning. Arts and culture are good for our schools, our communities, our economy, and our souls, you might say.

Many elected officials and members of the public see arts and culture as a frill, a luxury for the few. So, public funding for arts and culture is the first to be cut in tough economic times. Can you run a business when you lose one of your major customers and your revenue drops by as much as 50 percent in one year?

Successful arts administrators, the leaders of nonprofit cultural organizations, have mastered the skills of fundraising, earning ticket revenue, cultivating significant donors, writing grants, and managing expenses. The successful arts administrator will devote considerable time and energy to cultivate a $10,000 donor. However, how much time will he or she invest to keep the $10,000 arts agency grant available?

Sometimes cultural leaders neglect the strategic importance of political advocacy, as they are pressed to meet the demands of running their organizations and programs. They may quietly expect increased support during boom years and are shocked at sudden and severe cuts during the lean. Public opinion polls consistently show that people like the arts, respects its institutions, and support arts education. Why don't politicians recognize that? In an informal meeting, a gubernatorial candidate, when asked why he didn't have a position on cultural funding, simply said, "There are no votes in it."

Cultural advocacy needs to harness the good feelings expressed in opinion polls into votes, so that appreciation for the arts can be transformed into a priority that motivates voters.

Successful advocacy can change the perception of arts and culture from a frill to a necessity. As a society, we set our priorities through the government budget process. We may say we love arts and culture, but the proof is where we as a people choose to spend our tax dollars. Successful advocacy does more than increase budget lines; it teaches the public how to value arts and culture.

As a cultural leader, you are part of a significant and unique industry. However, your organization will benefit with others through increased funding and increased perception of value. Nonprofit cultural organizations have shared economic interests and must pursue a common political agenda.

WHAT CAN BE ACHIEVED THROUGH ADVOCACY?

Public funding through state and local arts agencies for operating support, project grants, and programming.

Public funding through appropriation, bond financing, or loans for capital grants to facilities for repairs, acquisition, and new and expanded facilities.

State and municipal investment in infrastructure projects, such as roads, sidewalks, parking, and signage that improves public access to cultural organizations.

Laws, policies, and regulations, including zoning and building codes for safe, accessible cultural facilities.

Increased investment in arts education for youth pre-K through twelfth grade in school and after school.

Government nonart agencies supporting and advancing the role of the arts through collaborations that promote education and youth development, tourism, economic and workforce development, community development, affordable housing, and other agendas of state government.

Legislation that enhances the operating environment, as well as expands revenue and resources for all segments of the cultural community—such as nonprofit reporting requirements, state tax deductions for charitable contributions, endowment incentive programs, stabilization grants, cultural facilities renovation, and arts education curriculum mandates.

Zoning that allows artists to find space to live and work.

Tax laws that are more favorable to individual artists, such as allowing artists to deduct the market value of donated works.

First Amendment rights of free expression are protected.

Advocacy is often defined as coordinated efforts to affect public policy in the political arena. However, advocacy is more than communication with elected officials. Since public policy derives from the political perception of what the public wants, then effective advocates must communicate with the broader public. So, advocacy can also achieve:

- **increased business support for arts and culture,** ranging from the small business owner who places a playbill ad to large corporations willing to underwrite programming;
- **encouragement of community and charitable foundations** to include cultural grants in their portfolios; and
- **changing the perceptions of the media** to increase the recognition of the value of arts and culture. The media shapes the broad public understanding of our society and is integral to any advocacy campaign.

Successful advocacy will help to create the environment where your cultural organization can pursue its mission and serve your community. The Advocacy Continuum sidebar outlines a range of advocacy activities which would enable your organization to achieve various end goals.

This continuum outlines a range of activities defined by the level of your commitment. Starting from the top are activities that are relatively easy, inexpensive, and straightforward. As you progress down the list, the activities require greater commitment of time, dedication, and resources. As you gain advocacy experience, you and your colleagues will become skilled at all the tasks outlined here. However, if you feel like a newcomer to advocacy, begin with the activities at the top of the chart.

Advocacy Continuum	
Information	Write newsletters, online briefs, etc. Tell your story to the public without links to an agenda.
Workshops/Training	Undertake advocacy discussion and training. Enable people through training.
Speakers Programs/Forums	Inform key audiences about your advocacy efforts (address noncontroversial topics).
Research	Conduct research to measure community value, including economic impact, etc. Create leads to positioning papers.
Position Papers	Use the research to guide policy positions as outlined in position papers. Communicate the research to the public.
Advocacy Days	Establish advocates on a local and statewide level. Develop a shared agenda and common message.
Agenda Setting and Public Policy	Set an advocacy agenda targeted to national, state, or local government.
Awards to Politicians, Business Leaders, and Others	Recognize past support and effort. Develop champions for your cause.
Accountability Organizing	Get candidates to state their opinions and commit to action or support. Publish the information about candidates or officials without offering support. Track official actions and votes taken after legislators are elected.
Endorsing Candidates	Publicly endorse one candidate over another based on voting records or opinion surveys. (This cannot be done by a nonprofit. Also, endorsing candidates is risky; your candidate may lose and your endorsement may antagonize other candidates and their supporters.)
Campaigning	Contribute personal money to a candidate's campaign. Volunteer to work in the campaign. (This cannot be done by a nonprofit.)
Lobbying	Hire a lobbyist. Register as a citizen lobbyist. Work at the statehouse to affect legislation and legislators.
First Amendment Issues	Arts and culture often sit on the fault lines of intense societal disagreements. Taking sides carries the risk of earning enmity. Not taking sides carries the risk of losing your self-respect Learn how to walk the line. Learn how to responding to public attacks on the arts based on misinformation, bias, or preference.

ARTS AND CULTURE AS A PUBLIC ISSUE

In 1780, the Commonwealth of Massachusetts adopted the first state constitution. Written by John Adams, later the second president of the United States, the Massachusetts Constitution became a model for the United States Constitution. In the Massachusetts Constitution, Adams establishes that the promotion of the arts, literature, and sciences is a shared responsibility between public and private institutions.

> ...It shall be the duty of legislatures and magistrates, in all future periods of this commonwealth, to cherish the interests of literature and the sciences...to encourage private societies and public institutions, for the promotion of agriculture, arts, sciences, commerce, trades, manufactures, and a natural history of the country...

Adams sought to do more than create a system of government structures in his draft of the Constitution; he had his eye cast to the future. He worked to create a foundation that would allow this new political society to grow and mature. In a letter to his wife Abigail, Adams described his vision of how a maturing society would be reflected in his own family:

> I must study politics and war that my sons may have liberty to study mathematics and philosophy. My sons ought to study mathematics and philosophy, geography, natural history and naval architecture, navigation, commerce and agriculture, in order to give their children a right to study painting, poetry, music, architecture, statuary, tapestry, and porcelain.
>
> —John Adams, letter to Abigail Adams, 1780

In the generations since John Adams, arts and culture have been private endeavors. Culture was a private matter maintained by and for the rich, and only the wealthy had access to what was defined then as "fine arts." Two generations ago, funding arts and culture was not a public issue subject to public policy.

This changed in 1965 when the National Endowments for the Arts (NEA) and Humanities (NEH) were established. To meet federal requirements for receiving NEA funds, the 50 states and three territories quickly established state arts agencies. In the short span of 41 years, every state and most major cities have devoted public funds to support arts and culture using a wide variety of funding mechanisms. State and local funding far exceed the federal NEA appropriation. In 2002, states allocated $411,557,737, nearly four times as much as the total NEA budget, according to the National Assembly of State Arts Agencies' Legislative Appropriations Database. New York City's municipal appropriation for arts and culture nearly equals the total NEA budget. Through budget appropriations from federal, state, and local governments, the arts and culture—like health, housing, transportation, and the environment—are now recognized as a public policy issue.

Culture, then, is part of the public debate. The laws, regulations, and budget allocations that benefit arts and culture are also subject to the constant tug and pull of political debate. Public funding for the arts, sciences, and humanities rises through boom years with little debate, and during leaner times—such as in the early 1990s and the early part of this century—state and federal funding was slashed, and in some cases, nearly eliminated. Political priorities shifted to stimulating state economies through job creation and budget balancing. State spending was scrutinized for "return on investment." For many states, cultural funding was an easy target, even though cultural spending was typically less than .5 percent of a state's total budget.

Advocates for favorable arts policy must understand these political changes and demonstrate the public value earned for public investment.

FOUR LEVELS OF GOVERNMENT

In the United States, the four levels of government—federal, state, county, and municipal—each affects cultural organizations in specific ways. These four levels have jurisdiction over specific geographic areas. Your location and concern dictate which level of government can address your problem. The lines of authority can blur on some issues like health care and education, but in general each level of government affects cultural organizations in different areas of operation.

The **federal government** provides direct funding to cultural organizations through grants and earmarks, and provides indirect subsidy by granting tax-exempt status. It is the federal tax code that allows the formation of tax-exempt organizations known under the tax code designation as 501(c)3. Nonprofit status allows donors to take a federal income tax deduction for gifts to the nonprofit, tax-exempt organization. The tax deduction allows a donor to take money that he or she would have paid to the government in taxes and give the money to a public charity. Therefore, tax deductible contributions are a form of public support.

The federal government also provides funding for cultural organizations through other federal agencies, such as the Department of Education (see The Art of Fundraising chapter for a list of federal agencies that support the arts). The federal government often uses its funding power to require states and local governments to adopt specific policies. For example, schools seeking federal funding must comply with Title IX regulations requiring gender equity in disbursements. As discussed above, most state arts agencies were created after 1965 in response to a federal requirement that states have an art agency to qualify for NEA funding. Under current law, the NEA must direct 40 percent of its funding to state arts agencies.

State governments are a major source of the public funding for cultural organizations, both through NEA funding directed to state arts agencies and funding appropriated by state government. There is a wide disparity in state funding for arts and culture. Some states provide generous support to arts and culture, while others don't. State governments must balance their budgets, so when state revenues fall during tough economic times, state spending falls. Consequently, state cultural funding has seen many peaks and valleys, with increases in prosperous times, followed by funding cuts during lean times. States can also assist arts and culture through tourism promotion, percent-for-art programs, and statewide arts education mandates, among others.

Local governments—counties, cities, and towns—provide the largest source of public funding for the arts, nearly double the amount of direct state and federal support combined in 2004.[1] Furthermore, local governments make critical decisions that affect cultural organizations. Local governments control the nuts and bolts of day-to-day operations, providing mundane but critical services such as police and fire protection, garbage removal, water, utilities, parking, and street repair, which impact the budget and daily operations of a cultural organization.

Local governments are also critical to long-term planning through zoning regulations, building and fire codes, and infrastructure investment. For example, a performance hall may want to expand its load-in facilities, requiring city permission for new construction. Or the performing hall might seek to expand its seating and ask the city to increase nearby parking facilities. Local governments can also assist in promoting cultural organizations through directional street signs or streetlight banners.

OTHER ADVOCACY AUDIENCES

Advocacy is more than working to influence public policy. The maintenance and development of our cultural resources is, as John Adams wrote, a shared responsibility between individuals, the private sector, and the public sector. We must advocate—effectively communicate the value that arts and culture create—to multiple audiences, including charitable foundations, large and small businesses, the media, and individuals.

Foundations are many and varied and are dedicated to promoting the public good through their giving. Cultural organizations contribute to the public good and strengthen communities. Through advocacy, we can persuade more foundations to include arts and culture in their funding priorities.

Though **businesses** are not established to promote the public good, they often recognize that a stronger community creates a better economic climate for business. Businesses can assist cultural organizations through sponsorships, program advertising, employee incentive programs, and direct contributions. Consider the broad spectrum of businesses in your area. Neighborhood restaurants benefit when people come to your evening programs. A large corporation may want to name the new wing of your museum to enhance its image as a good corporate citizen. Progressive business leaders learned long ago that attending to their community enhances business in the long run.

Nonprofit cultural organizations are also businesses, concerned about costs, payroll, capital investment, and long-term planning like any other business. Cultural leaders should participate in community and business forums like the chambers of commerce or local service clubs where they can make connections with other business leaders. These forums offer advocacy opportunities to describe the community value of your organization. Working effectively with business leaders also can also connect you with individual donors.

The media—newspapers, radio, television, magazines, and the Internet—shape how we see our society with a daily barrage of news, stories, data, and images. The media creates the context for political debate and monitors (and even creates) public perception that is then interpreted by political leaders. One good story in the newspaper will create a perception in the minds of thousands of readers. Effective advocacy must always have a media strategy. Always communicate with the press, formally and informally. Develop a relationship with your local media. Tell your story so that it serves your goals, but never dissemble. A long-term relationship with a reporter requires that you be honest, helpful, and prompt (they are always on deadline). It seems impossible to make your voice heard over the deluge of news report daily, yet the media needs new stories everyday—it is the definition of news. Consequently, the media needs you as much you need its coverage. For more information about how to work with the press, see the Marketing the Arts chapter.

We are a society of individuals, each with one vote. However, we often overlook the vital advocacy we can do with the people we meet everyday—friends, family, acquaintances, and strangers. Each individual is potentially more than one vote and more than one opinion. The smart advocate knows that when you share your story with one person, you are also linking to an extended network. A wise campaigner once said, "Every election is won one vote at a time."

Cultural organizations interact daily with government, ranging from the mundane—garbage removal—to the sublime—receiving a federal grant for new programming. While each cultural organization will face distinct advocacy challenges based on circumstance, all cultural organizations must engage in advocacy to achieve its mission. Advocacy plays a critical role in building public understanding of the value of arts and culture and the role of government. As you advocate in the political arena, you are also communicating to the general public. And advocating with foundations, businesses, individuals, and the media will build broader public support that will help convince elected officials to support the arts and culture.

BUILDING A FOUNDATION FOR ADVOCACY

Some cultural leaders may be reluctant to approach government. They may mistakenly believe that the tax-exempt status of their organization prevents them from advocacy. Or they may be unfamiliar with and even intimidated by the political world. As leaders of nonprofit organizations, we work in a society dedicated to profit. Without profit, we feel that we lack the power to influence government. For an explanation of what is allowed, see the Appendix, found at the end of this chapter, for How Much Advocacy Can a Nonprofit Do?

Believing ourselves to be powerless is wrong and blinds us to the sources of political power that we do have and can cultivate. Make a quick list of ten of your friends. Each of those friends can add ten more. Your list of contacts quickly grows to 100 and more as you add in coworkers, neighbors, contributors, and so on. You have more power than you think. Your goal is to harness and apply that power. That is effective advocacy.

Building an Advocacy Network

The first step in your advocacy work is to take an inventory of your advocacy resources. Make a list of everyone you know, including family, coworkers, friends, and neighbors. You can call on those in your advocacy network for assistance in your advocacy campaigns. Think of all the places where you have reliable and supportive contacts throughout the realms of your life.

Quickly, you will see that most cultural organizations have excellent networks in the community, ranging from influential board members and retired volunteers to school teachers and vendors, and to patrons and contributors. All of these people believe in the mission of your organization and can be recruited to be your advocacy network.

Board of Directors/Trustees

Your board of directors is critical to the success of your organization and essential to your advocacy. Directors and trustees are usually community leaders and representatives of the people you serve. They have wealth, connections, experience, and expertise. They are your eyes and ears in the community as well as spokespersons to the community. They serve as board members not only because they believe in the organizational mission, but also because they recognize the community benefit your organization provides. This dual role enhances their effectiveness as advocates: they are not acting out of self-interest but are volunteers dedicated to the community and to the greater good. Furthermore, board members arrive with distinct community, business, social, or political connections, and thus can connect the cultural organization to many diverse circles of influence previously unreachable. Make advocacy a part of the board's responsibility, with regular discussion at board meetings and appropriate advocacy training.

What is Your Organization's Role in the Community?

As part of your advocacy inventory, your cultural organization needs to assess how it serves its community. Because political districts are based on geography, we will assume that the community you serve can be defined in geographic terms, such as the neighborhood, city, and region where you provide services. Obviously, your organization plays a cultural role in the community. Have you considered its economic, social, and educational contributions? Cultural organizations provide educational programs for school children, adults, and seniors. They anchor a neighborhood. And, like any other business, they create jobs generating tax revenue through its payroll. Here are some questions that will help you to assess your organization.

What role does your organization play in the community?

Who benefits from its services?

How many full and part-time employees are there?

What is the total payroll?

What are the total expenditures in the community?

Which local businesses are regular vendors?

Which businesses indirectly benefit from your organization, such as nearby restaurants, hotels, coffee shops, and bookstores?

Which schools and how many students benefit from the organization?

How does your organization foster a spirit of community in the neighborhood and town?

Which social service and civic agencies collaborate with or benefit from your organization?

Many of these questions ask you to address the local economic impact of your nonprofit organization. The mission of your organization is vital to you and your colleagues. However, as you advocate outside of the cultural world, you will find that not everyone shares your view of the importance and vitality of your organization's mission. Economic impact offers another measure of community value, one that is more readily understood in business and political spheres. Though your organization is nonprofit business, it is still a business with economic impact: making payroll, paying vendors, withholding income tax, paying utilities, filing tax reports. Your organization also provides economic impact through the spending habits of the audience that participates in its programs.

Defining economic value is critical to successful advocacy, but it is not the only way to describe the value created by your cultural organization. Your organization may educate young people, support tourism by drawing people to the region, help at-risk youth, provide senior citizens with opportunity for creative activity and intellectual stimulation, be a catalyst for neighborhood revitalization, or serve as a forum for cultural exchange to strengthen bonds between diverse communities.

Key Allies: Local, State, and National Advocacy Groups

You must include local, state, and national advocacy groups in your advocacy inventory. These groups have government contacts and strategic insights gained through experience with cultural issues and politics. Advocacy groups, like Americans for the Arts and state arts advocacy groups, have conducted valuable research to support and inform your advocacy. Americans for the Arts posts extensive information and current news on its website, www.americansforthearts.org, and links to advocacy software that allows arts supporters to send emails to elected officials quickly and efficiently.

Americans for the Arts was created in 1996 as a result of the merger between the National Assembly of Local Arts Agencies (NALAA) and the American Council for the Arts (ACA). Since 1996, Americans for the Arts has merged with other advocacy groups, including most recently the Arts and Business Council. In 2004, Americans for the Arts also merged two networks of state arts advocacy groups into a new State Arts Action Network (SAAN), currently with 37 member organizations.

Forty-two states have arts advocacy organizations—spending anywhere from $400 to $1 million on state advocacy each year—that can provide expertise and networks to facilitate both state and local advocacy. Many cities and towns also have local arts agencies dedicated to supporting arts organizations and coordinating advocacy.

By working with established advocacy groups, you join a network of similar arts organizations that share your goals and needs. In our political system, there is strength in numbers and advocacy groups increase your political effectiveness.

The value of your cultural organization grows out of its mission, but extends to other areas. Successful advocacy requires telling the full story, including the economic value of your organization.

KNOWING YOUR ADVOCACY GOALS

Once you can describe the cultural, economic, and community value created by your organization, you are ready to determine your advocacy goals. The broadest goal of cultural advocacy is to increase public recognition of your organization and of the arts and humanities in general. As arts and culture already fare well in public opinion polls, it is important to set tangible goals that support and advance your organization's mission. It may be a general goal, such as increased operational support from the state arts agency, or it may be specific to your organization, such as a zoning variance from the municipal planning commission. Setting your advocacy agenda will take some time. It must dovetail with your long-range plans: Are you planning an expansion in three years, are your audiences growing, are you shifting your programming to serve more schools?

Government actions affect cultural organizations in a myriad of ways beyond public funding. For example, budget cuts in your community could reduce subsidies for school bus transportation. Unable to absorb the costs, schools might eliminate field trips requiring a school bus. A change in the payment for buses might bring an immediate drop in attendance for your cultural organization. Tax laws have significant consequences for arts organizations. For example, one state tried to close a loophole in the state income tax withholding laws and, in the process, inadvertently drafted a bill that would have forced cultural organizations to withhold tax on all temporary and contract employees.

Advocacy pays off in the long run. You may not see immediate benefits to your organization because government moves slowly and serves constituencies more than individual organizations. Your advocacy will assist other cultural organizations as well as yours. In addition, the advocacy you do today will not necessarily provide a return next week, next month, or even next year. But advocacy does bring results. The NEA would not have been created without advocacy, and, without the NEA, would we have 56 state and territory arts agencies? Making advocacy a part of your daily work will pay benefits down the road—for your organization and for your associated organizations across your state and the nation.

PLANNING AND EXECUTING THE CAMPAIGN

Setting the Agenda

Setting the agenda for your advocacy is comparable to the needs assessment discussed in the Strategic Planning chapter. Consider how many ways your organization interacts with government at all levels. How do government policies help or impede your organization's mission? In your assessment, determine which issues are the most important. This assessment will range from the nuts and bolts of daily operation (garbage removal, street signs, utilities, and so on) to the visionary (substantial grants for capital improvements). Here are some examples of typical government interaction for a cultural nonprofit.

- Bonded loan pools for economic development
- Changes in insurance regulations, such as liability, unemployment, and health insurance for employees
- Entertainment tax on tickets
- Federal and state filing requirements
- Federal grants from NEA, Institute of Museum and Library Services, Department of Transportation, and more
- Fire and building safety inspections
- Food and beverage licenses

When to Hire a Lobbyist

Many people seem to believe that a lobbyist is a cross between the Wizard of Oz and Harry Houdini—a magic power broker who can slip behind the curtains, pull the right strings, and, presto, his will is done. Others may believe that a lobbyist is a snake oil salesman whose tonic evaporates overnight. No matter what they think of lobbyists, people still believe that the solution to their advocacy problems is to rush out and hire an expensive lobbyist.

A lobbyist cannot solve all your problems, but there is a time to hire a good one and there is a time to keep your checkbook in your pocket.

The first step in making the decision is to define your legislative goals. What do you hope to achieve? Are these goals that can be realized in the short term, in the next few years, or the long term? Are you launching an advocacy campaign? What can you do yourself and where do you need help?

An experienced lobbyist can assist in all aspects of advocacy: design your campaign, devise strategy, write and prepare lobbying material, provide training, assist in developing your advocacy network, set up constituent meetings, coordinate media relations, and, of course, do the traditional buttonholing of key legislators. A good lobbyist is a reliable source of political information, able to get the right information to the right person at the right time.

Like buying a car, do you need a Cadillac or do you need reliable transportation?

Lobbyists come in all varieties and sizes—from large firms to one-man shops, from expensive to reasonable, from back-slapping door openers to expert strategists. Like any profession, lobbyists have their specialties and their distinct personalities and styles.

Find one that matches your expectations, your budget, and your style. Interview as many as you can. Come armed with questions and listen carefully to the questions they ask you. These questions will help you gauge your current political standing and provide a reaction to your current strategy.

In the interview, potential lobbyists will want to know about your advocacy network—how many people support your cause and how committed they are. They will want to know if you have advocates in key legislative districts, and if you can activate your network to write letters, make phone calls, and visit the State Capitol. They want to know if you have voters behind your cause. Because it is the voters in their legislative districts that have the most influence over legislators' decisions. They want to know if you've done your homework.

The time to hire a lobbyist is after you have built an advocacy network; it doesn't have to be extensive, merely passionately committed. The time to hire a lobbyist is after you have met your legislator. (After all, you don't need a lobbyist to introduce you to your own state senator.) The time to hire a lobbyist is after you have set your advocacy goals, completed an inventory of your advocacy resources, and sketched the broad outlines of your campaign.

Armed with this knowledge, you can begin asking around about lobbyists. You want a lobbyist who understands the legislature, who has a solid reputation for integrity, and who can help you fill the missing pieces of your advocacy inventory. Most of all, find lobbyists with whom you can work.

A lobbyist will not solve all your problems, but the right lobbyist can be the important ally you'll ever have.

Government-supported infrastructure, such as access roads

Operating support grants

Payroll taxes

Police and public safety

Publicity opportunities through convention and visitors bureaus

School funding for student field trips

Tax incentives for charitable contributions

Tourism signs on state highways and sign permits

Water and sewer capacity

Zoning variances

As you look at this list (and your own), you may know how to apply for a grant from your state arts agency, but you scratch your head about bonding, insurance regulations, or federal funds from unexpected sources. In setting your agenda, you don't need to know the answers to all these questions. Instead, you need to learn whom to ask. One of the best sources is an elected official, typically your state legislator.

After you've completed your list, set your priorities from two perspectives. First, what is the most beneficial and most urgent for your organization? Your assessment of advocacy goals must be coordinated with the organization's long-term goals. Rank your goals by urgency, strategic importance, and timing. Is your first priority more parking? More operating support? Better nighttime security? A capital loan for new construction? It may be that your first goal is more parking, but does that fit with your goal of building an addition in three years?

The second perspective is a realistic assessment of what you can achieve. Which of these goals can be solved by a phone call or a meeting? Which goals require a longer time to achieve? What can you achieve in conjunction with your state advocacy group? What can you achieve with key allies? For example, if your priority is increased operating support, then you should join forces with your state advocacy group.

You will be frustrated in your advocacy if you cannot balance what is possible with what is the ideal. Politics has been called the art of the possible and no elected official—no matter how brilliant or powerful—can make all your dreams come true.

Setting your agenda takes time, and it will evolve as you learn what is feasible by informally consulting board members, staff, leaders, and officials. Your agenda is formed by blending what is best for your organization with what is politically possible.

Making a Specific Request

You've defined your agenda. Now define what you are asking for in the clearest terms possible. You may have identified capital funding as your goal. However, in your formal meetings with elected officials, you need to be specific: we need a capital grant for $3.7 million which will be matched two-to-one by private funding to expand our educational wing. Or, our audiences have grown so much that we need the city to help us find 32 more parking spaces within a two-block radius of our art center. Or, I would like you to reduce filing costs for small nonprofit cultural organizations by voting yes on the public charities bill, House Bill 4234.

Creating the Message

The first step is to know what you are asking for. The second step is to answer why—not just why it is good for your organization, but more importantly why it is good for the elected official's constituency. Your message serves not only as a rationale for your request, but also as a call to action. You need to explain why an expansion of your facility is good for the community. To receive public support, you must demonstrate public benefit. For example, in Massachusetts, a campaign for cultural facilities funding argued that the state's aging cultural facilities formed the infrastructure for tourism, the state's second largest industry. The message linked investment in cultural facilities as a strategic investment in the broader economy.

As explained elsewhere in this chapter, there are many ways to measure the public benefits from arts and culture. Creating the campaign message means capturing the most significant public benefits in a concise, memorable way. Everyone—especially a politician—is inundated with messages clamoring for his attention. You don't need to outshine Madison Avenue. But you need clarity: this funding will allow us to create five full-time jobs and allow 125 low-income students to participate in our after-school programs.

The message and its accompanying justification will shift depending on the audience. If your elected official is committed to economic development, emphasize the jobs created and the amount of local spending. If he or she is working on juvenile justice issues, talk about how you serve at-risk youths. In a campaign for facilities funding, emphasize different benefits based on each legislator's interests. Here are three messages designed for three different legislators.

> Facilities funding will provide much needed capital support to help the concert hall in your district repair its roof.
>
> Facilities funding will create a lot of construction jobs, particularly for skilled, union workers in your district.
>
> The art museum in your district provides significant after-school education for school children. This money will allow that program to have its own facility.

The message answers the first questions everyone asks: what's in it for me and why should I care? You are passionate about your work, but never assume that the world shares your view of the inherent value of arts and culture. Many do, but often the ones who don't are sitting in the Legislature or Congress. Always remember that public dollars must be invested for public benefit, and the more tangible the benefit the easier it is for politicians to understand.

Campaign

Now design your campaign. The first question to ask is, who decides? Who has the power to enact your proposal or address your concern? Is it the zoning board, the Legislature, a bureaucrat in the Department of Education, or the city council? Is it one person or a majority of the Legislature?

Usually, you will be trying to persuade the majority of a deliberative body, like a legislature or county board of supervisors. With any deliberative body, you can choose a variety of strategies to build a majority (50 percent plus one) for your side. You can try to persuade the leadership, such as the Speaker of the House or a powerful committee chair, to champion your cause. Legislators need favors from leadership and will often support an initiative because their leadership supports it. This is known as an "inside" strategy.

Another tactic is to bring political pressure from outside the deliberative chamber, demonstrating popular support among voters. This entails a grassroots campaign which could include personal letters, visits, emails, postcards, rallies, petitions, and letters to the editor of your local newspaper. (See the hierarchy of contact described on page 51.) A grassroots campaign requires that you build and activate your advocacy network.

Every political situation is different. Your strategies and tactics will vary according to the situation and your resources. Design a campaign to suit your goals.

A campaign is a set of planned and coordinated activities to map out who will do what tasks and when will they be done. The following are typical campaign activities:

- Schedule meetings with your core activists.
- Collect and interpret any necessary research, such as economic impact studies.
- Identify your supporters and how you will communicate with them (for example, a phone tree or email network).
- Strategize ways to connect with decision makers.
- Develop a newspaper strategy, including press releases, editorial endorsements, op-ed pieces, and letters to the editor.
- Develop a media strategy to put your spokespersons on the air.
- Write a one-page summary of your goals and their values to distribute to decision makers.
- Meet with decision makers.
- Coordinate letter writing campaign to decision makers.
- Organize a rally at the Capitol, such as an arts advocacy day.
- Celebrate your victories.
- Thank everyone involved, particularly decision makers.

Knowing Your Elected Officials and Legislators

People enter public service and politics for honorable reasons: they want to help people and make a contribution to society. Along the way, they encounter endless demands on their time and energy, long hours, and frustration. Merely becoming a candidate is enough to make some people (including the opposing political party) instantly distrust them. Yet, at their core, every elected official entered politics to make a difference for their constituents. Therefore, most legislators want to help you.

However, politics, like most relationships, is a two-way street. You will succeed in your relationships when there is mutual benefit. You will know what you hope to achieve, but what does your legislator need?

Legislators and elected officials want to help people, and they need to be recognized for their contributions. To do their jobs, elected officials need the voters to get to know their values and goals. This communication and recognition develops into the political capital necessary for the elected official to represent the voters. They make decisions all the time based on how their choices will earn or lose recognition for their work. Recognition comes in many forms but ultimately political recognition depends on elections. In order to achieve their goals (and yours), your legislators must be elected (and re-elected.) Therefore, their goals include satisfying 50 percent plus one of the voters in their district. Their job is to represent the district that elected them. They may want to work for the greater good of all of society or of the entire state, but their job is to serve the interests of the people in their district. As former Speaker of the United States House of Representatives Tip O'Neill said, "All politics are local."

Therefore, you must establish a relationship with the legislators for which you vote. You should develop a relationship with your legislators just like you would with major donors. As with donors, your first steps are to learn about your legislators—their background, the issues on which they focus, their ambitions, and their political records. The more you learn about them, the easier it will be to connect your issue to their concerns. For example, if one is concerned about the economy, your discussions with him or her will focus on the local economic impact of your cultural organization. If one is interested in education, emphasize the educational services your organization provides.

The one consistent message you want to convey to your legislators is the many ways your organization benefits the people of their district. This includes the inherent value of your mission, as well as how many local people are served, how many tourists are drawn to the area (boosting the local economy), how much is spent on local vendors, how many people work for the organization, how much tax revenue is generated, and so on.

For a summary and details of this process, see the Appendix for Establishing a Relationship With Your Legislator.

You cannot develop a relationship in one 15-minute meeting during advocacy day at the Capitol. It takes time and persistence. Invite your legislators to events; invite them to tour your facility. Always remember that legislators need recognition, so never pass up an opportunity to introduce and thank your legislators to the audience. Ask legislators to speak at appropriate events. Any time that you can put legislators in front of an audience and make them look good, you are assisting them.

Legislators must win elections. You can help legislators to do so, just as you can ask legislators to help you fulfill your mission. You can and should become involved in campaigns so that your friends and allies win elections—the political recognition that counts the most. Become involved in an election as a private citizen. By law, you cannot use the name, facilities, or staff time of a 501(c)3 in support of a candidate for elected office. However, you do not give up your first amendment rights when you work for a nonprofit. Away from your job, you have every right to fully participate in elections.

There are three ways to get involved in campaigns.

First and foremost, you must vote. It is the core of our democracy.

Contribute money to your candidates' campaigns. You don't need to give a lot of money; candidates welcome all contributions because it represents a commitment to their candidacy. Consider hosting a fundraising event for your candidate, even if all your guests write small checks. This gives the candidate needed campaign funds and a chance to meet voters. Your fundraiser could be a neighborhood coffee, a cookout, or a cocktail party at someone's home. (A 501(c) 3 organization can offer its facilities to a political event only if it makes the same opportunity available to candidates of all political beliefs. If the museum is rented for a political event, then any political organization must be offered the same rental terms. A 501(c) 3 organization cannot sponsor a political event. Therefore, host your political events separate from your cultural organization in private homes or commercial establishments.)

Volunteer to work in the campaign. Candidates may not immediately remember every contributor, but they never forget the volunteer who walked the streets with them. Offer to go door-knocking with your candidate or help organize an event. If you're not comfortable knocking on doors, volunteer in the campaign office. There is always more work to be done in a political campaign. One of the most valuable tools in legislative campaigns is writing postcards to friends urging them to vote for your candidate. For the right candidate, you should activate your local advocacy network to rally voters.

Meeting in Person

Ideally, you have met your legislators in the district. (For step-by-step details on how to structure an effective meeting, see the Appendix for Meeting Your Legislator to Make the Ask.) They may in session at the Capitol and you need to approach them on your issue. Or you may have an urgent issue that occurs before you have met your legislators or elected officials. What's the most effective way for you and your advocacy network to communicate? Legislators receive a barrage of communication so they quickly learn to prioritize. The most important communications come from constituents in the district.

The most effective communication is meeting with legislators in their office. This allows for discussion and both sides can gauge the intensity of commitment. Prepare for your meeting by designating speakers, honing your talking points, and writing brief, yet informative materials on your issue. Do your homework, even if you've already met your legislators: On which committees do they serve? What are their political interests? Read about your legislators on websites and political almanacs. Ask your state advocacy group and ask people in the district. (Board trustees can be good sources of knowledge about the community and its leaders.) Knowing each legislator allows you to tailor your message and shape the conversation.

Begin with a specific request: We are here to ask for your support on House Bill 4234. Keep your talking points precise. Allow time for the legislator to ask questions. If you don't know the answer to a question, say so and promise to provide the information as soon as possible. Do not expect the legislator to make a commitment to your request right away. Legislators need to balance many conflicting interests, and any worthy issue requires time for consideration. End the discussion by repeating your specific request and thanking the legislator for his or her time and consideration. Give the legislator your briefing material, which contains a succinct summary of the pertinent information about your issue. You should be able to explain your request and its benefits in five minutes or less. Be informed, because you want your legislator to value you as a resource for information about the arts community.

Keep the meeting on track. You are there for one reason—asking for support for House Bill 4234. If the legislator wants to discuss baseball or an unrelated issue, gently return the conversation to your issue.

Legislative meetings should be short and concise. The demands on the legislator's time are intense. In a typical day, a legislator must bounce from meeting to meeting and from subject to subject. Follow up your meeting with a thank you note.

Sometimes you will be asked to meet with the elected official's staff. Talking to staff members can be as valuable as talking to the elected official. Get to know the official's aides: they can be helpful.

Communicating in Writing

We live in an era of instant communication, but e-mail and the Internet have not surpassed the effectiveness of old-fashioned human communication. As you decide how best to communicate with your legislators, recognize that the more you put of yourself into the communication, the more authentic and effective it is.

If you can't meet with your legislator, write a letter. (In a time crunch, letters can be faxed.) Identify yourself as a constituent and include your address. Make your letter straight and to the point. Communication with legislators should always be clear and concise.

A personalized email is also effective. Include your street address so that the legislator knows that you are a constituent. Personalize your communication so that you are sure that it is read. State why you care and what your relationship is to the issue. State how the issue impacts the legislator's district.

Stating your views clearly is the first priority of your personal letter or email. One of the primary goals of your personal letter or email is to begin a dialogue with the legislator. You can help ensure a response by making a request, such as asking for information, a copy of the bill, or for help. A personal request helps to lift your letter out of the pile of opinions to be counted and moved to the correspondence file.

Form letters, postcards, and standardized emails are less effective. How committed are you to your cause if you can only spare a few seconds to communicate it? However, form letters, preprinted postcards, and stock emails are sometimes counted by staffers, particularly if there are many from inside the district.

How many letters does it take to have an impact on a state legislator? Not as many as you may think. Depending on the size of the district, five to ten letters on the same subject will get the legislator's attention.

The least effective advocacy tool is probably the petition. Legislators know that most people will sign anything and that petitions promise almost anything. A good way to measure the effectiveness of your communication is to ask how much energy did you put into it: did you sign something at the grocery store, click on a website, or did you sit down and compose a thoughtful letter?

Here is a **hierarchy of contact,** from the most to the least effective.

1. Make personal contact with your legislator either face-to-face or by phone. Tell your own story in your own words about why this issue is important.
2. Write a letter telling your own story and concerns.
3. Participate in a postcard drive but still include a personal message.

4. The least effective is a postcard or petition drive where all you do is sign your name.

Always treat legislators with respect. They have sacrificed their time, and sometimes endured personal financial cost, to serve you. Legislators are not paid well, typically making much less in public office than they could in their chosen profession. You, then, need to find a balance between respect and persistence. Legislators have private lives and families. Respect that. There is a time and place for discussion of your issues. Say hello to your legislator in the grocery store, but pick another time for debate and discussion. Treating your legislators with respect also shows respect for the office and the institutions of our democracy: they are doing the people's work. Furthermore, treating elected officials with respect is more than good manners: it's good politics. You never know when the tides will change and the legislator who opposed you on one issue becomes your new ally on a different issue.

See the Appendix, Sample Statewide Campaign for Cultural and Heritage Facilities Funding, for campaign steps and a timeline for an actual bill filed in the Commonwealth of Massachusetts to establish a Cultural Facilities Fund.

Making Advocacy Part of Your Daily Mission

Elected officials make decisions based on their perception of the public good, often interpreted as what benefits the most people in their district. Their perception of what the public wants grows from a variety of sources, such as the media, public opinion polls, and political advisors. For most elected officials, the most important sources are the conversations, both formal and informal, with voters in their district. To an elected official, anyone is a potential voter. That's why arts advocacy must go beyond elected officials. The average voter in a casual conversation helps a legislator understand what's best for the district.

Therefore, the more you spread the word about the public benefit of your issue, your organization, and the arts in general, the more likely elected officials will recognize the value of the arts. Advocacy works one voter at a time. Cultural leaders, whether volunteer trustees or paid staff, should make advocacy a part of their daily mission. The process of converting elected officials into active supporters begins with earning public support. Arts advocacy will be successful in the long run when the average voter understands the benefits of government support for the arts.

Public funding for arts and culture has an impact on the economy. It has an impact on education. It spurs economic development. It sparks revitalization of neighborhoods. It supports the cultural resources that attract tourists. To succeed in these broad and diverse missions, the cultural community needs support through public policy that provides adequate funding, infrastructure support, arts education in public schools, and a chance to participate in the debate on the future of our commonwealth.

Arts and cultural organizations contribute far more to our communities than jobs and economic impact. They are integral to education, serving as classrooms during and after school. They provide programs that give at-risk youth and disadvantaged citizens the empowerment of self-expression. They are the distinctive institutions that build community pride. They challenge our assumptions, open our eyes, and nourish our society.

Though it is impossible to measure these values and rewards through simple statistics, the depth and breadth of contributions made by cultural organizations are easy to recognize. Arts and cultural organizations are good for our schools, our communities, our economy, and our souls.

The cultural community must engage in consistent advocacy that public investment in arts and culture benefits all the citizens for the common good.

ENDNOTES

1. According to Americans for the Arts, in 2004, local governments provided $740 million to arts and culture, compared with state governments at $272.4 million and the NEA at $121.7 million.

APPENDIX

HOW MUCH ADVOCACY CAN A NONPROFIT DO?

Nonprofit organizations have every right to engage in advocacy. You can (and should) talk to your elected officials about anything related to your work, including the necessity of government funding. Many cultural leaders misunderstand their advocacy rights and mistakenly view the legal limitations as a prohibition.

Here's what a nonprofit **can** do:

Advocate on behalf of its political and economic interests within a limit.

Here's what a nonprofit **cannot** do:

Take a position for or against any candidate for elected office.

What is the limit on nonprofit advocacy? Section 501(c) 3 states that a tax-exempt organization will lose its tax-exempt status and its qualification to receive tax-deductible contributions if a substantial part of its activities are carried on to influence legislation. "Substantial part" is not defined in the tax code; however, the suggested IRS guideline is five percent of total expenditures in pursuit of the nonprofit's mission.

Definitions

The five percent limit. Expenditures are considered to be all of the activities conducted by a nonprofit organization, including its annual budget, staff time, and even volunteer time. The chance of a cultural organization ever exceeding the five percent limit is highly unlikely. For example, if its annual budget is $500,000, the organization could spend as much as $25,000 on advocacy alone and remain within the guideline.

Influencing legislation. Attempts to influence legislation can be on a grassroots level or through direct lobbying. Grassroots lobbying is an effort to affect the opinions of the general public or any segment thereof. Direct lobbying involves communicating with any member or employee of a legislative body or with any government official or employee who may participate in the formulation of legislation.

Attempts to influence legislation do *not* include:

- making available the results of nonpartisan analysis, study, or research;
- examining and discussing broad social, economic, and similar problems;
- providing technical advice or assistance (where the advice would otherwise constitute the influencing of legislation) to a governmental body or to a committee or other subdivision thereof in response to a written request by that body;
- appearing before, or communicating with, any legislative body about a possible decision of that body that might affect the existence of the organization, its powers and duties, its tax-exempt status, or the deductions of contributions to the organization; and
- communicating with a government official employee other than communication with the purpose of influencing legislation.

An escape clause. In the unlikely event that your organization has exceeded the five percent guideline, the IRS can reclassify your organization to comply with IRS rules. This is called a 501(h) election. Section 501(h) permits certain eligible 501(c) 3 organizations to elect to make limited expenditures to influence legislation. Limited expenditures are defined as 20 percent of the total expenditures of the nonprofit's budget to achieve its educational purposes.

Under 501(h), donors will still be able to take a tax deduction for their contributions to your nonprofit, and your nonprofit will also continue to be eligible for donations from other 501(c) 3 funding organizations such as foundations.

A 501(h) election requires a vote by the board of directors and must be accomplished before the close of your fiscal year.

Rights of private citizens. As a private citizen—separate from your nonprofit—you have all the rights provided by the Constitution to petition, advocate, and communicate with your government. And you have the right to fully participate in elections. As a private citizen, you can contribute to campaigns and make public statements separate from your organization. Make contributions and volunteer your time to candidates who support arts and culture. Make it clear that your contribution is linked to their support for your issues. Business leaders seek support for their business issues by giving money as a private citizen.

In your official capacity, you can be an effective advocate within the broad limits of the IRS suggested guidelines. (As of this writing, the five percent suggested guidelines have not been established by law or legal precedent.) As a private citizen you can fully participate in the political process. Speak up on cultural funding; support the issues that support your organization.

Source: *Tax-Exempt Status for Your Organization.* (March 2005). IRS Publication 557. Retrieved from www.irs.gov/publications/p557/index.html

ESTABLISHING A RELATIONSHIP WITH YOUR LEGISLATOR

You must establish a relationship with your legislators so that, over time, they get to know you and your organization. Take these steps to start building a relationship with your elected officials before you have an urgent issue. It is important to begin the process before you call on them for a specific request. (Sometimes the urgency of your issues doesn't allow time to establish a relationship. Use the guidelines outlined below in Meeting Your Legislator to Make the Ask. In urgent circumstances, devote two-thirds of your meeting to the request.) Further guidelines—including key talking points for your one-page summary and meeting—are below.

Schedule a meeting with your legislator in his or her district.

Notify your statewide advocacy group in advance.

Develop a one-page summary of key points for each legislator.

Emphasize economic impact, educational services, and community value.

Send a thank you note and maintain contact from time to time.

Report to your advocacy network.

Building a relationship with your legislator is a lot like stewardship for your donors. For example, invite your legislator to tour your institution, appear at an event, observe an educational workshop, or just sit down to talk. It is appropriate to address your legislator by his or her title: Senator Jones or Representative Smith. Through these meetings, you want your legislators to learn how your cultural organization contributes to their district.

Examples
Your organization contributes to the **local economy** (jobs, payroll, local vendors).
It supports **education and children** (school tours, after-school programs, in-school presentations, curriculum development).

It is strongly supported by the legislator's **constituents.**

Address the following key points with your legislator:

1. The **mission** of your organization, including what audiences you serve.
2. Number of **employees**, and the size of your payroll.
3. Number of **visitors/audience per year** and where they come from—international, out-of-state, in-state, and local visitors.
4. **How long** the organization has existed.
5. **Plans for the future,** such as physical expansion, remodeling, new programming, capital campaigns and so on.
6. **Local economic impact.** If you do not have economic impact information, discuss it anecdotally. For example, your organization has an impact on nearby restaurants and hotels.

7. **Educational programs.** Make note of how your organization serves education through after-school programs, school visits, curriculum assistance, teacher training, life-long learning, and others.
8. The **role of local/state/federal cultural funding** for your organization, including how much money your organization has received, how it is used, what you have lost when the funding was cut, and how state cultural funding helps raise additional money. Talk about the importance of state funding for the arts, sciences, and humanities.
9. Be sure to mention your **membership in your statewide cultural advocacy group.**
10. Describe **how your nonprofit business works**—how much of your operating budget comes from earned income, endowment, grants—and how much money has to be raised each year.

Prepare a one-page letter or summary of the key points to discuss with your legislator. This will help you organize your thoughts and create an information sheet specifically designed for your legislator.

Learn what you can about each of your legislators before the visits. Do they have any arts experience, are they interested in the humanities, what did they study in college, do they have school age children, and so on. By understanding each legislator's interest, you can focus your discussions on what interests them most (just like you would a prospective donor.)

Discuss with each legislator how they can help in public appearances—can they speak at a board meeting; present awards at a show; draft a letter for an exhibition booklet or playbill? Think of ways you can make your legislators look good.

After the visit, send the legislator a thank you note. Then stay in touch. Put your legislators on your mailing list. Give them a call when there is an opportunity to appear before the public or any gathering with a significant number of voters. Keep them informed of developments and long-range plans. You are cultivating allies for mutual benefit. So, in addition to outlining your goals, you should work to understand each legislator's goals—building a better community and getting re-elected.

MEETING YOUR LEGISLATOR TO MAKE THE ASK: STEP BY STEP

After you have established a relationship with your legislator, the time will come when you meet to ask the legislator for a specific action—i.e., vote yes on your bill or support a 22 percent increase in state cultural funding. Your meeting will be short—probably no more than 15 minutes. Prepare for the meeting, know what you are asking for, and then make a list of the three most important points that your support your request.

Examples

1. "Our Cultural Organization" has a significant impact in your district, and we need state cultural funding to continue this work.
2. Cultural funding through the state arts agency gives valuable, unrestricted operating funds that we cannot replace through the private sector.
3. We believe strongly that our work benefits the community and that we could do more with more resources. We ask you to support an increase to the state arts agency appropriation so that we can have more resources to better serve our community and your district.

Try to arrive at the legislator's office a few minutes before your appointment. You will probably have to wait a few minutes. Be patient: legislators have harried schedules with back-to-back meetings that sometimes run long.

Always introduce yourself to the legislator, even if you're sure that he or she knows you. Introduce everyone in the group, and include their affiliations. For example, "this is R. Dent Artslover, co-chair of "Our Cultural Organization's" board of directors." Or "I am R. Dent Artslover, executive director of "Our Cultural Organization," but you may know me from volunteering on your campaign." Any context that you can give the legislator is helpful.

Keep the introductions brief.

Address the legislator as either Representative Jones or Senator Murray. This is a courtesy that shows respect for the office.

After the introductions and when you are seated in the meeting area, begin your discussion by thanking the legislator for taking the time to meet with you and then return to your three advocacy points. Be succinct. Legislators appreciate clarity and brevity.

Devote the brief time that you have to your issue. Watch out for digressions. Sometimes a legislator will avoid an issue by artfully changing the subject. Politely return the discussion to your issue: That's certainly interesting, Senator, but we're here today to thank you for your support and to ask you to support a 22 percent increase in cultural funding.

The legislator may have questions. Answer them as briefly as possible so that you can get back to your three points. If you cannot answer questions right away; tell your legislator that you will get the information as soon as possible.

When it is time to leave, make sure that you do the following:

1. Thank the legislator for the meeting. (There are dozens of people who want a meeting on any given day.)
2. Invite your legislator to one of your next events.
3. Ask your legislator one more time to support your request.

After the meeting, send a quick note thanking the legislator for the meeting and for considering your request. (Repeat your request in the thank you note.)

SAMPLE STATEWIDE CAMPAIGN FOR CULTURAL AND HERITAGE FACILITIES FUNDING

The sample advocacy campaign outlined here reflects strategy and steps implemented in 2005 to file a bill to establish a Cultural Facilities Fund in the Commonwealth of Massachusetts. The Fund will offer capital grants, loans, and planning assistance to help nonprofit cultural organizations renovate, expand, and repair their facilities, and to increase contributions from private funding sources.

The bill was developed because the cultural community in Massachusetts had identified a growing crisis of inadequate cultural facilities due to age and deferred maintenance. (The average age of the state's cultural facilities is 93 years.) Cultural organizations need substantial financial support to address issues of building code compliance, fire safety, handicapped accessibility, energy efficiency, and improvements and expansions. This campaign plan was designed to achieve the filing of a bill in the state legislature to provide cultural facilities funding.

January

Develop a legislative advocacy strategy based upon the new committee appointments in the House of Representatives and Senate. Identify a list of targeted legislators who chair key committees or hold positions of leadership.

Develop a fundraising strategy for private sector match requirement. Develop a steering committee of business and cultural leaders in tandem with this fundraising strategy.

Take the first steps to form an advisory committee of cultural leaders from organizations throughout the state. Recruit board leaders from cultural organizations, with an objective of two organizations per targeted legislator and two board members from each organization.

Meet with historic preservation leadership.

January–March

Meet with potential fundraisers.

Identify a key business leader to co-chair the campaign.

Conduct a telephone survey of cultural organizations with facilities to document facility needs and develop a database of maintenance issues for cultural institutions in the targeted legislative districts.

January–February

Invite business leaders to the February steering committee meeting.

Research public support for funding of cultural and historic buildings preservation.

Schedule a series of speeches for Chambers of Commerce from January–September 2005.

Explore partnerships with tourism and lodging industries.

Recruit a university or foundation to donate or commission a public opinion poll.

March–April

Continue to grow the steering committee of business and cultural leaders. Continue to work on private sector match.

Collect documentary photos through site visits to cultural facilities identified in the telephone survey. Photos will be used in collateral material and in the rally planned for the statehouse.

Obtain the support of key municipal leaders, including the mayors of targeted municipalities.

Identify mayors to participate in a Mayor's Forum to be held in September.

Develop collateral material, including a list of examples of cultural institutions in need of support. Possibly develop a top ten list of threatened organizations.

Develop a database of potential supporters in each targeted legislative district, including board members of each institution, major suppliers, volunteers, and employees. This would be done with assistance from members of the advisory committee.

Schedule meetings with industry and association leaders and high tech and biotech councils.

Conduct a private discussion with an editorial writer for the state's largest newspaper.

May

Continue to grow the steering committee of business and cultural leaders. Continue to work on private sector match.

Have the university collect polling information.

Schedule 40 Legislative site visits in targeted districts.

June–August

Continue to grow the steering committee of business and cultural leaders. Continue to work on private sector match.

Conduct site visits with local representatives and state senators in the targeted legislative districts.

Generate local press coverage for each visit.

September

Continue to grow the steering committee of business and cultural leaders. Continue to work on private sector match.

Meet with editorial boards of newspapers in targeted legislative districts.

Present at the Mayors' Forum press conference and deliver mayors' letters.

Generate press coverage in media.

October

Meet with editorial boards of newspapers in targeted legislative districts.

Hold statehouse event with coalition advocates. Have advocates meet with representatives and senators.

Announce fundraising goal.

Recognize donors.

Obtain sponsors and cosponsors of the legislation. Have key cultural leaders from the districts of targeted legislators meet with and ask their legislators to cosponsor the legislation.

File the bill.

Campaign Steps Coordinated with the Legislative Process

Organize key supporters to testify at House and Senate Committee hearings.

Implement grassroots advocacy strategy.

Collect letters of support addressed to legislators from the trustees and directors of nonprofit cultural organizations. Letters should be on the business, professional, or personal stationery of the individual trustee. These letters will be collected at the campaign headquarters to be delivered by hand at the right political moment.

Begin email campaign through the advocacy group's website and an advocacy software, such as that licensed through Americans for the Arts. Target: 1,000 emails over two months.

Coordinate a letters-to-the-editor campaign in support of the bill.

Host a series of political fundraisers in private homes for the bill's legislative sponsors and leaders.

Organize a series of meetings with business leaders, cultural supporters, and key legislators.

Organize an advocacy rally at the statehouse.

After the bill passes each chamber, send a thank you note to all the legislators who supported the bill.

Celebrate!

PART TWO

Fundamentals of Managing Arts Organizations

CHAPTER 4

Strategic Planning

4

CRAIG DREESZEN

Most of us have encountered arts organizations that maintain the same tired programs for years, oblivious to a dramatic decline in attendance at these events. We may also know organizations which react to each new problem as a crisis with no idea how to respond—or change direction each time leaders change. In contrast, successful organizations—community arts organizations or multinational corporations—typically possess something in common: a compelling vision and strategy. These organizations are guided by a clear sense of priorities and are able to adapt to changing circumstances without losing their way. They may be propelled by the inspiration of an individual who captures the imagination and commitment of others, or they may reflect the collective ideas of a group that has framed a common dream.

If the members of an organization—from the president to the newest volunteer—share an understanding of what that organization values and where it is headed, they will more effectively realize their shared intentions. An empowering vision expands personal dreams into ones that can unify, inspire, and mobilize people and resources. Translating that vision to priorities, strategies, and actions is what strategic planning is all about.

So what is strategic planning? Strategy is a term so commonly used in so many contexts, that it is much misunderstood.

Noted organizational theorist Henry Mintzberg offers the following definition of strategy in *Strategy Bites Back*, "...strategy is a plan—some sort of consciously intended course of action, a guideline (or set of guidelines) to deal with a situation." Michael Allison and Jude Kaye define strategic planning as: "a systemic process through which an organization agrees on—and builds commitment among key stakeholders—priorities that are essential to its mission and are responsive to the environment. Strategic planning guides the acquisition and allocation of resources to achieve those priorities."

When you are immersed in a vision, you know what must be done... But you may not know how to do it. You experiment, err, try again, yet there is no ambiguity.

—Ed Simon, president and chief operating officer, Herman Miller

A strategy may be the result of an intentional plan, or it may result from an experiential or intuitive sense of what works. In this chapter, we will explore how strategy develops as part of a deliberate process that engages leaders and stakeholders in defining a plan to guide future decisions.

WHY PLAN?

Strategic planning is a process through which an organization articulates what it may accomplish in the future, what needs it hopes to meet, and how it plans to do so. Strategic planning answers questions like: Who do we serve and what do they want? What difference do we want to make? What are our priorities? Where should we invest our time and money for best results?

A learning organization is a place where people are continually discovering they can create their reality.

—Peter Senge, business strategy writer

Planning informs and excites people about an organization's work, motivating staff, boards, and volunteers. Planning helps an organization to communicate the potential impact of its work to funders, potential partners, and audiences. Planning helps an organization allocate scarce resources—people, funds, and facilities—to accomplish its goals. Planning defines the results an organization hopes to achieve and provides the basis for measuring how well it achieves them. Planning helps protect an organization from potential artistic, financial, or political catastrophes. It is both a process that clarifies a group's intentions and a product, the written plan. Arguably the planning process is more important than the produced document.

KEEP PLANNING SIMPLE

Thinking about planning while attempting to keep up with daily tasks and financial and personnel restrictions can be overwhelming. Certainly, if you are in the midst of a crisis, deal with it you before undertaking strategic planning. However, if you are preoccupied with the mind-numbing details of daily operations, you may not notice opportunities or threats until it's too late. Planning can prepare you for some crises, mitigate others, and even prevent some catastrophes. Planning must be kept simple so that people will do it and it won't be ignored.

Most administrators intuitively use elements of the strategic planning process. It is impossible to organize a performing arts season, write a grant, or recruit volunteers without being able to plan. Any process that brings together the people who care about an organization to seriously consider its aims, audience, directions, and resources can serve as a model. The process doesn't have to be perfect. What is important is that it becomes an integral part of the life of the organization.

Planning at a Glance

In essence, a sound planning process mobilizes you to:

- gather together the people who care about your work;
- imagine what you could accomplish together, what the organization could become, and what difference it could make in the community;
- look around to identify what you do well or poorly, who your audience is and what they want or need, and your major threats and opportunities;
- determine what you will do and what you will not do;
- decide what steps will get you where you want to go, and what help and resources you will need;
- implement your plan; and
- evaluate, revise, and adapt your plan as you carry out programs and services.

Somehow, when we approach the task of systematically planning for an organization or community, all the discussion can make the task appear more complicated than it actually is. Planning is not as complicated as it seems. It's a bit like riding a bike. While bike riding is easy enough for a five-year-old to master, describing how to do it is more difficult. Everyday planning is also easy and we all do it. Keep this in mind. Like bicycling, the real work of planning is active and forward moving.

THE PLANNING PARADOX

Planning's fundamental paradox, which has always been true, is that the future is essentially unknowable. We plan to prepare for what cannot be known. In orderly times we forget this and plan with unquestioned assumptions about how we think the world will unfold. But when we think of planning as accurately predicting the future, we're defeated before we begin. When we think of planning as understanding community needs, clarifying our organization's values, and articulating the kinds of differences we hope to make for our constituents and communities, we're on safer ground. These things are less volatile than the political, economic, and social environment in which we work.

A plan is better thought of as a compass. With a general sense of direction we can navigate regardless of what changes we encounter in the terrain.

It is still very useful to forecast actions and their intended results into the future. This is essential in the current era of accountability for outcomes. What we can't do is get too attached to our predictions or follow planned strategies without constant adjustment to changing conditions.

We get in trouble when we use metaphors like blueprint and road map that reinforce the mistaken belief that planning is a reliably predictable, step-by-step guide to the future. The road changes—bridges wash out and new paths emerge. We need new metaphors. A plan is better thought of as a compass. With a general sense of direction we can navigate regardless of what changes we encounter in the terrain.

The planning paradox can be resolved. You don't have to know the future to plan. Except for the near future, plans have little to do with predicting exactly what will be done by when. Instead, when times are tough and changing fast, planning helps deepen understanding of people's needs, centers people in an organization around shared values and vision, and describes the results trying to be achieved. This makes planning more real and resolves a typical problem of plans languishing because they bear so little resemblance to the way things actually work out in the real world.

TYPES OF PLANS

One of the complicating factors in thinking about planning is that there are so many different kinds of plans: from the planning of routine operations to program planning and then major organizational change. The leaders of a local arts agency may create a program plan for an annual concert series where the scheduling, budgeting, process of artist selection, and marketing are routine. These same leaders could also undertake strategic planning to reevaluate their role as arts programmers in a community whose dance, theater, and music presenters are beginning to fill that need for the community. This nonroutine planning could dramatically transform the organization. This will be clearer after we define some types of plans. The intent of this chapter is that readers will understand strategic planning well enough to organize strategic planning for their nonprofit organization. We will also consider long-range plans, annual operating or work plans, budgets, business plans, program plans, and community cultural plans. See Figure 1.

Strategic Plan

Strategic planning is the means by which an organization makes choices about its overall priorities, who its constituents are and how they will be served, what difference

Figure 1: Common Types of Plans

Strategic Plan
Organization plan that documents an agreed mission, overall strategies, long-range goals, and short-term objectives for the next three to five years, stressing results and how they may be achieved

Long-range Plan
Organization plan that specifies mission, goals, and longer-range objectives, stressing the results expected more than the strategies to achieve them

Annual Work or Operating Plan
A more detailed work plan for the next 12 months that specifies short-term outcomes, tasks, responsibilities, deadlines, and costs. These are often organized by staff or program.

Business Plan
Strategic plan that includes revenue and expense projections for the duration of the plan and may include marketing strategies and an analysis of competitive position

Program Plan
Plan for a specific program, project (e.g., performance series), or component of an organization's operations (e.g., marketing or fundraising)

Collaborative Plan
Plan for a joint venture or collaborative project among two or more independent organizations, such as a school and local arts agency

Budget
Financial statement that specifies anticipated revenues and expenses consistent with a strategic plan, for a specified period, usually one year. Budgets may also be done for a single program or funding proposal.

Community Cultural Plan
Assessment and plan for a community, county, or region's arts and culture. It can be general or specific, as in a cultural economic development plan.

the organization hopes to make, and how it will achieve intended results. This is the most common type of organizational planning. Strategic plans recognize that organizations and the environments in which they operate are dynamic and unpredictable, requiring flexibility.

While it is useful to distinguish between long-range planning (where you're going) and strategic planning (where you are going and how you'll get there), in practice it is difficult to tell the destination from the path. Some planners and organization leaders use these terms interchangeably. It is common to see a strategic plan labeled "long range plan."

Long-range Plan

If you think of planning as a journey, a long-range plan focuses on the destination. It describes the future results you hope to achieve—goals and outcomes three to five years (or sometimes more) in the future. A long-range plan tends to assume that current conditions will continue. It is less common now that planners are less confident that their predicted results will hold true in an uncertain future.

Annual Work or Operating Plan

Many nonprofits and public agencies write strategic plans to include goals and the *major* objectives built on their goals, and then develop annual work or *operating* plans with more specific objectives and tasks. The work plan is updated each year. After three years (or sooner in a volatile environment), the organization renews its strategic plan.

A work plan contains specific operational objectives for the year with related tasks, persons responsible, deadlines, costs, and other details too specific for a strategic plan. Work plans might be developed for a single staff person, a program, or an entire organization.

Business Plan

Nonprofits are becoming more entrepreneurial and this is reflected in planning. When prospective donors asks to see an organization's business plan, they may mean a strategic plan that includes three years of projected revenues and expenses or a corporate business plan model that also includes an analysis of competition, market share, and market position.

Some nonprofits develop a strategic plan and then a separate three-year budget projection, which function as a business plan. A marketing plan may also complement a strategic plan. If the organization has multiple plans and budgets, just take care that these plans are consistent with each other.

Annual Budget

A budget is a kind of annual plan expressed in strictly financial terms. It should be influenced by, and reflect the priorities of, the annual operating plan. If the board has determined that arts education will be a greater priority next year, then the budget should reflect increased organizational resources of staff time and money spent on arts education. For more information on budgeting, see the Financial Management chapter.

Program Plan

Some plans deal with a single aspect of an agency's operations, such as an arts education program, marketing or fundraising plan, or facility renovation. See the Program Development and Marketing the Arts chapters for examples of program planning.

Program Plan Example: Procedures Manual

A simple *program* or *project* plan can be assembled as a procedures manual in a single binder or digitally recorded on a CD. A procedures manual for an ongoing program is a good example of a plan that emerges from experience. Rather than just projecting how a project might be done, the plan also documents what is being done and what needs improvement. For a volunteer-run organization this can be a breakthrough. Each lead volunteer amends the procedures manual before he or she passes it on to the next volunteer. It becomes easier to recruit volunteers and to assure well-managed programs. The following elements might be included in a procedures manual:

- Program objectives
- Planning and implementation schedule (often presented as a graphic timeline)
- Program tasks, including how-to guidelines
- Staff and volunteer job descriptions
- Funding sources
- Grant and contribution proposals

> The budget reflects the values of the mission statement, and if I see no link, I'm concerned that the project is probably not an appropriate one. If the mission is about supporting artists but the budget shows artists' fees as in-kind contributions, I rarely read on.
>
> —Maryo Gard, arts organizer, former associate director, Colorado Council on the Arts

- Projected budget and statement of actual income and expenses
- Samples of press releases and clippings, promotions, letters, contracts, brochures, advertisements, etc.
- Evaluation forms and results (compared to program objectives)
- Recommendations for changes.

The Cycle of Planning

It is not unusual for leaders of a strategic planning process to write an overall agency plan which deals with various aspects with differing levels of specificity. Some aspects—such as arts programming, fundraising, and marketing—may warrant considerable specificity, while other areas—perhaps staffing or facility improvement—might need more assessment and planning than can be completed during the organization's strategic plan. It is common to do a strategic plan in year one, then plan programs in the second or third year, and then renew strategic planning in the third or fourth year of the planning cycle.

Alternative Types of Agency Planning

Scenario Planning

Recognizing that the future is uncertain, some planners develop plans for two or more alternative scenarios. If you have ever had a "Plan B," you've done a kind of scenario planning.

> In a scenario process, managers invent and then consider, in depth, several varied stories of equally plausible futures... The point is not to 'pick one preferred future' and hope it will come to pass...nor...to find the most probable future and adapt to it... Rather, the point is to make strategic decisions that will be sound for all plausible futures. No matter what future takes place, you are much more likely to be ready for it...
>
> —Peter Schwartz, *The Art of the Long View*

Corporations use this kind of planning to anticipate how they will react if any of a number of variable conditions takes place For example, an arts center may prepare for two scenarios: in one, the capital campaign is successful and the facility is expanded; and the other scenario prepares for a less successful campaign and minor facility renovation.

Emergent Planning

Most planners anticipate future actions in their planning; they develop a plan that describes what they intend to do. There is another approach that Mintzberg called emergent planning. In this more intuitive approach, program managers run programs, try new initiatives, and observe and document what works and what does not. Emergent planning is a deliberate process of discovering a plan from experience. This is more sophisticated than what some planners call muddling through, in that planners are quite intentional about creating new written plans based on emerging experience. Program plans often use this method.

Collaborative Planning

You may find yourself planning for a program or larger initiative in partnership with other organizations; for instance, to develop arts education programs with schools. Other collaborative plans might produce statewide arts advocacy campaigns or a regional cultural tourism initiative.

> Vision plus information plus unforeseen events equals opportunity
>
> —Peter Senge

While many of the same strategic planning principles apply, there are some significant differences in collaborative planning. First, the partners will seldom have a common mission, so the partnership lacks this central organizing principle. Power among the partners may be unequal. Implementation is not under the authority of a single organization, and partners must create systems to determine how decisions are implemented, progress monitored, and results evaluated.

Community Cultural Planning

While an agency long-range or strategic plan should concern itself with the needs and resources of the community, or at least with the agency's audiences, community cultural plans are explicitly concerned with the cultural needs and opportunities of the entire community, transcending the interests of any one arts organization. Community cultural planning is a structured process for assessing a community's cultural needs and preparing a comprehensive plan to respond to those needs.

There are several types of community-wide planning. A community *arts* plan focuses specifically on planning to understand and encourage *artists, arts organizations* and their related funding, facilities, audiences, and educational and communications systems within a community. A community *cultural* plan is aimed at the *more broadly defined cultural interests* of a community, including areas like history and heritage, libraries, public celebrations, and interpretive science centers. Many cultural plans extend to urban design, including the look of streets and neighborhoods, and the preservation of historic buildings. More recently, communities are organizing plans for their creative economies. See the Arts and the Economy chapter for more information.

It is not unusual to combine elements of these types of plans. A local arts agency may conduct a community-wide cultural assessment and then create an agency strategic plan to respond to some of the issues raised in the broader assessment that most closely relate to the local arts agency's mission and capabilities.

PLANNING APPROACHES

Planning approaches vary by type of plan. In practice, short-term, project-specific planning is approached differently than long-term, visionary, or community planning. Short-term and specific plans are crafted more precisely and with a higher expectation of predictability than are longer-range and more comprehensive plans. Planning for ongoing operations is approached more routinely than is planning for organizational transformation.

The Benefits of Group Planning

Effective leaders are able to articulate a vision of what an organization can accomplish, possess the energy to work on behalf of that vision, and have the power to persuade others to support the effort. Why, then, shouldn't a leader just make plans and then convince the organization's board and staff to support them? Even if an individually-generated plan were as good as one created by a group, the apparent efficiency of individual leader planning may be undermined by the time and effort required to sell the finished plan to others. Involvement in planning leads to ownership and ownership can translate into commitment to do the work necessary to implement the plan. Even more important, plans that arise from vigorous discussions among board members, staff, and key stakeholders are better than solo work. Organizations and their environments are too complicated for any one leader to fully understand. Strategic thinking must be shared.

Ten Steps to Plan Collaboratively with Another Organization

The AES publication, *Learning Partnerships: Planning and Evaluation Workbooks,* and the online workshop, *Learning Partnerships: Online help for arts education collaborations,* lay out a detailed, ten-step process for collaborative planning. (Visit www.umass.edu/aes for more information.)

1. Prepare for partnership.
2. Explore a shared need.
3. Decide to act in collaboration.
4. Define goals.
5. Set objectives.
6. Describe activities.
7. Budget.
8. Plan fundraising.
9. Anticipate evaluation.
10. Summarize plan and timeline.

It is, of course, possible to involve board and staff members in token participation in planning where the leaders have predetermined the results. This Machiavellian sort of planning is usually recognized for what it is and backfires in the form of grudging support from board members, volunteers, and staff. When the work encounters obstacles, it is easy to give up on someone else's idea.

The difference between token and genuine participation in planning has little to do with the amount of time spent. A general sense of a group's priorities and intentions can be gathered in a relatively brief planning retreat or series of planning meetings. In genuine participation, the leader must be authentically open to new ideas, even those that may challenge the leader's own preconceptions. In a truly participatory process, a good idea gets tempered and improved, and a flawed one gets challenged and rejected. See the Fundamentals of Board Development chapter for more information on how a board can contribute creatively in planning.

What If Planning Provokes Disagreement?

The task of the planning team in the case of conflict is to clarify the implications of each choice in terms of fit with mission, fulfillment of community needs, financial implications, and audience outreach.

If board and staff members are largely united in their intentions and agree upon organizational priorities, the planning process can confirm this and provide the basis for coherent decisions on programming, marketing, fundraising, and volunteer recruiting. On the other hand, planning may reveal differing visions of an organization's mission and priorities and may even provoke conflict.

Board and staff members should debate priorities in a planning retreat or series of meetings. The task of the planning team in the case of conflict is to clarify the implications of each choice in terms of fit with mission, fulfillment of community needs, financial implications, and audience outreach. The planning team returns to a larger meeting of board and staff with a clearer picture of what the organization might look like if it moved along either of the proposed paths. There may be financial consequences for one choice that was not obvious when the alternative was first proposed. Or audience statistics may reveal a surprisingly high (or low) level of community support for one or the other option.

At times it is necessary to agree to disagree. Disagreements may be so profound that they prompt people to withdraw from organizations. While such conflicts are unpleasant, it is better to openly clarify what members of an organization believe in and are prepared to support than to allow conflicts to bubble up later when attempting to implement programs. It is usually better to achieve consensus on general principles. Then it becomes more obvious which specific decisions must be made.

THE LANGUAGE OF PLANNING

Planning terminology can be confusing. One person's goal is another's objective. Some commonly used definitions for planning terms are suggested below, but don't be overly concerned if people in your organization are more comfortable with others. What is more important is that, within an organization, people understand the language used in their plan and that a word like objective means the same thing each time it is used throughout a plan.

In general, planning terminology ranges from more general, inclusive terms to the more specific. Broad terms like *vision*, *mission*, or *purpose* describe an organization's ultimate intentions in the broadest sense. Goals describe desired long-term results. *Objectives* or *outcomes* describe more specific results to achieve in the short term. *Strategies* usually mean the organization's overall approach or methods that will realize goals and objectives. The most detailed short-term actions may be called *tasks*.

Terms Describing Beliefs

Values or principles. Values are core beliefs or assumptions about how the world works and what is important. In some plans, important values that define the organizational culture and inspire ethical action are stated as explicit values statements.

At Arts Kentucky...we believe that arts and culture:

- enrich the lives of our citizens;
- enhance the education of our children;
- strengthen the economic stability of our communities; and
- make Kentucky a better place to live.

We value:

- creativity, diversity, accessibility, inclusion, and artistic vision;
- freedom of speech; and
- the right of all citizens to experience and participate in the creation of art.

Assumptions. Some plans make explicit the organization's beliefs about the forces in the world that influence their plans. Plans may express assumptions about demographic, economic, political, social, or technological trends that organization leaders considered in planning.

Terms Describing Intended Results

Vision. A vision is a statement of an ideal or hoped-for future and describes what it would look like.

If you can imagine the essential difference your organization is trying to make or the kind of community you want to live in, you have a vision. Sometimes these are tightly crafted statements that complement the formal mission or they may be lists of idealized future results. Visions need not be practical. While not all plans articulate a vision, they can help to set the organization's sights high and provide context for a formal mission statement.

Hawai'i Community Foundation
We want to live in a Hawai'i where people care about each other, our natural resources, and diverse island cultures; a place where people's ideas, initiatives, and generosity support thriving, responsible communities.

Maine Performing Arts Network
Five years from now, the Maine Performing Arts Network will be the best source for Maine performing arts information, will serve more constituents and members, will directly support artists with touring funding, will have additional organizational capacity, will harness technology for information, networking and advocacy, and will be a consistent and vital advocate for the arts.

Mission. Mission is a long-standing statement of why an organization exists. A mission statement captures the purpose or ultimate result an organization hopes to achieve.

The mission answers fundamental questions: why an organization exists, whom it aims to serve, and what business it is in.

Maine Performing Arts Network
...maintains the communications, information, and assistance network that sustains Maine's community of performing artists and performance presenters. We work to enhance the artistic experience for Maine artists and audiences building more livable communities.

Young Audiences New York
...instills in young people from pre-kindergarten through high school an appreciation, knowledge, and understanding of the performing, visual, and literary arts.

Sierra Arts
...is a regional arts organization dedicated to enhancing the quality of life and human experience by supporting an environment where arts and cultural diversity thrive.

Slogans or tag lines. Organizations often condense their mission or vision into a very short, compelling phrase used as a memorable slogan or tag line. This is as much a marketing strategy as a planning issue. Especially if you choose to write a long mission statement, it is useful to capture the essence in a phrase that you reproduce on your letterhead, business cards, publications, website, email signatures, program notes, and fundraising materials.

Arts Extension Service: Connecting Communities and the Arts since 1973
Vermont Arts Council: We don't make art, we make art work.
National Arts Stabilization: Helping Arts Organizations Thrive

Goal. Goals are general, long-term, result-oriented statements consistent with the mission. They often describe the overall intended results of major program areas. If all goals are achieved, the mission is fulfilled. It is a good idea to lead with public-benefit goals and conclude with internal, capacity-building goals.

Maine Arts Commission Long-range Goals
Develop Maine communities through arts and culture.
Support full access to learning in and through the arts.
Encourage and support Maine artists.
Build the capacity of Maine's creative sector.
Develop art in public spaces.

Objective. An objective is a specific, measurable, and achievable short-term result consistent with a goal. Objectives are similar to goals in that objectives describe desired future results. Objectives, though, are more specific than goals and predict results in a shorter time frame—often a year. *Performance goals* are specific objectives to be measured through evaluation in a given fiscal year. Objectives also are anticipated outcomes. The terms *objective* and *outcome* may be used interchangeably (*objective* is used more often in planning and *outcome* is used more often in evaluation). This demonstrates the close relation between planning and evaluation.

Objectives should describe an intended observable result. A good test is to ask what specific changes in people or the world you expect to observe. See the Program Evaluation chapter for more information on the relation of planned objectives to observed outcomes.

Ask what specific changes in people or the world you expect to observe.

An effective objective should meet four conditions.

1. Be specific about what will be achieved.
2. Describe anticipated changes in the world or in people.
3. Be achievable (realistic and feasible).
4. Be time-bound (describe when will it be achieved).

Example
Increase new and renewal subscriptions by two percent by mid-May.

Terms Describing Intended Methods

Strategy. Strategies are general approaches or methods an organization utilizes to fulfill its plan. Strategies describe the overall means to accomplish goals and objectives. They answer *how*.

Examples
The arts agency will shift activities from presenting arts events to providing information and services for arts presenting and producing organizations.

The theater will cultivate more individual local contributions and rely less on public agency grants.

Tasks and actions. These are activities which contribute to the achievement of goals and objectives, expressed in terms of who does what by when. Tasks are specific jobs to accomplish objectives.

Example
The artistic director will present his proposed budget for the upcoming season of concerts to the board of directors for their approval by the March 15th meeting.

Assessment. In the context of strategic planning, assessment is the process of observing constituent needs, organizational health, and environmental trends. Assessment may also be used to describe the monitoring and evaluation of programs to see what works and what doesn't, and to evaluate results at the conclusion of programs.

An assessment is a reality check. In planning, assessment is thought of as information gathering in preparation for taking action. In practice, assessment, decision-making, and action are intermixed. Here, assessment is a specific step that identifies internal strengths and weaknesses and external threats and opportunities, concluding with a list of critical issues.

HOW TO PLAN: THE AES EIGHT-STAGE PLANNING PROCESS

Almost any planning process is beneficial if it regularly brings together people who care enough about an organization to answer important questions: How are we doing? What needs are we trying to meet? In what do we believe? If your organization already has an effective planning process in place, stick with it. However, organizations without one often want to begin with a tested process known to work. AES uses the following eight-stage planning process. It is simple, flexible, and can be adapted for a quick or more comprehensive process.

The AES planning process relies upon the combination of a small planning team or committee to organize and one or more planning retreats to engage the board and professional staff. The planning committee organizes the effort, and one or more of its members may actually write the plan. Assessment can be comprehensive or simplified. The planning retreat is a one-day (usually four to six-hour) or overnight meeting.

The eight-stage planning process should be undertaken to initiate an organization into a cycle of ongoing planning. The sequence of steps can vary. An organization that knows its constituency very well may organize an envisioning retreat instead of doing an external assessment, while one that is less sure of its community needs may want to organize interviews and focus groups before having its first planning retreat.

After planning becomes part of the organization, assessing, monitoring, adapting, and planning become ongoing activities. With practice, planning is not a separate activity but a fundamental way of working. It becomes second nature and intuitive. If planning is seen as a way to systematically learn about and adapt to changes in the organization's environment, the planning organization becomes a learning organization—one in which learning is an internalized value.

Who's on First?

If planning is seen as a way to systematically learn about and adapt to changes in the organization's environment, the planning organization becomes a learning organization.

Each organization will determine who is most able to take responsibility for each stage of planning. The board usually starts and concludes the planning and is ordinarily the final, approving authority. In some public commissions, the commissioners are advisory and ought to participate in planning even if they are not called upon to approve the finished plan.

While the board is ultimately responsible for planning, the professional staff should have key leadership roles. In some organizations, the board and staff together focus on the larger issues of mission, goals, and overall strategy, while staff may be primarily responsible for objectives and annual work plans. In the best case, the board and staff are partners in planning. In all-volunteer organizations, committee chairs may provide the staff perspective. Reviewed below are the sequence of events involved in strategic planning and the roles of board and staff in carrying them out.

1. Board and staff initiate the plan by organizing and appointing a planning committee.
2. Organizations needing outside help find and contract with a consultant.
3. Board and staff participate in an initial planning retreat to discuss vision, mission, values, and questions that should be resolved in planning.
4. The planning committee leads a community assessment if required.
5. Board and staff gather in a second planning retreat or series of planning meetings to make sense of assessment results and make decisions about priorities. A volunteer or professional consultant facilitates.
6. The planning committee (and/or planning consultant) writes the draft plan.

7. The board considers the draft, amends it if needed, and approves the plan. If necessary, the planning committee writes a second draft before final approval.

STAGE 1: ORGANIZE

A planning effort requires organization. Typically one or more board or senior staff members decide that the organization would benefit from planning and initiate discussion with other board members and staff. They consider the scope and scale of the plan, candidates for the planning team, and the time and funds needed for the effort. They decide how to involve the full board and staff. At a subsequent board meeting, the idea is raised and support sought. If there is professional staff, the project is introduced to them at a staff meeting.

To prepare for planning, some initial topics need to be considered.

Time commitment. When should planning start and finish? What time period should the plan cover? A simple plan can be accomplished with a single planning retreat, a few days of writing, and a board meeting. A more comprehensive plan may take six to nine months. Ask how comprehensive the plan should be and match the time commitment to the scope of planning. The stage that requires the most time is seeking constituent input in the external assessment.

Process. What process should be used to gather together the information needed for the plan? At what point should the assessment be made? Will it involve people outside the organization—through interviews, focus group meetings, or surveys—or will the board and staff assume they know the community, audiences, funders, and potential collaborators and competitors well enough to proceed?

Planning team. Who will lead the planning effort and who should be on the team? AES recommends using a small planning committee. (See the Online Companion for this chapter for Should We Use a Consultant. See the last page of the book for the Internet address.) Recruit people for the planning committee who can write, as well as those who represent a balance among the interests and constituencies served by the organization. A small, balanced group is needed to finish the planning work started at a retreat or series of planning meetings. The planning committee will not develop the plan by itself; it will organize the rest of the organization to do so.

Budget. What funds are required and from what sources will they be drawn? If a professional consultant or retreat facilitator is used, this will be the major expense. Consultants are sometimes helpful but not always necessary. Other expenses may include refreshments for the retreat and any assessment meetings, flip charts, photocopying, and postage. State and local arts agencies and community foundations often offer funding for planning. If you plan to seek a grant to underwrite your planning effort, this step will have to be accomplished well in advance of the start of planning.

Planning retreat(s). Reserve the retreat date on people's calendars. Allow enough time to collect information, including audience research or community assessment if they are part of your planning process.

Retreat site. Select an attractive, easily accessible location where people will be comfortable and productive. Retreats may be held in corporate boardrooms

Figure 2: The AES Planning Process

STAGE	WHAT	WHO	HOW
1. Organize	Recruit planning team, budget, determine scope, and collect background information.	Chief executive and board president	Organize meeting.
2. Envision	Discuss vision, values, and who you are and what you believe in (to be expressed in a set of governing ideas).	Board and staff	Hold planning retreat for stages 2-4.
3. Assess	Discover current internal and external conditions. Simple plans involve only board and staff; more team-comprehensive plans assess community members' needs directly.	Board and staff	Conduct retreat and/or planning interviews, focus groups, surveys, and public hearings. Review records.
4. Establish Goals	Explore alternatives and choose desired results and most likely ways to achieve them. These may be expressed through mission, goals, objectives, strategies, and budgets.	Board and staff or planning team	Hold planning retreat and subsequent series of planning meetings.
5. Write the Plan	Write first draft; revise, review (board and staff), check with constituents, and revise final draft.	Planning team	Write, revise, and rewrite.
6. Approve and Commit	Confirm board approval and organizational commitment to implement. Distribute plan widely.	Board, staff, and volunteers	Explain, promote, and public.
7. Implement	Determine who does what, and at what cost. Then do it.	Staff and/or volunteers	Link plan to budgets and program decisions.
8. Evaluate and Adapt	Regularly ask how you are doing. Monitor progress on objectives. Make course corrections as conditions change. Recycle through the planning process.	Staff and board	Recruit champions for goals schedule discussions, and monitor progress.

(to encourage hard work), in private homes (to encourage informality and sociability), or at conference centers (to encourage productivity or make the retreat more of a special event).

Necessary materials. You will need an easel and large flip chart, markers, and masking tape. In addition, have on hand copies of existing plans, budgets, mission statements, audience statistics, sample promotions, etc. Refreshments are essential. (See the Appendix for a Planning Retreat Checklist as well as a Sample Planning Retreat Agenda.)

The next three stages may be covered in part or in their entirety at the planning retreat. However, if your board and staff do not adequately represent the community you serve or wish to serve, an external assessment step is probably necessary. In that case, this process works best if the assessment is conducted before the planning retreat. Assessment becomes the second step and Envision becomes the third.

STAGE 2: ENVISION

This may be the most important step in the planning process. It is here that members of the group ask the most fundamental questions: In what do we believe? Why does this organization exist? What difference, ultimately, do we wish to make in this community? What is our vision for the future? What will that envisioned future look like?

For an organization with a clearly established vision, this step becomes an opportunity to introduce new board and staff to that vision and to remind everyone of the important work of which they are all a part.

The Importance of Vision

A sense of vision—one that is meaningful, articulate, and widely shared by members of an organization—is a powerful force in planning. A vision, a clear sense of mission, and core values are more valuable in a rapidly changing environment than a detailed set of tasks that may become quickly outdated. A planning retreat which achieves a clear sense of a desired future is well worth the effort. But how do we find one?

Stripped of all the jargon, planning is, in essence, a creative act. A planner, like an artist, imagines what might be and then goes about to make it so.

Recall your vision. Sometimes discussions among founding members or a review of early plans and promotions will reveal a powerful founding vision which may have been forgotten. Ask members to recall why it was that they joined the organization to regain a sense of this founding vision.

Recognize the vision of a leader. Sometimes arts organizations are blessed with a visionary leader. This is frequently the case for arts-producing organizations formed to support the creative work of a choreographer, music director, or curator. This envisioning stage can encourage the visionary leader to communicate her or his artistic vision to the rest of the organization's members.

Create a new vision. For arts organizations sustained by community needs for artistic programs and services, this approach may be the most successful.

It is difficult for most people to express their visions. While a vision must ultimately be expressed in writing, it often needs to emerge from a less literal process. Too much talking and writing may inhibit more imaginative thinking. A planning retreat should include envisioning exercises to assist people to tap their right-brain creativity. These may include the use of drawing, metaphors, storytelling, games, and guided visualization. (See the Appendix for the Sample Planning Retreat Agenda.)

It's likely at this point in the retreat (or in a succession of planning meetings) that the vision exists as a series of key words and phrases, perhaps some drawings or charts. Try to condense onto one or two flip charts the essential parts of the visioning exercises. Post the mission statement on a flip chart alongside the written elements of the newly described vision.

Envisioning a Theater

An actress in Maine attended an AES planning workshop to learn how to start a theater company in her rural community. She had worked in other theaters and knew how they operated. There were a number of people interested in participating, but she was having considerable trouble getting started. How does one create an institution? She was daunted.

After she described her dilemma, it occurred to the instructor to ask if she could act and organize the production of a play. Of course she could. He suggested that she assume the role of an artistic director, imagine a scenario of her theater company in business, and then cast players in the roles needed to get the theater established.

But the theater isn't real yet, she said. He asked her at what point it would be. Would it be real after they had built a theater, after they had produced their first play, or after they had a year's productions behind them?

Why not create it now? He suggested that she announce that a community theater had been started and that she was its artistic director. She was to print some business cards, call a meeting of interested community members, and plan its first production. She was to assume the role and act the part.

Soon after she announced on her new letterhead that it worked just as she had imagined. She had tapped the creativity of the art she knew so well.

Compare the emerging vision with the existing mission statement. If the mission remains consistent with the language emerging as a vision, planners can reconfirm the mission. Some of the words and phrases generated in the retreat can be used to interpret the mission in promotions, fundraising appeals, and communications with volunteers or staff.

The comparison of the mission and vision may prove the mission to be out-of-date. In that case, the group should discuss whether it needs to revise the mission. It should resist the temptation to write a new mission statement as part of the retreat. Rather, the planning committee should work with the intentions of the retreat participants. The committee should return to the board and staff with one or more versions of a revised mission for their consideration.

An inspiring vision is crucial. But the vision must balance with a clear-eyed look at where the organization is and how it is doing.

STAGE 3: ASSESS

An accurate assessment of your current situation—both internal and external to the organization—is the usual next step in planning. While assessment is considered here as a discrete phase in planning, the leaders of any successful arts organization are constantly observing and assessing what is going on within the organization and its community and adapting operations as required. In addition to this ongoing assessment, a deliberate taking stock of current conditions is a part of a strategic planning process.

The eight-stage model assumes two assessment possibilities.

Questions to Inspire People to Express a Sense of Vision and Mission

What most inspires you about our work?

Recall an incident when you observed this organization at its finest.

When have you seen us doing the best work we were meant to do?

What business are we in?

If we went out of business, what would be the ultimate cost to our community? What would be lost?

How You Might Ask Questions

During a retreat or planning meeting, a facilitator asks one of the above questions.

Ask each individual to briefly write down one or more answers.

After individuals have worked alone for a time, ask people to form groups of two or three and share their stories. Planners call these purpose stories.

Ask a representative from each group to summarize stories that are typical of their group's discussion.

A facilitator summarizes themes and patterns from the discussion by writing keywords and phrases on a large pad of paper.

Compare the elements of these visions to the current mission or purpose statement.

If the formal mission statement seems to fit these stories, group members now have a better understanding of what that dry language now means. If the mission seems out of synch with the values that group members most often described, this suggests that the planners may need to revise the mission.

1. Board and staff represent the community or constituencies served by the organization and understand their needs.
2. The organization's leaders may not represent or may not understand all of what the constituency needs.

The first case assumes that you are in close frequent contact with the people you serve and you understand their concerns. It may be possible to develop a good plan without extensive community assessment. However, planning and the organization are usually improved through the relationship building that happens when you go out into the community to ask about people's interests and needs and how your organization can help serve them.

External assessments fulfill two important functions: gather information and build relationships.

If the group's leadership does not itself reflect and understand important resources or constituencies, then external assessment is essential for the planning to be authentic. Beyond the obvious advantage of the planning information you will gather, there are other critical benefits. Plans inevitably change, but if you've built relationships in planning, you can adjust. There is also a political or public relations benefit from constituent assessment. Your organization becomes visibly concerned with understanding community needs. This may put you on the radar screens of people who may be in a position to help you implement your plans. Many arts leaders find they are able to reach funders, political leaders, school officials, and newspaper publishers to ask questions in assessment in a way they could never do if they were asking for help.

External assessments can be accomplished by sampling the opinions of representatives of key funders, audiences, and potential collaborators through interviews, focus group meetings, or surveys. Internal assessments can be done by reviewing financial reports and evaluation results, by asking questions of staff, volunteers, and board members, and by identifying assessment issues as part of a planning retreat.

Internal Assessment

Records. Before going out to the community to gather more data, look at what you already have. Some information may originally have come from external sources and may be useful in your assessment.

Financial statements. The current year's budget compared with actual expenses to date provides valuable assessment data. Get an even better sense of financial trends by reviewing the three previous operating statements (statements of annual income and expenses). While much can be learned from a look at how specific line items change, summarized charts may be more useful for strategic planning—for example, a pie chart showing the sources of income and the major expenses or a simple line chart with total income and expenses over a three or four-year period.

If the data show changes, ask why. If ticket sales rose and then fell, ask if there were programming or promotion changes that could explain the variation. The point of the financial analysis is to help make strategic decisions in planning.

Evaluation reports. Consider the findings of program or service evaluations in planning.

An arts agency board debated the wisdom of partnerships with nonarts agencies. A table, showing the relative amount of money that partners invested in the arts agency and directly to artists through employment contracts, quickly settled the debate.

Grant panelist comments. Comments and scores about an organization by grant panelists may provide good assessment data. Consider what they say about your organization, good and bad, during planning.

Attendance statistics. A summary of attendance at programs, events, and services can be useful. Organize visitor tracking data, inquiries for information, ticket sales, etc., into summary charts or tables and then ask what the information reveals.

Self-assessment questionnaires. It can be quite productive to ask questions of board and staff to elicit a clearer sense of what is working and not inside an organization. Or you can frame questions specific to the issues you know to be of concern. Consider using a self-assessment instrument. (See the Online Companion for this chapter for a Self-Assessment Questionnaire you can use or adapt. See the last page of the book for the Internet address.) The scoring of anonymous responses can identify issues that people might otherwise be hesitant to raise. More important than scores is that the questions provoke reflection. Circulate assessment questions a couple of weeks before your first retreat to stimulate critical thinking about the organization's strengths and weaknesses.

For information on framing *open-ended* questions or *fixed-response* questions, see the Program Evaluation chapter.

Interviews. Administer assessment questions in one-on-one interviews or small group discussions. In one large arts center, the director met with small groups of professional and support staff, regular volunteers, and teaching artists to discuss their concerns and suggestions for planning. Then he summarized these discussions during a planning retreat for senior staff and board members.

Strengths, weaknesses, opportunities, and threats (SWOT). Invite board and staff members to brainstorm and consider internal organizational strengths and weaknesses and external threats and opportunities. Planners call this step a *SWOT analysis.*

A SWOT analysis is best done as part of a more thorough internal and external assessment. However, in an abbreviated planning process, a SWOT discussion could be done in a planning retreat context. This will work as an *external* assessment only if the board and staff understand their community well enough. If they understand the general intentions of important funders, the interests of audiences, the concerns of neighbors, and the likely impact of competitors and partners, then they might skip more thorough external assessment.

There are two popular methods: brainstorming and nominal group process.

Brainstorming. The objective of brainstorming is to get as many ideas as possible from group members in a short time. The facilitator invites the group to think about the organization's internal strengths and weaknesses and external threats and opportunities. While ideas are being expressed, judgment should be suspended. People should feel free to propose whatever comes to mind, even if it seems far-fetched, bouncing new ideas off earlier ones. The facilitator or an assistant jots down key words or phrases to keep track of each idea as it is introduced.

If the group gets stalled, suggest some categories of ideas within the broader headings. It may help to focus first on the internal strengths and weaknesses and then on the external threats and opportunities.

It is easier to tone down a wild idea then to think up a new one.

—Alex Osborne, inventor of brainstorming

In most SWOT sessions, internal strengths and external opportunities get intermixed. Don't worry. Just mark an "S" next to each strength and an "O" next to each opportunity. A threat may also be seen as an opportunity and vice versa. If the issue is both a threat and an opportunity, mark it "T/O." Brainstorming concludes when many issues have been identified and the pace of new suggestions slows.

Sometimes a group falls into a pattern of just listing problems. A perceptive facilitator will prompt for some strengths and ask if some of the threats don't also suggest opportunities. Don't gloss over real problems, but the productivity of the retreat will be compromised if everyone is depressed by a litany of problems without relief.

A variation on brainstorming is to break into smaller groups of five or six people and have each group brainstorm its own list. After a period of perhaps 40 minutes, the full group reconvenes and each small group reports on its assessment.

Nominal group process. In this variation, members of the group are invited to individually write out a list of strengths, weaknesses, opportunities, and threats. After 15 or 20 minutes, the facilitator asks each person in turn to identify one issue. Like group brainstorming, each issue is summarized on a flip chart until all ideas have been expressed.

Nominal group process is good for getting everyone to participate and is easier to facilitate. This approach, however, does not take advantage of group synergy. The people are only "nominally" a group. Brainstorming is good for generating ideas, as it builds on group enthusiasm. But brainstorming is more challenging to facilitate, with lots of ideas being tossed out at once.

External Assessment

Often important community interests are underrepresented by an organization's board or staff. Direct community input may be needed to identify and understand needs or test potential support for new initiatives. In these situations, the planning process should be adapted to conduct community assessment prior to the planning retreat/envisioning stage.

The three standard external assessment tools are *interviews*, *focus groups*, and *surveys*. A staff and board may conduct interviews and focus groups, though the outside perspective and research skills of a consultant may prove useful. Any complicated surveys should be designed and administered with the advice or help of experienced survey researchers. For further detail on conducting focus groups and surveys, go to the Online Companion for this chapter for How to Run a Focus Group and Steps of Survey Research (see the last page of the book for the Internet address.)

Interviews. A good interview requires some preparation and skill. First, determine what information is needed, whom to ask, and how to formulate questions. Typically, external perceptions are sought regarding community needs and interests, opportunities and threats, and potential resources.

The people most frequently sought out for assessment interviews are community leaders—people who can represent the interests of larger groups of people, such as religious leaders and community organizers. Spokespersons, however, may not always fully understand the interests of their constituency, so it is a good idea to interview multiple leaders, if possible, or include some constituent types as well.

For guidelines on conducting interviews, see the Program Evaluation chapter.

Focus groups. Interviewing a focus group—several carefully selected representatives of a constituency with common interests or affinities—is a simple way to determine what a large number of people are likely to think about a given subject. You can gain a general sense of preferences—What kind of entertainment does your family prefer?—or reactions to specific programs—How did you like the jazz concert?

See the Program Evaluation chapter and the Online Companion for this chapter (see the last page of the book for the Internet address) for more information on how to run a focus group. See also the Appendix at the end of this chapter for suggested Planning Questions.

Surveys. Surveys are commonly used to collect assessment information from large numbers of people. They can be simple cards distributed in program notes to audience members, surveys sent by email or mail to representative samples of a population, exit polls (a combination of survey and interview), or telephone polls of randomly selected households. As more people use the Internet, more planners are using Web-based surveys combined with emailed requests to participate. As more people screen telephone calls, telephone polling is declining.

See Steps of Survey Research in the Online Companion (go to the last page of the book for the Internet address), the Program Evaluation chapter for detail on survey design, and the references in the bibliography for excellent books on survey design.

For general population surveys of the type needed for a community cultural plan, it is highly recommended that you seek professional advice. An experienced consultant or graduate student at a school of business or sociology may design or conduct a survey.

Identify Critical Issues

Conclude your assessment by reducing all the information you have gathered into a short list of critical issues to resolve in planning. If your assessment was limited to a brainstormed list of SWOT issues in a retreat, you can do this quite simply. Post all of the flip charts around the room and invite participants to walk around, reflect, and make notes about what issues seem to be the most significant. Then determine group consensus through discussion. Another method is to hand out colored markers or adhesive dots and ask people to put a red dot next to critical issues and an orange dot by important ones. The issues with the most red dots are likely to be the most critical.

If your internal and external assessments are more thorough, it is best to go through the data and look for themes, patterns, problems, and opportunities to be raised in the planning. It is best if the assessment is presented as a written report that concisely summarizes critical issues for planning. See the Program Evaluation chapter for information about how to organize and interpret assessment data.

Conclude the Assessment Stage

The assessment concludes with planning team consensus on a pared down list of critical internal and external issues that must be considered during the remainder of the planning process. A local arts agency might conclude its assessment with a recognition that they are sustained by an effective staff, a well-connected board, and a reputation for quality programs and services; and that they are challenged by inadequate information about community artists and arts organizations, and their audiences do not sufficiently include the community's growing Latino and Asian-American populations.

At this point the most important work requiring the broad participation of the organization's board and staff has been completed. While the retreat has not yet delved into specifics, critical issues have been identified. Important principles have been established that will guide the planning team as they proceed to work out long-range goals and more specific objectives and strategies. The simple act of articulating organizational values, vision, and critical issues helps volunteers and staff to recognize opportunities and to resolve problems as they arise.

Stage two (envisioning) and much of stage three (assessment) may be completed in a single planning retreat. If the facilitator keeps an eye on the clock, the agenda, and people's energy, it is often possible to take further advantage of the organization's gathered leadership in a retreat. Before people disperse it is helpful to move on to the next stage of the process: planning more specifically for the next two or three years.

STAGE 4: MAKE DECISIONS

Write or Revisit the Mission

A mission statement becomes the fundamental principle or foundation of your strategic plan. If planning is leading to the creation of a new organizational mission, you will need to write one. If there is an existing mission, determine if it should be revised. You should consider mission as part of an envisioning exercise early in your planning retreat, but also revisit your mission as you approach the conclusion of your planning.

Develop or Refine Goals

The vision expresses what could be; the mission expresses why the organization exists; the assessment describes what is; and goals are future conditions that, if met, help to realize the vision or resolve critical issues. Goals tend to describe public-benefit programs and services. Many plans also include organizational capacity-building or administrative goals.

The vision expresses what could be; the mission expresses why the organization exists; the assessment describes what is; and goals are future conditions that, if met, help to realize the vision or resolve critical issues.

Goals may not be clear at the end of a single retreat. It is possible, though, to elicit some directions specifying what the organization wishes to accomplish over the next two or three years. Then the planning committee or consultant writes goals based on their notes and observations from the retreat. Alternatively, the leaders can be convened for a second retreat that focuses on goals and objectives.

It is a common mistake for planners to draft goals that describe symptomatic problems or superficial solutions. For example, an artist advocate and planner might have the following interaction, with the planner trying to move to a more fundamental and long-range goal.

Advocate: Our goal is to renovate the front room of the arts center to serve as a local artists' gallery.

Planner: If this goal were resolved, what would that get us?

Advocate: It would provide artists a place to exhibit.

Planner: A more fundamental goal might therefore be: To provide for local artists opportunities to exhibit their work. What would that get us?

Advocate: If they had opportunities to exhibit their work, more people would see their work, and the artists could make more sales.

Planner: A still more basic goal statement might be: To provide opportunities for local artists to connect with their audiences.

With such a fundamental goal, many programs may help fulfill the goal: renovate the gallery, publish a map of local artist studios, encourage the local artist guild to hold open studios, work with the local newspaper to feature local artists, etc. By seizing on the first obvious project as a goal, the planners may limit their thinking and subsequent programming.

A group can make headway in articulating long-range goals by breaking into smaller task forces with each one working on a separate program or goal area. In each case, the planners prepare rough notes for the planning committee to refine. (See the Goals/Objectives Worksheet on the Online Companion. Go to the last page of the book for the Internet address.) It is probably wise to limit the number of goals an organization commits to in its strategic plan. Many good plans have only three to five long-range goals.

Set Priorities

The critical results of the assessment should present organization leaders with strategic choices: How can we respond to the changing needs of our diversifying population? Should we discontinue a favorite program that is no longer funded?

There is a distinct shift in emphasis as the planning process moves from assessment and envisioning to decision-making and problem solving. Assessment is expansive and questioning. Exercises to elicit vision and clarify mission are not constrained by limitations of resources. Now the planners must answer questions raised in the assessment, solve problems, and determine priorities. This stage can be the most challenging part of planning. It can also be the most rewarding as organization leaders solve problems and resolve ambiguous questions.

Decision-making will occur throughout the planning process. Many planners prefer to determine overall strategies first (shift from arts programming to arts services), then establish goals (provide capacity-building information and services to the arts community), and then define specific objectives (establish a central ticketing office by the start of next year). With clear goals and defined objectives, planners can determine a work plan for the first year with detailed tasks, deadlines, responsibilities, and evaluation measures. Such planning moves deliberately from general principles to specific actions.

Other planners start at the detailed level of programs and services (create a central ticketing service). They then consider what goals and strategies are implied by that and other operational decisions, as described earlier in Mintzberg's emergent planning model. Planning often blends deliberate decision-making with emergent strategies as leaders plan ahead and also learn from what works and does not.

Define Critical Questions

Decision-making starts with a list of the decisions to be reached. What are the critical questions and issues that surfaced in the assessment and that must be resolved in planning? What specific opportunities and problems do you face? If the assessment raised dozens of questions, prioritize the few, most compelling questions that must be resolved. Resist the temptation to pursue every interesting problem or to delve into the details of specific programs or operations. Many opportunities to answer major questions are wasted on debates about details.

Talk It Through

The simplest method for group decision-making is to sit down and talk through the planning questions. Conversation works best for uncomplicated decisions. Start by defining the question and then explore several possible solutions before settling on the best decision. There are risks to decisions by conversation. Sometimes the first suggested option is accepted as "good enough" before better, more subtle options are even considered. The most articulate people may dominate and ignore good advice from others. "Group think" may lead to poor decisions: if no one in a group takes the initiative to voice a reservation about a proposal, then others with doubts may also not speak, and the group makes a bad decision that most do not support.

There are several structured ways to engage a team in problem solving, but don't ignore the old fashioned way of sitting around a table to talk about it.

Resolve SWOT-defined Issues

If SWOT analysis was used in the assessment stage, now determine which of the identified issues are critical and within your power to influence. Then plan how to maximize strengths, minimize critical weaknesses, respond to the best opportunities, and avoid the most dangerous threats. This often provides just enough structure to planning discussions that you can make decisions and choose priorities. There is a risk, however, that this simple analysis will ignore the interrelationship among these forces.

Kevin Kearns, in *Private Sector Strategies for Social Sector Success* (2000), cited by Allison and Kaye in *Strategic Planning for Nonprofit Organizations*, recommends using SWOT to look for relationships among strengths, weaknesses, opportunities, and threats. Try to match strengths with opportunities. An organizational strength (track record of successful arts programming for kids) combined with an opportunity (demographic projections of increasing numbers of children) suggests a strategic choice to invest in children's programming. An area of organizational weakness (no experience coordinating centralized services) and an opportunity (community need for central ticketing) requires a decision: strengthen organizational capacity, collaborate with another organization, or ignore the opportunity. Kearns suggests further that areas of strength provide the means to mobilize to defend against external threats (strong capacity to organize advocacy can defeat threatened public arts funding cuts). If threatened in areas of weakness, the strategy may be to control the damage.

List Pros and Cons

A time-honored way for a group to make decisions is to simply frame the question, brainstorm alternative solutions, shorten the list of options to the few most feasible solutions, and then list pros and cons for each alternative response or solution. This may reveal your best choice.

Compare Alternatives to Agreed Criteria

You can create a matrix or grid to compare options against criteria. (For an example, see Figure 3.) This allows for more sophisticated analysis of alternative solutions. Determine by what criteria you will judge the alternatives. Common criteria include:

- fit with the mission (always the first criterion);
- fit with overall strategy and/or goal;
- addresses documented and unmet need;
- fiscal feasibility (capacity to earn more than it costs or be funded);
- staff capacity to implement; and
- facility capacity.

Depending on the issue, problem, or opportunity at hand, alternatives may be compared to other criteria such as the potential to increase organizational visibility, increase organizational capacity, develop partnerships, increase earned revenue, etc.

To rate each alternative against each criterion, the simplest approach is to put yes, no, or question mark (need more information) in each cell. Or determine a numeric score: a +3 for an option that excellently matches a criterion, +2 for very good match, down to -3 for an option that seriously undermines a criterion. Criteria may also be weighted so that "fit with mission" carries more relative weight than "increase organizational visibility." Then each column of numbers is totaled to get relative scores for each option. If criteria are weighted, then the result of each column is multiplied by the number representing that criterion's relative weight.

Figure 3: Comparing Options Against Criteria

Question: What capacity-building programs and services should we offer?

Criteria	**Fits mission** *(weighted 2x* other criteria)	**Staff can handle**	**Advances core strategy: shift to services**	**Fiscally feasible**	**Score**
Option 1: Create central ticketing	3	-2	3	-2 *requires two-year subsidy*	0
Option 2: Start nonprofit management training program	3	-1	3	0 *revenue neutral*	5
Option 3: Provide consulting services	2	-3	3	2 *earns money*	4
Option 4: Create website with links to other resources	3	3	3	3 *very good cost/ benefits*	12

CompassPoint's Dual Bottom-line Matrix

Allison and Kaye describe a decision tool that helps planners evaluate decisions based on two bottom lines: impact of the decision on the mission and on financial viability. A good decision would have high positive impact on the mission and high financial viability. An option that had low impact on the mission and low financial viability should be carefully considered. A program in that quadrant of the matrix would be a good candidate to close down or give to another agency. (See Figure 4 for a sample matrix.) This tool may be particularly useful if your planning decision is to start a new program or keep or discontinue an existing program. Decide if the program has a high or low impact on mission and high or low financial viability and place it in the appropriate quadrant. Then make a decision guided by the matrix.

Be careful, however. These types of decision-making tools may suggest an illusionary precision of results. Much depends upon your assumptions. When you evaluate the

Figure 4: CompassPoint's Dual-Bottom Line Matrix (used by permission)

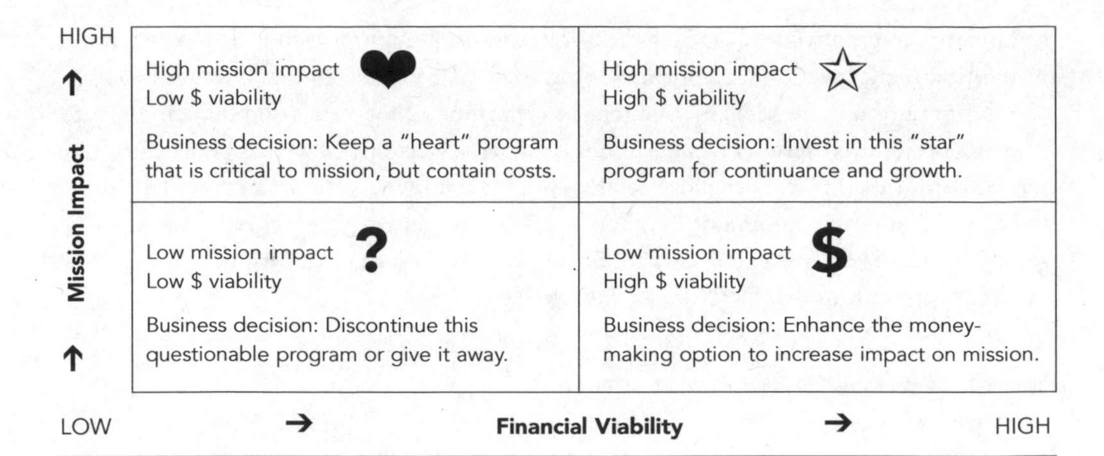

results of an exercise like this, use your judgment. Ask if it makes sense. Ask what the results suggest. Creative problem solving often defies the tools planners invent to bottle it.

Document Priorities and Decisions

Document decisions as each are determined in planning. Many planning committees run in circles rehashing the same questions because no one recognizes or writes down decisions. (See the Fundamentals of Board Development chapter for a discussion of group decision-making). If you have an existing plan, you may wish to annotate it as you go with revisions or additions: amend a goal, write a strategy, adopt a new objective, or note a task. Or you can simply write down the decision and later integrate any changes in the strategic plan. If in doubt whether you're writing a strategy, goal, or objective, simply label the decision an "intention" or "priority" and later sort out how it fits into the hierarchy of the written plan. If you haven't yet made a decision, but have narrowed choices to two options, record them both with a note to decide later.

Define Objectives

While some planning decisions become expressed as goals or strategies, more often the answers to planning questions may be written in the plan as objectives. Objectives clearly state intentions and set specific targets for board, volunteers, and staff to reach. This may be the first time in the planning process that some bottom-line, results-oriented staff and board members get interested! The elusive stuff of vision gets translated into how many of what kinds of programs are offered when, and at what cost.

This is the stage of planning when the board and staff make the tough decisions to set priorities, determine what programs the organization will start or discontinue, and allocate scarce resources among competing demands. This process can be untidy and uncomfortable as tough questions are raised and may appear to be getting even more ambiguous. Some people's favorite programs may not survive. Trust in the process and accept that decisions will become clearer as you move through planning. Acknowledge when questions have been resolved and note that the list of ambiguous problems is getting shorter.

Specific objectives anchor the plan to the real, immediate needs and opportunities of the organization and its constituency. This is where the expressions of high purpose answer the question, So what are we going to do about it now? At this point, goals become linked to resources to realize them.

> Who will organize and lead the program?
>
> How much will it cost?
>
> Where will the funds come from?
>
> If we do this project, what demands will it make upon staff time, facilities, and supplies?
>
> Which objectives are important enough to merit scarce funds and time?
>
> When should this objective be achieved?

Here competing priorities are balanced. Some priorities move forward as immediate objectives for the organization and community. Others are postponed until more resources can be secured.

Japanese management doesn't prescribe specific measurable objectives. Rather, leaders try to communicate a business philosophy—how to deal with customers, employees, competitors, world role—that allows individuals to determine their own objectives as they operate under any circumstances, no matter how unusual or new.

—William G. Ouchi

But specificity has its limits. Because conditions inevitably change, a plan that projects overly specific objectives too far into the future may soon be out-of-date. To balance short-term specificity with long-term flexibility, many strategic plans project detailed objectives for the upcoming year and more general ones for the period thereafter, and then update annual work plans each year by specifying objectives.

When you write objectives, you are setting the conditions for evaluation. If your objectives are specific and observable, you can evaluate the extent to which each is achieved. This will make evaluation simpler. See the Program Evaluation chapter for more on the relationship of planning to evaluation.

Link the Plan to the Budget

A budget must be developed that translates the next year's objectives into anticipated revenues and expenses. A first-draft budget will likely reveal that all the objectives can't be realized as first hoped. The budget process provides a forum for debating the relative merits of competing objectives and programs.

It is helpful to organize the planning process so that it parallels the organization's budgeting process. The planning team can then focus upon programmatic objectives, which the financial staff or committee converts into a budget. (See the Financial Management chapter for more on budgeting.)

STAGE 5: WRITE THE PLAN

Writing the plan is a dynamic phase of the planning process. The rigor of crafting words to clarify emerging directions and to identify dilemmas serves to ground ideas. It is not necessary that the planning committee leave a retreat with clear consensus on the organization's intentions or instructions for every element of the plan. Often it isn't until the planning team begins reworking retreat notes into the draft plan that areas of consensus and disagreement become apparent.

Format Options for the Finished Plan

Option 1: Narrative Format
Commit to a policy of inclusion in every program, with particular attention to the unique needs of rural artists and rural communities. In the first year, convene a meeting of the Rural Arts Panel to explore alternative programs for rural arts advancement if federal support is not available.

Options 2: Outline Format

1. Commit to a policy of inclusion.
   1.1 Serve the unique needs of rural communities.
   1.2 Explore alternatives to federal funding.

Option 3: Graphic Format
Goal 2: Remove barriers to access.
Objective 2.1: Commit to a policy of inclusion in every program with particular attention to artists of color and rural artists.

	FY2007	FY2008	FY2009
Tasks	Convene a panel of artists to assess needs	Evaluate impact of changes.	Complete accessibility plan.
	Make changes as indicated.	Secure additional funds for a full accessibility plan.	Establish artist fellowships.
	Hold four regional forums.	Hold a state conference.	

Who Writes?

Writing can be done primarily by one writer (chief executive, planning committee member, or the consultant), with the rest of the planning committee serving as editors; the planning committee can write jointly; or sections of the plan can be delegated to various committee members. How you proceed depends on the skills and working styles of the committee. You may find that the single writer/multiple editor approach produces a more coherent, readable plan.

The Drafting and Review Process

Write drafts of the plan soon after each planning retreat or meeting while ideas are still fresh and momentum is strong. Express points of agreement clearly. Convey beliefs about which the group feels strongly. Earmark for additional deliberation issues on which there is disagreement. Outline the implications of various goals on courses of action that must still be decided. Keep it simple! Aim for brevity, conciseness, accessibility, and a usable document.

The planning committee or consultant works up a first draft from the flip charts and from their own notes. (See sidebar, Format Options for the Finished Plan.) The draft is distributed for consideration at a scheduled board meeting or a second planning retreat. At the meeting, portions of the plan with broad support are confirmed, allowing enough time for thorough discussion. Alternative goals or versions of goals are debated. Here the objective is to focus and reach closure on unresolved issues. The board should try to reach consensus in principle and let the planning committee revise the draft plan.

The planning committee meets again and incorporates these changes into another draft. The second draft, if approved by the board, becomes the strategic plan. If there is disagreement about the intentions of the group or need for further clarification, these are debated until there is consensus or an agreement to disagree. The plan is revised and finalized, copied, and distributed.

Consider two versions of the finished plan. Many planners produce two versions of their strategic plan. A simple outline or graphic version communicates the key points of the plan. This version, laid out on a single page or as a brochure, is then produced in quantity and distributed widely. Every staff and board member, volunteer, and committee member gets a copy. Copies of this plan are included in funding requests and made available to audiences, municipal officials, and community partners.

A more comprehensive version of the plan, either in narrative form or in outline plus narrative, is produced to guide the organization's policymakers and those responsible for day-to-day operations and decision-making. Goals, objectives, and strategies are explained in greater detail in this version. Objectives for the upcoming year are linked to the budget so that various commitments are backed by line items in the budget.

STAGE 6: APPROVE AND COMMIT

The governing board ordinarily approves the final draft of the plan. Since board members have been a part of the planning process from the start, this process should be harmonious. It should be an opportunity to celebrate the organization's new or renewed commitment to a shared sense of purpose and the clarification of strategies which will be pursued to help fulfill that mission. This stage should also be the occasion to present the entire strategic plan in overview. Some board and staff members will not have participated in every planning step and some may have only a partial understanding of the plan, appreciating primarily those portions with which they are most closely associated. The strategic plan is meaningless unless members of the organization understand it and commit to carrying it out. Accordingly, the leadership should work to assure that everyone understands the group's intentions as expressed in the plan. If the plan can succeed in realigning the efforts of individual members toward a commonly shared sense of purpose, significant energy is released that can accomplish that purpose.

If the plan is a community cultural plan, the approval and commitment process should include a well-orchestrated publicity campaign and a celebratory arts and public relations event that presents the plan.

Design and Print the Finished Plan

The finished plan should be attractively presented with good graphic design. Recruit a graphic designer to produce a professional-looking document. It need not be slick to respect aesthetic quality. Consider incorporating visuals into its design.

Produce enough copies of the abbreviated version to distribute it liberally. Produce enough of any comprehensive version for all board and professional staff, with some in reserve for new people. Many organizations also publish a summary version of their plans on their website.

STAGE 7: IMPLEMENT

In the context of planning, implementation of the plan makes it operational, mindful of the priorities expressed within it. Considering implementation as a discreet final stage suggests that planning is separated from action. In fact, the process is more circular. Assessing, monitoring, adapting, and implementing are ongoing and simultaneous processes.

Decisions to act—that is, to implement—may occur at any point in the eight-stage process. For example, ideas are frequently expressed at the planning retreat that make such obvious good sense that staff resolve to implement the idea immediately, not waiting for the finished plan. Still, as strategic planning is mostly devoted to describing how the organization will relate to the future, most implementation follows the conclusion of the strategic planning process.

Avoid the Fate of Abandoned Plans

Following are some tips to help ensure that the strategic plan doesn't collect dust on the shelf and instead becomes a useful tool which will inform and guide the organization's leaders and members.

Use an authentic, inclusive planning process which fosters investment in the plan's success.

Keep the planning process and product simple. Planning should produce a few core strategies and goals. Take advantage of enthusiasm for the project and start and conclude the planning process in a short time, with no more meetings than are necessary. In the assessment stage, remember that you can never know enough to plan as thoroughly as you might wish, so be content with information that is "good enough." It will change anyway. Few people will read long planning documents. Write the plan simply and succinctly. As E. B. White suggests, "Make every word tell."

Think strategically and adapt. A plan does not substitute for judgment. No plan can predict the future. Think strategically and creatively, and adapt as conditions change. Don't be quick to abandon a good strategy every time you encounter a problem, but be willing to adapt plans as you observe what works and what does not.

Go public with your plans. By publicly committing to your strategic plan, you have put yourself under some pressure to implement it.

Keep your "eyes on the prize." Keep the objectives of your plan before you. People who find they never have time for the crucial tasks that will help realize important goals should heed Stephen Covey's advice, "Don't prioritize your schedule; schedule your priorities." Post your one-page plan above your desk or somewhere you'll see it often. The most useful plan is the note-covered copy that you keep tucked in your appointment calendar. Highlight priorities, cross off strategies that haven't worked, check off accomplished tasks, and make notes about potential new objectives.

Recruit champions. Identify people who care about the issues expressed in your plan and ask them to advocate for the implementation of specific elements. The board member who is a parent concerned about arts-in-education can become the advocate of your new arts-in-education goal. She or he would work with staff to ensure that education programs are developed and get into the budget.

Link fundraising and spending decisions to the strategic plan. A plan that is not related to the budget can scarcely be called a realistic plan. If you don't plan to raise money for and spend money on activities to achieve planned goals, they probably are not your real priorities.

Acquaint new people with the plan. As new board members, staff, and volunteers join your organization, make it a point to orient them to your priorities as expressed in your plan.

STAGE 8: EVALUATE AND ADAPT

How are we doing? and What difference did we make? are the questions at the heart of evaluation. The point of planning is to help make a difference by supporting improved programs and services for a positive impact on the community. The inevitable question then is, Did we?

Strategic planning is an ongoing, dynamic process of action, observation, and reflection. Evaluation and adaptation are presented here as the final phase of the process. In practice, however, evaluation commences at the assessment stage of planning, and adaptation is something leaders do every day to cope with new information and unforeseen developments.

Schedule periodic reviews of the plan. Armed with evaluation information, review progress on important plan objectives. Ask the advocates of planned programs to provide progress reports and note suggested changes in the plan at regular staff and board meetings. Many groups schedule an annual planning retreat for the benefits of planning and evaluation.

Planning and then not evaluating is like producing a play and then not asking how good it was, or planning a game in football and not keeping score.

Use evaluation to adapt the plan. Ongoing informal evaluations and periodic formal reviews provide information essential to keeping organizations on course. Your strategic plan was your best guess about how the future would unfold. Evaluations show how it is in fact unfolding. Adjust strategies accordingly.

See the Program Evaluation chapter for specific program evaluation methods.

THE LEARNING ORGANIZATION

This chapter has offered instruction on how to organize a strategic planning process. Once such a process has become a way of doing business, planning becomes simply an increased capacity to learn—what Peter Senge described as the *learning organization.*

Planning adaptively means being tightly committed to your principles and your vision of what the organization can accomplish while being loosely committed to your specific plans to get there. This is what Robert Waterman and Tom Peters in their search for excellence call the *simultaneous loose/tight* principle. Mindlessly sticking to specific strategies that no longer make sense is one of the acts that give planning a bad reputation. Regularly recreate your strategies as you learn from experience, but don't regularly recreate your value system or your sense of ultimate purpose.

Know what you believe in and care about. Know what difference you want your organization to make in your community. Keep your eyes and ears open for evidence about how you are doing—financially and in terms of audience impact and quality of programming—and look for unforeseen problems and opportunities. Waterman, in *The Renewal Factor*, says that opportunities knock often but show up disguised as problems. Staying attuned to your vision for the organization plus regularly gathering information about how the organization is doing positions you to take advantage of opportunities. Learn by planning and you'll be able to recognize fruitful opportunities. Effective planning becomes second nature in a learning organization.

REFERENCES

Allison, M., & Kaye, J. (2005). *Strategic Planning for Nonprofit Organizations* (2nd edition). Hoboken, NJ: John Wiley and Sons.

Barry, B. W. (1997). *Strategic Planning Workbook for Nonprofit Organizations* (Rev. ed.). St. Paul, MN: Amherst Wilder Foundation.

Bryson, J. M. (2004). *Strategic Planning for Public and Nonprofit Organizations* (3rd ed.). San Francisco and Oxford, England: Jossey Bass.

Bryson, J. M., & Alston, F. K. (2004). *Creating and Implementing Your Strategic Plan: A Workbook for Public and Nonprofit Organizations* (2nd ed.). Jossey-Bass Public Administration Series. San Francisco: Jossey Bass.

Dreeszen, C., Aprill, A., & Deasy, R. (1999). *Learning Partnerships: Improving learning in schools with arts partners in the community.* Washington, DC: The Arts Education Partnership.

Dreeszen, C. (1998). *Community Cultural Planning Handbook: A guide to community leaders.* Washington, DC: Americans for the Arts.

Dreeszen, C. (2001). *Learning Partnerships: Planning and Evaluation Workbooks and Online Help for Arts and Education Collaborations.* Amherst, MA: Arts Extension Service.

Dreeszen, C. (1999). Who's on First: Resolving Problems of Implementation in Public Sector Planning. *Lessons Learned: A Planning Toolsite.* Washington, DC: National Endowment for the Arts: Retrieved from www.arts.endow.gov/pub/Lessons

Drucker, P. (1990). *Managing the Nonprofit Organization: Principles and Practices.* New York: HarperCollins Publishers.

Mintzberg, H., Ahlstrand, B., & Lampel, J. (2005). *Strategy Bites Back: It is far more and less, than you ever imagined.* New Jersey: Pearson Prentice Hall, 26.

Mintzberg, H. (1994). *The Rise and Fall of Strategic Planning.* New York: Free Press.

Mintzberg, H. (1987, July/August). Crafting Strategy. *The Harvard Business Review*, 66-75. Harvard Business School Publishing.

National Endowment for the Arts. (n.d.). *Lessons Learned: A Planning Tool Site.* Retrieved from www.nea.gov/resources

National Endowment for the Arts. (1985). *Surveying Your Arts Audience.* Washington, D.C.: Author.

Peters, T. J., & Waterman, R. H., Jr. (2004). *In Search of Excellence: Lessons from America's Best-run Companies.* New York: HarperCollins Publishing.

Schwartz, P. (1991). *The Art of the Long View: Planning for the Future in an Uncertain World.* New York: Doubleday.

Senge, P. (1990). *The Fifth Discipline: The Art and Practice of the Learning Organization.* New York: Doubleday.

Stevens, L. (1987). *The Community Cultural Assessment Work Kit: Vol. 1. Conducting a Community Cultural Assessment.* Amherst, MA: Arts Extension Service.

Stevens, L,. (1990). *Developing a Strategic Cultural Plan: A Work Kit.* Bacon, B.S., Dreeszen, C., & Krieger, K. (eds.). Amherst, MA: Arts Extension Service.

Warshawski, M., Barsdate, K. J., & Katz, J. (2000). *A State Arts Agency Strategic Planning Tool Kit.* Washington, DC: National Assembly of State Arts Agencies.

Waterman, R. H., Jr. (1987). *The Renewal Factor: How the Best Get and Keep the Competitive Edge.* New York: Bantam.

Wolf, T. (1999). *Managing a Nonprofit Organization in the twenty-first century.* New York: Simon & Schuster Inc.

APPENDIX

PLANNING RETREAT CHECKLIST

Background Materials

The following materials may be culled from grant applications, final reports, and file cabinets. Assemble as many of them as possible as resources for the planning committee. Look for trends, articulate expressions of your organization's intentions, and search for hints about threats and opportunities, etc. It's not unusual to find a better version of your mission in a press release or brochure than in your formal statements.

Critical materials:

- ☐ Mission statement
- ☐ Bylaws
- ☐ Existing or previous plans
- ☐ Previous financial statements (a three-year period shows trends)
- ☐ Current year's budget

Helpful materials:

- ☐ List of current and two years' previous programs and services
- ☐ Numbers of participants for each program
- ☐ Press releases and promotions (look for good descriptions of organizational purpose, values, intentions, etc.)
- ☐ Audience or participant evaluations

Optional materials:

- ☐ Grant applications (especially narrative sections for basic operating support grants that describe organizational purpose and priorities)
- ☐ Final reports to funders
- ☐ Annual organizational reports
- ☐ Recent consultant or technical assistance reports
- ☐ Results of recent audience research or survey

Preretreat checklist:

- ☐ Ask the planning team to refine ideas and rough drafts from the retreat schedule into a written plan.
- ☐ Schedule planning committee meetings after the retreat and a due date for the draft plan.
- ☐ Schedule the retreat date well in advance and enter it on board and staff member calendars.
- ☐ Reserve a comfortable meeting place (retreat site, board room, or residence).
- ☐ Select a retreat facilitator—either a group member or outside consultant.
- ☐ Collect and distribute background information: mission, existing plans, relevant audience statistics, etc.
- ☐ Prepare and distribute preliminary agenda. Specify start and finish times.
- ☐ Collect tools: flip charts and easel, tape, markers, and worksheets.
- ☐ Arrange for refreshments and meal.

SAMPLE PLANNING RETREAT AGENDA

1. **Purpose (10 minutes)**
   The president first explains the purpose of the retreat, its role in the overall planning process, and steps to be taken, and then introduces the facilitator who will manage the remainder of the meeting (may be a designated group member or professional).

2. **Process (10 minutes)**
   The facilitator presents an overview of the day's agenda and the retreat process—facilitator's role, opportunity for full participation, likelihood that problems will be raised that won't be satisfactorily solved, etc.

3. **Participant Introductions (20 to 30 minutes)**
   A common approach is to say, Please introduce yourself and tell us why you have chosen to work with this organization. A variation is to ask each person to find someone else whom he or she would like to know better. Once the group is divided into pairs, each takes a turn interviewing the other, asking for information about the person's background and their role in and hopes for the organization. The facilitator keeps track of time and announces when they should shift roles (about five minutes each) and then asks each person to introduce to the group the person she or he interviewed. (Facilitator must be prepared to cut people off to use time economically.)

4. **Warm-up/Visioning (20 minutes)**
   Serious discussions about an organization's purpose are difficult to generate until people get used to thinking imaginatively and individuals cohere into a working group. Here are some favorite AES warm-up exercises:

   Drawing. (This is best done in small groups.) Draw a picture of the organization as a success. Post the drawings and discuss implications. Variation: Draw it as it exists now and will be in the future.

   Metaphors. Invite participants to meet in small groups and consider the following series of questions: Imagine this organization as a vehicle: What kind is it? Over what kind of terrain does it travel? What powers it? How full is the fuel tank? What parts tend to break down? Who is driving? Who is riding? Where is it headed?

   Guided visualization. Invite members to take an imaginary journey through their community in the near future when the arts organization will have succeeded. What do they see?

5. **Vision/Values/Mission (one hour)**
   Recalling the warm-up exercise, invite group members to talk about visions and values that seem to be shared by members of the organization. As people talk, the facilitator records key words and phrases on the flip chart. This can be approached with a larger group (more than 12) as a brainstorming exercise, quickly generating ideas without discussion, or with a smaller group as an informal discussion. After everyone's ideas are

noted on the flip chart, discuss and underscore with contrasting color markers those that are most compelling. Write key words and phrases on another flip chart and post.

Compare the existing mission statement (written in advance on a sheet of newsprint) with the newly articulated vision and values. Discuss whether the mission is still relevant or if it may need to be reconsidered and rewritten by the planning committee for board consideration. Resist the temptation to write a new mission as a large group. It seldom works.

6. **Assessment (30 minutes)**
   Conduct a SWOT Analysis (internal strengths and weaknesses and external threats and opportunities). Ask members to name the organization's internal strengths and weaknesses and to record them with a key phrase on a flip chart. Mark each with an "S" or "W" to indicate whether it is a strength or weakness and an "S/W" when a factor is both. Don't be concerned if internal and external factors get all mixed up. Just record the issues as they are named.

7. **Critical Issues (30 minutes)**
   Review the SWOT list and underscore critical items requiring planning. People can vote by show of hands, by putting a check on the flip chart by their most critical issues, or by trying to reach consensus through discussion. Write the critical issues on a flip chart sheet and post.

8. **Advice to Planning Team on Goals (30 minutes)**
   Quickly review the vision, values, and critical issues. Discuss long-range goals consistent with the mission, vision, and values, and which could resolve some of the most pressing critical issues. People will be tired. Don't try to write out the goals precisely. Simply record key ideas as raw material for the planning committee to work with as they start to write the draft plan. Write out the rough draft goals on a sheet of newsprint and post.

9. **Wrap Up and Look Forward (10 minutes)**
   At this point everyone is tired. Some may feel more confused about organizational priorities than when they started. It is wise to remind people that they have grappled with a lot of information in a short amount of time and that there is no need to wrap up each step in a tight summary statement. That is the job of the planning committee or consultant. Take down all the flip charts except for visions/values, critical issues, and draft goals. Remind the group of all they have accomplished. Reintroduce the planning committee. You may want to invite others to join the committee if they would like to participate in the next step. Announce the next meeting of the planning committee and the date by which a draft plan will be circulated to board and staff for consideration.

PLANNING QUESTIONS IN PLAIN ENGLISH

Questions that help identify people and institutions that should care (your stakeholders)
Who do we say we serve?
Who do we really serve?
Who should we be serving?
Who would care if we went out of business?

Questions that may help clarify values
What do we care so much about that we can't compromise?
What do we believe in?

Questions to evoke a sense of vision or purpose
What difference do we hope to make in this community?
What do we want our organization to become?
What, ultimately, do we want to accomplish?

Questions to assess conditions
What do we do well?
What could we do better?
What are our internal strengths?
What are our weaknesses?
What opportunities are there in our community of which we might take advantage?
What are threats to our organization or the cultural community (economic, political, social, technological, environmental)?
What do each of our major stakeholders need? How do we know?

Questions to help develop long-term goals
What do we want this program/organization to look like in three years?
What should each of our major programs accomplish in the long term?
List the three or four major problems we or our constituents face and describe the solution to each as an intended goal.

Questions to help develop short-term objectives
For a particular program, what specifically do constituents want us to accomplish in the next year?
What specific changes or improvements do we want to see in place by the end of this year?
What observable outcomes should we be able to observe if the program succeeds?
What results could be measured or counted?

Questions to discover strategies to achieve goals or objectives
Consider the situation now (answers to questions about current conditions) and what we want the situation to be (our goals or objectives).
What specific steps can we take to get from the current to the desired situation?
What factors are helping accomplish [a specific goal or objective]?
What factors are working against accomplishing it?
What can we do to reduce those factors that aren't helping?
List the most feasible as strategies.

CHAPTER 5

Board Development

CRAIG DREESZEN

5

Boards of directors, composed as they are of a changing mix of people with all their hopes and failings, are challenging to analyze and improve. When you think you finally understand your board, new board members join and the complexion alters. Even experienced consultants and trainers are wise to recall the observation of Sandra Hughes of BoardSource: "When you've seen one board, you've seen one board."

Members of boards can be called board members, trustees, steering committee members, or (in public agencies) councillors or commissioners. Boards govern nonprofit organizations and govern or advise public agencies. They may work with professional or all-volunteer staff. The most common type of board in community arts work is the governing board of a professionally staffed nonprofit.

Board members provide leadership, funding, connections, and skills. They represent the interests of their community and exercise accountability. Ideally, a board energizes the organization and serves its constituents. Some boards do not live up to this promise, or worse, get bogged down in tedium or conflict.

Effective organizations usually credit a strong board as a key to their success, while struggling agencies often cite problems with their boards. Arts service agencies report that the most frequent calls for help from arts organizations regard boards and money. The most frequently prescribed cure for both problems may be board development.

A FLEXIBLE APPROACH TO BOARD DEVELOPMENT

A board development text such as this one confronts a basic paradox. Board service is not an innate skill; board members must learn what they are expected to do and how to do it. At the same time, each board is different. Each has evolved from a unique combination of artistic vision, community needs, resources, and leadership personalities. In addition to the variation among boards, each board itself changes. Most tend to evolve over time from an entrepreneurial to a more collaborative approach to leadership. The best advice on board development would be tailored to the current specific circumstances of each board.

Organizations are dynamic. They grow and evolve, responding with both structural and procedural changes to different internal connections, such as new or lost resources, staff changes, new ideas, and plans.

It is impossible to successfully prescribe generic solutions that will work for each board at each stage of its development. This chapter will instead provide a framework to help you examine what works and how your board could be improved. Boards are so individually distinctive that you should think twice before changing something that works just because this book or someone outside the organization advises another way of working.

Most of this chapter is devoted to improving board members' understanding of their role and governing processes. Most readers of this text may be attempting to learn how to work with an existing board of directors, although the principles apply as well to a start-up board. More experienced readers, who are in a position to significantly influence their organizations, will want to attend particularly to the concluding section that questions basic assumptions about organizational structures and refer to the books suggested in the references.

A BOARD'S GOVERNING RESPONSIBILITIES

Most nonprofits have ambiguous expectations of their boards. Often board members confuse their governing role with the many other important functions that board members fulfill as individuals and volunteer staff in their organization. This is particularly true for all-volunteer and understaffed organizations. Board members also bring differing expectations from their corporate, civic, and other nonprofit board experiences.

Three Modes of Governance

Richard Chait, William Ryan, and Barbara Taylor, in *Governance as Leadership*, introduced the idea that a nonprofit board operates in three leadership modes: fiduciary, strategic, and generative.

The fiduciary governance can be watchful and cautious, strategic governance can be open and analytical, and generative governance can be intuitive and creative.

Fiduciary governance. Boards are legally liable to fulfill their fiduciary responsibilities. They must assure fiscal accountability, monitor tangible resources, make sure the law is fulfilled, and watch for problems that would threaten the solvency of the organization. Board committees are organized around functional areas like finance, governance, and personnel.

Strategic governance. In this more visionary role, boards work closely as partners with staff to strategically shape the organization's future by organizing temporary teams around strategic priorities. While many organizations engage in strategic planning, to govern strategically the entire board must be fully engaged and not just authorize and approve a plan.

Generative governance. The concept of generative governance is not as familiar, though some nonprofit boards operate in this creative leadership mode. Boards that govern in a generative leadership mode consider their organization's values and principles, ask fundamental questions about whom is being served and how well, identify and frame problems and opportunities, and seek to discover sense and meaning in the organization's work. According to Chait et al., "As long as governing means what people think it means—setting the goals and direction of an organization and holding management accountable for progress toward those goals—then generative thinking has to be essential to governing. Generative thinking is where goal-setting and direction-setting originate."

Chait et al. also argue that each mode or type of governance is associated with a different mindset. The fiduciary governance can be watchful and cautious, strategic governance can be open and analytical, and generative governance can be intuitive and creative. Each of these has its place, and an effective board must operate in all three modes.

Most board development writers, this one included, have urged clarification of roles that stresses a division between governance and management. Boards govern and staff manage operations. This clarity helps prevent board micromanagement of programs and operations and assures accountability. The governance/management separation of authority works especially well in the fiduciary mode. However, in the strategic or generative types of governance, the roles of the board and staff are less distinct and more partner-like.

If board members and staff often engage in collaborative problem solving and strategic thinking, then strategic and generative governance may not be distinctly different modes of governance. Advice to boards that they should intentionally engage in generative governance is especially useful if boards are accustomed to responding to finished plans and proposals from chief executives.

Fiduciary Responsibilities

Fulfill the Law

The one unavoidable fiduciary expectation of all incorporated nonprofit boards or public commissions is that they assure fulfillment of certain legal requirements. In many cases, staff or individual board officers will actually fulfill the legally required tasks, but the board is legally responsible to see that each is done.

BoardSource (formerly National Center for Nonprofit Boards) describes below the legal expectations of board members.

Duty of care. The duty of care is commonly expressed as the care that an ordinarily prudent person would exercise in a like position and under similar circumstances. This means that a board member owes the duty to exercise reasonable care when he or she makes a decision as a steward of the organization.

Duty of loyalty. The duty of loyalty is a standard of faithfulness: a board member must give undivided allegiance when making decisions affecting the organization. This means that a board member can never use information obtained as a member for personal gain, but must act in the best interests of the organization.

Duty of obedience. The duty of obedience requires board members to act in a way that is consistent with the mission and goals of the organization. A basis for this rule lies in the public's trust that the organization will manage donated funds to fulfill the organization's mission.

Collectively, board members must:

- govern the organization in keeping with the charitable purpose for which the organization was incorporated;
- assure that annual reports are filed with the state;
- assure that federal income tax returns are filed and earnings of contracted workers are reported (consult IRS 990 and 1099 forms to determine current regulations);
- pay payroll and social security taxes for employees; and
- fulfill contracts.

Because of the duty of care, individuals or corporations suffering financial loss or personal injury as a result of alleged negligence may sue board members.

Be Accountable

The board is the central link in an organization's system of accountability. Externally the board is accountable to the government on behalf of the public. The government entrusts the board with public funds in the form of grants and with the privilege of collecting tax-exempt contributions. The board is accountable to funders to fulfill their requirements and to implement grant-funded projects as promised.

The board is also crucial to internal accountability. In an effective organization, board members and professional and volunteer staff are actively accountable to each other to fulfill their responsibilities in keeping with policies, plans, and budgets. Board members govern on behalf of organization or community members who "own" the nonprofit. In a volunteer organization, committee members and volunteers may be accountable to an individual board member—typically a committee chair—who, in turn, is responsible to the full board. In staffed organizations, volunteers and support staff members are responsible to senior staff who, in turn, are responsible to the board.

Ensure the Financial Well-being of the Organization

We entrust boards to be responsible for the short- and long-term fiscal health of the organization. Boards fulfill this responsibility by fundraising, budgeting, and overseeing the group's financial management.

Raise funds. A nearly universal expectation is that board members will give and get money to help support program, operating, and capital expenses. A common recommendation is that all board members make, what is for each, a significant annual personal cash contribution. All should also participate in some way to support efforts to solicit contributions from individuals and businesses. Some board members can make fundraising calls, while others are better able to write letters, but all should participate. See The Art of Fundraising chapter for more information.

Budget. The board must approve budgets. It may be that a finance committee or staff member will actually draft the budget, but the board should be sure that the budget both protects the organization's financial interests and furthers its purpose. Board members should insist that budgets are clearly presented and explained. While budgeting may be seen as a primarily fiduciary responsibility, it is also strategic. Organizational plans and priorities should be clearly expressed in financial terms through annual operating and program budgets. A common mistake is to agree on a priority in planning (e.g., reach more underserved community members with subsidized tickets) and then fail to budget for the costs required to implement that priority.

Oversee financial management. Day-to-day financial transactions are ordinarily the responsibility of the treasurer or staff. The board is responsible to see that financial controls are established and applied. The board sets financial policies to determine how money is accounted for and how expenses are approved. The board should regularly compare revenues and expenses to budget projections. If revenues drop or expenses rise above amounts budgeted, the board takes corrective steps—usually reducing expenses. Some boards have been publicly embarrassed and put legally at risk when they learn of dangerous deficits too late to act. See the Financial Management chapter for more information about budgeting.

Leadership Responsibilities

Govern and Lead

Board members help shape an organization's vision, express that vision in plans, and represent and advocate for the interests of the organization throughout the community. The board, a step removed from the details of the day-to-day operations of committees or staff, can take the longer view: What are the core organizational values? What are the goals? The board is primarily concerned with values and ends—where we are going—and staff and committees are more concerned with means—how we will get there. In a staffed organization, the board is responsible to govern and the staff is responsible to manage. In some organizations, the chief executive is the primary leader. In others, it is the board. In the best case, the board and staff partner in leadership.

In many all-volunteer organizations, however, the board may do everything. The same people who plan programs may also manage every detail of their operation. The challenge of leadership is to rise above the details to see the larger picture, to reserve time from managing to also govern. Otherwise everyone may end up rowing with no one steering. The board's central role in planning is further explained in the Strategic Planning chapter.

Represent the Community

A board that reflects the diversity of its community can govern the organization to serve that community's variety of interests. A board also keeps its organization in touch with its community and constituencies—artists, funders, audiences, and community partners.

If the organization needs to work closely with the public school system, it is helpful to have an educator on the board. If funds are to be raised from corporations, the board should have access to corporate leaders. Be wary, though, of recruiting community members to the board to represent a constituency if they are not also passionate about the organization's mission and do not bring leadership skills. An organization seldom can recruit board members to represent every constituency served. Some boards seek two members of an underrepresented constituency, such as youth, so that an individual will not feel isolated. Seek out formal and informal advisors, plan inclusively with the community, and get board and staff out into the community to hear concerns.

ARE EXPECTATIONS OF BOARDS REASONABLE?

Board members are volunteers who are expected to lead, govern, raise funds, oversee finances, and assure internal and external accountability. It is a common complaint that boards do not fulfill their roles. Before taking steps to improve the board, it seems appropriate to ask how reasonable those expectations are.

The central board function of fundraising is a tough responsibility. Arts organizations are attempting to sustain levels of programming and service that have been growing, sometimes over decades. There is an increasing gap developing nationwide between the quantity and quality of arts programs and services offered and the human and financial resources that a community can provide to sustain them.

George Thorn, of Action Research, argues that "…most organizations [are] attempting to function at about 30 to 50 percent above the floor of realistically available and achievable human and financial resources." Increasingly, the board is being called upon to fill the gap by raising even more contributed funds to replace lost or reduced public grants.

In tight economic periods, arts organizations cut back staff due to decreased funding. Many of these seek to sustain programming levels by asking board members to manage programs previously run by staff. Such a strategy risks board members becoming so consumed with their volunteer staff roles that they neglect their governing responsibilities or quit in fatigue.

Sometimes it is reasonable to expect increased fundraising and volunteer work from the board. A more successful remedy may involve a combination of reduced programs and expenses along with additional help recruited for specific operational tasks. The Strategic Planning chapter will help you organize a process to determine priorities and make tough choices.

TWO STRATEGIES FOR BOARD DEVELOPMENT

Two fundamental strategies for improving a board if it is not effectively fulfilling reasonable expectations are to improve the board's understanding of governing and its own governing processes, or to revise the organizational structure.

The first strategy focuses on how a board understands its role, who occupies leadership positions, how board members relate to one another, and how they do their work. Examples of procedural change would be to develop a new statement of governing responsibilities or design a new system for identifying and recruiting board members.

The second strategy involves restructuring the board itself. Examples of structural changes range from a simple reduction of the number of board members or elimination of standing committees to a more comprehensive overhaul of structure as outlined at the end of this chapter.

Structural changes have the most potential for impact. Dramatic structural change can sometimes be just the jolt needed to bring the organization into alignment with its contemporary environment. In other cases, too many changes at once can so disrupt and discomfort board and staff members that they fail to provide the arts programming and services for which they were organized.

Strategy 1: Improve Governance Understanding and Processes

Two approaches to improve board processes are to improve the effectiveness of current board members and their interaction with staff and volunteers, and to recruit additional people.

The First Approach: Improve Effectiveness of the Current Team

A common error is to recruit additional board members into a poorly functioning organization without also improving the way they work together. If board members don't understand what is expected of them or if they don't get the information they need to do their jobs, recruiting more people may only worsen the situation. In other cases, the existing team may have neither the skills nor the inclination to make the required changes, and the fresh perspectives of new board or staff members may be required.

Another common board development error is to assume that the only way to recruit people with the requisite expertise is to elect them to the board or to hire them. It may be more effective to invite people to undertake specific tasks as committee members, task force team members, or volunteer consultants. A growing trend is to engage people with special skills to handle specific short-term tasks in ad hoc task forces rather than recruit people to the board or create standing committees.

Clarify board responsibilities. Perhaps the most contentious issue in board development is ambiguity of responsibilities for governance and management between the board and staff. Making two lists—one for the board (governance) and one for staff (management)—is helpful to focus board energies on policy and other governing tasks that only a board may do. Such clear descriptions also help prevent individual board members from meddling in day-to-day operations or second guessing staff operational decisions. However, the need for vision, leadership, insightful questions, and creative solutions transcends board and staff roles.

One risk—especially for a small, understaffed, or all-volunteer organization—is that the board attends too much to management of programs and operations and too little to governance. One simple technique is to schedule regular governing or planning meetings when the agenda includes only strategic questions and policy issues: What are the pressing community needs? Whom do we serve and whom have we left out? How well are our services fulfilling our intentions? What external threats and opportunities should we address? These sessions could be cast as an annual planning retreat, quarterly taking-stock meeting, or an hour at the start of every other board meeting. A board might reinforce that they are in a governing mode by a change of meeting location. The metaphor is often applied that the board must change hats, sometimes wearing a policy maker hat and sometimes a volunteer staff hat.

Balance policy and operations. A separation of the responsibilities of governance and management serves as the fiduciary function of check and balance. This distinction is not absolute since staff may exercise considerable leadership and the board may do many management tasks as volunteers. An insistently strict division of duties may

Summary: Governance and Management Responsibilities

Governance (Board)	Management (Staff and Volunteers)
Manage policy and planning	Advise on policy and planning
Advise on operations	Manage operations
Concerned with ends	Concerned with means
Account to the public, law, and bylaws	Account to the board
Plan mission, goals, objectives	Plan objectives, tasks, annual work plans
Hire and supervise chief executive	Hire and supervise staff and volunteers
Assure fiscal stability (raise funds, oversee budgeting, and monitor financial performance)	Manage finances (handle accounting and reports, write grants, and support board fundraising)

reduce the cooperative benefits of board and staff working together, each contributing his or her expertise in support of the central artistic vision.

An experienced staff will not only implement board policies, but will also advise and partner with the board as it sets policy. Board members, in return, will help staff with operations, usually continuing to serve as occasional volunteer staff. When board members don their volunteer staff hats, they are no longer governing; they are assisting staff in operations. The distinction is that a governing board, as a collective body, supervises the senior staff; the gallery director supervises an individual board member helping paint a gallery. Most confusion about roles and responsibilities arises from a lack of clarity about who is helping or advising and who is ultimately responsible for a task.

Note that some writers, including John Carver, do not agree that flexible roles make sense. This author is persuaded by Chait et al. that strategic and generative leadership require shared responsibilities among board and staff that defy entirely clear separation of powers.

Each board's responsibilities are a function of its history and circumstances, as well as the skills and personalities of its members. Therefore, each organization needs to discuss and determine for itself what is expected of its board.

How to Help Board Members Understand Their Roles

In order for board members to operate effectively within an organization, they must clearly understand their roles and responsibilities. These responsibilities should be shared with prospective board members as part of the recruitment process, orientation, and distributed to all board members in the board manual.

There are also other ways in which boards can deepen understanding of their roles and responsibilities.

Arts conferences and board development workshops are excellent ways to cultivate skills in board members with leadership potential, as well as expose board members to other arts leaders.

Readings on boards and board development, including the books and websites listed in the references, should be recommended to the board.

Board development or governance committee (or perhaps a single board member) organizes board responsibility discussions and oversees the identification, cultivation, recruitment, and orientation of new board members.

Participation in an exercise can help boards clarify their roles and then discuss their responsibilities. Their decisions should be documented in writing. (See Figure 1.)

Board responsibilities change as the organization evolves and as external circumstances change. Reconsider board responsibilities annually.

Whenever a serious problem arises related to ambiguity of responsibilities (missed opportunity or someone's sense of authority overstepped), approach the problem as an opportunity to address the larger issue of distribution of responsibilities rather than assigning blame.

Figure 1: Two Exercises to Clarify Board Responsibilities

Adapted by permission. Chait, R. P., Ryan, W. P., & Taylor, B. E. (2005). *Governance as Leadership.* BoardSource and Wiley.

1. Board's critical role. Imagine the board is meeting five years in the future and celebrating achievement of a critical objective: [insert a priority objective from your plan.] With that success in mind, complete the following sentence: This result would not have been achieved if the board had not…

2. Small group discussion. Present the following questions to the board in order to sort tasks into those that only the board may fulfill (governing) and those that are anyone can fulfill (managing). Convene small discussion groups of three to five people to determine their responses. Then ask each group to present their recommendations for governing, managing, and volunteer tasks. Use uncertainty or disagreements as opportunities to clarify the essential roles of the board. It is much better to debate a list of duties now than fight over authority later. Seek consensus with a summarized list of the board's governing responsibilities. The list of activities that board members may do in their capacity as volunteer staff may be important, but competent volunteers may do them. The board development committee should then draft a statement of board governing responsibilities for the full board to consider, amend, and adopt as policy.

What are the essential governing responsibilities of our board of directors?

What are the responsibilities of an individual board member to contribute to good governance?

What expert help, advice, or volunteer work would it be helpful for board members to do that helps but is not part of official governing responsibilities?

What should board members avoid doing?

If you have an executive committee, what board responsibilities are delegated to the executive committee?

Avoid the dilemma of the president and chief executive competing for leadership authority. In most cases, the president looks outward toward the community, cultivating partners and support. The executive looks inward to oversee programs and operations. They will advise each other, but the wise president will defer to the professional staff's judgment on organizational operations. If the executive is taking the organization off course, this is cause for collective board intervention. Remember, though, that the board supervises the executive as a body. This supervisory authority may be delegated to an executive or personnel committee. An individual board member, even the president, cannot pull rank on staff.

For more on creating a constructive partnership between the board and chief executive, go the AES Online Companion for this chapter (see the last page of the book for the Internet address) and see Constructive Partnership: Board and Chief Executive, excerpted from *The Source: Twelve Principles of Governance that Power Exceptional Boards.*

A useful rule of thumb is that the board speaks as a body or not at all.

Roles in transition. A board that works well with an experienced president or chief executive must adjust when either resigns. A board used to trusting the leadership of a seasoned executive will find itself much more actively involved in leadership during a transition to a new executive. In small organizations, the transition following the departure of a professional chief executive may require the board to temporarily take a more hands-on management style. As the new staff executive matures on the job, the board increasingly lets go of operations until they are back to managing policy. A board may use a leadership transition to take stock and confirm the organization's mission and priorities or make a significant shift. William Bridges' book, *Managing Transitions: Making the Most of Change*, is a good resource for navigating significant organizational change.

Policy Development is a Primary Board Responsibility

Policy development is an essential responsibility of boards and reflects what is important to the organization as a whole. Policies are written statements approved by the governing board that are used to guide individual and group action toward organizational goals and objectives. A test of the need for a policy and of how well it is written is: Will the policy help staff make subsequent decisions related to this issue?

Policies allow for leadership continuity despite turnover. By setting policies to guide staff or volunteer action, the board is relieved from making day-to-day operational decisions. By setting limits, policies permit freedom of action within those limits. They simplify decision-making and provide for more consistent decisions. The protection that policies provide to staff from political and personal pressures is very important.

> Mayor: Why didn't my niece get accepted into your exhibition?
>
> Gallery Director: According to our exhibition policy, a jury of peers makes the selections. I am sorry, but the matter is out of my hands.

Policy Governance®, a prescriptive board system adopted by some state arts agencies and larger cultural institutions, is a proprietary theory of board governance developed by John Carver. Organizations adopting this model operate within explicitly defined roles for the board and chief executive. When done well, this system leaves little room for ambiguity. It best suits larger organizations with a professional chief executive and adequate additional staff so that the board can focus entirely on governing through policy. This system is less useful for working boards, where board members also serve as volunteer staff, and is inappropriate for advisory boards. The Carver system stresses the board's fiduciary role to assure accountability and may limit its potential to engage in generative leadership.

Policies of Interest to Arts Organizations

Board operating policies encompass how board members should function in relation to each other and to paid staff and volunteers.

> Board members are expected to attend all regularly scheduled meetings (four to six per year) and to serve on at least one committee.
>
> Board decisions will be made by consensus and confirmed by formal vote.

Management policies concern planning and overall operation of the organization, as well as establishing accountability, responsibilities, budgets, and fiscal procedures.

> The operating budget for the upcoming fiscal year shall be approved by the board at least one month prior to the end of the current fiscal year.
>
> Year-end statements will be reviewed by an independent auditor.

Personnel policies relate to recruitment, affirmative action, selection, placement, training and development, discipline, compensation, grievances, termination, and fringe benefits. (See the Personnel Management chapter for more information.)

Staff members are entitled to a formal performance appraisal each year.

Professional policies deal with professional actions of staff members in relation to performance of their organizational duties, confidentiality, and ethical standards.

It is the duty of board and staff members to act in the best interests of the gallery. Part of that duty is to exercise confidentiality on matters conveyed to the board.

Artistic and program policies pertain to an organization's programs and type and scope of artistic activity.

The gallery is committed to representing the fine artists and craftspeople emerging from the four-county region whose work meet the artistic standards of the director.

In all programs, the arts agency has a policy affirming and supporting artistic freedom of expression.

Artistic policy in arts-producing organizations is a special case. A dance company, theater, or music ensemble is frequently founded by an individual artist. The organization provides the support that allows the choreographer, director, or musician to produce his or her work. A board is recruited to help institutionalize and sustain the organization, support the artistic vision, and fulfill the law. Such a board would not ordinarily develop an artistic policy on its own.

The board which attempts to set artistic policy may find itself in conflict with the founding artist or current artistic director. Some argue that arts programs should be solely the responsibility of the artistic director. The board of a producing organization would affect artistic policy only through the selection of an artistic director. Arts programs would also be subject to the board's financial controls. A community arts board, however, often has dual obligations to its art and community. The board may need to collaborate with its artistic personnel to balance artistic and community development goals.

Build a Sense of Team

Even an understanding of responsibilities does not assure that individual board members will work together as a team. Members of any small working group such as a board require time to get to know each other, build trust, clarify roles, accept leadership, work out conflicting interests, and learn how to make decisions.

A group needs to have some history together before it becomes effective. One classic description of group process—found in J. S. Heinen and E. Jacobson's *A Model of Task Group Development*—predicts that a new group will spend time to form, then storm (encountering and resolving conflicts), then norm (working out effective procedures), before they can effectively *perform* as a group. Recognizing this process helps keep perspective when a group struggles at first.

Working groups, such as boards of directors, have two parallel group dynamics: accomplishing organizational tasks and meeting the needs of the members themselves. To accomplish tasks, board members identify problems, determine agendas, consider alternatives, and make decisions. A skillful chair or meeting facilitator can help the group advance through its tasks. At the same time, a social and emotional dynamic is being played out. Who is that new person? Should I volunteer? Who does he think he

Kathleen Fletcher, in *The Policy Sampler: A Resource for Nonprofit Boards,* describes a variety of policies.

Anti-discrimination

Capital expenditures

Check signing and cash disbursement

Confidentiality

Conflict of interest

Expense reimbursement

Grievance

Indemnification

Investments

Nepotism

Sexual harassment

is, taking charge like that? These dynamics are as much a part of the board meeting as the tasks, yet they sometimes go unacknowledged.

If a board meets infrequently or only to conduct business, team building will proceed slowly. Create opportunities for less formal gatherings. If board members laugh together, sometimes they can later debate the tough issues and still like and respect each other. Board members who care about each other work better together.

Consider team building activities.

Plan pre- or post-meeting gatherings with cocktails or a potluck supper so people can get better acquainted.

Hold a reception before or after an arts event. This helps people get acquainted and connects them with the programs of the organization.

Conduct a board retreat. A facilitated retreat can address issues of board responsibilities apart from or within the context of strategic planning, with the added benefit that board members get to know each other. Program the retreat loosely enough to encourage important informal conversations. See the Strategic Planning chapter for information on retreats.

Ask board members to write one-paragraph biographical sketches. Provide these sketches—along with a list of board members, their addresses and phone numbers, and the names of spouses or partners—to the entire board.

Periodically "check in" with people to see what is happening in their lives as a preliminary to conducting business.

Identify one or more board members who concern themselves with the human, emotional side of board development. Ask them to call a board member who missed several meetings to see what is going on, or speak with the person who doesn't participate in board discussions.

Celebrate successes. People want to be a part of a winning team, and they need to be reminded when the organization is doing good work.

Manage Meetings

Meetings are occasions when both group task and social needs of the board are accomplished. Most people have plenty of experience with agonizing meetings that waste people's time and fail to accomplish important work. Since meetings are so central to the board's work, learning how to make meetings productive and rewarding is important.

Respect board members' time. Arrange meetings that thoughtfully consider busy volunteer schedules. Meetings lasting more than two hours suggest that committees or staff should do more work between board meetings. A national trend suggests that boards are meeting less frequently than once was the case. BoardSource reports that on average, nonprofit boards meet six to nine times a year. They should also meet annually in a retreat.

Conduct some business electronically. Boards are increasingly doing business electronically. Be sure that your bylaws accommodate virtual meetings. Agendas, minutes, and reports are often distributed by email, and actions requiring quick response are handled through email exchanges. National organizations sometimes conduct entire board meetings with conference calls, videoconferences, or email exchanges. Organizational websites sometimes have password-protected areas where board members can post communications and drafts of policies and plans. Do take care that no one is disenfranchised by lack of Internet access. Consider also the limitations of electronic communications and avoid working through conflicts or distributing sensitive information by email. Virtual meetings work best when good personal relations are built and maintained through face-to-face contact.

Select a skilled meeting leader. Any gathering of more than three people can benefit from a facilitator. Usually the president facilitates the meeting. If the president's skills don't include meeting management, consider appointing a meeting facilitator or rotating the task. The facilitator manages the agenda and time; guides discussions, reining in a long-winded speaker or drawing out a reticent one; clarifies issues; tests for consensus; and recognizes decisions.

In some groups, the president controls access to discussions by recognizing people who want to speak. In others, the president only intervenes when someone can't get a word into a lively debate.

Work with an agenda. Board members appreciate receiving an agenda in advance of the meeting. In many organizations the president or executive committee along with the chief executive develop the agenda in advance of the board meeting. The first item should be a confirmation of the agenda. Consider important items brought forward by board members that aren't yet on the agenda. Schedule important issues early. As the meeting proceeds, watch the time. If a discussion is taking longer than anticipated, consider the impact on the rest of your business.

Figure 2: Agenda Outline

Agenda Item	Presenter	Time Required	Tab in Binder	Outcome Wanted (Discuss or vote)	Action Taken

There are different types of agendas.

Traditional. This type of meeting is used to approve minutes, give reports, revisit old business, conduct new business, etc. This is what people are used to. Unfortunately, it forces the board to look backwards to what has been. New thinking is relegated to the end of the meeting and may be cut short if the rest goes over time.

Operating. Operating meetings are organized around major operations, i.e., finance, programs, or marketing. The meeting time is organized according to the areas of major work. This promotes better use of time than the traditional agenda, but does risk that the board oversees management, instead of governing.

Planning. The meeting is organized to discuss progress on each of the organization's goals. This is a fine way to assure that the plan is lived, not filed away. This approach is ordinarily blended with one of the other models to accommodate business unforeseen in the plan.

Functional. This agenda starts with action items, then moves to matters that require discussion, and concludes with routine reports. This approach puts the important matters first.

Tabular. A graphic presentation can be used for any of the agenda styles. (Figure 2 is an example.) In this format, the agenda itself can be used to note actions taken in the meeting minutes.

Timed. A prediction of how much time should be allowed for each agenda item can be incorporated into any agenda style.

Consent. Consent agendas have long been used in government to streamline board meetings, yet the idea is relatively new to nonprofits.

As described by Alice Sturgis in *The Standard Code of Parliamentary Procedure*, organizations having a large number of routine matters to approve often save time by use of a consent agenda, also called a *consent calendar* or *unanimous consent agenda*. This is a portion of the printed agenda listing matters that are expected to be noncontroversial and on which there are likely to be no questions.

Before taking the vote, the president allows time for the members to read the list to determine if it includes any matters on which they may have a question, or which they would like to discuss or oppose. Any member has a right to remove any item from the consent agenda, in which case it is transferred to the regular agenda so that it may be considered and voted on separately. The remaining items are then unanimously approved en bloc without discussion, saving the time that would be required for individual votes.

By dealing with lots of information, reports, and routine action matters at once, the board can reserve time to discuss policy. Board members must take care, though, that they read the proposals on the consent agenda carefully so that they fulfill their governing responsibilities.

Provide information in advance. Board members need to have information prior to meetings so as to make decisions in a timely and concise manner. They will likely not read voluminous reports. Sarah Hughes of BoardSource recommends providing vital information in a one-page "dashboard report" that just shows critical facts. See Figure 3: Arts Agency "Dashboard" Report.

Agree on how to make decisions. Parliamentary procedures, such as described in *Robert's Rules of Order*, are only one way to run a meeting. In large groups, such as an annual meeting of members, parliamentary procedure is a useful technique. It is also useful for crucial policy and financial decisions.

Figure 3: Arts Agency "Dashboard" Report
(Quick assessment of critical indicators)

Examples of Indicators *(Adapt to suit your specific needs.)*	**April 2007**	**April 2006**	**April 2005**
New members			
Total members			
Number of grants written			
Grants receivable			
Grants received			
Earned revenues			
Administrative expenses			
Program expenses			
Other financial details			
Endowment balance			
Bank balance			
Audience numbers			
Other measures of interest			

Most board decisions, however, are more creative and effectively managed by consensus. A formal, parliamentary motion for a specific action tends to fix the group on one alternative too early in a discussion. A bad idea gets proposed as a motion, amendments are offered and debated, and the only way to proceed to a good solution may be for the motion-maker to withdraw the motion or for the group to defeat it (and the person) by a vote. Consensus is a less formal process that is closer to the way people actually work together. A problem is clarified, alternatives are proposed in a brainstorming-like fashion, and alternative solutions are discussed until the best options become clear. The president or another board member tests for consensus by such suggestions as: I hear a lot of support for inviting key constituents to our fall board retreat. Have we reached a decision? If people agree, the matter is decided. If not, there is need for more discussion.

Recognize when the group has made a decision. At the conclusion of a discussion, the president should acknowledge that a decision has been reached. Restate the decision. If the business item has financial or legal implications, or if people are more comfortable with formal rules of order, confirm the consensus decision with a motion and a vote. At the conclusion of a meeting, review decisions that have been reached.

Document decisions. Decisions should be recorded in writing and promptly distributed as minutes. Meeting minutes can be genuinely useful if they record decisions rather than whole discussions. Minutes should not include a summary of the discussion, only decisions made and actions required. The trend is toward shorter minutes. They usually need not be more than one page in length. Decisions that require action should acknowledge who does what by when and, if necessary, at what cost. If no one can be identified to take action, acknowledge that the group has not made a decision to act.

Monitor and follow through on agreed actions. A useful assumption is that even the best-intentioned board member needs encouragement or a reminder to complete board assignments. The minutes highlighting decisions and actions become a tool to provide that encouragement and to monitor implementation.

Monitoring Tips

When preparing to send out minutes, for each person with a task pull their copy and highlight the portion of the minutes that summarizes the agreed-upon action.

Recruit a board member to monitor the fulfillment of important board or committee tasks. This is a good assignment for a vice president. The monitor should make timely calls to inquire on the status on tasks in process. This is a huge improvement over the belated, What, you missed the deadline?

Dispense with the routine reading of the minutes at the next meeting. Instead, determine the status of all of the action items.

Produce a timeline. A graphic summary of important tasks and key dates is a useful task-monitoring tool. The timeline is consulted by staff and committee chairs and brought out at board meetings for a quick visual overview of work before the board. Seeing all projects and key tasks on one chart also helps to pinpoint bottlenecks and people being overburdened with work.

Learn to manage conflicts. While it is beyond the scope of this chapter to teach conflict management, the issue must be addressed. Conflicts are virtually inevitable and are sometimes useful. Conflicts tend to be about policy, programs, or personalities.

Conflicts can identify important differences that need to be aired and resolved. A fundamental misgiving about the mission can manifest itself as a conflict over a detail. Rather than smoothing over the disagreement, leaders should use this opportunity to have a substantive discussion about the organization's purpose and its policies, programs, or procedures. Conflicts that are personality clashes also need attention.

In any conflict, two factors need balancing. One is a concern for the relationships of the people involved, and the other is a concern for the task or the principle at stake. If the cause of the disagreement (the color of the membership brochure) is relatively less significant than the relationships, one party concedes or both agree to disagree. If the principle is vital (the policies and measures for genuine inclusion of people of color), it may be worth risking the angry resignation of a board member in a win/lose solution.

Sometimes the best solution is to ignore the minor conflict. More often the best course is to develop a win/win solution that meets the interests of all parties. It is important to look beyond the specific positions taken by people to the interests they all have in common. Look for a solution that satisfies the common interests rather than pitting one position against the other. (For further discussion, see *Getting to Yes Without Giving In* by R. Fisher and W. Ury.)

The Role of the President

The leadership provided by an effective president is a key ingredient of a successful organization. In all-volunteer organizations, the president may act like a chief executive. In a staffed organization, the president complements the chief executive.

The president provides a focal point for the various branches of an organization—a lever to bring the organization into balance, and a catalyst for action. The president should have an overview of the organization's purpose and management process, and may be the public spokesperson. He or she is the one person, in addition to the chief executive, who is concerned with the organization as a whole and with its process of fulfilling its mission. To maintain an overview and to manage in the relatively little time available as a volunteer leader, the president must work by motivating others to act. To be effective, he or she must avoid getting bogged down with tasks that should be the responsibility of staff or volunteer workers.

The duties of the president, as prescribed in the bylaws, might include:

- manage the board of directors;
- oversee recruitment and orientation of board members (with governance committee);
- call for and conduct board meetings;
- prepare board agendas (with executive staff and/or chief executive);
- appoint ad hoc committees and committee chairs;
- represent the organization to the public; and
- serve as the liaison between board and staff.

Equally important are the key leadership, visionary, people-managing roles of the president:

- provide leadership to help the group identify its mission and goals;
- monitor the overall process of organizational governance and policy fulfillment;
- identify and recruit board members who can contribute to the organization's success;
- inspire and motivate board members, staff, and volunteers to willingly fulfill organizational goals;
- manage conflicts;
- represent the organization to the public; and
- look out for future threats and opportunities.

The Second Approach: Improve Boards by Recruiting New Members

The Recruitment Process

The first step in board development has been to ensure that the existing team understands its role and the way it works together on behalf of the organization. However, community arts organizations often do not have enough depth of leadership on the board or staff. When that is the case, the organization may need to recruit new members.

Any strategy to improve the governing process will eventually involve the identification and recruitment of new board members. Without conscientious attention to the recruitment process, however, boards tend to perpetuate themselves by recruiting people just like the ones who now serve. This leaves the same gaps in skills, representation, contacts, and resources. A better approach is to identify the organization's governing needs and find people who help meet those needs.

Create a board development or governance committee. Replace the short-term nominating committee with a year-round leadership development committee, which would oversee the profiling, recruitment, and orientation processes. This group could include a board member (someone in line to be president would be a good choice), a staff member, and someone with an outside perspective. In some organizations, the governance committee organizes board training, talks with nonperforming board members, and helps manage conflicts.

Profile governance needs. Produce a written profile of the skills, contacts, resources, and representation needs of the board. (For the Board Profile Grid, see the AES Online Companion for this chapter. Go to the last page of the book for the Internet address.) Next, compare the existing board to this profile and summarize characteristics missing from the current board profile (or attributes that will be lost when member terms expire). Report to the board. Needs not met now become the priorities for recruitment. Keep in mind, though, that some needs can be fulfilled by recruiting people to serve as advisers, on committees or temporary task forces, or in other capacities. Only a few identified candidates would ordinarily be approached to join the governing board of directors.

Chait et al. remind us to seek board members who can lead and not to aim for a "Swiss army knife" board with every conceivable skill represented. Look for people who bring multiple attributes. It is dangerous to an artistic mission to recruit people who bring only financial expertise without some artistic sensibility. It is patronizing to invite a person of color who does not also bring needed skills or provide access to resources.

Identify stakeholders. It is wise not to limit recruitment to people immediately known to board members. List community types who ought to have a stake in the organization's success. Few people will make the commitment required of a board member unless they perceive they have a stake in your success. People who do not care about your mission should not be entrusted with board membership. This stakeholder analysis can serve fundraising, membership development, and marketing functions as well.

Name potential candidates. With recruitment priorities in mind, look at the list of stakeholders and think of individuals who provide the priority attributes and who may see themselves as having a stake in your organization. People who fit into more than one category of stakeholder are more likely to appreciate the benefit of volunteer service.

If specific, qualified stakeholders cannot be identified, the recruitment committee should seek advice from people who know your arts organization and people who represent prospective stakeholder groups. The complete list of prospects should be reviewed and prioritized by board and staff members.

Sample Stakeholder Analysis

This stakeholder analysis was done by a New England children's theater.

The theater operated in a barely adequate church basement. The board was wholly composed of theater professionals and parents who did not have access to potential contributors. Among the identified stakeholders were parents and a local publisher of a children's magazine. Looking at the clusters, a board member realized the obvious: a senior executive of the publisher had a child who participated in the theater. This individual provided the link to the corporate community. The board development retreat concluded with the president's decision to invite the executive to lunch. That lunch concluded with an agreement by the executive to invite a group of the executive's friends to another lunch. That lunch concluded with an agreement to form an advisory board to the theater which would plan corporate fundraising. Within two years several corporate leaders joined the theater board and the advisory board was disbanded. The contacts provided by these new board members eventually helped yield contributions sufficient to buy and refurbish a performance facility.

Decide on individuals and invite them. Make a short list of the most qualified candidates. As in fundraising, board recruitment is best conducted by someone known and respected by the candidate. If no board or staff member knows the candidate well, determine who would be the most persuasive. Inform and invite candidates.

Assemble a fact pack that helps a candidate to decide whether or not to accept your invitation. Such a kit might include a mission statement and plan, program descriptions, current year's budget and past year's financial statements, board and staff list, a statement of board responsibilities, and a schedule of board meetings.

Make a call to the candidate. Most people are flattered to be asked. If you have done your homework, this will lead to more conversation. The best way to do this is face-to-face; second best is an extended telephone conversation.

Meet to discuss the organization, why the candidate is being asked to help, and the benefits and responsibilities of board membership. This discussion is similar to a fundraising call, where you are trying to persuade the prospect of the value of your work, and to a job interview, where both parties can assess whether this is a mutually beneficial commitment. Determine the candidate's interests and how they may be served through your organization. This is an important step in later assigning the board member responsibilities. If you want something specific from the candidate, this is the time to ask.

> One arts center, seeking someone to fundraise, recruited a woman who had just raised $5 million for the hospital. At her first board meeting she exclaimed to her dismayed colleagues how happy she was to be working with the arts and how tired of fundraising she had become.

Invite the candidate to join the board. If there is initial interest and the match between the candidate and the organization seems good, extend the invitation. Your bylaws may specify that the invitation must be in the form of a nomination to be confirmed by a vote of the board or members. It may be that the candidate will need to think about your offer and consult family members or an employer before responding. In that case, leave the fact pack and call back at a specific date.

Elect or appoint new board members. Each organization's bylaws will specify how to formally approve new board members.

Board Orientation

New board members do not become productive team members without some deliberate orientation and team building.

Board manual. The materials identified earlier as a board member recruitment fact pack form the core of a board manual. Create a digital version or assemble the materials in a three-ring binder with index tabs so that changes can be easily incorporated.

Sample Contents

Mission statement and strategic plan

Brief history of the organization

Program descriptions

Current year's budget and past year's financial statements

Bylaws

Major policies

Standing operating procedures

Statement of board responsibilities

Board member list

Staff and committee chairs list

Biographical sketches of board members

List of major funders

Calendar of upcoming events, including a schedule of board meetings.

Orientation meeting. The president and chief executive or the governance committee should meet with new board members to orient them to their responsibilities, the organization's ways of working, and to current projects or issues being considered. This can be a separate meeting or can precede the first regularly scheduled board meeting.

Social gathering. A luncheon, dinner, or reception in honor of the new board members is a courteous gesture that may accelerate team building. Make sure to introduce the newcomers and to provide opportunities for people to meet each other.

Board development and planning retreat. An annual planning retreat can serve both to advance the organization's planning and to build a team. Such an event takes time, energy, and perhaps money to do well, but can yield significant results. See the Strategic Planning chapter for more information on retreats.

Buddy system. Some groups find it helpful to assign a more senior board member to be a buddy to the new board member. Such a partner provides a direct and personal source of information, encouragement, and support in the first months of board service.

Specific assignments. People respond better to a request to "organize a team to raise $2,000 from downtown business" than to "do what you can to raise money." Assign one or more specific responsibilities.

Ongoing board development. Attention to board development does not end with the recruitment and orientation of new board members. This is one of the reasons many organizations have board development or governance committees instead of nominating committees. Someone should be charged with ongoing attention to how the board is functioning as a team. Personal attention to the human needs of board members goes a long way.

Keep Good Board Members

Board members most commonly resign because they misunderstand what is expected of them or never feel themselves to be an important part of the team. In some boards, board members feel uninvolved since the president or executive committee makes most important decisions.

Often, too, key board members care a lot, work hard, and burn out. As one weary board president bluntly put it, "Our arts council recruits good people and sucks them dry." Burned-out board members and volunteers may only find relief by dropping out completely.

Learn to delegate. Boards that spend too much time on programming and administration, and too little on policy and planning, may need to delegate detailed operational decisions and tasks. Set aside meetings or portions of meetings for policy discussions. Indicate that the board is serving in its governing role by changing seats and meeting locations. In addition, if you delegate and involve more people periodically for shorter assignments over a longer period of time you can spread the workload and help prevent burnout. A good friend of the organization could serve on a cultural planning task force one year, coordinate a fundraiser the next, take a year off, join the board for two years, and then retire to be an occasional advisor.

Here are additional measures to retain good board members.

Help them meet their needs. Try to understand why they are motivated to volunteer and match them to opportunities to fulfill those needs.

Share successes. People like to win. Bring to the board any positive news or feedback.

Involve board members actively in decision-making. If you persist in bringing predetermined issues to the board, you'll lose board members. Executive committees should be cautious of assuming too much authority and undermining the participation of other board members.

Help them develop. Invite board members to professional conferences, management development workshops, and networking meetings.

Recognize them. Acknowledge the interests and the work of board members at public functions or in your publications.

Thank your board members. Never take them for granted.

Involve people in many different ways. Any organization needs multiple options to engage people in their work. Recruiting individuals to the board is only one way to attract expertise. Consider these options:

- a pool of volunteers under the direction of a volunteer coordinator (see the Volunteers in the Arts chapter);
- short-term, task-specific volunteers referred by such agencies as Business Volunteers for the Arts, Society of Retired Executives, or other local service organizations;
- ad hoc committees, project teams, or short-term task forces organized for a specific task and then disbanded;
- consultants or volunteers working in a consultant-like role to accomplish specific tasks (funds for paid consultants are often available from state and local arts agencies or foundations); and
- peer advisers (local arts leaders trained to do short-term consulting and referred by a number of state arts agencies and statewide assemblies of local arts agencies)

Strategy 2: Change the Governing Structure

The preceding section explored strategies to improve governing and managing processes. However, it may be that procedural changes alone don't make enough difference to create an effective governing system. Structural changes may be required. Think of how an organizational chart would show all players (board, committees, staff), their responsibilities, and how they relate to each other.

Structure should relate to the organization's mission. A major change in goals or program plans may suggest a corresponding structural reorganization. For example, some organizations facing financial crisis have responded by abolishing their fundraising committee. Fundraising was too important to delegate to a committee, so it became everyone's priority.

Structural changes can be minor or dramatic. Simple structural changes could be the creation or elimination of some standing committees, the creation of new officer positions, or a change in the number of board positions. More significant changes could be reducing the frequency of board meetings, eliminating the executive committee, or appointing the chief executive to the board as a voting member. A radical change might be reducing the board to the legally required number of members, who become charged solely with assuring the organization's fulfillment of legal requirements.

Rethink Old Assumptions

Before considering specific structural changes, it may be helpful to question commonly held assumptions about nonprofit boards. Beyond what is required by law, there is nothing carved in stone about the way boards, committees, and staff are organized.

Consider some common assumptions and some alternative thinking.

Assumption—An organization should be steeply hierarchical, with information flowing up to a few leaders (board) and decisions flowing down to the staff.

Alternative—People in an organization can relate to one another as peers. Information is communicated throughout the organization at all levels. Decisions are, as much as possible, entrusted to the people who are closest to the action. While important policy decisions may be reserved for a governing board, everyone should have an opportunity to contribute to important decisions.

Assumption—An organization needs standing committees and every board member should be assigned to one.

Alternative—Create only those committees that are essential and convene meetings only when necessary. Eliminate conflicts or redundant efforts by removing committees that mirror staff functions. BoardSource promotes the idea of a "zero-based committee structure." Like the parallel concept for budgeting, each committee should be justified each year or discontinued.

Consider flexible committee structures. A committee can be a single board member who invites some friends to work on a fundraising event or who develops a proposal for a communications policy. A committee meeting can be a conference call or email exchange. A volunteer working in the role of a consultant can fulfill a governing task, such as designing a membership campaign. A temporary task force can be convened just for the life of a project. Ad hoc committees and task forces are becoming more common than standing committees. As a general rule, resist the temptation to set up a standing committee.

Assumption—More board members means more contributions.

Alternative—Recruiting someone to the board may help assure her financial contribution, but it commits the board member and the organization to each other with all the trappings of other board responsibilities. Consider instead cultivating a large number of contributors who have a stake in your organization's success and who commit themselves to giving.

Assumption—"But the bylaws say we can't."

Alternative—Bylaws have a clause that allows them to be amended. Use it.

EXAMPLES OF ORGANIZATIONAL STRUCTURES

These models of alternative organizational structures may stimulate your own thinking. A successful structure should evolve from an organization's unique history and community environment.

All-volunteer nonprofit organizations. The all-volunteer nonprofit can be structured in various ways. One variation is the board plus executive committee. The executive committee typically meets more frequently than the board and acts on behalf of the board. The full board is more concerned with policy and the executive committee with oversight of operations. In a staffed organization, the executive committee relates more directly with professional staff than does the rest of the board. In an all-volunteer organization, the executive committee may serve as the volunteer staff.

Another variation is the governing board plus advisory board. An advisory board may be formed to connect your organization to community leaders who offer expertise, perspectives, and contacts not found on the board or needed for particular programs. They can be convened periodically for discussions, or called upon by staff or governing board members for advice on specific issues. In the latter case, the advisory board enables key community leaders to be available for occasional requests for help or advice.

Characteristics of Nonprofit Boards:
Excerpts from the Nonprofit Governance Index (2004)

BoardSource conducts periodic surveys of nonprofit chief executives and board members from all types of organizations. Here are some highlights from 1999 and 2004 studies.

Board structure
The average size of board is 17 members, and the median size is 15.

Women are 45 percent of surveyed board membership.

Minorities are 15 percent of boards.

Most board members (68 percent) serve three-year terms. Nearly half (48 percent) may serve only two consecutive terms.

Fundraising
Over half (55 percent) of boards require personal financial contributions.

More than one third (36 percent) report 100 percent board giving.

Over half (52 percent) require board members to identify donors or solicit funds.

Less than a quarter (22 percent) of board members report that fundraising is one of their board's primary roles, though most (88 percent) make annual monetary contributions.

Board roles
Most boards see themselves as policy-makers (69 percent).

Boards also see themselves as an oversight body ensuring accountability (44 percent).

A quarter of boards (24 percent) see fundraising as primary role.

Chief executives most often ranked fundraising (37 percent) as the area their boards most need to improve. New board member recruitment and orientation (21 percent) is the next most common need for improvement. Fundraising (28 percent) and recruitment (32 percent) are the two greatest areas of board dissatisfaction.

The majority of boards (53 percent) have fewer than five standing committees, most often executive, governance, finance, and development.

Board policies
Most boards hire an external auditor (81 percent).

Over three quarters of boards have a conflict of interest policy (76 percent).

Few boards reimburse members for expenses to attend meetings (14 percent).

The chief executives sit as voting members in 18 percent of boards.

Less than half of boards (42 percent) formally assess their own performance.

Most boards (80 percent) annually evaluate the chief executive.

Most boards set term limits (65 percent).

Board meetings
Board members spend most of their time on policy (33 percent) or planning (32 percent).

Less than half of boards spend any time on crises (48 percent), and only 39 percent spend any time on minor management issues.

Median number of board meetings is seven per year.

Board members spend on average five hours or more on committee business each month.

Board recruitment
Nearly all board members (91 percent) report that fit between organizational mission and personal interests is one of the most important reasons for joining a board.

Fewer than half (40 percent) are formally oriented.

Managing or administrative director. Within a staffed organization, a managing director administers the policies and programs of the board. The role of the managing director can range from a supportive, almost clerical role in support of board initiatives to one where the director assumes a leadership role.

Managing director plus artistic director. As organizations grow, artistic staff is sometimes hired to manage artistic programs, and the managing director's responsibilities are limited to administration. Sometimes the two staff are peers who together report to the board. In other cases, either the managing or artistic director is the more senior staff.

Chief executive. The title of chief executive connotes a staff person more generally responsible than either a managing or artistic director. In a large organization, the chief executive may have supportive management and artistic staff. In a smaller organization, the chief executive may possess overall programming and artistic responsibilities and may be assisted by board members and non-governing volunteers operating in the capacity of volunteer staff.

President/chief executive officer. A trend in larger, well-established community arts organizations is to promote the experienced chief executive to be the president and chief executive officer. He or she assumes much of the policy-making responsibilities of the president, as well as the administrative responsibilities of the chief executive. The board president is retitled "chair" or "chairperson."

Some Alternative Structural Models

Staff driven with a nominal board. An organization that does not depend much upon individual or corporate contributions may reduce its board to the legally required minimum and ask that it simply ensures the fulfillment of the organization's legal responsibilities. It might meet once a year for the legally required annual meeting, authorize the staff to sign contracts, note that tax reports have been submitted, and sign the annual report to the secretary of state. Otherwise it serves as adviser to the staff.

In a variation, the nominally governing board is supplemented by a larger advisory board, which may help provide specialized advice, representation, access to constituencies or resources, and fundraising assistance to the staff.

Ad hoc task forces. A traditionally structured board organizes committees as they are needed. These are often called task forces or ad hoc committees to distinguish them from standing committees. When the project is completed the team disbands.

Artistic and governing boards. Some artistic producing organizations create both a governing board and an artistic one. The artistic board assumes the responsibilities that would be fulfilled by an artistic director in a larger organization.

Board composed of all members. Alternate ROOTS is an example of an organization whose board is composed of every member. Similar to a cooperative, the board of some 200 members meets annually in a conference-like setting to make policies and plans for the organization.

Nonprofit board plus a profit-making subsidiary. Some nonprofits have organized profit-making companies. Typical of these are craft organizations, which, because of tax regulations, have been required to separate their retail marketing operations from their nonprofit educational programs. In some cases, the same professional staff supports two separate boards. In others, there is considerable—even complete—overlap between the memberships of the two boards. Over time some of these subsidiary boards have grown so independent of the parent organization that they have split completely away and become wholly independent entities.

Special Cases: Public Commissions and Coalitions

Public commissions. A quarter of local arts agencies nationally are public commissions. In some, the commissioners function like a nonprofit board of directors. They set policy, direct staff, and are ultimately responsible for the commission.

In other towns and cities, the commissioners merely advise staff and elected officials. The professional staff is accountable to the mayor, city manager, or city council. In these cases, the structure and governing procedures explicitly acknowledge the political role of a local arts agency. Problems arise when the commissioners don't understand their role. Especially problematic are commissioners who should be advising, but assume their role to be governance and supervision. In one city, the professional staff director of the arts commission had to seek a legal opinion from the city attorney to convince her commissioners that their role was to advise the staff and mayor.

Coalitions and networks. Local arts agencies that are organized as coalitions of other arts organizations are yet another special case. Here the board of directors may comprise representatives of the member organizations. As such, these board members must learn to consider their collective interests and may encounter conflicting pulls on their time, energy, and loyalties. Avoiding conflicting interests while fundraising for the coalition and for the represented organization can be particularly difficult.

In these two cases, the board and staff may have a limited role in recruiting new commissioners or board members. In a public commission, the mayor appoints new commissioners. In a coalition agency, the member organizations may select their representatives.

Cautions Regarding Structural Changes

Experiment with incremental changes. See what works, and then expand upon what is successful and discard what fails. You may wish to live with a change for a while before entrenching it in your bylaws or articles of incorporation. Successful organizations are perhaps more effectively grown than built.

The Internal Revenue Service and funding agencies may prefer organizations with traditional boards of directors. Be prepared to do a lot of explaining if you innovate with other structures. It may be that you'll operate with an innovative board but describe it in a more standard format to funders.

CONCLUSION

This chapter is likely to have raised as many questions as it has resolved about fundamental assumptions and long-accepted board models. Summarized here are the key suggestions for board improvement.

Engage board members in creative problem solving and strategic thinking.

Help board members get better acquainted with each other.

Host a social gathering of board and staff members.

Manage meetings more effectively.

Document decisions and follow through on commitments.

Help board and staff understand the governing responsibilities of the board.

Create a board development or governance committee.

Create a board manual.

Review the committee list.

Organize a board development/planning retreat annually.

REFERENCES

Bridges, W. (2003). *Managing Transitions: Making the Most of Change* (2nd edition). Cambridge, MA: Da Capo Press.

Chait, R. P., Ryan, W. P., & Taylor, B. E. (2005). *Governance as Leadership: Reframing the Work of Nonprofit Boards.* Washington, DC: BoardSource and Wiley.

Carver, J. (1997). *Boards that Make a Difference: A New Design for Leadership in Nonprofit and Public Organizations* (2nd edition). San Francisco: Jossey-Bass.

Drucker, P. (1992). *Managing the Nonprofit Organization: Principles and Practices.* New York: HarperCollins Publishers.

Fisher, R., & Ury, W. (1983). *Getting to Yes: Negotiating Agreement Without Giving In.* New York: Penguin Books.

Fletcher, K. (2000). *The Policy Sampler: A Resource for Nonprofit Boards.* Washington, DC: BoardSource.

Heinen, J. S., & Jacobson, E. (1976). *A Model of Task Group Development in Complex Organizations and a Process of Supplementation.* Academy of Management Review, 1, 98-111.

Huges, S. (1999). *To Go Forward, Retreat! The Board Retreat Handbook.* Washington, DC: BoardSource.

Robert, H. *Robert's Rules of Order.* Stilwell, KS: Digireads.com Publishing.

Sturgis, A. Revised by American Institute of Parliamentarians. (1988). *The Standard of Parliamentary Procedure* (3rd ed.). McGraw-Hill, Inc.

BoardSource. *The Source: Twelve Principles of Governance that Power Exceptional Boards.*. Washington, DC: Author.

Wolf, T. (1999). *Managing a Nonprofit Organization in the Twenty-first Century.* Simon & Schuster Inc.

RESOURCES

BoardSource—This is probably the best source of practical information, tools and best practices, training, and leadership development for board members of nonprofits. Much of it requires a paid membership. The website's Q & A section and Glossary offer good summaries of frequently asked questions.
www.boardsource.org

Independent Sector—This is a good source of nonprofit-sector trends. Independent Sector sponsors research and creates resources so staff, boards, and volunteers can improve their organizations and better serve their communities.
www.independentsector.org

Governance Matters (formerly Alliance for Nonprofit Governance)—Governance Matters engages and informs nonprofit leaders on governance issues and improves board governance.
www.governancematters.org

The Nonprofit Genie—This program of the California Management Assistance Partnership is a frequently updated source for information and resources for nonprofit organizations.
www.genie.org

The Board Café—The Board Café is an electronic newsletter with short articles of ideas, information, opinion, news, and resources for board members of nonprofits.
www.boardcafe.org

About Nonprofit Charitable Organizations—This website offers start-up help, and financial, funding, and legal information of interest to staff and boards of directors.
www.nonprofit.about.com

CHAPTER 6

The Art of Fundraising

6

HALSEY M. NORTH AND ALICE H. NORTH

This chapter is written to demystify the fundraising process. It describes the key elements—from basic fundraising events through sophisticated capital campaigns. Your organization may be ready to tackle a large campaign or your first request for gifts from members. Whatever the scale of your fundraising, you should be familiar with all of the alternatives.

A small, all-volunteer arts agency will find this chapter as instructive as the largest arts organization. The same principles apply to the approach of a corner grocer for an in-kind donation of refreshments for the opening reception and to the approach of a corporate CEO for the $20,000 sponsorship of a concert. The prospect is identified, contacted, and cultivated over time, presented with a well-considered idea, asked for the contribution, and thanked, and the relationship is sustained. The larger donor takes more research and cultivation and expects the idea to be presented as a tight case statement supported by financial reports. But the same clarity of purpose and decisiveness of approach is necessary for the smallest potential donor.

Those of you who work in arts commissions as part of a local government should read this chapter with the following four ideas in mind:

1. Making a case for the community impact and worthiness of your agency's work for public support is much like making a case for private contributions. The ongoing cultivation of private donors has its parallel in the public sector with the year-round preparation for the annual municipal budgeting process.
2. Cultivation of the public and their elected officials parallels the development of supportive relations with corporations, foundations, and individual donors.
3. Public commissions usually seek funds from outside local government sources. They write grants to state, regional, and national agencies and foundations. Some have arranged to seek contributions from businesses and individuals as well by setting up a nonprofit organization or making arrangements for a dedicated municipal fund or community foundation to receive donations.
4. Arts commissions often advise their constituent arts organizations on fundraising and sometimes regrant funds themselves and should, therefore, know the principles of effective fundraising.

AN OVERVIEW OF SOURCES AND STRATEGIES

Earned revenue from sources such as admission tickets and participation fees, sales, and advertising provides the largest proportion of most arts organizations' income. A strong foundation of unrestricted earned income should be a central part of any organization's funding mix. However, it almost always costs more to produce arts programs and sustain organizations than can be earned through tickets, sales, and other earned revenue. Effective fundraising is therefore essential.

There are essentially four sources of contributed funds for the arts:

Individuals and small businesses

Corporations

Governments

Foundations

Individuals are widely documented as the largest source of contributed revenue. Understanding how to raise funds from individuals not only yields the most contributions, but also applies directly to raising funds from other sources. Consequently, this chapter will explain how to raise funds from individuals, and then will adapt the approach for corporations, foundations, and government grants.

FUNDRAISING IS "RELATIONSHIP BUILDING"

Think of fundraising as an opportunity to share your passion about an arts organization with others you know. Successful fundraising is built on the infectious enthusiasm of a few dedicated volunteers who can show their acquaintances that a gift to the arts organization will not only benefit the community but also the donor.

Passion bends reality! The passionate support of volunteers can make the impossible possible for an arts group. Achieving that support takes time, organizational skills, and commitment. Fundraising is a continuous process. Asking for money is just one component. Fundraising is informing and educating prospective donors, keeping them interested and involved, and showing them how they can help.

People give money to people they know and trust. At its very core, all fundraising is built on the personal relationships and links between individual people. *Individuals* give money—whether they are representing themselves, corporations, foundations, or governments. People give money to people they know and trust. Many people equate fundraising with grant writing. Grant writing is only a small part of what is needed to be a successful fundraiser, and successful grants are often the end product of a personal relationship which has been established between the representative of a funding organization and an arts organization.

Never ask a stranger for money! Successful fundraising results when an organization develops relationships with potential donors *before asking* for money. The basic principle is never to ask a stranger for money.

Fundraising is nurturing a sense of ownership and trust over time. It is "friend raising," enabling people to feel such a part of your organization that they feel a sense of ownership. With ownership comes a sense of responsibility for the organization's financial well being.

Think of the needs of the donor. You develop a relationship with a potential donor by thinking about the donor's perceptions and needs, not the needs of the organization. The basic principle is: speak to the needs of the donor.

Your organization's needs are not a motivating force for a donor. Individuals, corporations, foundations, and governments all give to support their own needs or to fulfill their own agendas.

Find out what interests the donor has and think through how the donor will benefit by giving. A corporation, for example, may want visibility and an individual newly arrived in town may want opportunities to meet people.

The key is to define your organization's dreams in such a way that potential donors can buy into them. They need to know what they can do to help and how they will benefit.

Who Will be Interested in Giving to Your Organization?

Donors are asked to give to many different causes and organizations. Those to which they contribute are ones in which they have developed a special intellectual or emotional interest or, even more importantly, one in which they have become involved or from which they have benefited.

In general, arts organizations that had established strong relationships with individual donors before the emotional turmoil of September 11, 2001, kept those donors because their donors had a sense of "ownership" and responsibility. Many of those donors were determined that the organizations they supported would thrive in spite of September 11. One donor to an arts center said to us, "It is my patriotic duty to make certain the arts center raises the money it needs." On the other hand, arts organizations that had passive mail-based relationships discovered their donors' loyalties had shifted to disaster relief and other human service causes.

Individuals give about 83 percent of the total dollars given in the United States to nonprofit organizations.[1] For you, these individuals can be those who attend your events and enjoy the art you produce as well as the friends, neighbors, and acquaintances of your volunteers. You, your board members, and other volunteers can help to strengthen your arts organization by exciting these individuals to *join* you in giving and asking others to give.

When you study fundraising, you are learning how to develop a systematic approach for developing relationships with people. It is the human element of personal relationships that makes fundraising an "art" rather than a "science."

Gifts from individuals are the key to successful fundraising; 68 percent of the gifts from individuals go to organizations to which the donor belongs.

Whether your organization is volunteer-run, has a one-person staff, or is so huge that it has lots of staff, the same principle applies—fundraising is about relationships between individual human beings.

THE FIVE ELEMENTS OF SUCCESSFUL FUNDRAISING

As you focus your organization's fundraising energy on developing relationships with donors, realize that there are five elements that are crucial for successful fundraising.

1. **Case.** A clear, compelling reason why your organization is raising money, what you are going to do with it, and who will benefit. Need is not a compelling factor. Most potential donors want to understand why their gifts will make a positive difference.
2. **Confidence.** Both in the organization and its board and staff, and that their gifts will be well used.
3. **Constituency.** A sufficient number of prospective donors who are capable and willing to give major gifts to the organization at a level that meets the

organization's needs. Otherwise, the organization will operate at a level that the constituency is willing to provide.

4. **Leadership.** Access to effective volunteer leaders with clout in the community who are capable, available, and willing to commit the time and energy needed to make your fundraising successful. Leadership is often the most difficult fundraising component to put into place. Leaders will often give money but not time or, more usually, leaders will give time but do not have the clout or money your organization needs. The key is to find a balance of both. If you have to choose, go for the clout or money and support the leadership effort with additional staff or volunteer efforts.
5. **Organizational fundraising capacity.** Staff with enough time, knowledge, and organizational resources dedicated to the development of donor relationships, and key volunteers with the power, influence, and financial resources needed to raise funds successfully.

WHY PEOPLE GIVE

As of 2005, the number of 501(c)(3) organizations in the United States exceeded one million.[2] Most of them do good and important work. Individuals, businesses, foundations, and governments are besieged with requests. Why should they give to your arts organization and not something else?

Fundraising for the arts is different from other forms of fundraising. Individual donors to organizations such as the United Way, hospitals, American Cancer Society, American Red Cross, and Salvation Army generally hope they won't have to "benefit" from the services such organizations offer.

Arts and cultural organizations offer donors opportunities to support things not only where they will benefit directly, but also where being involved will be fun, exciting, and personally enriching. The arts can offer joy, hope, education, and improved quality of life. The arts can help people feel good about themselves. As arts organizations, we can ask people to invest in the quality of their own lives. Even better, we can ask them to invest in the quality of life for the next generation.

You can position your organization to foster active involvement and participation in ways which simply are not available to other nonprofits in the United States. This is an advantage you will want to utilize.

People will only give to your arts organization if you are doing demonstrably good work—but they will not give *because* you are doing good work (so does the Red Cross). People as individuals and in businesses, foundations, and the government will give to you because they:

- know the people asking for the gift and like, trust, and respect them; and
- perceive that they and/or the community will benefit from the work of an arts organization.

The best way to develop prospective donor confidence in the organization is to involve them in some way—through governing boards, advisory boards, committees, support groups, and special events, etc. Such involvement can bring them into the "family."

The Importance of Face-to-Face Visits

Personal visits and face-to-face discussions are also good ways to cultivate people's interest. By involving a person in the development and creation of ideas and solutions, a potential donor can become emotionally involved in the success of those ideas and solutions. People give more and are more likely to give when asked in person.

Personalize your solicitation! The more people give, the more personalized the approach must be. Personal calls raise more than phone calls. Phone calls raise more than letters. And personalized letters and handwritten notes raise more than form letters.

INCORPORATE LONG-RANGE PLANNING INTO YOUR FUNDRAISING PLANS

Potential donors will want to know what your organization is going to do with their money. You can't be vague with donors—you need to be able to tell them clearly what you are going to be able to accomplish with their support.

Planning defines your organization's future so funders can buy into it. It shows how the donors' money will be used and how the community will benefit. Planning also gives potential donors confidence because they will realize your organization has been thoughtful in determining what it would accomplish and how much would be needed to get the job done.

New philanthropists in the United States have grown up in an entrepreneurial era. They have a hands-on approach to their work and their philanthropy. One of the most effective ways to engage them in your organization is through the long-range planning process. When potential donors are involved in helping to determine what an organization is trying to accomplish and become emotionally involved in the success of the organization, they are much more likely to give at a level to ensure success.

START FUNDRAISING FROM THE INSIDE

Raise money from the inside out! Start your fundraising with your organization's own board of directors. Each board member should be asked for and should give a gift which is, for him or her, an important gift. This is easier said than done. Board members often say, "I give time, I give my expertise, I give up hunks of my life working for this organization, and now you want me to give money?" Yes!!! It takes cash to run a nonprofit organization. If your board members are unwilling to give cash to your organization, why should others support it? Your board members should demonstrate a strong leadership commitment to your organization which is demonstrated to the rest of the community, in part, by their personal financial commitment.

Reasons to start your fundraising with your own board members include:

Each board member should give, what is for him or her, an important gift.

- 100 percent board giving builds community confidence;
- a board member campaign teaches your board members how to ask and how it feels to give;
- a board member campaign helps your organization test its "case" for giving, refine its fundraising materials, and train staff on how to organize a fundraising effort; and
- your board members will become much more effective fundraisers once they have given and can say, "Won't you *join me* in supporting…"

Boards which, when they recruit new members, instill the "expectation" that all board members will give are more likely to be able to announce 100 percent board participation in the organization's fundraising.

Not all donors are equal in importance to a fund drive. Large, early gifts to a campaign help to build volunteer and staff confidence that the campaign will succeed.

RAISE MONEY FROM THE TOP DOWN

Larger donors will set the pace. Once you have started raising money from your own board, then you can begin to approach your largest potential donors. Focus on the BIG gifts first. The larger donors will set the pace of giving for your campaign. Go to these large donors before you go public and announce a goal because the size of the gifts from these early donors will, to a large extent, determine how much you can raise and the goal that can be set. These early, large gifts determine your fundraising fate because:

- 75 to 95 percent of all the money you raise will come from ten to 15 percent of your donors, usually 50 to 100 prospects; and
- these 50 to 100 prospects will usually be solicited by ten to 15 individuals.

In essence, effective fundraising consists of a few of the right people (leadership) asking people they know and can influence (constituents) to give.

Fundraising, by its very nature, may seem elitist. You will target your fundraising to those who have the most capacity to give. Only individuals, foundations, corporations, and governments with accumulated assets can contribute substantial amounts of money. Focus on their gifts first, and then broaden your base of support by going after smaller gifts.

Smaller gifts do matter. You can demonstrate your broad-based community support with larger numbers of contributors, even if individual gifts are modest. Your funding agencies will value the numbers of contributors in addition to the total amount of gifts. Note too that people who admire your work may be encouraged to increase their initial contributions in subsequent years.

POSITION YOUR ORGANIZATION FOR SUCCESSFUL FUNDRAISING

There are several key elements which need to be in place to enable you to raise money successfully.

Mission

Why do you exist? First, you need a clear, concise mission statement specifying why the organization exists. A commonly agreed upon mission helps focus the energies of the board, staff, and volunteers. It ensures that the community is receiving a clear message about the purpose of the organization. Mixed messages about mission can confuse potential givers. Make certain your mission can be stated clearly during a fundraising call so that prospective donors will know to what purpose you will be using their money.

Strategic Plan

What are you going to do? Who will get it done, when, and at what cost? If your organization has established priorities in a strategic planning process as is recommended, these should be reflected in your fundraising goals.

The plan will also help you make a convincing case to funders who will have more confidence in your organization if they know you have thought through the options, established the priorities, and determined who will do what, when, and at what cost.

Funders want to know how you will be spending their money, and a multiyear plan helps give them the answers they want.

Funders will also be reassured when they can see your fundraising history, how much you need to raise, and a reasonable projection estimating the sources of those funds. The details give an organizational plan credibility. Funders can see that you have a strategy to bring your vision from a dream to a possible future reality.

Financial Information

Show donors you will spend their gifts wisely. Clear financial information, in the form of Statement of Activities (operating statement) and Statement of Position (balance sheet), demonstrates an organization's ability to manage money. (See the Financial Management chapter for more information about how to prepare these financial statements.) Figure 1 in the Appendix is a sample summary of historical and projected cash flow. It gives two years of financial history, the current budget, and six years of projections (two years is often sufficient). This sweep of information gives donors an understanding of your organization's operations, stability, and financial needs—current and projected.

You will notice that Figure 1 places expenses first and income second, reversing the format used by profit-making corporations. We recommend this format because it differentiates your organization as a not-for-profit enterprise and focuses a reader's attention first on the *cost of the art*, and then on how much money it takes to support those programs and services. This format enables you to put your request of a potential donor—and the level of that request—into the context of an overall plan.

Financial information can be presented as backup for a written request or taken along on a fundraising call as evidence of thoughtful planning. In either case, it will strengthen a potential donor's confidence that a gift will be well spent.

Case for Giving

Once you have developed a succinct mission, a clear multiyear plan, and businesslike financial projections, you will have the information you need to create a document known as the *case for giving*, *case statement*, or simply the *case*.

The case for giving outlines how your organization will serve the community, your qualifications to do so, how the donor will benefit, how much money you need to raise, and why. The case describes the programs and services your organization will provide and the funds needed to carry them out. It does not need to convince a prospective donor of the value of supporting the arts—that can be done, if needed, as part of the in-person call. Instead, the case focuses on how your organization will strengthen the community and the quality of life for the donor and the donor's children, family, employees, etc.

The case can be summarized in a single page or it can be printed in a multipage document which can contain, as appropriate:

- the community leadership and volunteers involved with your organization as board members and working on the fund drive (this list acts as a stamp of community endorsement);

- the mission of the organization, why you are raising money, and the amount of money being raised;
- the project's budget, how the community benefits, how donors will benefit and be recognized for their gifts; and
- your organization's goals, achievements, and financial health.

Make the case larger than the organization! From a fundraising standpoint, it is important to think about your organization in a larger community context. What is your organization's contribution to your community in terms of impact on the economy, downtown revitalization, quality of life, schools and education, corporate recruitment, or tourism? Package your organization's needs and dreams in such a way that donors can relate to you in terms of their own needs. Make the case larger than the organization. Give people a sense of how they can help your organization make a difference that benefits them.

Annual Report

Show the donor you know what you are doing. An annual report is useful for showing what your organization can accomplish. It can list your volunteer leadership, professional staff, what you do for the community, and what it costs. It can state your mission and include clear and succinct financial information. It can outline next year's goals, discuss future plans, and list and thank donors.

Organizational Attitude

Give fundraising the time it deserves, and incorporate fundraising into the everyday life of your organization. Every board member must be involved with fundraising at some level at appropriate times.

The act of giving money—like the act of participating in creating the long-range plan—enables people to feel that they are a part of the family, that they are important to the success of a worthwhile organization. Fundraising involves marketing, membership, and the cultivation of resources—leadership, constituencies, and money.

Fundraising is not effective when it is rushed or done at the last minute because the money has run out. Such a state of panic does not build confidence in volunteers or donors.

Fundraising cannot be "tacked on" to an organization's already full work load. It has to be given staff and board time and resources as well as the money to pay for supplies, receptions, meetings, computer software, printed materials, annual reports, etc. Fundraising is an ongoing process that needs advanced planning. Successful fundraising takes time and attention on a daily basis.

Volunteer Leadership

To raise funds, you need time, money, power, and passion from your board and other volunteer leadership. To survive over the long run, your organization must have political and social access to the people who control public and private giving in your community, who can give as well as ask. This does not mean that every board member should have wealth and political clout. Your mission and commitment to the community may require that you also have artists and other community members of modest means. What you need is balance and a commitment from every board member and some key volunteers to cultivate potential contributors throughout the community, including those who have wealth and power.

Everyone enjoys being an expert. If you do not have "power people" involved with your arts agency, then you need to identify specific people who could help you develop an individualized cultivation strategy for each person you want to bring into the family. You can develop a series of small lunches, receptions, or special orientation meetings to ask for specific advice or help. Or you can ask them to work on projects, ad-hoc committees, an advisory board, etc.

Make volunteers feel important, and use their time wisely. The key is to use their time wisely. Recruit them using clear expectations (verbal or written). Enable them to feel helpful and important. Make certain they have fun, learn something, and enjoy the experience. Provide follow-up information by newsletters, notes, and phone calls.

To summarize, in addition to giving what is for them an important gift, campaign leaders should have:

- understanding of the case for giving;
- commitment to the organization;
- confidence the money will be used wisely;
- an opportunity to learn how to make a fundraising call;
- appropriate fundraising materials;
- clear tasks that are organized into doable bite-sized pieces; and
- the recognition and thanks they deserve.

Treasure your volunteer leadership! Good leaders are rare. Don't take them for granted once they are involved. Thank them often and in many different ways. Make them feel special and appreciated. Remember, you can't thank volunteers enough. And saying thank you leaves the door open to ask for their help again. See the Volunteers in the Arts chapter for more information about working with volunteers.

Staff and Office Resources

Fundraising requires professional or volunteer staff to provide the information and administrative support that board members and key volunteers need to raise funds.

For a larger organization, it is best to hire a part- or full-time staff member whose sole function is fundraising.

When staff functions are combined, fundraising often comes up short. Someone responsible for both marketing and fundraising, for example, will spend more time on marketing: it is more fun to write a press release than a gift request which might be declined.

Many smaller arts organizations find that they can hire excellent part-time help from the pool of parents who want to work from 10 a.m. to 3 p.m. so they can be home with their school-age children. When hiring or recruiting volunteer fundraising staff, look for:

- fundraising experience;
- organizational ability and attention to detail;

- writing skills; and
- ability to work with and motivate volunteers.

Also make certain that you have the computer support you need, including software for record-keeping and word processing. There are a number of fundraising-specific software packages on the market, some of which, if you need, can interrelate to ticketing, accounting, and scheduling software. Even the smallest arts organization can find a board member or key volunteer with an adequate computer system to support fundraising.

Constituency of Donors

Developing an ongoing process of cultivation to involve as many potential donors as possible is essential to effective fundraising. People usually do not give to strangers or causes with which they have no relationship. Your job is to bring potential donors into the family, develop their interest, and get them involved. Develop monthly newsletters, reminder postcards, annual reports, special receptions, preview parties, or post-performance gatherings. Develop guilds, friends groups, advisory boards, or volunteer committees. Try to involve as many community members as possible in your organization. If your arts organization is run with the input and involvement of only a few individuals, then those few people will be your only significant source of contributed income.

People do not give to causes or good work. They give to people they know, trust, and respect.

The section, Raising Money from Individuals, discusses how you can identify, cultivate, and focus your search for specific prospects. Keep in mind that the best prospective donor is someone who already feels like they are *part of the family*. The *next best* prospect is someone who is *beginning* to feel *part of the family*. This is because fundraising is, in part, the process of giving people a sense of ownership in your organization.

Legal Readiness

Donors are not able to deduct their gifts to you unless you are designated as a 501(c)(3) tax-exempt organization by the IRS. To receive this status, you need to be incorporated as a not-for-profit tax-exempt organization by your state government. Corporations, foundations, the National Endowment for the Arts (NEA), and state arts agencies can, generally, only give to 501(c)(3) tax-exempt organizations. If you do not yet have your tax-exempt status from the IRS, it may be possible to find a 501(c)(3) organization willing to accept gifts and grants on your behalf as a fiscal agent.

DETERMINE YOUR FUNDRAISING CAPABILITY

Is our board committed to fundraising? Do we have the key volunteer and staff support we need to make our efforts successful?

Before you can establish how much you are going to raise, you have to determine not only how much you need but also how much your arts organization is capable of raising. As you evaluate your fundraising capacity, remember that fundraising is built on the relationships between individual human beings. So, in a real sense, what you are evaluating is your organization's capacity to initiate, strengthen, and maintain relationships with people who can give money.

To determine your fundraising capability, begin by evaluating your organization's internal resources and its access to outside funding sources.

Does the organization have…

- board members/volunteers who have fundraising experience?
- board members/volunteers who have access to funding sources?
- board members/volunteers who are capable of providing leadership?
- advisors who can help provide information and assist with donor cultivation and solicitation?
- staff or dedicated volunteers who have the time and expertise to do the homework?
- computer capabilities or access to computers to do the record-keeping and reports?
- existing and prospective members/friends and donors who will give?
- the support of local businesses (including restaurants, stores, law firms, doctors' offices, real estate agencies, motels and hotels, grocery stores, etc.) in the area which know your work?
- the support of decision-makers in local and state governments whom you know and who will help you get funding?
- strong peer relationships with colleagues who will make grant decisions on local, state, and NEA panels?

The Six Sources for Raising Money

There are six primary sources for raising money. Determine which should be your organization's focus in order to maximize the amount of money you can raise given the time and energy you can put into it. Remember that gifts from individuals are how most nonprofits get the most money. Public grants and national foundation contributions may be a part of your fundraising mix, but there is no substitute for cultivating local individual donors. The six sources, in priority order, are:

1. contributions from board members, former board members, and other key volunteers;
2. contributions from other individuals;
3. net contributed income from benefits and special events;
4. contributions from local businesses and foundations;
5. grants from local, state, and federal governments; and
6. contributions from national corporations and foundations.

Individuals

For most arts and cultural organizations, the best results are achieved when funds are first raised from board members who are then enlisted to solicit, face-to-face, other key, potentially significant donors. For those organizations limited by the number of individuals they can send out to ask for money, solicit other individuals by personalized letters followed up by personal phone calls.

Why emphasize the "personal?" Because the basic component of successful fundraising is building and maintaining relationships.

Benefits

Fundraisers and special events are another source of funds for arts and cultural organizations. They can devour staff and volunteer time and take a lot of work. They require long-term planning to secure sponsorships, in-kind donations, and attendance that will generate maximum revenues and minimum expenses. They are most effective when they are run, from beginning to end, by a group of committed volunteers. The best benefits and special events can be a lot of fun and can help with donor cultivation and involvement.

Local Businesses and Foundation

Personally soliciting local businesses and foundations is very similar to asking local individuals for money. Success is based on cultivating a relationship with them. So, the key question to ask is: Do you have the manpower to develop and maintain good relationships with these folks?

If you have been working with the chamber of commerce and its arts committee is willing to help you launch your first local business fund drive, one option is to develop a cultivation and solicitation strategy for the 50 to 75 most likely business prospects.

Governments

Many nonprofit cultural organizations receive grant support from their local and state governments, and this area is worth exploring. Contact your state arts agency and get to know the staff. Ask them to help you understand what grant programs they offer that might help your organization. Once you have established a relationship with your state arts agency, then you may want to ask them if there are any grant programs at the NEA to which your organization should apply.

Another strategy that is often overlooked is to enlist the assistance of state and local legislators in your fundraising efforts. Does your organization's staff or volunteers know any local or state politicians who can help you organize a lobbying effort for a major grant from your city, county, or state government? If no one knows any local or state politicians but there is strong feeling that the city, county, or state government should support the organization, then the strategy may be to develop a cultivation plan. Decision makers will then get to know and become involved in the organization so you can ask them for money in the coming year. See the Cultural Advocacy chapter for more detailed information about relationship building with your legislators as well as advocacy campaign strategies.

National Corporations and Foundations

Proposal writing to national corporations and foundations is generally the least effective form of fundraising for nonprofit arts and cultural organizations. Exxon, for example, won't give to you because there is a gas station on the corner. National corporations generally give only when they have a factory in your community and its officers have a relationship with your organization. National foundations generally give when an organization is doing something unique which can have national impact or which can become a model for other organizations.

Create a Fundraising Work Plan

Figure 2 in the Appendix is a chart you can use to get an overview of your organization's fundraising options and capabilities. The left-hand column lists fundraising options the organization might want to consider; the other axis evaluates internal and external resources. You do not have to, nor should you, attempt all options. Decide what strategies are best for your organization.

Aim for success. Don't overreach. Fundraising success builds community, donor, and volunteer confidence so you can ask again.

Once you have evaluated your organization's internal capacity to fundraise, you will need to make some choices. What fundraising options will realistically produce the most money from donors for the time, energy, and resources your organization invests? You do not have to attempt all options. Decide what options your organization can undertake effectively. If you have a board of directors, it is recommended that your board undertake the option of a personalized campaign to raise money from board members and other key volunteers. Then, option by option, develop a work plan to implement each fundraising option, as follows:

1. Select the fundraising options your organization will undertake.
2. For each option:
   - list the tasks that need to be done to raise the money;
   - negotiate with the staff, board, and other volunteers who will do what tasks;
   - establish a timetable (who is going to do what, when);
   - determine the costs (the direct costs in dollars) plus the staff/board/volunteer time needed (who, number of hours, tasks) and consultants, if any (who, number of hours, tasks, cost); and
   - determine the funds expected to be raised from each option.
3. Set the total dollar fundraising goal for your organization.
4. Step back, review the plan, and ask whether it is realistic and feasible. Can your organization—staff, board, and other volunteers—actually do the work you have outlined?
5. Revise the work plan as needed.
6. Distribute the work plan to those who will do the tasks and ensure buy-in from all involved. Revise the plan as needed.
7. Regularly update everyone on tasks accomplished and costs/funds raised compared to the work plan.

Figure 3 in the Appendix offers a sample fundraising work plan. Included are examples of a board giving campaign, a membership campaign, and a special event.

Set the Goal

Now you can compare the dollar goal established in the fundraising work plan (how much you think the organization can raise) with the numbers in the financial projections (how much it needs to raise). The two numbers usually differ. Arts organizations often find that their needs outstrip their fundraising capabilities. Groups get into trouble by increasing their estimates of how much they can raise to equal the amount needed. A goal set too high can demoralize volunteers and put the organization at financial risk because it arouses unrealistic expectations that cannot be met.

The goal is a compromise between how much you need and how much your volunteers feel comfortable raising.

On the other hand, an organization which always reduces its staff or operations to reduce the demands on the organization's fundraising efforts will limit the organization's growth and ability to serve.

The goal should be a realistic stretch. The overall fundraising goal should be established by the board and staff as a compromise between the need and the fundraising capacity. The need should be lessened and the goal should be increased to slightly more than what the fundraising team feels is comfortable. The overall fundraising goal should at least balance the budget and be a realistic "stretch" for the fundraising team.

THE ROLE OF THE BOARD AND STAFF IN FUNDRAISING

Simply stated, the primary role of the staff in fundraising is to do the homework, while the role of the board is to do the solicitation.

Role of the Board

To build confidence and a sense of ownership, have board members help to develop the fundraising work plan and present it to the rest of the board for approval.

The board of your arts organization has the legal and moral responsibility to make certain the organization has the financial resources it needs to operate. When the board approves the budget, they need to realize that they are setting their own fundraising goal. If they do not feel they can make the goal, they should adjust the budget.

Have the board help develop a fundraising work plan. By participating in the development and approval process, board members are more likely to ensure that the fundraising work plan is implemented successfully.

Board members should ask each other. Board giving is essential. Many government, corporate, and foundation funders require 100 percent board giving before considering making a contribution to a nonprofit organization.

The amount a board member gives is also important. Board members should be recruited with the expectation that they will give, what is for them, an important gift. Set the expectation that board members give the organization an amount comparable to what they donate to the United Way, their place of worship, their college, or other nonprofits in which they are interested and involved. The actual dollar amount they give is not as important for setting the pace for giving as the perception that each and every board member is stretching to be as generous as possible. We are not suggesting that board members be required to give a specific minimum amount as a gift, but, rather, that each board member be challenged to maximize their personal giving commitment.

Personally, board members are more comfortable and effective as fundraisers when they have already given themselves and can say, "Join me!" Giving a cash donation strengthens board commitment to the organization and the fundraising process. Moreover, the giving enthusiasm of board members sets the pace of support for the organization.

In addition to setting the pace by giving, the board needs to accomplish these tasks.

Spend money to raise money.

Ensure fundraising staff and systems are in place. It is a board's responsibility to make certain the organization is investing enough of its resources in fundraising.

Staff time and fundraising information-gathering and record-keeping systems must be in place to help ensure success.

Identify and cultivate prospects. Board members introduce their friends, business acquaintances, and associates to the organization and excite them about the organization's work. The board needs to make certain there is an ongoing, systematic approach to gathering and updating information about prospective donors from board members, and utilizing board members to cultivate prospects.

Take the time to show prospects you care about them before you ask them to give.

Advocate with local governments and businesses. The board is the "good housekeeping seal of approval" for your organization. Board members' ability to talk about the organization knowledgeably and with enthusiasm will go a long way in convincing others to give. Board members are your best advocates to work with local government officials and businesses for support.

Be passionate. How a community thinks about an organization is often determined by the hundreds of brief remarks and discussions people hear at meetings, social gatherings, and events. This gossip can set the tone for what community members think about your organization when they are approached for money. The board of an organization in small- and medium-sized communities can, to a very real extent, influence the tone of the community's perception by talking about the organization with enthusiasm and passion.

Board members should be passionate advocates.

Solicit gifts in a thoughtful manner. Board members often want to ask others for gifts by phone or letter. It is easier and, on the surface, more efficient and less time-consuming. If board members want significant gifts from individuals, businesses, or foundations, however, they need to make the request in a considered and thoughtful manner. Taking the time to do it right will pay off in the long run. Expedient fundraising may create frustration, failing to produce the kinds of gifts the board needs to succeed.

Say thank you. Board members can help keep donors interested by thanking them when they see them as part of their everyday work life. You can't thank a donor too often, and a thank you from a board member is much more powerful than a staff thank you. Board members can also help by writing personal notes or making phone calls to donors to thank them.

Role of the Staff

You need to cherish your volunteers and make certain you maximize their effectiveness and personal satisfaction by giving them the staff support they need. Good staff back-up is the key to good volunteer involvement. If you do not have adequate staff time dedicated to fundraising, then you need a few dedicated volunteers to fulfill the support role that staff would normally provide. Volunteers can help advocate for the organization, identify and cultivate prospective donors, and ask for money. Staff can support fundraising volunteers in these efforts with:

- background materials;
- data on potential donors;
- training materials;

- individualized solicitation letters;
- examples of thank-you letters;
- their presence on calls;
- confirmation calls for appointments;
- information on developments and funds raised to date;
- the calendar of meetings, appointments, and follow up;
- agendas for meetings; and
- meeting spaces, names tags, refreshments, and clean up.

Trust is an important part of fundraising. Volunteers need to know that they can rely on the fundraising staff. Donors need to trust in the people to whom they are giving. As a result, consistency in the fundraising staff is another element to consider when your organization is working to strengthen its fundraising efforts. The trust needed for successful fundraising is built upon hours and hours of staff time and dedication to building the relationships needed over time—with volunteers and donors.

Because relationship building takes so much time—as do day-to-day homework, information-gathering, and record-keeping—fundraising is not a project that can be dumped on top of everything else the staff is doing. To be successful, arts organizations must invest more and more money to hire and train fundraising staff. Each organization needs to make certain it has adequate staff or dedicated volunteer fundraising leaders in place to develop ongoing relationships with volunteers and donors; support volunteer fundraising efforts; organize the homework, making certain the record-keeping and accounting systems are up-to-date and accurate; and write grants and proposals.

If your organization is staffed by a single individual or if your organization has no staff, you must still find ways to provide the same fundraising support as is provided by a development director in a larger organization. Consider these alternatives.

Recruit an exceptional volunteer to lead a time-limited fundraising campaign.

Seek the loan of secretarial help from a local corporation or public agency.

Seek the loan of database-design or data-entry personnel.

Contract with an independent fundraiser to help staff your fundraising campaign.

Seek the help of a fundraising consultant to advise how to manage your fundraising. Note: Be clear about whether you are seeking advice or supplemental staffing. Most fundraising consultants are in the advising business.

Seek a donor to invest in fundraising staff.

Fundraising is 90 percent homework and ten percent solicitation. It is the staff's responsibility to give the board/key volunteers the support and information they need to do their jobs successfully. The staff collects, organizes, and produces information (the homework) and then develops the letters and materials needed for the board to implement the cultivation and solicitation process (the solicitation).

The reality is that the staff cajoles, prods, educates, and pushes board members and other volunteers to complete their fundraising tasks. The staff should do the following.

Make certain that board members learn how to ask for money.

Organize the fundraising tasks into doable, bite-sized pieces. When we ask board members to "fundraise," they often don't. The task is too open-ended. When we encourage them to "cultivate and solicit five people they know for gifts similar to their own," they usually respond positively.

Organize the homework. Make certain a board member has all the information needed to make a successful call—that the right solicitor is asking the right prospect for the right amount for the right reason at the right time.

Organize and develop the fundraising materials—solicitation letters, case statement, prospect information, pledge cards, receipts, brochures, newsletters, and calendars.

Create giving opportunities with benefits. It is easier for board members to ask prospects to join them as a patron member or a sponsor of a special event.

Say thank you for fundraising as well as for giving.

In summary, the staff is the glue that holds the fundraising effort together—setting up the meetings, gathering the information, educating the volunteers, and saying thank you. The board members and key volunteers are the community liaisons who say; "The work of this arts organization is important. Please join me in supporting it to enrich the lives of our children and the quality of life in our community!"

RAISING MONEY FROM INDIVIDUALS

As noted earlier, gifts from individuals account for more than 83 percent of U.S. philanthropic dollars.[3] Your organization's ability to keep potential individual donors happy and satisfied is fundamental to its future fundraising success. An organization has cultivated and involved a donor well when that donor believes the organization is an important part of his or her life.

Basically, what most donors want from a relationship with a nonprofit arts organization is to:

- be thanked in an appropriate and thoughtful manner;
- feel good about themselves and what they have done;
- be confident that their money will make a difference;
- feel special with access to select privileges, people, savings, or experiences not generally available to others; and
- have a sense of satisfaction, recognition, importance, appreciation, belonging, and being part of the family.

Six "Rights" of Fundraising

—the right person asking

—the right prospect

—the right amount

—the right reason

—the right time

—the right way

In general, individuals give money to people they know and trust for organizations in which they have a personal interest. The size of the gift will be influenced by:

- their capacity to give;
- their level of interest in the organization;
- who asks them for the gift; and
- the manner in which they are asked.

Your organization cannot influence an individual's capacity to give, but it can influence their level of interest, who asks, and the thoughtfulness of the ask. To develop an effective individual gifts campaign, you need a two-phased process.

Phase 1: Research, Planning, and Cultivation. Identify the highest potential individual donors and find out their needs and interests. Determine the best way to position your organization potential donor by potential donor, develop a connection, and get them interested.

Phase 2: Solicitation. Have people whom potential donors respect and trust ask them for a gift face-to-face in a thoughtful manner.

Phase 1: Research, Planning, and Cultivation

Step 1: Work Plan

Develop a work plan for the individual gifts campaign. Determine how much you need to raise, how many volunteers you need to recruit, how many prospects you need to identify, how you will cultivate the prospects, and the approaches you will use to ask them for money.

Step 2: Staff Support

Determine the staff support you need and have for the fundraising effort. Limited staff support will limit your fund drive efforts. Is your organization expecting too much from its current staff or do you need to commit additional staff time? Do you need to hire fundraising staff or do you need to free up more of the chief executive's time to devote to fundraising? Often, hiring fundraising staff (or staff to free up the chief executive's time) is a cash-flow issue rather than an expense issue. You should be able to expect competent fundraising personnel to more than pay for their salary and expenses after the first year because they should increase the organization's capacity to raise money.

Step 3: Job Descriptions

Develop job descriptions for staff, board, and volunteers so each person in the individual gifts campaign knows what their role will be and the timetable for getting work done. Deadlines are important in fundraising because they help give a sense of urgency so the work gets done in a timely manner.

Step 4: Prospect Lists

Begin to develop prospect lists for different elements of the campaign. Who are the prospects with the highest potential that require special personal attention? Who are the intermediate givers who will respond to some personal cultivation? Who are the others you should solicit by mail?

You have limited staff and volunteer time available to solicit gifts from individuals, so you want to develop a fundraising work plan to give you the greatest dollar return for the time invested.

The two primary sources of individuals whom you can solicit for your arts organization are:

- those who are involved or benefit from your services, such as audience members, constituents, board members, guild members, committee members, other volunteers, artists, students, alumni, parents of students, friends, group members, organizational members, etc.; and

- people known personally by your board members, other key volunteers, and staff.

To find those potential donors who can and are most likely to give, you first have to do some donor research and organize the information you have.

Step 5: Prospect Research

Do prospect research to gather as much information as possible about the prospective donors you have identified. Take all the lists of the names of people you serve—those who support you, encourage you, volunteer for you, get your newsletter, attend events, etc.—and gather them together with an annotation of where the name came from and their relationship to your arts organization. Then, using staff and key volunteers who know your community well, divide these lists into three categories:

- **high potential—**worth the time for personal cultivation and solicitation;
- **medium potential—**worth a personalized letter and telephone follow-up; and
- **little potential and don't know—**solicit by mass mail and telephone campaigns.

Once you have completed this broad-brush-stroke sort, you can begin to refine your placement of donors into appropriate solicitation categories.

First, review your high-potential list and make certain it is less than 200 names. Enter these names on a form similar to Figure 4 in the Appendix. (It takes about two hours for two to three volunteers to review 100 names on such a set of worksheets. If you have more names than that, you may want to have two sets of worksheets.)

The more potential a donor has, the more time you want to spend getting to know and cultivating them.

Then ask a number of your staff members and key volunteers to review these worksheets and tell you (or your development staff or designated volunteer) as much as possible about the prospective donors. Do they actively participate in the arts? What is their occupation, interests, perceived worth, community involvement, and history of giving to other organizations? Is there anything else it would be helpful to know?

Another approach to developing a list of high-potential donors is to ask your board members and key volunteers who they know who has the capacity to give generously and who might be interested in your organization. Sit down with each board member and key volunteer and go through their Palm Pilot with them, noting names, addresses, and phone numbers on a worksheet such as is given in Figure 4. Ask them to tell you anything helpful to know about the donors. Also discuss lists of potential prospective donors that you have drawn up. Does the board member know any of the names on the lists? Then, using the upcoming year as a time frame, ask them to divide the resulting names into the three prospect categories.

Ask board members, other key volunteers, and staff who they know and can involve in your organization.

Determine who is best to cultivate their interest in the organization, who is best to ask them for a gift, and what is the best strategy for cultivating and asking for the gift.

Step 6: Recruit Volunteers

Once you have done enough research to know the potential donors you want to cultivate and solicit face-to-face (and the best people to solicit them), you are ready to recruit the volunteers. The average fund drive volunteer can solicit between five and seven prospective donors. So, if you have 100 prospects that you want to cultivate and solicit face-to-face, you will need 15 to 18 dedicated volunteers. Actually, you may need to recruit more volunteers: experience shows that volunteers are more effective, especially for major gifts prospects, when they work in teams of two people. These teams can consist of a volunteer and a staff person or any effective combination of board members, key volunteers, previous donors, or staff members.

The average volunteer can solicit five to seven people face to face.

In a typical campaign, some wonderful volunteers may solicit 15 to 20 prospects and others may have to be hounded to follow through on only one or two prospect solicitations. So, determine how many volunteers you will need, recruit a chairperson or co-chairs, and work with the chairperson or co-chairs to identify and recruit the volunteers they believe will be effective and who they can motivate to do a good job. The volunteers can then review the list of prospective donors, tell you who they can help call upon, and give you additional information on the prospects.

Step 7: Case for Giving

Based on how much your organization needs to raise, and your capacity to raise these funds from your community, develop a compelling written case for giving—what will be accomplished with that money. If you need unrestricted annual operating support, look at your programs and services and package your need in a way that captures people's attention and calls out things in which prospective donors might be interested—such as subsidizing tickets for school children, enhancing the quality of productions, providing scholarship support, or strengthening the staff so you can take more artists into the schools.

As you write the case, include how your organization will benefit. For example, discuss the quality of education in the schools, the community's quality of life, economic development, downtown revitalization, corporate recruitment, and providing people with educational, enriching, and entertaining opportunities.

Step 8: Fund Drive Materials

Create the printed fund drive materials in such a way that they serve a two-fold purpose: (1) they inform potential contributors about the organization and help build confidence that contributions will be well utilized; and (2) they are tools designed to help the volunteers go on calls with confidence that they have in hand all the key information they need to complete a successful call. Fund drive materials can include:

Create fundraising tools to make the volunteer's job easier.

- case statement;
- personalized letter requesting the gift;
- pledge form;
- volunteer information sheets;
- answers to most frequently asked questions;
- thank you letters;
- contribution acknowledgment and tax receipt forms;
- annual report; and
- record-keeping sheets for calls, gifts, and acknowledgments.

Step 9: Establish Information System

The person responsible for fundraising should oversee the creation and maintenance of a file—both electronic and hard copy/desk files—on each prospective high-potential donor. Establish a system to collect and enter information continuously into these files. Everyone having contact with these people on behalf of the organization needs to know how to feed information into the system so that the files are always up-to-date.

Phase 2: Solicitation

Step 10: Solicit the Board First

Start the fund drive with a board campaign, that is, board members asking other board members (and former board members asking other former board members) for gifts.

Board members can set the pace of giving.

Step 11: Solicit Fund Drive Volunteers

Concurrently with the board campaign, solicit the other volunteers who have agreed to work on the campaign. Arrange this effort so everyone has a chance to go on a call and experience being called upon before they start solicitations in the broader community. If your volunteers, and board members, have successful fundraising experiences with each other first, then they will have more confidence as they begin to approach prospects who are not as close to the organization.

Step 12: Solicit Major Gifts

Once the board and fund drive volunteers have been solicited, you can then move on to the select group of prospects who are capable of giving your organization larger gifts. The major gift prospects should be cultivated before they are asked for money. They should be personally invited to special events, receptions, private dinners, etc., where they can learn more about your organization before they are solicited. Remember the basic fundraising principal: never ask a stranger for money. Make certain the prospective donors know about your organization and how they personally or the community will benefit from your work.

Figure 5 in the Appendix lists steps and offers pointers for making a fundraising call to an individual. We recommend you use it, or something similar, as a basis for training board members and other volunteers.

Step 13: Announce the Campaign Goal

Once your organization has an understanding of how generous these advance donors will be, then you can project forward how much you will raise from a broader, public campaign. At this point, publicly announce a campaign goal that you have confidence in achieving. The publicly-announced goal may be more or less than the actual need. It is often less than the organization had hoped to raise, but it is better to make a goal and even exceed a goal than to fail trying to raise too much.

Remember that 75 to 95 percent of all the money raised will come from ten to 15 percent of your donors.

Step 14: Launch the Broader Campaign

Once you have publicly-announced a goal and launched the campaign, then you can go after a broader range of gifts using personalized letters, telephone calls, mass mail, special events, and grant writing, etc.

Step 15: Acknowledge Donors

It is crucial that each donor be thanked properly, with major donors being acknowledged on multiple occasions. Proper thank-yous are personalized thank-yous.

All donors should be thanked by the appropriate staff person who sends the formal acknowledgment for tax purposes. Major donors should also hear from the solicitor and the president. Hand-written notes—even if at the bottom of a personalized, computer-generated letter—are effective ways of making the donor feel special. At the beginning of the campaign, thank volunteers in advance for their hard work and, at the end of the campaign, thank them in writing and with some kind of celebratory event.

DEVELOP A "FRIENDS OF…" PROGRAM

People like to join or belong to groups. How do you position your arts organization so people will want to join and be identified as being a member?

It is easier for a volunteer to offer benefits and to say "join me" than to ask for a specific amount of money.

By developing a "Friends of…" or membership program, you are giving people an opportunity to "join." You are also creating a structure of benefits which make people feel special and involved. It is important to build a structure where people receive more benefits the more they give—thus encouraging them to give generously. The package of benefits will be different for every organization.

This kind of friends/membership structure helps formalize your organization's cultivation of donors. The newsletter, benefits, and special events will keep donors informed and make them feel special. The benefits can be important, too. You will attract some people you did not know to the higher levels of giving. For current friends/members, you will have mechanisms for involving them and encouraging them to give at higher levels. For potential donors, volunteer fundraisers will be able to say, "Join me as a sponsor. It will give us a good opportunity to see more of each other!", which is even easier to say than "Join me in giving $250 to a wonderful arts organization."

Make the benefits meaningful to the donor and of minimal cost to the organization.

This kind of program is usually promoted through a mass-mail effort, but it can implemented more effectively through personalized letters, phone calls, and, at the higher levels, personal visits from volunteers.

Friends/membership programs take a lot of work. You have to write and send the newsletters, host the receptions, and provide the special tickets, dinners, and parking if you offer them. Start them out as volunteer-run programs. As they grow, hire staff, at least on a part-time basis, to provide the services you offer. The prompt, complete provision of these services and making people feel special is the best cultivation (fundraising) you can do.

TAX-DEDUCTIBILITY OF CONTRIBUTIONS

The IRS requires not-for-profit organizations to make clear, at the time contributions are solicited, exactly how much the donor can take as a tax deduction. The federal law is summarized in *IRS Publication 1771, Charitable Contributions—Substantiation and Disclosure Requirements*, which is available online at www.irs.gov. The law requires organizations that receive tax-deductible charitable contributions to:

> **Provide written acknowledgment to donors for any single contribution of $250 or more so the donor can claim a tax deduction.** Cancelled checks are no longer acceptable. Such acknowledgements must express the amount of a cash contribution and a description (but not the value) of a noncash contribution.

Example Benefit Structure

GIFT	CATEGORY	BENEFITS
$50	Donor	Member card + monthly newsletter + advance notice of events + volunteer opportunities
$100	Patron	All the above + recognition in the annual report + quarterly preview seminars and receptions
$250	Sponsor	All the above + advance ticket purchase capability + priority access to special trips + private receptions with artists
$500	Sustainer	All the above + access to house seats + private tours of exhibits with curators + recognition in monthly newsletters
$1000	Producer	All the above + special reserved parking privileges + annual dinner with the board
$1000+	Benefactor	All the above + use of the Green Room for a private party + curbside parking at all events

The valuation of such donated noncash property is still the responsibility of the donor. Note: Even though the law only requires a written acknowledgement if a gift is $250 or more, consider doing it for all gifts. Donors will appreciate having the receipt, and you can take advantage of the opportunity to communicate, say thank you, and let donors know how much you value their support!

Provide written disclosure to donors with a description and good faith estimate of the value of goods or services received *in exchange* for a single contribution in excess of $75. Written acknowledgments would state: "In exchange for your contribution, we gave you [description] with an estimated fair market value of [$__]" or "No goods or services were provided in exchange for your contribution."

The IRS allows full deductibility of a contribution and no written disclosure when:

- the goods or services given to a donor are considered insubstantial and meet either the "token exception" or "membership benefits exception" (see *IRS Publication 1771* for the current dollar amounts considered to be insubstantial); or
- there is no donative element involved in a particular transaction, such as a typical museum gift shop sale.

The benefits described on the previous page would be considered insubstantial. The written acknowledgement would state: "No goods or services were provided in exchange for your contribution."

If you have questions after reading *IRS Publication 1771*, seek advice from your organization's accountant or lawyer.

METHODS OF INDIVIDUAL GIVING

Individuals may choose from a number of methods for making contributions. Larger gifts may require longer payment periods or more sophisticated methods of payment.

Gifts that Would Benefit the Organization Now

Cash gifts. These can be in the form of checks made payable to your organization or pledges paid over a period of time. The pledge form should state who the donor is, how much they are giving, and the date(s) when they will make the gift.

Matching gifts. Your donors or their spouses may work for or serve on the board of a company which will match their gift. Have your donor contact their company's matching gifts officer, if appropriate.

Gifts of appreciated securities. Larger gifts are frequently paid with long-term capital gains securities, which can provide donors with a more attractive income tax benefit. If your organization has the potential to attract gifts of securities, develop a relationship with a stock broker who will offer free or reduced-price services in facilitating the transfer and sale of the securities.

Gifts of tangible personal property. Gifts that are useful to your organization, including real estate, can provide donors with an immediate tax deduction and, if qualified as a long-term capital assets (held for a year and a day), offer avoidance of capital gains tax, removal of the assets from the donor's estate, and, if appropriate, elimination of maintenance costs of the property. Valuation for income tax purposes can require an independent appraisal. The deduction is limited to 30 percent of adjusted gross income. Excess beyond 30 percent can be carried forward for five additional years.

Charitable lead trusts. This planned giving method can enable a donor to reduce gift and estate taxes, leave property to heirs, *and* make a contribution to your organization. The donor contributes assets to a trust and sets an amount or fixed percentage that is paid to your organization for a specific period of time. At the end of the time period, the trust is dissolved and the property returned to the donor or the donor's designated beneficiaries, thereby removing the assets from the donor's estate. This and other planned giving transactions can be complex and offer the opportunity to involve professional advisors as volunteers with your organization.

Gifts of life insurance proceeds. A donor might decide to liquidate a life insurance policy no longer needed for family protection and give the proceeds to your organization. This would give the donor an immediate tax deduction (for the value of the gift) and would reduce the donor's estate and inheritance taxes by removing the asset from the donor's net worth.

Gifts that Would Benefit the Organization in the Future

Bequests/giving through a donor's will. A donor may make a bequest to your organization by preparing a new will or adding a codicil amending an existing one. A bequest is not subject to federal or state estate or inheritance taxes and is, in fact, deductible in calculating the taxable estate. There is no limit to the amount of that deduction. The following language is appropriate for making an unrestricted bequest: "I give ["the sum of ____ dollars" or "all or _____percent of the residuary of my estate"] to [organization] for its general corporate purposes."

Charitable remainder trusts. These enable a donor to contribute to the future of your organization, retain lifetime annual payments, and generate significant tax benefits. The donor makes an irrevocable gift of cash or marketable securities and sets an amount or fixed percentage that is then paid to him or her, providing life income for the donor (and a survivor). For an *annuity trust*, the amount is set when the trust is created, either as a fixed percentage or a set dollar amount of the then fair market value of the trust assets. For a *unitrust*, the amount is a fixed percentage of the fair market value of the trust assets as determined annually.

Charitable gift annuity. A donor can make an irrevocable gift of cash or marketable securities for which your organization contractually guarantees to pay a specified annuity to the donor and/or another beneficiary for life. The donor receives a charitable deduction and other tax benefits (which depend on the type of gift) and, in return, secures a stream of income for life, often at the rate of return recommended by the American Council on Gift Annuities when the charitable gift annuity is set up. If the donor didn't need income now but wanted to secure income sources for retirement, a *deferred gift annuity* would allow for a gift and charitable deduction now with higher income payouts due to deferring the payments for a period of years.

Gifts of life insurance. A donor can name your organization as a beneficiary of all or part of the proceeds from a life insurance policy. Or the donor can give a paid-up policy, a new policy, or a policy on which you are still paying—naming the organization as sole owner and beneficiary—and take a deduction for the "present value" of the policy (approximately the cash surrender value or the cost basis, whichever is less). In these instances, the donor diminishes his or her estate and inheritance taxes by distributing part of his or her net worth during his or her lifetime. If the donor continues to pay the premiums to maintain the life insurance policy, he or she will also be able to deduct the premium payments as charitable contributions. A donor can also use life insurance as a replacement asset.

Gifts of real estate, reserving the right of occupancy as long as donor and spouse live. A gift of a remainder interest in a personal residence can entitle a donor to an income tax deduction of the asset's fair market value, an avoidance of capital gains tax, and the removal of the asset from his or her estate. To qualify, a donor must make the gift now rather than in a will. Through a "reserved life estate contract," a donor can reserve the right to occupy the property during his or her (and a survivor's) lifetime, while making an immediate and irrevocable transfer of title to the organization. Any real estate transaction is complex and should be reviewed with both the organization and a donor's financial advisors.

This outline is prepared as a guide to planning. Donors should be encouraged to consult their own legal, accounting, and other professional advisors as they consider the best possible ways to benefit their individual tax situation.

SPECIAL EVENT FUNDRAISING

Special events can help your organization raise money creatively while attracting new members, developing new leadership, and providing opportunities for publicity. Special event fundraising can also be the fastest way to bankrupt your organization. Numerous arts organizations boldly decide to host a special event, spend lots of money on it, and then wake up to realize they did not focus enough energy on developing strategies for selling tickets.

Pros and Cons to Special Event Fundraising

Pros
They are fun.
They cultivate prospects.
They attract new friends.
They get volunteers involved.
They raise money.

Cons
They are hard work.
They take staff time.
They take volunteer time.
They cost money.
They can lose money.

Below are key points to consider with special events.

Plan ahead. (Select your chairperson up to 14 months in advance, enabling him or her to help on the preceding year's event and to start planning early for a successful event.)

Start small.

Set the fundraising goal early and stick to it. Do not compromise later on.

Evaluate the risk (expenses, break-even point, number of sales needed at what ticket price to reach your financial goal, potential for loss or net profit).

Seek as many donations as possible of space, labor, food, beverages, entertainment, auctioned items, favors/gifts, and printing.

Maximize volunteer involvement.

Recognize and thank everyone involved.

Keep the mailing list updated.

Special events have a life cycle of about seven years. Do not try to do something new every year. Build on the experience of past years until the event starts losing energy or no longer attracts the volunteer support it needs to succeed.

Always remember that the purpose of a fundraising special event is to raise money. Set the fundraising goal and do not compromise. If the volunteers want to fancy things up a bit, let them pay for it or seek donations. Do not spend any money you do not have to. Some examples of special events are silent auctions, dinner and dance events, walk-a-thons, private film screenings, and meet-the-artist receptions. Be creative and try to link the event to your organization's mission (i.e., if you are a music organization, build your event around music). Give yourselves plenty of advance time.

RAISING MONEY FROM LOCAL AND NATIONAL CORPORATIONS

Cultivation and solicitation of *locally-owned* businesses is similar in approach to raising money from individuals. You focus on the owners/decision-makers and do the same kind of homework, cultivation, record keeping, planning, and follow-through. Help them feel more like family and less like strangers.

The approach for *national corporations* with manufacturing plants or branches in your area will be different because the motivations for giving will be different. Often, plant/branch managers are from out-of-town and are emotionally uninvolved with the local community. They may look at your request and ask themselves, Does this make me look good in the community or the home office? Does it put me at risk? Does it meet our guidelines? Local managers have a limited contributions budget over which they have discretion. Normally, they can award grants of $1,500 to $2,500. Larger grants usually have to go to the home office but need the blessing of the local facility to have any chance of success.

As you approach businesses for gifts, be aware that there are a number of ways in which businesses can support your efforts. There are four primary types of support.

Philanthropic gifts. Tax-deductible as charitable deductions, these come out of the contributions budget or a separate corporation foundation. Corporations and foundations often have specific policies and guidelines for grant applications. Decision-making may take one to six months.

Corporate giving comes more easily when you first involve one or more executives in your work: they can help to position your request.

Sponsorships and ads. These are often (but not always) considered marketing expenses and can come out of budgets other than for contributions. They are typically sought through the marketing, community, or public relations department. An ad sale might take a month; however, sponsorship solicitations and negotiations can take considerably longer. Allow a minimum of three months, six or more for larger corporations.

Employee matching gifts. Some corporations offer programs to match the gifts their employees make to nonprofits like yours. Others have a matching gift program restricted to gifts to higher education. Such funds come out of the contributions budget.

In-kind contributions. These are gifts of goods and services—paper, printing, newsletter mailings, office furniture and equipment, graphic design work, computer help, accounting services, space, office supplies, loaned secretarial services, loaned executives, food, lumber, hotel rooms, or rental cars for visiting artists. The expenses associated with such gifts are tax-deductible as part of the normal course of doing business, and this is often the easiest type of corporate support to attract. Often a frontline manager can make such a decision without getting elaborate upper management approval.

In-kind gifts can lead to future cash gifts.

You will get more from a company if you first involve some of their key executives in your organization. They can guide you through the process of asking for various kinds of gifts from different departments within the company. We recommend the following strategy when asking national corporations for support.

Do research.

Prioritize and select the most likely prospects.

Try to identify contacts of board and staff at the corporations.

Cultivate the individuals identified on the local level.

Ask for help positioning the gift request at national headquarters.

Ask for the gift (make a formal proposal).

Receive and acknowledge the gift.

Maintain contact.

Ask for help positioning the next gift.

RAISING MONEY FROM FOUNDATIONS

Focus your efforts on raising money from *local* foundations which you know already have an interest in your community. You will raise more money per hour of time invested with local foundations than you will with national foundations.

Approach *small family foundations without professional staff* in the same manner as you would an individual. In these cases, the foundation is usually just a mechanism for giving which has certain personal tax advantages.

The staff of foundations can often direct you to other potential donors if you ask.

For *established foundations with professional staff*, a more formal approach is required.

Do research through such places as:

- The Foundation Center, a nonprofit that provides extensive information on foundations, including which ones give to the arts and which ones give to the arts in your state. Its website and publications are excellent. Publications are found at most public libraries. It also has research centers across the country. www.fdncenter.org
- *The Chronicle of Philanthropy*. Published biweekly. www.philanthropy.com
- Websites of larger foundations and places such as GrantsStation. www.grantstation.com
- Colleagues with similar situations.

Develop a list of appropriate foundations, including those which fund organizations in your region/community, the type of work you are doing (arts, education, beautification, urban renewal, senior citizen projects), and the type of fundraising you are doing (annual operating support, project support, endowment campaigns, capital improvements, renovations).

Review the list and develop cultivation strategies. Meet with key volunteers to review the information gathered. Find out whether your volunteers know individuals on the staff or boards of the foundations. If no one knows anyone at the foundation, search within your organization's family of supporters for someone who does. Never ask a stranger for money! Once you make a personal contact, develop a cultivation strategy for each foundation to educate the foundation about your arts organization and how you serve the community. You will also need to learn about the foundation, what they fund, their guidelines, timelines, funding preferences, and criteria for funding decisions.

Review a draft proposal with the foundation. Based on this research, respond accordingly to the foundation's guidelines. Some will welcome an initial phone call. Others will require or encourage a letter of inquiry summarizing your request in order to determine whether a full proposal should be invited. Others may be willing to critique a draft proposal. In this case, you can ask how to strengthen or revise the request to best meet the foundation's needs. Then finalize the proposal and submit it to the foundation for review. If you take this step, build in at least six to eight weeks before any deadline to give the foundation time to review and to give you time to revise.

See the subsequent chapter, Essentials of Proposal Writing, reprinted with permission from The Grantsmanship Center, for information on how to develop a funding proposal.

Write a thank-you letter. Once the foundation makes a decision, say thank you in writing, even if the response is negative. Once you know the foundation representative, you can ask why your application was rejected. The answer may be simply that there were more good requests than could be funded. Reapply if you get any encouragement from the foundation.

Maintain contact. Maintain contact with foundation representatives. Make certain they get your newsletter, invitations to openings, etc. Keep them up-to-date on how your arts organization is serving the community.

RAISING MONEY FROM GOVERNMENTS

Raising money from government agencies or other public funding sources is also a process of identifying the right people, cultivating them, and having them help you get funding. Each level of government requires a different approach.

Local Government Funding

Local government fundraising equals politics and the art of persuasion through lobbying.

City and county governments can be your best prospective funders if you organize those who believe in your work to help you lobby for government funds. Identify who has the power and makes the decisions on how local public funds are spent. Develop a cultivation strategy for each decision-maker. Make them understand how your organization serves the community and that you have a powerful constituency that supports your organization's work. Because many good organizations ask for money, make certain you are capable of making the politicians look good.

Local government funding can be delivered through:

- line item direct funding;
- local government departments such as libraries, school systems, and parks and recreation departments;
- community development funds;
- dedicated or special taxes such as ticket taxes, cable franchise fees, entertainment taxes, hotel/motel taxes, special tax districts, and voluntary tax check-offs;
- general county funds; and
- local access to federal community development funds (community development block grants), historic preservation, social service, and more. (Talk with municipal staff in various departments to see what sources you might tap through them.)

State Government Funding

State funding for the arts comes primarily through your state arts agency. Call your state arts agency and ask for guidelines and assistance to understand how and to what you should apply. The staff members are there to help you, and you will enjoy getting to know them. Typical state arts agency funding programs for arts organizations might include:

- project support;
- general operating support;
- artists-in-schools or in residence;

- technical assistance funds; and
- touring performance/exhibition funds.

In most states, peer panels recommend which grants should be funded. While it is ultimately the quality of your proposed project or use of funds that will reap a positive funding decision, it helps if peers in other arts organizations in the state know you, your organization, and the good work you are accomplishing.

Other avenues of state funding can include:

- line item direct funding;
- state government departments such as education, tourism, economic development, human services, humanities council, community development, rural development, rural health, and historic preservation;
- going through states to access federal funds; and
- state income tax check-offs.

See the Cultural Advocacy chapter to learn about advocacy principles and practices that can help secure local or state public funds.

Government Sources

U.S. Dept. of Agriculture
U.S. Dept. of Commerce
U.S. Dept. of Defense
U.S. Dept. of Education
U.S. Dept. of Energy
U.S. Dept. of Health and Human Services
U.S. Dept. of Housing and Urban Development
U.S. Dept. of Interior
U.S. Dept. of Justice
U.S. Dept. of Labor
U.S. Dept. of State
U.S. Dept. of Transportation
Advisory Council on Historic Preservation
Appalachian Regional Commission
Corporation for National and Community Service
Environmental Protection Agency
Federal Emergency Management Agency
General Services Administration
Institute of Museum and Library Services
National Endowment for the Humanities
National Science Foundation
Save America's Treasures
Small Business Administration

Federal Government Funding

The NEA is the most visible source of federal arts funding.

Local arts agencies can access some federal sources (some NEA funds are set aside for this purpose) through their state arts agencies or statewide assemblies of local arts agencies.

The NEA stresses quality, excellence, and professionalism in its funding considerations. You should have unique, special, or strong programs before you consider spending your limited fundraising time approaching the NEA. The NEA funds only specific, definable activities by professionally-staffed organizations. To learn about the NEA's current grantmaking areas, visit online at www.nea.gov. Talk to NEA staff before you apply.

As with state funding, NEA funding recommendations are made by peer review panels, so it can be helpful to be known nationally by your peers in the field. The best way to do this is by participating actively in national and regional conferences.

Other federal government sources. Listed in the sidebar are some of the other federal departments and agencies that offer arts funding opportunities. Collaborations and partnerships with other organizations—often local government agencies—are essential for access to most of these federal grants.

Expand Your Options through Partnerships

Requests for funding are often strengthened by collaborating with other organizations.

Don't just consider arts sources. Be alert to opportunities in your own community to create innovative collaborations which can expand your resources, programming, and audiences. Local arts agencies around the country have partnered with such groups as school systems, universities/community colleges (good sources of interns, too), civic organizations and clubs, restaurants, radio/television stations, cable television systems, other businesses, chambers of commerce, schools of business, libraries, churches, festivals, rescue squads, volunteer fire departments, home extension service programs, outdoor recreation facilities and parks, tourist development authorities, planning departments, historic preservation agencies, community centers, transportation agencies, prisons, economic development organizations, elder care facilities, the United Way, health and social services agencies, and human services.

HOW TO WRITE A PROPOSAL

Your state arts agency, the NEA, and some foundations and corporations have their own forms to fill out or guidelines to follow when you apply for funds. Follow the guidelines carefully. You do not want to give them an excuse not to fund you.

If you are writing a grant request to a foundation or other source without particular guidelines, keep your request short (two or three pages plus appendices).

For a more detailed explanation of how to develop an effective proposal, see the next chapter, Essentials of Proposal Development, reprinted by permission from The Grantsmanship Center.

BUILD ONGOING RELATIONSHIPS

Maintain the relationship so that donors are never strangers again.

Once you have received a gift or a grant, you have the opportunity to create an ongoing relationship with the donor, which can produce major amounts of money in the years to come. Fundraising is built on trust and the development of ongoing personal relationships. Always be open and honest with your donors. Keep them informed about your successes, problems, and planning. Avoid surprises. Work to make certain they understand what is happening within your organization, and, if possible, involve them in ways they can feel helpful and supportive. Help your donors realize that a gift to your organization will enrich their lives.

ENDNOTES

1. Draper, L. (2005, January/February). Philanthropy in Action. Where the Money is: Topping Overlooked Sources of Support for Nonprofits [Electronic version]. *Foundation News & Commentary*, 46, 1.
2. Cohen, T. (2005, May 1). Each 501(c)(3) is Now. *The Nonprofit Times.*
3. Draper, L.

APPENDIX

Figure 1a: Annual Operating Projections for the Capital County Arts Center

Figure 1a: Annual Operating Projections for the Capital County Arts Center

Summary of Historical and Projected Cash Flows—Confidential/for Planning Purposes

Fiscal year ending June 30:	**Year 1** Actual	**Year 2** Actual	**Year 3** Budgeted	**Year 4** Projected	**Year 5** Projected	**Year 6** Projected	**Year 7** Projected	**Year 8** Projected
CASH DISBURSEMENTS:								
PROGRAM & OPERATING COSTS ***(cost of the art)***								
Programming	417,411	439,380	457,135	479,992	503,991	529,191	555,650	583,433
Facilities	287,727	302,870	318,014	333,914	350,610	368,140	386,547	405,875
Administration	209,500	220,526	206,119	216,425	227,246	238,609	250,539	263,066
Other operating costs	93,015	97,910	96,658	101,491	106,565	111,894	117,488	123,363
TOTAL CASH DISBURSEMENT	**1,007,653**	**1,060,686**	**1,077,926**	**1,131,822**	**1,188,413**	**1,247,834**	**1,310,225**	**1,375,736**
CASH RECEIVED:								
EARNED INCOME:								
Programming income	378,225	398,132	418,039	438,941	460,888	483,932	508,129	533,535
Facilities income	94,430	99,400	104,370	109,589	115,068	120,821	126,862	133,206
Operating interest	12,845	13,500	14,175	14,276	15,390	16,159	17,245	18,007
Endowment income	58,880	62,000	65,100	68,000	71,000	74,550	78,000	82,000
Total Earned Income	**544,380**	**573,032**	**601,684**	**630,805**	**662,345**	**695,462**	**730,236**	**766,747**
CONTRIBUTED INCOME:								
Board members	31,825	33,416	36,980	38,829	40,770	42,809	44,949	47,197
Other individual members	103,844	109,036	106,529	111,855	117,448	123,321	129,487	135,961
Corporate members	51,300	53,865	40,000	42,000	44,100	46,305	48,620	51,051
Corporate sponsorships	36,720	38,506	37,600	39,480	41,454	43,527	45,703	47,988
Foundation grants	85,500	90,775	90,000	94,500	99,225	104,186	109,396	114,865
State grants	21,085	22,139	25,000	26,250	27,563	28,941	30,388	31,907
County grants	57,000	59,850	60,000	63,000	66,150	69,458	72,930	76,577
City grants	4,750	4,988	5,000	5,250	5,513	5,788	6,078	6,381
Income from fundraising events	72,248	75,860	76,050	79,853	83,845	88,037	92,439	97,061
To Support Operating Needs	**464,272**	**488,436**	**477,159**	**501,017**	**526,068**	**552,371**	**579,990**	**608,989**
TOTAL CASH RECEIVED	**1,008,652**	**1,061,468**	**1,078,843**	**1,131,822**	**1,188,413**	**1,247,833**	**1,310,226**	**1,375,737**
Net Cash	999	782	917	0	0	0	0	0
							8 2002 The North Group	

Figure 1b: Capital and Endowment Campaign for the Well-Established Arts Center

Figure 1b: Capital and Endowment Campaign for the Well-Established Arts Center
Summary of Historical and Projected Cash Flows—Confidential/for Planning Purposes

	Actual	Actual	Budgeted	Budgeted	Construction				Campaign
Fiscal year ending June 30:	**Year 1**	**Year 2**	**Year 3**	**Year 4**	**Year 5**	**Year 6**	**Year 7**	**Year 8**	**TOTALS**
CASH DISBURSEMENTS:									
PROGRAM+OPERATING COSTS: ***(cost of the art)***									
Production	1,617,367	1,606,136	1,581,723	1,746,372	1,798,763	1,852,726	1,908,308	1,965,557	
Administration	196,110	211,668	184,032	215,976	222,455	229,129	236,003	243,083	
Other operating costs	209,772	213,872	166,781	216,417	222,910	229,597	236,485	243,579	
Total Program+Operating Cos	**2,023,249**	**2,031,676**	**1,932,536**	**2,178,765**	**2,244,128**	**2,311,452**	**2,380,795**	**2,452,219**	
CAPITAL NEEDS:									
Construction costs+equipment purchases					548,320	596,230	935,142	693,230	2,772,922
Architect+theatre consultant						166,375	166,376		332,751
Development+marketing			28,179	159,342	57,300	25,000			269,821
Financing costs					15,274	98,821	60,582	17,736	192,413
Endowment					775,000	975,000	1,000,000	1,250,000	4,000,000
Total Capital Needs	**0**	**0**	**28,179**	**159,342**	**1,395,894**	**1,861,426**	**2,162,100**	**1,960,966**	$7,567,907
Campaign Loan Retirement						347,000	600,000	275,907	1,222,907
TOTAL CASH DISBURSEMENT	**2,023,249**	**2,031,676**	**1,960,715**	**2,338,107**	**3,640,022**	**4,519,878**	**5,142,895**	**4,689,092**	
CASH RECEIVED:									
EARNED INCOME:									
Ticket sales	1,123,467	1,028,915	1,057,710	1,353,280	1,393,878	1,435,695	1,478,766	1,523,129	
Concessions	20,858	21,131	20,000	20,000	20,600	21,218	21,855	22,510	
Advertising	69,017	71,309	60,000	65,000	66,950	68,959	71,027	73,158	
Rentals+Miscellaneous	172,067	203,489	139,280	153,880	158,496	163,251	168,149	173,193	
Foundation distribution		43,144	74,000	41,000					
Total Earned Income	**1,385,409**	**1,367,988**	**1,350,990**	**1,633,160**	**1,639,925**	**1,689,123**	**1,739,796**	**1,791,990**	
CONTRIBUTED INCOME:				***Campaign need: $7,567,907***					
To support operating needs	560,807	585,638	507,500	497,500	512,425	527,798	543,632	559,941	
To support program needs	77,659	80,400	85,000	95,000	97,850	100,786	103,809	106,923	
Proposed Capital Campaign			25,000	125,000	977,300	1,401,375	2,800,000	2,239,232	$7,567,907
Total Contributed Income	**638,466**	**666,038**	**617,500**	**717,500**	**1,587,575**	**2,029,958**	**3,447,441**	**2,906,096**	
Campaign Loan proceeds					414,291	808,616			1,222,907
TOTAL CASH RECEIVED	**2,023,875**	**2,034,026**	**1,968,490**	**2,350,660**	**3,641,791**	**4,527,697**	**5,187,237**	**4,698,086**	
Cash in Excess of Disbursements	626	2,350	7,775	12,553	1,769	7,819	44,342	8,994	

Figures 2: Evaluating Internal Resources

Figure 2: Evaluating Internal Resources

Organization: ______________________ Completed by: ______________________ Date: __________

Fundraising Options to Consider (in priority order)	Do we know how?	Do we have needed staff time?	Do we have needed volunteer time?	Do we have needed space/ equipment?	Do we have needed prospects?	How much can we raise?	How much will it cost?	Should we do it?
1. Board/key volunteer gifts								
2. Individual gifts								
a. Personal solicitation of major gifts								
b. Membership campaign								
1) Personal solicitations								
2) Personalized letters								
3) Telephone follow-up								
4) Mass mail campaigns								
3. Fundraisers/benefits/special events								
4. Personal solicitations								
a. Local businesses								
b. Local foundations								
5. Cultivation and grantwriting								
a. Local governments								
b. State government								
c. Federal government								
6. Cultivation and proposal writing								
a. National corporations								
b. National foundations								
Other								

Figure 3: Fundraising Work Plan Example

CAPITAL CITY PERFORMING ARTS CENTER FIVE-YEAR PLAN

GOAL: To increase annual contributed income by 250 percent from $77,100 to $1,927,500

1. Board Solicitation

Plan and rationale. Our 18 board members have been pushed hard to give to their maximum over the last five years. They have given to the annual fund drive and capital campaign. There is little room for improved giving. Each board member is required to give to the best of his/her ability.

Strategy. Continue to have the board chair solicit the executive committee members and to have the executive committee members solicit other board members. All solicitations will be made in person.

Time commitment.

Chief executive	five hours to help with "prospect research"
Development director	ten hours
Board chair	six hours
Executive Committee members	four hours each

Timetable. Board solicitation is to be completed within the month of September.

Direct cost. Minimal

Projected Income.	Year 1	Year 2	Year 3	Year 4	Year 5
	$37,100	$40,000	$47,000	$58,000	$65,000

2. Individual Gifts Solicitation

Plan. Start small, build a strong base, and give our board and staff experience in raising money from individuals. By Year 5, achieve 400 high-level members, assuming we keep cultivating current members as we add more.

Enhance membership benefits. New seven to eight member Individual Gifts Committee improves special privileges/benefits provided for those at $50 to $1,000 levels of membership.

Personal solicitation. Given new benefits, board members submit information on 15 individuals/couples capable of memberships at $100+ a year. Staff compiles list and eliminates duplicates. Committee discusses list, prioritizes top 80 most-likely prospects, and determines who is best to cultivate/solicit each one. Those "best" personally invite prospects to attend a special show and private reception. That night, solicit prospects to become members at $100 to $1,000 a year. Repeat each year with new prospects.

Mail campaign. Committee arranges for those next on the list to receive letters with hand-written notes from people they know, inviting them to become high-level members ("Please join me as a Patron-level member"). Committee organizes phone follow up by "best" person for mail prospects who did not respond. Start calls with "thank you" for past support and/or participation. The calls should be made within a month after mailing.

Time commitment.

Development director	30 days of coordinating, motivating, following up, record keeping, and list/letter preparation
Individual gifts	two meetings +
Committee members	five performances with guests + two evenings each for phoning
Other board members	two performances each with guests + two evenings each for phoning

Direct cost. Supplies and mailings, $3,800; receptions, $1,850; and 160 complimentary tickets

Projected income.	Year 1	Year 2	Year 3	Year 4	Year 5
Personal solicitation	$14,000	$25,000	$35,000	$48,000	$55,000
Mail + Follow-up	$6,000	$9,750	$13,500	$18,500	$20,000

3. Special Fundraising Event

Plan and rationale: Establish a gala cocktail party, sit-down dinner, and show as a special event to kick off the season. Involve up to 150 people and get donations in a way that is not extra work for our technical crew. We have already recruited to the board the head of food service at the Capital Hotel and his wife, former president of Junior League, specifically to establish this event as an important community occasion. They will recruit the Gala Team from prominent couples on the subscription list.

Strategy. Secure a headline artist. Charge for dinner and tickets. Gala patrons can secure best seats in the house through the development director. Use this opportunity to get current and potential donors into the theater who don't have the time to come on a regular basis. Make the evening very special.

Time commitment.

Development director	Several days for Gala Team back-up, invitations, ticket-related phone calls, ticket and dinner arrangements, and helping with marketing and publicity
Co-chairs and Gala Team members	One meeting + time to address envelopes and write personal notes to tuck in invitations + gala evening

Timetable. Secure commitment of Capital Hotel, headline artist, and co-chairs up to 13 months ahead.

Direct cost. Pay Capital Hotel for set-up, flowers, food, clean-up, etc.—an agreed upon $5,000 (rest of their cost is a contribution).

Projected net income.	Year 1	Year 2	Year 3	Year 4	Year 5
	$20,000	$30,000	$35,000	$40,000	$52,750

Figure 4: Prospect Research Chart

Figure 4: Prospect Research Chart **(intelligence gathering and cultivation!)**

Organization: ______________________ Completed by: ______________________ Date: __________

Prospect	Giving history	Capable of gift of	Likely gift	Best solicitor	Comments
1. Names					
Address					
Phone					
Email					
2. Names					
Address					
Phone					
Email					
3. Names					
Address					
Phone					
Email					
4. Names					
Address					
Phone					
Email					
5. Names					
Address					
Phone					
Email					

(complete 1st 2 columns ahead of time)

Figure 5: Steps for Making a Fundraising Call on an Individual

Ask in a face-to-face meeting.
Solicit gifts in a thoughtful manner, not casually.

Cultivate the prospect, and ask face-to-face if you are asking for a lot of money.

Be prepared and brief.
Know as much about the prospect as possible.

Be clear about the amount or range of money you are requesting.

Have a personalized letter with you which asks for a specific amount or range (and includes the pledge form).

Include attachments explaining the fund drive/organization which the prospect can review later.

Be confident, positive, and passionate.
You are not begging; you are sharing an opportunity to enhance your organization and to satisfy the prospect's need.

Focus on the prospect's needs.
Successful fundraising speaks as much to the needs of the donor as it does to the needs of the arts organization.

Ask up front for a specific amount or range of money.
Mention a need or goal of the prospect which the gift will satisfy (based on your research). Lead with the strongest opportunity. (Mentioning more than one may give the prospect a chance to shoot down your request.)

Don't fill the silence after you make the request.
Give the prospect a chance to respond.

Then continue based on the response.

Involve the potential donor in the development of the idea/proposal so the donor is emotionally involved in its success.

Remember that everyone wants to be a worthwhile member of a worthwhile organization.

Mention that the amount requested may be high or low.
It is only a suggestion.

Only the prospect knows the appropriate gift level.

Follow up with a thank-you letter.
Follow up even if the prospect turns you down.

In fact, thank donors every time you can.

Saying thank you gives you the right to ask again.

"Involve" the donor and follow through to make the contribution an annual gift.

CHAPTER 7

Essentials of Proposal Writing

7

NORTON J. KIRITZ

The grant proposal package to a *foundation* or *corporate* funder will usually contain these three elements:

1. **Cover letter.** Signed by the chairperson of the board of a nonprofit agency or the top authority in a governmental agency, the cover letter describes the program and tells the grantmaker how important the grant would be to the community served by the applicant agency. The cover letter demonstrates the board's strong support of the proposed program, which is essential in gaining foundation grants.
2. **Grant proposal.** The body of the proposal may be as modest as one page (in the case of a foundation that limits requests to a page) or it may be quite voluminous. It may be in letter form or it may be more formally presented. The format described in the following article will help to assure that necessary items are included and that they are presented in a logical manner. It can serve as your proposal format where the funding source has not provided one—as is often the case with foundation proposals. *But it should not be substituted for any format required by a foundation.* If the funder asks you to follow a set format, do it!
3. **Additional materials.** These should be limited to the items required or requested by the funding source, supplemented by only the most important addenda. Reviewers don't grade proposals by the pound, so save your postage.

The proposal package to a *government* funding source will usually contain these three elements:

1. **Letter of transmittal.** A brief statement (two to three paragraphs) signed by the highest level person within your organization. It summarizes the request and the amount asked for, and it may indicate the significance and importance of the proposed project. It should indicate the support of your board of directors. It should also convey the approval of the request as reflected in the signature of the board chairperson (possibly along with that of the executive director/chief executive officer).
2. **Grant proposal.** A proposal going to a government funder is usually much lengthier than one going to a private foundation. The funder's guidelines will contain the sequence to be followed in writing the narrative portion. Quite often, government agency guidelines will also describe exactly how each section of your proposal will be weighed. This tells you what the reviewers look for and it helps you to organize your thoughts. Follow the guidelines meticulously, because the reviewers will. Proposals are often disqualified simply because the applicant failed to follow specific instructions. Proposals for government grants may also contain unique forms, such as face-sheet forms where the entire

project, names of key staff, budget, numbers of people impacted by the project, etc., are indicated, along with various assurance and compliance forms pertaining to issues such as handicapped accessibility and civil rights. It is important to understand which items must be submitted with your proposal and how they are to be completed, so read the instructions carefully.

3. **Additional materials.** These might include job descriptions, résumés, letters of support or commitment, your IRS tax exemption designation, an annual report, financial statement, or similar documents required or requested by the funder. This section (or Appendix) can be extensive when a funding source requests a great deal of information. There are instances in which the funding source will request copies of certain agency policies and procedures, copies of negotiated indirect-cost rates, etc. Generally, this will happen only once, and for refunding packages to the same public agency, you will probably not need to resubmit the same documents.

We suggest the following basic format for planning all of your proposals. Thinking through the various sections should enable you to produce everything that either a private or government funding source will ask of you. It will also enable you to develop a logical approach to planning a program and writing the proposal for getting that program funded.

Proposal Summary

Introduction

Problem Statement

Program Goals and Objectives

Methods

Evaluation

Future Funding

Budget

Appendix

The Summary is a critical element of any proposal—not just something to be written as an afterthought.

PROPOSAL SUMMARY

The Summary is a critical element of any proposal—not just something to be written as an afterthought. There may be a box for a Summary on the first page of a federal grant application form. (It may also be called a "Proposal Abstract.") In writing to a foundation, the Summary should be the first paragraph of a letter-type proposal, or the first section of a more formal proposal. The Summary should succinctly describe who you are, the scope of your project, and the cost.

The Summary is probably the first thing that a funding source will read. In fact, it may be the only thing that some people in the review process will read—so make it clear, concise, and specific.

INTRODUCTION

In this part of the proposal you introduce your organization as an applicant for funds.

More often than not, proposals are funded on the basis of an applicant's reputation. The Introduction is where you build your credibility and make the case that your organization deserves to be supported.

What gives an organization credibility in the eyes of a funding source? That may depend on the nature of the funding source. A traditional, conservative foundation might be more impressed by persons of prominence on your board of directors, how long it has been in existence, or how many other funding sources have been supporting it. A progressive funding source might be more interested in a board comprised of community representatives rather than corporate bigwigs, or in organizations that are new and promising rather than old and established.

Potential funding sources should be targeted because of their possible interest in your type of organization as well as their interest in the kind of program you are proposing. You can use your proposal's Introduction to reinforce the connection you perceive between your interests and those of the funding source.

Here are some of the things you can talk about in your Introduction:

- how you got started—your purpose and goals;
- how long you have been around, how you've grown, and the breadth of your financial support;
- unique aspects of your agency—the fact that it was the first organization of its kind in the nation, etc.;
- some of your most significant accomplishments as an organization or, if you are a new organization, some of the significant accomplishments of your board members or staff in their previous roles;
- your success with related projects; and
- the support you have received from other organizations and individuals (accompanied by a few letters of endorsement which can be attached in the Appendix).

Remember, in terms of getting funded, the credibility you establish in your Introduction may be more important than anything else. But here, as in all other parts of your proposal, be as brief and specific as you can be. Avoid jargon and keep it simple.

PROBLEM STATEMENT OR ASSESSMENT OF NEED

From the Introduction, the reader should know your areas of interest—the field in which you are working. Now you will zero in on the specific problem or problems that you want to solve through your proposed program. If the Introduction is the most important part of your proposal in getting funded, the Problem Statement is the most important element in planning a good program.

If the Introduction is the most important part of your proposal in getting funded, the Problem Statement is the most important element in planning a good program.

The Problem Statement or Needs Assessment describes the situation that prompted you to write this proposal. It should refer to situation(s) that are outside of your organization (i.e., situations in the life of your clients or community). It does *not* refer to the internal needs of your organization, unless you are asking someone to fund an activity to improve your own effectiveness. In particular, make sure you don't describe

Many grant applicants fail to understand the difference between problems and methods for solving problems.

your lack of money as the problem. Everyone understands that you are asking for a grant. That's a given. The funder wants to know what external situation will be addressed if you are awarded the grant. That is what you should describe—and document—in the Problem Statement.

A Problem Statement is used to address such issues as homelessness, school dropouts, teen pregancy, and the like. A Needs Statements deals with with less tangible subjects. It is especially useful for programs that are artistic, spiritual, or otherwise value-oriented.

Don't assume that everyone knows the urgency or the dimensions of the problem you are describing. The funding source has no assurance that you will be able to deal with the problem if you fail to demonstrate your understanding of it. Use some appropriate statistics. Augment them with quotes from authorities, especially those in your own community. And make sure that you convey a knowledge of the problem in your area of service, not just on a national level. Charts and graphs will probably turn off the reader. If you use lots of statistics, include the key figures in your Problem Statement and save the rest for an Appendix.

In the Problem Statement you should present the following:

Make a logical connection between your organization's background and the problem or needs you propose to address.

Clearly define the problems or needs you intend to address. Make sure that what you want to do is feasible—that it can be done by your agency within a reasonable time and with a reasonable amount of money.

Demonstrate the existence of the problem or needs by including credible evidence, such as statistics or statements from groups in your community who are knowledgeable about the problem, from prospective clients, from other organizations working in your community, and from professionals in the field.

Be realistic—don't try and solve all the problems in the world in the next six months.

Note: Many grant applicants fail to understand the difference between problems and methods for solving problems (or between needs and methods for satisfying needs). For example, an agency working with the elderly in an urban area said that what the community needed were vans to get the elderly to various agencies. They determined that this "need" existed because not enough seniors were able to get to the local Social Security office or access health services. What the organization had done was to immediately jump to a "method" by which seniors would now be able to receive services. But, of course, there are other methods for accomplishing the same end. For example, what about the possibility of working with institutions to decentralize services? Alternatively, volunteer advocates could work with seniors, acting on their behalf with some of these service providers. Ultimately, buying vans might be the best method, but it is clearly a method and not a problem or a client need. Be very cautious about this. If you find yourself using "lack of" statements in the Problem Statement, you are probably equating the problem with the lack of a method. This starts you on a circular reasoning track that will work havoc with your planning process.

GOALS AND OBJECTIVES

A good proposal flows logically from one section to another. Your Introduction can establish the context for your Problem Statement. Similarly, the Problem Statement will prepare the funding source for your Goals and Objectives. [Editor's note: Please see the Strategic Planning chapter for more information about goals and objectives.]

Goals are broad statements, such as:

> Develop additional resources to provide AIDS information to bilingual populations.
>
> Reduce underemployment rates among adults.
>
> Increase availability of resources to address the problems of adolescent pregnancies.
>
> Create an environment in which folk art is fully appreciated.
>
> Enhance self-images of senior adults.

These types of statements cannot be measured as they are stated. They suggest the general thrust of a program. They are not the same as Objectives.

Objectives are specific, measurable outcomes of your program. Objectives are your promised improvements in the situation you described in the Problem Statement. When you think of Objectives this way, it should be clear what your Objectives should look like. For example, if the problem is that certain children in your school read at least three grade levels below the norm for their age, then an objective would be that a certain number of those children would read significantly better when you have concluded your program. They would read better than their classmates who had also been reading poorly, but who did not have the benefit of your intervention. These *outcome* Objectives should state who is to change, what behaviors are to change, in what direction the changes will occur, how much change will occur, and by what time the change will occur.

If you are having difficulty in defining your Objectives, try projecting your program a year or two into the future. What differences would you hope to see between then and now?

Many, if not most, proposals state that the purpose of the program is to establish a program or provide a service. This results in Objectives that read like this: The objective of this project is to provide counseling and guidance services to delinquent youth between the ages of eight and 14.

The flaw in this sort of Objective is that it says nothing about outcome. It says nothing about the change in a situation that was described in the Problem. Objectives should be specific, estimating the amount of benefit to be expected from a program. If you are having difficulty in defining your Objectives, try projecting your program a year or two into the future. What differences would you hope to see between then and now? What specific changes would have occurred? [Editor's note: Please see the Program Evaluation chapter for more information about outcomes-based measurement.]

Outcome objectives should not be confused with *process* objectives. You may be used to seeing statements like, "The objective of this training program is to offer classes in automotive repair three times each week, for a period of 36 weeks, to a group of 40 unemployed individuals," or "The objective of this program is to provide twice-weekly counseling sessions, for a period of 18 weeks, to no less than 50 parents who have been reported to Child and Protective Services for child abuse."

Those are process objectives, and they belong in the Methods section of your proposal. They tell what you will do. They do not address the outcome or benefit of what you will do. If you do not distinguish between these two kinds of ojectives, you will not be able to gauge the changes attributable to your program. Remember, you are proposing your program in order to make some change in the world, not to add one more service to a world already overcrowded with services and service providers.

METHODS

Now you are ready to describe the Methods you will use to accomplish your Objectives. The Methods component of your proposal should describe, in some detail, the activities that will take place in order to achieve the desired results. The Methods section of the proposal is where the reader should be able to gain a picture in his/her mind of exactly how things work, what your facility looks like, how staff are deployed, how clients are dealt with, what the exhibits look like, how the community center recruits and assigns volunteers, or how a questionnaire is administered and the results interpreted.

There are two basic questions to be answered in the Methods section: (1) What combination of strategy and activities have you selected to bring about the desired results? (2) Why have you selected this particular approach, of all the possible approaches you could have employed?

Justifying your approach requires that you know a good deal about other programs of a similar nature. Who is working on the problem in your community or elsewhere? What Methods have been tried in the past and are being tried now and with what results?

Considering alternatives is an important aspect of describing your methodology. Showing that you are familiar enough with your field to be aware of different program models and showing your reasons for selecting the model you have selected will add greatly to your credibility.

Showing that you are familiar enough with your field to be aware of different program models and showing your reasons for selecting the model you have selected will add greatly to your credibility.

Your Methods section should describe who is doing what to whom, and why it is being done that way. Your approach should appear realistic to the reviewer, and not suggest that so much will be performed by so few that the program will be unworkable. Unrealistic programs do not win points for good intentions.

EVALUATION

Evaluation of your program can serve two purposes. *Outcome* evaluation is used determine how effective the program is in reaching its stated Objectives. *Process* evaluation is used to make appropriate changes or adjustments in your program as it proceeds. [Editor's note: Please see the Program Evaluation chapter for more information about evaluation methods.]

Measurable Objectives set the stage for effective outcome Evaluation. If you have difficulty in determining what criteria to use in evaluating your program, take another look at your Objectives. Chances are they weren't very specific.

Many Evaluation plans are subjective in nature. Subjective Evaluations tell you how people feel about a program, but they seldom deal with the concrete results of a program. For example, the Evaluation of an educational program that surveyed students, parents, teachers, and administrators of the program would be eliciting attitudes about the program. It would not speak to a statistical improvement in performance attributable to the program. Subjectivity also invites your own biases to enter into an Evaluation, especially if you feel that continued funding depends on producing what looks like good results.

One way to get a more objective Evaluation is to have an outside organization conduct the Evaluation for you. Sometimes it is possible to get an outside organization to develop an Evaluation design that can be submitted to a funding source as part of your proposal. This not only can suggest a more objective Evaluation, and if the evaluating institution has an impressive reputation, it can also enhance the credibility of your proposal.

It is essential that you build an Evaluation plan into your proposal and that you be prepared to implement it at the same time that you start your program. It is very difficult to start an Evaluation at or near the conclusion of the program. By then, you may not know the characteristics of your clients when they entered the program.

FUTURE AND OTHER NECESSARY FUNDING

No grantmaker wants to adopt you. Funding sources want to know how you will continue your program when their grant runs out. If you are requesting funds to start a new program, or to expand an existing program, they want to know how you will maintain it after the grant funds have been spent.

A vague promise to continue looking for alternative sources of support is insufficient. You need a real continuation plan that will assure the funding source, to the greatest extent possible, that you will be able to maintain this new program once the grant is over. Indeed, if you are having trouble keeping your current operations up and running, you will probably have even more trouble maintaining a level of operation that includes additional programs. The grantmaker may be doing you no favor by funding a new project and putting you in the position of having to raise even more money next year in order to keep it going.

No grantmaker wants to adopt you. Funding sources want to know how you will continue your program when their grant runs out.

At this point in your planning you may realize that there is little likelihood of any other sources of support one or two years hence. Should you even try to implement a new program at this time?

Where should you be looking for future funding? Could you get a local institution or governmental agency to help support the program, should it demonstrate the desired results? Can you get such a commitment in writing? Can you generate funds through the project itself—such as fees for services that will build up over a year or two, subscriptions to publications, etc.? Are there third parties available to provide reimbursement for services? Are you expanding your non-grant fundraising activities? The best plan for Future Funding is the plan that does not require continued grant support.

Other Necessary Funding refers to what are sometimes *non-recurring grants*—i.e., one-time-only requests. Examples would be a request for a vehicle to transport your clientele or the purchase of a piece of medical equipment for your hospital. While these are not program grants, the funds you request are not all you will need either to utilize the vehicle or to operate the medical device. For the vehicle to be used, you must cover the costs of a driver, insurance, gas, and maintenance. Similarly, the medical equipment must be operated by trained personnel. The funding source will want to know if your are aware of what you need beyond the purchase requested in your grant, and whether you have the funds needed to cover these costs. It makes no sense to find a bus that will sit in your garage for a year.

BUDGET

The requirements for Budgets vary widely. Foundations usually require much less detail than government funding sources require. Our recommended Budget contains three sections: the first covers personnel costs, the second covers non-personnel costs, and the third covers indirect costs.

Budgets should be built from the ground up—that is, they should be based upon your Goals and Objectives as well as your proposed Methods. It is important to go through this exercise in developing a Budget. Without it, there is a risk of developing unrealistic or impractical requests, where program and Budget are unrelated.

This is how we suggest you structure your Budget.

Personnel

Salaries and Wages

In this section you can list all full- and part-time staff who will be working on the proposed program. Include the following information in columns running across the page.

Number of persons per title

Title

Full monthly salary

Percent of time employed during grant period

Number of months during grant period

Amount requested

Amount donated or volunteered

Total

If any of your staff are being paid out of another source of funds (for example, a staff person assigned to your project by a county agency), then you would total up their salary and put it in the "donated" column (also referred to as in-kind, local share, or applicant share).

The salary listed may represent the actual salary paid to a staff member, but not necessarily. If this is a new project, and if your organization has a multistep salary schedule for job classifications, you should request the mid-point unless you know in advance who will fill that position. That way, you have the flexibility to hire at any point along the range with the assumption that all staff salaries will average out toward the middle of the salary range. (This works if there are a number of positions in your project, not just one or two.)

How do you determine what the salary range ought to be? The federal government prefers that salaries be comparable to the prevailing practices in similar agencies in your community. To justify the salaries you build into your Budget you should obtain information from other local agencies regarding the salaries of persons with job descriptions, qualifications, and responsibilities similar to those of the jobs in your agency. You might go to the local city and/or county government, the school district, or United Way. By comparing the jobs in your agency with the jobs at other local agencies, you plan a salary for each position, and you keep the "comparability data" on hand, should you be asked by the funding source to justify your staff salaries.

Another item to be included in your Budget for most public agency applications is the matching support being contributed by your organization, or the donated services. They can either be personnel contributed by you (the applicant organization) or by a third party (another participating agency, a corporation giving you a loaned executive, students, etc.). In many cases this will involve the use of volunteers. You should place a value on the service being performed by that volunteer, e.g., plumber, attorney, carpenter, receptionist, etc. That value is based upon the function being performed by the volunteer, not on the professional background or education of the volunteer. A physician volunteering time at a community center where he/she helps out painting the facility is shown at the hourly wage paid painters, not physicians.[1]

Government grantmakers sometimes require financial participation on the part of an applicant, e.g., 25 percent match. You may be able to make this contribution in cash or in-kind. If you are going to pay the salary of a staff member, that qualifies as *cash*. If you are using volunteers, or receive an executive on loan from a local corporation, that is *in-kind*. If you promise volunteers in your program, you are required to deliver the promised services, just as if the funding source were actually paying their salary. You will be asked to document the work they perform and to keep records of their time. Records may be audited in the case of a government grant. Always be able to document five to ten percent more than the required percentage match just in case you are audited and some of your volunteer time is disallowed.

Why is it important to develop a match (applicant share) and show the total costs of a project when some of the money or services are not being provided by the funding source? First, the government funding source wants to know that there is a commitment on the part of your agency—a commitment beyond just conducting the program. It helps for them to know there is some likelihood that you have resources with which to continue the program after funding has ceased. It also provides some clarity as to the precise cost in delivering a service. If the program were to be replicated elsewhere, and donated services were not available, it tells the funding source what the total cost would be. Finally, when you have local resources (volunteers, cash, staff, equipment, etc.), it reduces the amount of money required of the grantor, thereby allowing additional projects to be funded in other locations.

Fringe Benefits

In this section you list the fringe benefits your employees will be receiving, and the dollar cost of these benefits. Some fringe benefits are mandatory, but those vary from state to state, so you will have to determine what they are for your agency in your state.

Mandatory fringe benefits may include state disability insurance, state unemployment insurance, FICA, etc. They are usually based on percentages of salaries.

Some fringe benefits, such as health insurance, are calculated on a flat amount per month per staff member, and not on a percentage basis. As with your salary schedule, your fringe benefits should be comparable to the benefits offered in similar agencies in your community. While you will need to calculate fringe benefits for your own information, in some grant applications you simply indicate the fringe benefit total as a percentage of salary.

Consultant and Contract Services

This is the third and final part of the Personnel section of your Budget. In this section you include paid consulatants as well as unpaid consultants (i.e., volunteers). You can differentiate between the items that go here and those that go in Salaries and Wages according to the manner in which the individual or business normally operates. If a bookkeeping firm generally operates on a fee-for-service basis and is volunteering its services to your organization, that would fit best under Consultant and Contract Services. Essentially, be logical and if a Fed yells at you, change it. (Foundation persons never yell.)

Entries might look like these.

	Requested	Donated	Total
Bookkeeping Services @ $400/month x 12 months	$0	$4,800	$4,800
Contracted Fundraising Services @ $500/day x 10 days	$5,000	$0	$5,000
Trainer @ $450/day x 8 days	$3,600	$0	$3,600

Nonpersonnel

Space

In this section you list all of the facilities you will be using, both those on which you pay rent and those which are being donated for your use. Rent you pay, or the valuation of donated facilities, should be comparable to prevailing rents in the geographic area in which you are located. In addition to actual rent, you should also include the cost of utilities, maintenance services and renovations, if they are absolutely essential to your program, insurance on the facility, telephones (number of instruments needed, installment cost, and monthly cost of instruments), and out-of-town facilities needed. Include these items in line item fashion like this:

	Requested	Donated	Total
Office Space (900 sq. feet) @ $1.25 foot/month/ x 12 months	$13,500	$0	$13,500
Facility insurance @ $600/year	$0	$600	$600

Rental, Lease, or Purchase of Equipment

Here you list all the equipment, donated or to be purchased, that will be used in the proposed program. This includes office equipment, desks, duplicating machines, computers, etc. Use discretion. Try to obtain as much donated equipment as you can. It not only lowers the funder's cost, but it shows the funder that other people are involved in trying to make the program happen. Read guidelines closely when working with government grant applications, especially as to their definition of "equipment" and the restrictions that apply. For example, equipment is often defined as something costing more than $500 per unit and/or having a lifetime of greater than one year. In addition, there may be prohibitions against purchasing equipment, and you may be encouraged to lease rather than purchase.

Supplies

This generally means "desktop" supplies, such as paper clips, pens, stationery, etc. If you have any unusual needs for supplies—perhaps you are running an art education program, a sheltered workshop, or some classroom activity requiring lots of educational materials—then have a separate line item for such supplies. This component can also include publications, subscriptions, and postage.

Travel

All transportation-related expenses are included here. Don't put in any big lump sums which will require interpretation or raise eyebrows. Include staff travel at per diem rates approved by your agency and/or the state or federal agency to which you are applying, ground transportation, taxi, reimbursement to staff for use of their automobiles, consultant travel costs, use of agency vans or automobiles (if this has not been included under equipment), etc. Be sure that you use per diem rates (covering hotel and meals) which are appropriate for the location. Attending a workshop in Iowa will be considerably less expensive than attending one in Manhattan.

Other Costs

This is generally a catch-all category which includes items not reasonable to include elsewhere.

Examples

Bonding of employees

Tuition for classes

Professional association dues

Printing (unless this was included under Consultant and Contract Services)

Indirect Costs

The federal government defines indirect costs as "those costs of an institution which are not readily identifiable with a particular project or activity, but nevertheless are necessary to the general operation of the institution and the conduct of the activities it performs. The cost of operating and maintaining buildings and equipment, depreciation, administrative salaries, general telephone expenses, general travel, and supplies expenses are types of expenses usually considered as indirect costs." While it is possible for all such costs to be charged directly—that is, to the line items listed above, this is often impractical, and you may group them into a common pool.

The federal government indicates that an Indirect Cost Rate is "simply a device for determining fairly and expeditiously…that proportion of an institution's general expenses each of its projects or activities should bear." An organization or institution can negotiate an Indirect Cost Rate (generally a percentage of Salaries and Wages or Total Direct Costs) with any federal agency from which it has received funds. This is an important issue, since many larger institutions find that every new project undertaken costs the institution money unless it is reimbursed for the indirect costs associated with operating the project.

For further clarification of Indirect Cost Rates, contact the federal office's regional comptroller or your program officer or contract officer to find out exactly how to go about negotiating Indirect Cost Rates. Once you have such a rate, there may still be instances in which the funding source refuses to pay indirect cost rates or places a cap (a maximum) on the percentage of total direct costs they will pay. Nevertheless, this is an area which should be thoroughly explored and understood.

APPENDIX

Addenda to a foundation or corporate proposal should be minimal. It is an imposition to make reviewers plod through pages and pages of "window-dressing" material. In the case of a government grant, however, the Appendix may well be longer than the body of the proposal. The Appendix should contain material which needs to be submitted to the funding source but which would detract from the continuity and flow of the proposal if it were included in the narrative. Ask yourself, "Do I really want the funding source to read/scan the census runs, flow chart, or job descriptions while reading the proposal?" If the answer is yes, then definitely include the item at that juncture. If the answer is no, then include the item in the Appendix and refer the reader to it.

Funding sources will usually stipulate the specific attachments they want you to include with your grant application. The following items are routinely requested.

Financial statements. Funding sources generally require an audited financial statement. Many smaller organizations do not routinely have an audit conducted, so an *unaudited* financial statement is developed by the agency's accountant or bookkeeper. It is important that applicants know whether the funding source will accept an unaudited financial statement. Call the program officer or other contact person at the offices of the funding source for an answer.

IRS determination letter. Your organization should have a letter from the Internal Revenue Service indicating its tax exempt status. It contains important information regarding the basis for your exemption and the requirements associated with maintaining it. In some cases, individual states also grant such exemptions, and copies of both letters may be appropriate for submission.

Indication of nonprofit corporation status. A copy of the receipt of nonprofit corporation status by the state in which your organization was incorporated may be required. In most instances, the favorable determination of tax exemption (above) will be sufficient in that it lists the name of the incorporated nonprofit organization.

Board roster. Funders are not simply interested in knowing the names of your board members, but who they represent. Are they ministers, doctors, bankers, social workers, building contractors? In the cases of retired individuals, indicate their former job or profession. In situations where organizations have board members who are welfare recipients, unemployed persons, students, etc., select an area of interest or specialty indicate that after their name. Don't just list a name without any affiliation.

Organization chart. This should include the proposed staffing pattern for the project for which funds are being requested, and should also include the larger agency/department/section to whom the new project personnel report. With large organizations, it is not critical that each position be indicated, but units or departments should be shown. In many instances it is more important that the funding source understand how the major functions of the organization are carried out, and how boards, committees, and staff interrelate.

Organizational budget. Some funding sources will require submission of an organizational Budget for the current or forthcoming program year. This organizational Budget differs from the Budget for the project itself, previously discussed. This allows the reviewer to put the grant request in a larger context.

Summary chart of key activities. Most public grant applications will require that you submit some form of timeline for major milestones or activities. This can be done in a variety of formats—Gannt charts, PERT charts, flow charts, etc., and can be done by month, quarter, or time elapsed from the initiation of the project. Whatever format you use, it should be clear and easily understood by the funding source.

Negotiated indirect cost rate. A copy of your agency's negotiated indirect cost rate should be included in the Appendix when you are citing a percentage amount for indirect costs. This is required when submitting public agency applications where such costs are being charged.

Letters of support or endorsement. Letters from elected officials or from other interested parties may be required by a funding source. Or your organization may decide that such letters are good indicators of support and include them in the Appendix.

In general, such letters should be addressed to your organization (executive director, board chairman, etc.) and sent along with the proposal. Letters should not be sent under separate cover to the funding source because they may not get there in time or they may not be filed appropriately with your proposal.

Résumés. Résumés/curricula vitae of key staff should be updated periodically. They should also be written in the same format. With the exclusion of academic and medical personnel, they need be no longer than two to three pages.

Job descriptions. While in some instances it is important to create a capsule résumé for inclusion in the body of the proposal, in most cases the description of positions should be an Appendix item.

ENDNOTE

1. Editor's note: Please see the Independent Sector website at www.independentsector.org/programs/research/volunteer_time.html for an estimated dollar value for volunteer time per hour.

The Grantsmanship Center (TGCI) was founded in 1972 to offer grantsmanship training and low-cost publications to nonprofit organizations and government agencies. TGCI conducts some 200 workshops annually in grantsmanship, enterprise development, and fundraising. More than 100 local agencies across the country host these workshops. TGCI alumni attend regular meetings in Los Angeles and other cities, receive continuing support from the TGCI organization, and benefit from technical assistance and other forms of support delivered through its website.

TGCI publishes *The Grantsmanship Center Magazine*. TGCI's "Winning Grant Proposals Online" collects the best of funded federal grant proposals annually and makes them available on CD-ROM. The TGCI proposal writing guide, *Program Planning and Proposal Writing (PP&PW)*, is available in short and long versions (this chapter represents the short version) and is a widely utilized publication with more than a million copies in print.

Essentials of Program Planning and Proposal Writing

P.O. Box 17220
Los Angeles, CA 90017
phone 213-482-9860; fax 213-482-9863
info@tgci.com

CHAPTER 8

Personnel Management Basics

8

AMY BRANNOCK

Successful arts organizations in the early 21st century are characterized by their ability to balance their artistic missions with the need to operate effectively in an ever-changing environment. Human resources play a critical role in the success of these organizations, yet few arts managers and volunteer board members are well versed in how to recruit, hire, supervise, evaluate, and retain staff—all of which are key elements of the human resources profession. Managing human resources in a dynamic, artistic, high-pressure environment requires both sensitivity to the organization's artistic raison d'être and strong managerial skills. One of the hurdles successful arts organizations face is the perpetual shortfall between their missions and the human capital needed to get the work done.

The wave of new arts organizations that followed the establishment of the National Endowment for the Arts in 1965—and the subsequent creation of state arts agencies in every state—was a period of explosive growth. Along with this growth came the realization that the simple structures of earlier arts organizations were no longer sufficient to support the evolving programs and operations of these more complex entities.[1] As a result, efforts to stabilize and systemize "best practices" for board development, management, and organizational structures emerged. While many of those practices are still relevant today, we now are challenged to create organizations that are agile enough to incorporate new insights, personalities, and generational values.

While there is a body of literature on personnel management for nonprofit arts organizations, there is no single model of organizational charts or board/staff relationships that is suited to every organization. Each organization should plan carefully, understand its mission and organizational culture clearly, and go about intentionally creating a personnel structure that uniquely serves its needs and reflects its values.

This chapter is a primer to guide board members and arts managers in the basics of personnel management, and is suited especially to organizations at an early stage of development—organizations hiring staff for the first time or replacing a sole professional staff person. For organizations that already have professional staff, the chapter concludes with a discussion on planning for leadership succession and the professional and personal qualities of arts leadership—key issues in today's nonprofit arts environment.

THE NONPROFIT WORK FORCE

Four groups comprise the nonprofit arts organization's workforce.

Salaried staff members provide ongoing services for important tasks and functions. The organization can expect high standards of these professionals and must provide ongoing supervision and evaluation. State and federal laws require that salaried staff members be provided with unemployment coverage, social security, and various other benefits.

Volunteers provide a source of free labor and expertise. The organization must devise other systems of rewards to keep them motivated. Recruiting, training, and retaining volunteers must be carefully coordinated with paid staff. They are an important part of the nonprofit arts workforce. Please see the chapter on volunteers for more information about how best to work with these committed individuals.

Independent contractors are hired for a specific period of time to perform a discrete task. The organization pays a flat or daily rate for the job and does not withhold taxes or pay benefits. Contractors can provide a cost-effective solution for a one-time service. However, it is not legal to hire people as independent contractors when their working patterns and responsibilities indicate that they should actually be categorized as staff members. A person who works in the office on a continuing basis, and whose work is directed by a board or staff supervisor, should be considered an employee even if he or she works only part-time. The Internal Revenue Service and many state divisions of employment security have regulations on the definition of an independent contractor, so be aware of these when contracting for services. If the work is short-term and the individuals enjoy more independence than other regular employees, the government agencies are usually satisfied. If the individuals do not fit the definition of an independent contractor, the nonprofit can be required to pay back taxes, unemployment compensation, and fines.

Outside organization service providers provide a discrete service on a fee basis, e.g., financial management, equipment maintenance, cleaning, etc.[2]

PERSONNEL POLICIES AND PRACTICES

Lines of Authority and Accountability

In a small organization, it may seem that an organization chart is unnecessary, but as an organization grows, it is necessary to establish lines of authority and of reporting as well as chains of accountability. An organizational chart (see figure 1) graphically illustrates the approved chain of command, although it no longer has to be the traditional hierarchical and corporate structure with boxes on top of boxes. Today, organizational charts may look like space ships and three-ring circuses. An organizational chart can take any shape, as long as it truly reflects your organization's structure.

Board Responsibilities

Sometimes a problem arises when individual board members supervise support staff or make direct requests for assistance on organizational matters. When there is a chief staff executive, board requests for assistance from support staff should go through the executive. In organizations where the sole employee is an administrative assistant or secretary, a board member may treat that person as a personal assistant. Establish a policy that clarifies if, how, and when board members may directly call upon staff for

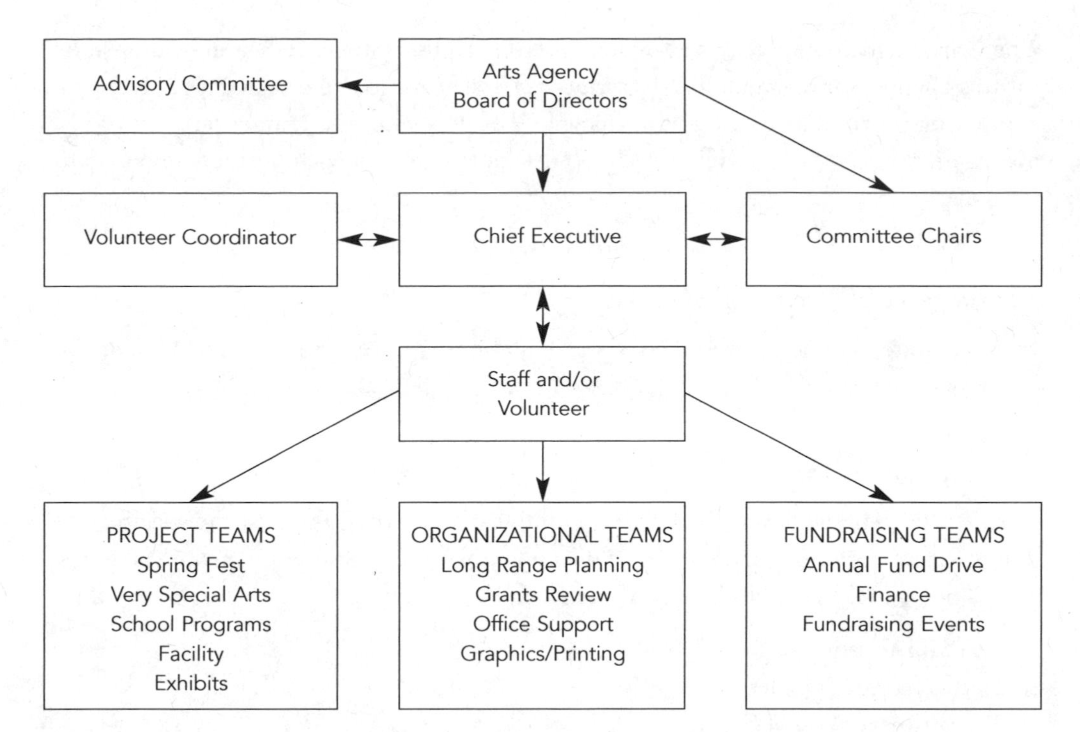

Figure 1: Smalltown Arts Agency Organization Chart

assistance. For example, a policy might state that requests always be funneled through the chief executive.[3] Alternatively, the board chair or personnel committee chair may have the authority to assign certain types of tasks to staff.[4]

See the Board Development chapter for more information on board responsibilities.

Personnel Committee

The personnel committee is responsible for establishing personnel policies and procedures, drawing up the organization chart, writing job descriptions, and recommending a salary range—all for approval by the board. It can also serve as a search committee when needed. Sometimes the committee stands alone; other times it is a function of an executive committee. The personnel committee is the chief executive's ally, liaison, and representative to the full board. Its duties are to:

- work with the chief executive to review job descriptions, personnel policies, compensation and benefits;
- take policy revisions to the board for approval;
- represent the chief executive to the board for requests for new positions;
- handle grievances as designated in approved grievance procedures; and
- conduct the chief executive's annual performance evaluation.[5]

Job Descriptions

Too many nonprofit arts boards have unrealistic expectations of new employees. They expect a "white knight" to come in and cure all existing problems, raise all the money, set up the chairs, and scrub the toilets! Thinking through job descriptions, assigning duties, and estimating the time necessary to perform those duties will help avoid this pitfall.

Wanted: A multifaceted and experienced individual—effective in marketing, arts programming, fundraising, financial management—to double the budget each year for the next three years. Must develop a warm and caring relationship with artists, volunteers, and board. Salary: $15,000–$18,000.

There are many examples of well-written job descriptions. (See the Online Companion for this chapter for a Sample Job Description.) Take care to avoid taking a model from another organization and using it unchanged. Every organization, and every arts manager's job, is different. Tailor each job description to suit each position, and update it regularly.

A job description typically includes three components.

1. A general description of the job
2. A statement about who the person holding the job reports to and who he or she will supervise
3. A list of specific responsibilities and functions needed to carry out the duties of the job[6]

It is helpful to break down the description into categories and then list the specific duties within each category. Shown below are examples of some of the major categories into which a chief executive's responsibilities fall.

Administration
Financial management
Programs and services
Fundraising
Planning
Public relations

Why take the time to write job descriptions at all when the organization is small, or when the job descriptions have to be redrafted every time there is staff reorganization? Thomas Wolf, in *Managing a Nonprofit Organization in the Twenty-First Century*,[7] outlines three reasons.

The process of writing job descriptions can reveal that the responsibilities envisioned for a single person are unrealistic. In addition, once all the tasks are written down, it is easier to shift responsibilities with a clearer sense of the total work needs of the organization and the time commitments of each staff member.

Job descriptions protect the employees. The job description clearly outlines what is expected of the employee and provides the basis for a fair evaluation of job performance.

Job descriptions protect the organization. The job description specifies certain expectations in writing that, if not met, offer grounds for disciplinary action or dismissal.

Personnel Policies

Personnel policies articulate employees' rights, expectations, and responsibilities. The clearer the policies, the fewer misunderstandings will arise. Well-designed policies provide continuity through board and staff turnover. They guide board and staff to act predictably, consistently, fairly, and legally.

When developing workplace policies, management must carefully balance the organization's needs with those of the employees. The American Association of Museums has developed *The AAM Guide to Writing an Employee Handbook*. It suggests that organizations "adopt policies that ensure its health and well-being, permit it to comply with all legal requirements, protect it from harm or loss, and highlight the special benefits of…employment."[8]

A nonprofit arts organization's operations, including its personnel policies, are regulated by a wide range of federal, state, and local laws. Employer compliance with federal, state, and local laws is not negotiable. Failure to properly administer any law can be costly in potential monetary penalties, a tarnished reputation, a compromised relationship with employees, and the time it takes to untangle a legal mess. This book cannot thoroughly address all of the laws relevant to every organization. It's a good idea to regularly enlist the expertise of an employment attorney to interpret relevant laws and adapt policies accordingly.

Personnel Policies

A comprehensive set of personnel policies includes:

Employment Practices
Equal employment opportunity
Affirmative action
Americans with Disabilities Act
Sexual harassment
Hiring, orientation, and promotions
Work eligibility, immigration law compliance, new employee probationary period
Work for hire, outside employment
Wage and salary administration, pay periods, payroll deductions
Overtime, compensatory time
Performance, disciplinary, and grievance policies
Performance appraisals
Disciplinary actions and grievance procedures

General Work Conditions
Parking, dress code, professional conduct
Attendance and punctuality, inclement weather, emergency closings
Work schedule, timekeeping, meal and break periods

Security
Emergency procedures
Security, protection of property
Violence in the workplace

Health and substance abuse policies
Drug- and alcohol-free workplace, smoking
Life-threatening illnesses in the workplace
Staff health and safety, first aid

Benefits (see section on Benefits that follows)

Leaves of Absence
Family and medical leave
Bereavement
Personal leave
Jury duty
Voting in elections
Military leave and military reserve duty

COMPENSATION AND BENEFITS

The greatest challenge many arts boards face is how to find the resources to pay adequate and competitive salaries.

While nonprofit compensation is low overall compared to the corporate and government sectors, it is even lower in the arts. In 2002, Americans for the Arts published a study of executive compensation in the nonprofit sector based on findings from the National Center for Charitable Statistics and Guidestar.[9] The report stated that in 1998 the median annual salary of top executives in the nonprofit sector was $42,000 compared with $31,000 in the arts, ranging from $43,000 for museum directors to $23,000 for chief executives in performing arts. Maximum salaries ranged from $502,000 in the performing arts to $234,000 among supporting arts nonprofits.[10]

The study also found that while executive compensation in the arts varies by an organization's activities, other factors—most notably the age of the organization and fundraising efforts required of executives—are significant determinants of executive pay.[11] And while executive pay in the arts relates to an organization's activities, age, and fundraising, the study found that the most important determinants in executive compensation in the arts were organization size and location.[12] An Americans for the Arts survey of local arts agency salaries and benefits found that the average salary of full-time chief executives of local arts agencies was $54,309 in 2001.[13]

If salaries in the arts are lower than those in most other nonprofit arenas, and certainly lower than those in the corporate and government sectors, then what makes people want to work in the arts? While money is a valid motivator and a powerful predictor of job satisfaction, one study suggests that arts employees differ from their for-profit counterparts due to the value these employees attach to performing a beneficial service to their community. Strength of this desire may not only draw them to the organization, but keep them there as well.[14] However, this altruism may be changing with a new generation of emerging leaders who are concerned with the balance of work and personal life as well as earning an appropriate level of compensation in a competitive marketplace. This new reality heightens the nonprofit arts sector's challenge of attracting new leaders to the field.

How does a board decide on salary? BoardSource suggests that to evaluate the appropriateness of executive compensation, one should consider:

- the size and complexity of the organization;
- the mission, geographic location, and financial condition of the organization;
- the qualifications required for the job; and
- compensation at comparable organizations.[15]

Once job duties, time needed to do the tasks, and skills, experience, and qualifications are determined, the next step is to check with other nonprofits in the community to see what similar positions are paid. The United Way, YMCA, library, parks and recreation department, visitor's bureau, and chamber of commerce are good guides. Contact state arts agencies and professional organizations at the state and national levels—such as Americans for the Arts, the American Association of Museums, or the Association of

Performing Arts Presenters—to see what up-to-date research exists. The local offices of the U.S. Department of Labor Statistics also issue national and local salary scales.

It should be noted that the compensation of the five highest-paid managers of the organization is required on the IRS Form 990, an informational tax form that nonprofits must file each year. The 990 is a public document that must be made available by mail or at the organization's office when requested by members of the public, including journalists. For this reason, compensation can't be considered a private matter, and all board members should be aware of the implications.[16]

Benefits

It is up to the board to see that the organization provides a benefit package that will attract excellent employees and retain them. Here are some examples of typical benefits.

The following are required by law:
Social security
State disability insurance (in some states)
Unemployment insurance
Workers' compensation

The following are optional:
Car allowance and parking
Club memberships
Disability benefits
Employee assistance program
Flexible benefit plans ("cafeteria" plans)
Flexible spending accounts
Health and dental insurance
Holidays
Life insurance
Professional development
Retirement and pension plans
Sick time
Vacation benefits

Nonprofits are increasingly looking to benefits and other rewards, financial and nonfinancial, to attract and retain quality employees. The two Americans for the Arts studies mentioned in the Salaries section report that only a fraction of arts organizations supplement base salaries with benefits plans. In 1998, only 26 percent of the arts groups surveyed reported contributions to employee benefit plans or deferred compensation of their chief executives, only seven percent provided them expense accounts, and there was a wide variation depending on the type and size of the organization.[17] On the other hand, in 2001 the majority of local arts agencies provided benefits to their employees such as insurance, paid time off, incentives, and retirement savings plans.[18]

As arts organizations compete more directly with for-profit companies for workers, the hiring and retaining of employees is becoming more competitive, according to a study by the Arts and Business Council of Greater Philadelphia.[19] The 2002 study found that more groups in the Philadelphia area were giving bonuses and offering retirement plans, in addition to the tradition of offering health-care benefits. Some are raising funds to offer 403(b) plans, the nonprofit version of the 401(k) retirement savings plan. Some provide unconventional benefits that for-profit companies might shy away from. These include perks such as attending theatre rehearsals, discount tickets to performances, or bringing children and dogs to work.

A 2002 CompassPoint study of nonprofit turnover and vacancy in the Silicon Valley/San Francisco Bay area suggests the following strategies to attract and retain employees:[20]

> **Salaries and benefits.** Strive for competitive salaries with other nonprofits, as well as with similar jobs in the corporate and government sectors.
>
> **Retirement benefits.** The benefit correlating most highly with chief executive and senior staff retention is a retirement plan.
>
> **Organizational culture.** Aspects of organizational culture include how conflict is treated; formal and informal hierarchies; multicultural awareness and support; the quality and location of the work space, building and employee security; and availability of appropriate supplies, equipment, and technology.
>
> **Professional development.** In addition to formal training programs, coaching and mentoring support from supervisors and peers can be supported with varying degrees of structure and formality within an organization or from service organizations.

Another recent survey suggests that employees' absences can be curbed, and job satisfaction increased, by new approaches to benefits and working policies.[21] For example, some organizations are reconsidering what a "work week" looks like. That may mean providing flexible hours, compressed work weeks, time off for school events, or other arrangements that help employees strike a successful balance between personal demands and their jobs. Giving employees more control over their time by providing paid time-off programs that let employees use their leave time for whatever reasons needed—personal, vacation, family, or sickness—can provide employees with a bank of hours to be used for various purposes instead of traditional separate leave accounts. Other effective programs include job sharing, telecommuting, and child care referral programs.

PLANNING TO HIRE A CHIEF EXECUTIVE

Among the board's primary responsibilities is to select, evaluate, and, if necessary, terminate the appointment of the chief executive. Be sure that the board has done some soul-searching and really understands and buys in to the mission and direction because the new chief executive will be expected to work energetically and wholeheartedly to fulfill that mission. Before writing the job description or appointing a search committee, the organization must assess its current condition and agree on its future direction. Most often, the board wants a chief executive that can take the organization to the next level.

Determine what qualities the organization is looking for. What is the desired leadership style? What characteristics will be a good fit for the organization's culture?

Nello McDaniel and George Thorn suggest that a good approach to planning for the search process is for the board to ask itself, Are we prepared to answer the insightful questions that good candidates are going to ask?

> Are the vision, mission, and values of the organization clearly articulated? Is there understanding and agreement throughout the organization?
>
> Is the next evolution of the organization defined? Is there understanding and agreement throughout the organization about the direction?
>
> Is the board actively participating in fundraising? Are board members making significant financial contributions?
>
> Is there a positive working relationship between board and staff?
>
> What is the leadership structure? Is there specific delineation of authority and responsibility?
>
> Is there a comprehensive description of the community and the current condition of the organization?
>
> Is there a long-range plan? Is there a planning process?
>
> Is there an in-depth and complete presentation of budgets and balance sheets? Is there a deficit? How is it financed? What is the plan to retire the debt? Are there cash reserves, lines of credit, or restricted funds?[22]

Whether boards are looking to hire a new chief executive, or the executive is hiring other staff, organizations need to determine what specific tasks need to be performed. Once they have been identified, don't assume that all of the important tasks need to be performed by salaried staff.

Search and Selection

Time and Money

When planning to hire new staff, remember to budget for the expenses related to bringing on staff as well as the time it will take to hire a competent employee for the position. You'll be spending money on the job search, taxes, insurance, travel, professional development expenses, paid vacations, and holidays. There will also be expenses in maintaining a comfortable office conducive to effective work, and which presents a professional image to the community. Also remember to budget for next year's raises and cost-of-living increases.

Depending on the situation, the time and money required from the initial announcement of a job opening to the new employee's first day on the job varies. Smaller organizations, particularly those looking for an administrative assistant or their first paid staff person, may choose to restrict their search to local candidates. In those cases, an organization can have a new employee on the job in a month or two, with little financial investment beyond an ad in the local newspaper and a few well-placed phone calls. On the other hand, the greater the position's responsibilities and the higher the qualifications it demands, the more expensive the search will be. Some organizations hire a search firm whose services can ensure a vigorous process to publicize the opportunity as well as make field contacts to identify qualified and interested candidates. When a professional search firm is enlisted, expect to spend a minimum of six months and pay headhunter fees. It is important to allow sufficient time to find the right person. Consider the following when you set a schedule for your search process.

If you're placing ads in national trade publications, it takes at least a month for the ad to appear in print. Electronic vehicles usually require less.

Candidates need time to submit application materials.

Plan time to review resumes, check references, and conduct screening interviews.

Schedule interviews for finalists. If candidates are coming from out-of-town, allow time to coordinate travel schedules.

Make a decision, negotiate the contract, and allow time for the candidate to give the current employer sufficient notice and arrange to relocate.

The budget for a search depends on whether the scope of requirements is beyond community resources, how in depth the process will be, and whether the services of a professional search firm are used. Plan to spend money on:

- advertising;
- postage for correspondence;
- printing information packets for candidates and duplicating candidate materials for the search committee;
- finalists' interview travel costs;
- long distance phone charges for screening interviews, reference checks, and calls to finalists; and
- relocation expenses for the new employee.

The Search Committee

Carrying out the activities of hiring a chief executive is often the responsibility of a designated search committee of the board. This committee is sometimes augmented by individuals outside the board who can lend needed perspective or expertise. Serving on the search committee requires time and effort to accomplish the following activities:

- establish the search budget and schedule;
- create the job description (See the Online Companion for this chapter for a sample job description. Go to the last page of the book for the URL.)
- advertise the job opening;
- set a deadline for applications;
- establish application screening and interviewing schedule and procedures;
- decide criteria to use in considering current employees for a posted position;
- check references;
- prepare information packets for candidates;
- coordinate candidate correspondence and logistics;

- define parameters for negotiating salary and benefits; and
- negotiate the offer and contract with the selected candidate.

The kinds of people to consider for the search committee are:

- people with knowledge of and commitment to the organization;
- people with knowledge of human resources and personnel;
- people who can maintain the confidential nature of the search;
- an employment attorney;
- the organization's current chair and chair-elect; and
- a senior-level staff person who is not a candidate for the position and who is considered fair and appropriate. The current outgoing chief executive should not serve on the committee.

The board will need to adopt procedures for the final selection and determine who makes the final decision. Either the full board makes the decision based on the search committee's recommendation, or the board delegates authority to the committee to select the person to whom the executive position will be offered.

Reaching Qualified Candidates

If the search committee is conducting its own search (as opposed to hiring a firm), it is important to get the word out about job openings. There are many potential sources to help promote to and identify candidates.

State arts agencies, statewide arts advocacy and service organizations

Americans for the Arts

National Assembly of State Arts Agencies

National Endowment for the Arts

Regional arts agencies (Arts Midwest, Mid-America Arts Alliance, Mid Atlantic Arts Foundation, New England Foundation for the Arts, Southern Arts Federation, Western States Arts Federation)

Arts discipline-specific national, regional, and statewide service organizations

ArtSEARCH: The National Employment Service Bulletin for the Arts

New York Foundation on the Arts *Jobs in the Arts* online national jobs resource

Nonprofit job listings, such as *Access: Networking in the Public Interest* or *The Chronicle of Philanthropy*

Employment Security Commission

Newspaper and internet advertising

Internet search

Personal referrals

Professional Search Firms

Looking for a new chief executive takes time, contacts, and an enormous amount of effort. It does not always make sense to have the board take on this task or even expect the search committee to handle the details of the search. Hiring a search firm may be the right decision when:

- the search is national or it is important to cast a wide net for candidates;
- board members do not have the capacity or the time to get involved personally;
- it is important to give special credibility to the process and eliminate conflicts of interest; or
- you need help structuring the process, drafting a job description, clarifying the expectations, and defining the position profile.[23]

Checking References

Former employers and references listed on a candidate's resume are not always the most reliable sources about job applicants. A potential employee usually only offers names that will provide glowing testimonials. Furthermore, current and former employers may be reluctant to talk about issues related to an employee's performance for fear of litigation.

Even though it is very important to talk with people who have worked with and for applicants, some organizations never call references. And when they do, they rarely go beyond the names provided by the applicant. But if there's a fib in a resume or a serious problem in a potential employee's past, it's a lot less painful to discover it before he's been hired.

Some human resources professionals believe that the best way to learn about an applicant is to go beyond listed references and consult colleagues in the candidate's current workplace or within his or her professional circles. Should you adopt this route, obtain permission from the candidate *before* calling someone not listed as a reference to ensure that you are not revealing that your candidate is job hunting before he or she has made the announcement to his or her current employer.

There is a current trend to run credit and background checks on potential executive hires.[24] While having a $50,000 credit card balance isn't a crime, it's better to know that ahead of time when a candidate is applying for a job that pays a $38,000 salary. Before a final decision is made on any candidate, talk with everyone who can help the search committee evaluate the candidate's potential performance.

The Interview

Initial screening of the candidates who survived the resume review and reference check can be done on the telephone. Once the list has been pared down to a few promising applicants, it's time to bring them for an in-depth, onsite interview.

The search committee should decide the format and schedule for the interviews. Spend enough time with each to get to know them well. It's a good idea as well to invite as many people as possible—other board members, volunteers, artists, arts and community leaders—to the interviews.

Consider the following options or a combination of these approaches.

> Appoint one "master interviewer" who asks all the candidates the same questions, and then follows up with a less formal meeting with the entire search committee.

The Interview—Questions to Ask and Issues to Avoid

Questions to Pose or Revise to Suit Your Needs

How would you go about becoming known and respected by the leadership in our community?

What do you think are the most relevant factors likely to affect the future of organizations like ours in the next three years? How would you position us to take advantage of positive trends and minimize the impact of negative ones?

What role do you think this organization should play in the community? state? national landscape?

What are the greatest issues in budgeting and financial management for a multiservice nonprofit arts organization with a variety of funding sources?

Two months prior to the end of a fiscal year you receive word that your revenues will be 20 percent less than anticipated. What steps would you take to resolve the problem?

What do you expect of a good board member? staff?

What responsibility in this position do you think would stretch you? Do any cause you concern?

Describe your current position. What do you enjoy the most/least about it?

What have been your greatest accomplishments in your current job?

What are your greatest strengths, and how have you used them in your current position?

What are your weaknesses? What have you done to improve upon them?

Why are you considering leaving your current job?

What was the greatest challenge in your career, and how did you resolve it?

Do you feel that you have a good understanding of what this job entails?

Why do you think that you are suited to this position?

What do you think is likely to make the difference between success and failure in this position?

How does this position fit into your overall career goals?

If you were offered and accepted this position, how would you manage your first month?

How is supervising volunteers different from supervising paid staff?

How do you recognize the contributions of others in your organization?

Why do you believe that your skills, abilities, and experiences are a good match for this organization?[25]

Issues that Can Be Interpreted as Discriminatory

Age

Arrest record

Conviction record

Credit rating

Education (You may not disqualify a candidate who does not have a specific degree unless you can prove that the particular degree is the only way to know if the candidate can perform the job. You may ask about degrees, coursework, or equivalent experience that would better qualify the candidate for the job.)

Disabilities or health conditions

Marital and family status

Military record (Do not ask about the type of military discharge. You can ask about military experience if it relates to the job being sought.)

Name and national origin (Do not ask questions to find out about a person's national origin, ancestry, or prior marital status. You may ask if the person has ever worked under another name and whether she or he is legally eligible to work in the United States.)

Organizations (Do not ask about memberships to determine the race, color, religion, sex, national origin, age, or political affiliation of the candidate.)

Race

Religion

Sex[26]

Conduct one-on-one interviews (or "several-on-one") by members of the search committee.

Conduct an interview by the full committee.

Hold meet-and-greet functions with other board members, staff, artists, arts leaders, and community leaders.

During these interviews, the organization will be assessing the candidates, and the candidates will be evaluating the organization. Organize informal gatherings such as dinner with board members the night prior to the formal interview or attendance at an arts event. In addition to a tour of the organization's facilities, arrange for a tour of the broader community. Arrange for appropriate hospitality and make them feel welcome. Have someone meet them and serve as escorts if they are from out of town. Include significant others in appropriate activities and arrange to entertain them during the interview process. Whatever the set of activities, it is important to treat all candidates equally.

Ask questions that will help you learn the applicant's history and experience, job knowledge, abilities and skills, attributes, and commitment to your mission. Understand, though, that certain interview questions are illegal and can be interpreted as discriminatory. In order to avoid even the appearance of discrimination or preference, all job requirements and interview questions must relate to the candidate's ability to perform the job in question.

Evaluating Candidates and Making the Selection

It is a good idea to develop standardized ratings and comment sheets on which to record the reactions of search committee members as well as other board, staff, and community members who talked with the candidates. After each onsite visit, collect and tally the sheets and return them to the search committee for discussion. After all the interviews have been completed, carefully rank each finalist against the priorities you have agreed upon for qualifications and attributes. Making the decision on whom to hire requires consensus-building on the part of the committee. It is essential for future harmony and the strength of the organization to have everyone's wholehearted agreement. If no one person emerges as the right match for the job and the organization, start the search again.

Once a candidate is approved, the board chair or search committee chair presents the organization's offer. If during the course of the negotiations there is a need to redefine the parameters, they must be submitted to the board for approval.

Contracts

Once the offer has been accepted, organizations should draft a formal employment contract. A formal contract provides security to both the executive and to the board, and makes absolutely clear the details of the compensation arrangement and the mutual expectations of the two parties. As of 2002, about one-fifth of nonprofits had formal employment agreements with their chief executives.[27] The employment contract also offers some added security to both the executive and the organization by demonstrating the organization's commitment to the executive. Remember it is common to include a "probationary period" in the language of the contract—anywhere from three to six months—where the candidate's contract may be terminated by either party for any reason. This enables the candidate and the board the added security of an "out" should things go awry.

ASSESSMENT OF THE CHIEF EXECUTIVE [28]

The board delegates the management and administrative duties to the chief executive. That conveys a lot of authority and a large dose of trust. However, the board does not abdicate itself from the overall responsibility of oversight and duty of ensuring the health of the organization. To ensure that the right person is running the operations, regular performance reviews should take place. Performance evaluation benefits the chief executive, the board, and the entire organization.

Performance evaluation benefits the chief executive, the board, and the entire organization.

Chief Executive Benefits

Constructive feedback is the best guide to show what works and where change is needed.

Self-evaluation as part of the process forces the chief executive to reconcile his or her own weaknesses and strengths—and then to improve them or to build on them.

Clarifying expectations for the coming year establishes priorities.

Board Benefits

Supporting the chief executive is one of the board's main duties; performance evaluation should validate it.

The evaluation process enhances communication between the board and the chief executive.

Evaluation facilitates the board's oversight function.

Organizational Benefits

Performance evaluation helps gauge whether there is a good fit between the organizational goals and a chief executive whose role is to achieve them. Evaluation ensures that the right hands are guiding the organization in the right direction.

Elements of a Productive Performance Evaluation

Three key elements ensure that the performance evaluation is well structured: job description, annual expectations, and process. Like any evaluation, the practice is cyclical in nature. Any shortcomings must be incorporated into the next evaluation cycle to feed into future improvement efforts.

A clear and unambiguous job description that clarifies the primary duties and responsibilities of the position forms the basis for the evaluation.

Annual expectations identify the priorities and specific projected accomplishments for the coming year. They must be mutually agreed upon by the chief executive and the board, and they serve as the final device for assessing achievements or shortcomings.

The evaluation process must fit the organizational culture and enhance the working relationship between the board and the chief executive. Who is involved, what tools to use, how to communicate—the board and the chief executive determine their preferred options in order to use the results as a building block for the future.

Who Participates?

The full board must be familiar and feel comfortable with the evaluation results, but the actual process may be handled by a committee, task force, board chair, or eventually even by an outside facilitator. A self-evaluation of the chief executive is an integral part of the process. Other feedback may come from senior staff, key constituents, funders, or other stakeholders if the board wants to use a 360-degree approach. The 360-degree feedback review involves collecting perceptions about an individual's job performance from a number of sources normally chosen on their opportunity for firsthand interaction with the individual. By increasing the number of evaluations, a more balanced and comprehensive view of an individual's overall job performance is possible.

Timing of Evaluation

The evaluation may be conducted at the end of the fiscal year. There also may be intermittent discussions as long as it is understood that constructive criticism is part of positive feedback and evaluation relates to previously set goals. Documentation of the discussions and agreements protect both the board and the chief executive if disagreements or misinterpretations occur.

Process

A comprehensive assessment looks at qualitative and quantitative factors that shape individual performance. Some of the concrete areas that demand attention include the chief executive's success in meeting the overall goals, strategic alignment with the board's directives, accomplishment of management, programmatic and fundraising objectives, fiscal management, and his or her relationship with the board, staff, and the community.

The process can be informal or structured. There are comprehensive and simple questionnaires available for board members to fill out. (BoardSource provides sample forms, open-ended questions, and tally sheets useful for nonprofit arts organizations. See Resources at the end of the chapter.)

Board members should rely on predetermined objectives (derived from the organization's strategic plan or annual plan of work) when forming their opinions on the accomplishments. Usually their comments are compiled, tabulated, and shared with the chief executive and, with the chief-executive's self-assessment, provide fodder for discussion. If the board seeks opinions from outsiders, their comments are integrated into the feedback.

Some boards may want to be less structured about the process, but still need to ensure that continuous or intermittent feedback reaches the chief executive.

WHEN TO HIRE THE FIRST PROFESSIONAL

How do you know when your arts organization is ready to hire its first chief executive? There isn't a rule or formula based on budget size, or scope of programs, or the organization's evolution. Many all-volunteer organizations function effectively for many years without paid staff. But for many, the scope of activities expands to the point that the board needs staff support.

Before making the leap into hiring the first professional chief executive, consider the following:

Where is the organization now, and where is it going?

What tasks need to be done?

What type of position is needed: clerical, administrative assistant, program coordinator, chief executive?

Will the position be full- or part-time?

What are the salaries and benefits of comparable positions in similar institutions—on local, statewide, and national levels?

How much can you afford to pay staff while continuing to present your current programs?

What office space and equipment will your new employee need to do the job effectively?

What paperwork will need to be filed in order to become a legal employer in the eyes of the state and the federal government?

Is your board ready to adapt to the changes that will come about when staff is hired?[29]

Arts consultant Cheryl Yuen states that "effective staff is a key ingredient in building an effective local arts agency… There is significant evidence that staffing advances the LAA in ways that board leadership is unable to do. Some advantages of staffing are:

- Recognition in the community of the seriousness of the organization's mission and activities. It indicates that the local arts agency is an organization that intends to serve and stay the course.
- Development of the capacity to move ahead more quickly. Effective staff will be able to follow up on opportunities more readily and maintain ongoing activity."[30]

The decision to hire staff should be based on a sound analysis of the organization and what it really needs to fulfill its mission. Hiring staff to do the things board members don't want to do or can no longer sustain through volunteer effort doesn't exempt board members from all previous responsibilities. A classic example is the organization that hires a chief executive because board members don't like to raise money. The board may expect the executive to not only raise funds for programs and operations, but will "raise his own salary" too. This isn't fair to the organization or the employee. Although a chief executive may assume some and even significant fundraising responsibility, fundraising continues to be a key board responsibility so that the executive can spend time and energy on activities that fulfill the organization's mission.

Changes in Board Responsibilities

When the first paid staff person is hired, some board members may find it difficult to shift from being deeply involved in the day-to-day management of an organization to taking on a governance role. On the other hand, sometimes the board steps back too far and expects the new staff person to do everything that many volunteers had done before, from keeping records to running programs to raising money. Boards need to be flexible and to reevaluate and change board/staff responsibilities as the organization evolves. With the hiring of the first professional staff, board roles should gradually shift to be more focused on governance and less on operations. (See the Board Development chapter.)

LEADERSHIP SUCCESSION—THE NEXT GENERATION

Given the relative youth of the nonprofit arts sector and of the many organizations within it, it is no surprise that we are at the point of a generational transfer of leadership on a scale that has never before occurred. A professional leader's departure can be the most challenging and important change in an organization. For many organizations, the impending change represents the first step beyond a founder, a step Theatre Communications Group Executive Director Ben Cameron describes as "a step especially fraught with problems and challenges."[31] For others, the transition represents another kind of crisis, particularly when a departing chief executive has been especially strong, or perhaps even more so when the organization is left in the wake of serious management problems.

Planning for Succession

Succession planning is a process for ensuring that the most qualified person is always running the organization. Its aim is not necessarily to groom a successor or determine ahead of time who the next chief executive should be. A good plan proposes guidelines and options for action when that action is necessary. The steps of the plan are activated when the present chief executive leaves, planned or not.[32]

The board plays an essential role in succession planning—a proactive process to keep the management aligned with the mission and strategic direction of the organization. This is a process that the board should regularly discuss and update. Only then it is possible to create a positive succession culture that allows the board to react wisely and in a timely manner when it needs to support the present or choose the next chief executive.

Ways to ensure that succession is part of the board's ongoing discussions include the following.

Regularly update the strategic plan.

Include leadership succession as a regular part of strategic planning.

Do regular and periodic evaluations of the chief executive, the board's own performance, and whether the organization is meeting its specifically projected goals.

Keep the chief executive's job description and the organizational chart up-to-date.

Include a budget line item for transition expenses associated with changes in senior staff, including the chief executive. A common problem facing an organization during a transition is meeting unanticipated expenses associated with a search.

Keep records of previous executive searches so that the organization can learn from previous experiences and not reinvent the wheel.[33]

Circumstances of the Transition and Managing the Interim

It is important that a board understand the circumstances leading to a transition as they set about to find a new staff leader.

Was the change in leadership determined by mutual agreement, a board decision, or a decision by the current chief executive?

When is the departing chief executive's departure date? Will it be necessary to appoint an interim chief executive before a search can realistically be completed?

What is the organization's history of leadership succession? Have a number of chief executives left after a brief tenure? If so, the board needs to recognize this as a sign of an organization in trouble and take steps to repair the underlying causes.[34]

The board will likely need to determine how to handle the interim between the current executive's departure and the new leader's arrival. There may be an appropriate person on the senior staff who, ideally, has worked closely over a sufficient period of time with the current executive as part of the succession plan. If so, this person may be well suited to be interim director. He or she may also become an internal candidate for the position. Having this person in the interim director position can have several advantages. It allows the board time to be thorough in its search, avoids a leadership vacuum, and allows the board an opportunity to assess the acting director's ability to fill the position permanently. However, the risk is that the acting director may find it difficult to return to his or her former position when a permanent successor is hired.

It is also possible to hire an interim director from outside the organization, but this may require undue time and energy to get the person up to speed since he or she likely lacks the information and experience to run the organization. It also creates a double transition for both board and staff. On the other hand, it could become an effective trial run should he or she prove to be a promising candidate for the permanent position. The board should take care to make its expectations and conditions of the interim appointment clear to avoid an uncomfortable situation should it decide to hire someone else.

There are times when appointing a board member as interim director is the logical approach. While a board member will have a deeper understanding of the organization than an outsider, this solution may create difficulties if the board member becomes accustomed to running the organization. It is an awkward situation when a board member decides to become a candidate for the permanent position without the appropriate qualifications or when he or she is reluctant to let go of the reins when the new executive is in place. Some organizations require board members who apply for a permanent staff position to resign her or his position on the board. This may avoid any conflict of interest that could arise if she or he were not hired.

A final option is to assemble a transition team comprising a strategic combination of the board chair, board members, staff, and volunteers working together to run the organization until the new executive is in place.

Helping People Leave

How do we help current leaders—founders and long-term executives—leave an organization with dignity and grace? Some executives find themselves facing retirement age literally without the financial means to retire gracefully. Others, having given their lives to the arts, are unable to envision a sense of self apart from their ties to the organization. The departure of a founding director is especially challenging.

Cameron emphasizes the importance of facilitating the appropriate departure of long-term leaders in preparing for the future of an organization in transition.[35] The first step is to help a leader delegate responsibilities, both in order to instill and preserve important organizational information and as a transition for the individual. The next step is to celebrate the achievements of the past, pay proper homage by honoring the departing leader in a fitting way, and preserve the body of knowledge—creating a legacy of which the new leadership will be a part.

Despite the pain of separation, organizations must be strategic in balancing the needs of departing leaders with those of the new leaders who will undoubtedly implement change and set new directions. The third step is to help the organization itself move to the next chapter in its history without the central personality, especially in situations where there is a continuing affection for the former leader and where he or she is perceived as functioning at a high level. Boards need to shift from a desire to replicate a leader who has served them so well to an exploration of new opportunities.

Some organizations find overlapping terms helpful; others do not. Determine what will work best for your situation. If letting go is difficult for the departing chief executive, perhaps a meeting after the first few weeks of the new tenure is the best approach. However, the departing leader must give the new leader time and room to make the position their own. In the best of all possible worlds, a retiring founder or chief executive will be a tireless advocate for the organization well into the future in an appropriate way, but not as a board member. Undoubtedly a cordial relationship between the old and the new is ideal for the health of the organization.

Supporting New Leadership

Once a new person is hired, after many hours and an incredible amount of work, the board may be ready to dust off its hands, sit back, and let the new leader take the ball and run. Well, not so fast. The transition work is not over yet. The organization and the new employee are at a tremendously vulnerable stage. The board must now do everything possible to set up the new executive for success for the organization to succeed. Here are some tips for ensuring that the new executive and the organization have a "marriage made in heaven."

Create a sense of celebration around the arrival of the new executive. Communicate the excitement and sense of opportunity you feel about the hiring of your new executive to internal and external stakeholders. Plan a series of social events for him or her to meet the staff, the full board, and key arts and community leaders.

Create a transition team—composed of strategically selected board, staff, and volunteers—to educate the new executive about the organization and the community. While the new executive shouldn't be stifled by history, he or she needs to be sufficiently informed to build on prior success and consciously chart a new course for the future.

Check in regularly with the new executive to see how everything is going. Encourage open and honest communication; be candid enough to allow the executive to talk about any real problems.

Establish ground rules for board and executive interaction. Both parties should be frank about the kinds of communication each regards as useful and mutually critique the first few board and committee meetings and other interactions to ensure they are meeting each other's needs.

Introduce the new executive to all the "right" people: local elected officials, business and education leaders, donors, civic groups, schools and colleges, the chamber of commerce, media. Take him or her to meet arts administrators and attend their events. Make sure the new executive understands why these people and groups are important to the organization.

Be prepared to be supportive of all the issues families face when they relocate: finding the spouse appropriate work or volunteer activities, helping children adjust to new schools, and locating satisfactory housing are all issues that can affect job performance even though the new executive may love his or her new job.

Recognize that there will be an adjustment period for both the new executive and the board. Once the flurry of the former executive's departure and search is over, everyone wants things to settle down and be calm and stable. Realistically, that won't happen for a while. Despite the fatigue of the transition, the board will need to muster renewed energy. The wise board will feel enormous pride in the new leader it has chosen and excitement and commitment about the work ahead.

FINAL NOTES ON LEADERSHIP

Managing change is an inevitable part of any arts organization's survival and growth. Navigating rapid and sometimes unpredictable social, economic, political, and cultural changes in the environment demands imagination and courage from board and executive leadership as well as qualities that go beyond standard management and governance skill. Cameron suggests the following talents and sensibilities that distinguish leaders capable of ushering an organization through change.

Leaders recognize and change key organizational assumptions.

Leaders "create value through the power of their ideas, the depth of their commitment, and the authenticity of their character."[36]

Leaders have the ability—indeed the charge—to think long term.

Leaders focus on intangibles, vision, values, and motivation.

Leaders have the ability to synthesize and analyze complex ideas to provide a unifying, relatively simple vision that will inspire and galvanize others to follow.

Leaders recognize the importance of collective, rather than individual, energy and seek to instill larger team performance. While there is irreplaceable value in

> individual artistic genius, talent alone does not assure an ability to lead an organization; the ability to work collectively, rather than in isolation, is essential for leading an organization.
>
> Leaders get above and beyond the organization in order to see the total landscape, while management emphasizes immersion within.
>
> Leaders model achievement, integrity, courage, investment, and clarity through their own behavior.
>
> Leaders command power, authorship, significance, and love, and impart these gifts to others.
>
> Leaders provide three services: creation of forums in which meaning is created and communicated, arenas in which decisions are made for actions to be taken, and courts in which decisions are made about the appropriateness of actions in relation to goals.
>
> A leader links ongoing renewal to constant preparation for departure.
>
> Leaders know when to move, when to stand still, and when to stop.
>
> Leaders recognize that innovation always comes from the outside—for example, to enable us to see the issues of audience development through the filter of grassroots political organizing rather than merely through subscription renewal campaigns.
>
> Leaders are passionate about what they do.
>
> Leaders are clear about the core values of the organization, the ones worth fighting for."[37]

Boards are well served when they seek and nurture these qualities in staff leaders, but also when they consider their governance role as one that requires these same qualities of analysis, vision, creative thinking, and teamwork with staff.

ENDNOTES

1. McDaniel, N., & Thorn, G. (1992). *Work Papers 2. Arts Boards: Myths, Perspectives and New Approaches* (B. Carlisle, Ed.). New York: FEDAPT.
2. Wolf, T. (1999). *Managing a Nonprofit Organization in the Twenty-First Century*. New York: Simon & Schuster Inc.
3. There are many titles used for the chief executive in an arts organization—executive director, managing director, president and CEO, etc. For purposes of this chapter, the author has chosen to use the generic term "chief executive" when speaking of the professional staff person who is at the top of the organizational chart, and who reports directly to the board.
4. Weaver, C.C. (1993). *Let's Get Personnel: A Handbook for Arts Organizations* (A. Brannock, Ed.). Raleigh, NC: North Carolina Arts Council and North Carolina Association of Arts Councils.
5. Ibid.
6. Wolf.
7. Ibid.
8. Roosa, A.M., & Chin, P.L. (2002). *The AAM Guide to Writing an Employee Handbook*. Washington, DC: American Association of Museums.

9. The National Center for Charitable Statistics (NCCS), Philanthropic Research, Inc. (PRI)/GuideStar, and the IRS have created the nation's largest database on U.S. nonprofit organizations, National Nonprofit Research Database. http://nccsdataweb.urban.org/faq/

10. Twombly, E.C. (2002, December). *Executive Compensation in the Nonprofit Sector: A Focus on Arts and Cultural Organizations* (Monograph). Washington, DC: Americans for the Arts.

11. Arts organizations that were at least 20 years old paid their chief executives an average of $53,000 annually, compared with $30,000 for groups that were less than five years old.

12. Arts groups with at least $1 million in revenue paid their chief executives an average of $90,000 per year, compared with $12,800 annually for arts organizations with less than $100,000 in revenues. Furthermore, a group's location in major arts centers—Boston, Chicago, Los Angeles, New York, and Washington, DC—is also a key factor in setting higher executive wages. The median salary paid to executives in the arts in these cities was $39,000, compared with $30,400 for arts executives in the rest of the United States.

13. Americans for the Arts. (2003). *Local Arts Agency Salary and Benefits Survey Fiscal Year 2002: A Detailed Report about the Compensation Practices of the Nation's Local Arts Agencies with Paid Staff during Fiscal Year 2001.* Washington, DC: Author

14. Townsend, A.M. (2000). *An exploratory study of administrative workers in the arts: Are they really different from for-profit workers?* Public Personnel Management, 29(3), pp. 423-435.

15. BoardSource. (2005). *What constitutes excessive pay for chief executives?* Retrieved May 1, 2005, from www.boardsource.org/FullAnswer.asp?ID=91

16. Ibid.

17. Twombly.

18. Americans for the Arts, *Local Arts Agency Salary and Benefits Survey.*

19. Horn, P. (2002). *To Compete for Workers, Nonprofit Groups Look Beyond Salaries.* Knight Ridder Tribune Business News, p. 1.

20. Peters, J., et al. (2002). *Help Wanted: Turnover and Vacancy in Nonprofits, a San Francisco Bay Area/Silicon Valley Study.* San Francisco: CompassPoint Nonprofit Services.

21. Nonprofit World. (2005). *Don't Let "Sick" Workers Undermine Your Organization.* Nonprofit World, 2005. 23(1), p. 14-17.

22. McDaniel, N., & Thorn, G. (2005). *Leading Arts Boards: An Arts Professional's Guide for Creating and Leading an Effective Collaboration with Board and Volunteers.* Brooklyn, NC: Arts Action Issues.

23. Albert, S. (2000). *Hiring the Chief Executive.* BoardSource. Retrieved May 1, 2005, from www.boardsource.org/loginwelcome.asp

24. DiConsiglio, J. (2004). *Flirting with Disaster.* Board Member, 13(1).

25. Weaver.

26. Ibid.

27. Vogel, B.H., & Quatt, C.W. (2005). *The Nonprofit Board's Guide to Determining Chief Executive Compensation.* BoardSource. p. 92.

28. Pierson, J., & Mintz, J. (1999). *Assessment of the Chief Executive: A Tool for Governing Boards and Chief Executives of Nonprofit Organizations* (2nd Ed.). BoardSource.

29. Weaver.

30. Yuen, C.L. (1990). *Community Vision: A Policy Guide to Local Arts Agency Development.* Washington, DC: National Assembly of Local Arts Agencies.

31. Cameron, B. (2003). *Leadership Succession/Organizational Transformation. Succession: Arts Leadership for the 21st Century.* Chicago: Illinois Arts Alliance Foundation, p. 81–87.

32. BoardSource. *CEO Succession Planning.* Retrieved May 1, 2005, from www.boardsource.org/TopicPaper.asp?ID=128

33. Beidler, P.R. (2003). *Leadership Succession in Nonprofit Organizations: A Board Member's Viewpoint. Succession: Arts Leadership for the 21st Century.* Chicago: Illinois Arts Alliance Foundation, p. 110–118.

34. Ibid.

35. Cameron.

36. *Fast Company* magazine (as cited by Ben Cameron)

37. Ibid.

RESOURCES

Americans for the Arts
1000 Vermont Avenue NW, 6th Floor
Washington, DC 20005
202-371-2830
Fax 202-371-0424
www.AmericansForTheArts.org

BoardSource
1828 L Street NW, Suite 900
Washington, DC 20036-5114
202-452-6262 or 800-883-6262
Fax 202-452-6299
www.boardsource.org

National Center for Charitable Statistics (NCCS)
NCCS/PRI National Nonprofit Research Database
A program of NCCS, Philanthropic Research, Inc. (PRI)/Guidestar, and the IRS
http://nccsdataweb.urban.org/faq/

Society for Human Resource Management
1800 Duke Street
Alexandria, Virginia 22314
Phone US Only: 800-283-SHRM; Phone International: +1-703-548-3440;
TTY/TDD 703-548-6999
Fax 703-535-6490
www.shrm.org

CHAPTER 9

Volunteers in the Arts

9

PAM KORZA

Volunteers constitute a key resource for arts organizations. In a field where economic pressures make the flexible use of people and skills a must, volunteers can provide essential services at all levels from staff to board to one-time helper. They extend staff resources by assisting or even running ongoing programs and services, launching new projects, serving on committees, providing invaluable clerical or technical support, researching, and documenting. Volunteers may lend professional skills and advice—accounting, carpentry, graphic design—which can save arts organizations considerable money. And volunteers lend fresh and diverse perspectives and enthusiasm. In addition, volunteer involvement in your organization reflects the community's commitment to your organization, as well as your interest in having its input.

This chapter focuses on integrating volunteers into a cultural organization to support both ongoing and special activities. The principles presented regarding motivating, managing, and rewarding volunteers are equally applicable to your arts education committee chairperson, a college student intern conducting demographic research, or the helper who occasionally assists with bulk mailings. Considerations about recruiting, orienting, and managing board members as a specific type of volunteer are discussed in the Board Development chapter.

AGE-OLD MOTIVATIONS, CHANGING CONDITIONS

The enjoyment and artistic stimulation the arts provide have always attracted people to volunteer. In general, the things that motivate people to volunteer have remained much the same over time. They reflect an individual's values, needs, interests, and desire for self-fulfillment. Volunteer work offers opportunities to:

- help others and make a difference;
- learn new things and develop new skills;
- belong to a group or institution;
- be needed;
- have fun;
- grow personally and gain self-esteem;
- share skills, knowledge, or talents;
- gain meaningful acknowledgment;
- enhance one's public image;
- gain valuable career insights;
- make professional contacts;
- enjoy social contact with others; and
- support causes in which one believes.

The things that motivate people to volunteer reflect an individual's values, needs, interests, and desire for self-fulfillment.

Yet, while the desire to volunteer remains strong, the conditions that enable people to volunteer have changed dramatically in the past 25 years. Working adults, typically the most often tapped pool of volunteers, juggle demanding jobs and family obligations. Many are cautious about making long-term commitments they might be unable to fulfill. Today's volunteers want to serve responsibly within the limited amount of time they have to devote to volunteer activities.

For arts organizations to succeed at developing a volunteer base of support given such competing demands for volunteers' time, they must make volunteering as easy and accessible as possible. Volunteer programs, such as City Cares of America, have found the following operating principles important:

Arrange volunteer opportunities to involve short-term commitments and flexible hours.

Offer choices in terms of the types of jobs that suit both individual motivations and availability.

Minimize paperwork and procedures which might discourage busy people or those unfamiliar with institutional processes.

Diversify the volunteer pool to reflect the growing populations of people over age 55 and people of color.

Appeal to motivations unique to certain groups, such as young professionals' social interests or senior citizens' need to remain active contributing members of society.

THE NEED FOR A VOLUNTEER PROGRAM

To recruit discerning prospective volunteers, organizations must "sell" themselves. It is essential to plan ahead of time what you want and can offer. This means developing a serious, well-planned volunteer program.

Getting the Organization Ready

A first step in preparing your organization to fully incorporate volunteers is to assess staff attitudes and preconceived notions about volunteers.

Attitudes. The planned integration of volunteers into an organization may elicit from staff a variety of concerns and questions: Can we maintain our standards of quality with volunteers providing service? How much time will it take to effectively manage them? I've been burned before when I counted on volunteers who didn't come through; I'd rather do it myself. These concerns must be acknowledged and dealt with in order to agree upon the purpose of the volunteer program and to foster an environment in which volunteers are respected and nurtured, but also where policies and expectations are clear to volunteers.

The Independent Sector's 2001 report on volunteerism in the United States describes, for example, "mindset" barriers to youth involvement that must be addressed for a productive and enjoyable experience for both youth and nonprofit organizations. For organizations interested in engaging youth, it cites the importance of having open discussions about stereotypes that adults and youth have of each other; conducting exercises to practice "shared power;" understanding "dos and don'ts" behavior for adults on working with youth, and for youth on working with adults; and adopting decision-making processes that include youth in meaningful ways.[1]

Roles. Organization staff and board members should also clearly communicate their roles and degree of involvement in each volunteer's work. Who will coordinate the volunteer program—recruitment, placement, and tending to volunteer group needs? Assuming there is staff, what will be individual staff members' roles regarding interviewing, selecting, training, evaluating, and firing? Such planning also clarifies a volunteer's rights, for example, to have information that enables her to carry out her work, defining limits, responsibilities, and authority. This could include selecting artists for the arts agency's community gallery or negotiating advertising rates when selling ads for a program book.

Practical concerns. Also consider the following practical issues:

> **Work space.** Can you provide work stations, phones, office supplies, and computers to enable volunteers to be effective?
>
> **Accessibility.** Can you make volunteer opportunities accessible to people with disabilities or for whom transportation might be a problem (teens, seniors, low-income individuals)?
>
> **Policies.** What are your policies regarding reimbursement of expenses related to volunteering, benefits such as free or reduced tickets, or grounds for termination? Will you acquire volunteer liability insurance?

Components of a Volunteer Program

A successful volunteer program has the following components:

> **Purpose statement.** This statement describes why the organization includes volunteers.
>
> **Coordinator.** Someone, either paid or volunteer, should have primary responsibility for planning and implementing the volunteer program and monitoring volunteer needs.
>
> **Policies.** Policies can include reimbursements, insurance, free tickets to events and other perks, and termination.
>
> **Recruitment.** Volunteer recruitment requires methods and tools to identify and enlist prospective volunteers; discover volunteer interests, abilities, and experiences; and determine potential positions.
>
> **Selection and placement.** For proper placement, one must first determine which persons are most qualified or have potential for particular volunteer positions, and what positions are most suitable for each individual.
>
> **Training.** All volunteers should engage in an orientation process that prepares and equips them with the necessary information, knowledge, and skills to do an effective job.
>
> **Support.** Volunteers need ongoing guidance, support, recognition, and gratitude for their work.

Evaluation. Appropriate processes must be put in place to solicit volunteers' evaluations on their experiences. These evaluations should be used to make necessary changes to the volunteer program and keep it functioning effectively.

EVALUATING WHO YOU NEED AND WHERE TO FIND THEM

In order to be clear with potential volunteers about what specifically they can do, it is first necessary for you to evaluate your own organizational needs.

What are the specific jobs, tasks, or projects which require doing?

Is it more cost-effective to use volunteers or staff to accomplish activities and objectives? What is the potential to enhance or compromise the quality of programs and services with volunteers versus staff?

How can jobs best be broken down in terms of responsibilities, time commitment, difficulty, interest, and balance? For example, in trying to attract busy, working people, consider how jobs can be structured to be accomplished and monitored on weeknights or weekends when many people are more likely to be available.

What are the volunteer benefits associated with each job?

Are you looking for "members" with long-term needs (social, self-actualizing, learning, contributing) or "joiners" with short-term ones (social contacts, affiliation, status)?

Are you looking for "members" with long-term needs (social, self-actualizing, learning, contributing) or "joiners" with short-term ones (social contacts, affiliation, status)?

Job Descriptions

Drafting job descriptions serves several purposes. From your organization's standpoint, it forces you to summarize the work that needs to be done—assessing how many people are required, estimating work hours, projecting deadlines. It makes actual recruitment simpler and clearer. From the volunteers' viewpoint, it offers a more realistic picture of what they are getting into and what they can expect to gain by being involved in your organization.

The job description most often expresses an ideal. In recruiting it is important to remain appropriately flexible and to balance the pros and cons of what each applicant has to offer. Perhaps two people with complementary skills can do the job better than either one alone. Keep in mind the implications of compromises, however. Two people require twice as much oversight on your part, at least at first.

Allow room to grow. Aim for balance between specifying responsibilities and leaving room for the volunteer's own initiative to shape the job. See the sidebar, Sample Job Description.

Where to Find Volunteers

Sources of volunteers are many. It is useful to first profile who your current volunteers are since they reflect likely sources of new recruits. What are their characteristics? What has motivated them to volunteer with you?

Sample Volunteer Job Description

Job Title
Publicity Assistant for *On the Road Theater*

Job Description
Assist publicity coordinator with the following tasks:

- write press releases;
- write radio advertising copy;
- make and follow through on media contacts (feature writers, television, and radio personnel);
- arrange guest spots on local radio and TV shows;
- update media mailing and email lists; and
- orchestrate mass mailings and emailings.

Skills and Interests Necessary or Helpful for Job
Good writing and interpersonal communication skills
Computer skills helpful, but will train
Knowledge of and interest in theater preferred

Job Benefits
Receive intensive one-on-one training in various aspects of publicity
Gain knowledge of how a touring theater group functions
Gain free admission to all shows or one complimentary ticket per show

Training Provided
Copy writing
Targeting markets
Writing press releases
Information/mailing systems management
Developing media relationships

Hours per Week Recommended
Six to ten, depending on flow of local and regional tour schedule

Anticipated Length of Internship
Minimum six months or ongoing

Other Information/Comments
The intern will have the chance to work with and learn from a lively and credentialed promotion staff of two! She or he will also have opportunity to get to know the artists in the company during down time through special seminars set up for volunteers.

On the Road Theater can work with college students and appropriate college programs to help students earn college credit for this volunteer opportunity.

Staff Person:________________________ Date:__________

To focus your recruitment, determine the type of volunteers you are seeking, considering factors such as:

- special skills or knowledge (bookkeeping, graphic design, database management, research);
- particular ages and backgrounds (nearby residents, teens, people of color, seniors, low income, young professionals, people with disabilities); and
- numbers (for example, large numbers needed for a short-term opportunity such as a festival or fundraising campaign).

These factors will suggest likely places to look for qualified prospects, as described by the volunteer coordinator for a children's museum.

> It is important for the Children's Museum to recruit young people as volunteers. We wanted the youngest children who come to the museum to have role models from their community, and we needed the perspectives of young people as part of our team. Those who had grown up using the museum were a likely source of youth volunteers. We used our membership lists and also went to local junior and senior high school art classes. The Latino children who live in the community where the museum is located had not visited the museum much. We decided to put together a teen council comprising Latinos to advise us on programming, image, and other things which would help us better serve this community. We identified Latino youth with the help of the nearby church and a Puerto Rican neighborhood center.

Besides identifying skills and characteristics to define sources of volunteers, use your accumulated list of volunteer factors to help you to narrow down the field of prospects. Then conduct *targeted* recruitment.

Recruiting and Involving for Diversity

As communities experience increasingly diverse populations, there is value in diversifying your arts organization's volunteer base to reflect and connect with that diverse community. However, methods and approaches for recruiting and providing positive experiences that have worked effectively in more homogenous settings may not be as useful in more diverse environments. Arts organizations need to understand and be sensitive to cultural norms and life circumstances that may affect how various groups will respond to your organization and its volunteer needs. They will need to develop culturally-sensitive ways to reach these diverse groups. In an article for *The Journal of Volunteer Administration*, diversity consultant Santiago Rodriquez explained that in the United States, there are a great number of community-based organizations focusing on volunteer activities. But he explains:

> ...this phenomenon may not be representative of many other societies where extended family groupings, religious organizations, and government may play greater roles... Community-based volunteerism, for example, is relatively rare in the traditional Hispanic and Asian contexts—families and churches may play a greater role... Activities such as fundraising, how people are managed, and how decisions are made within groups are affected by different cultural norms. Diversity, then, is about learning to include different perspectives and processes so that the work of the organization can be as effective as possible.[2]

If people of color, senior citizens, people with disabilities, teens, people who are economically disadvantaged, or others are not frequenting your programs or using your services, it is almost a sure bet that they are not volunteering in or reflected in the leadership of your organization either. As is true in any effort to engage and involve diverse populations, you must first look at how you are currently serving the interests of diverse groups through your programs. You may find that there is work to be done that first ensures that your organization is relevant to various segments of the community.

Sources of Volunteers

Community and Professional Associations
Civic organizations

Church groups

Trade associations

Fraternal associations

Labor unions often offer union gatherings and newsletters for the purpose of publicizing volunteer opportunities; some labor unions provide expertise of union members.

Youth
Schools

Arts-related programs (dance schools, drum corps)

Clubs (scouts, 4-H)

Church groups

Vocational schools

Businesses and Corporations
Companies sometimes have an executive loan program which enables employees to provide expertise or consultation to community organizations on company time.

Business Volunteers for the Arts

People of Color
Urban League

National Association for the Advancement of Colored People (NAACP)

Ethnic organizations

Church groups

Political, advocacy organizations

African-American fraternities and sororities

College departments (African American, Native American, Asian, Latin American studies)

Neighborhood associations

Volunteer Agencies
City Cares of America

Business Volunteers for the Arts

Singles organizations

People Looking for Job Retraining or Career Skills
Unemployment office

Career counselors

Senior Citizens
Councils on Aging

Senior centers

RSVP (Retired and Senior Volunteer Program)

Nursing homes

Retirement communities

People with Disabilities
Statewide Very Special Arts (VSA) programs

Associations for Retarded Citizens

Schools and clubs for the deaf or blind

State agencies for deaf and hard of hearing and blind

College Students
Academic departments

Internship programs

Work/study programs

Sororities and fraternities

Clubs and service organizations

Campus arts organizations

Career services

Specialized Sources of Unpaid Workers
Prison inmates or individuals with community service sentences

U.S. Army Corps of Engineers (for traffic control, leveling earth, hauling major equipment, loaning and erecting tents)

In recruiting volunteers from diverse populations, be clear on why you are interested in including them in your organization. Are you seeking multiple viewpoints, better service to constituencies, enlightenment on issues or needs, or simply to better reflect your community? Be sure your reasons are authentic and clear to you before you begin a recruitment plan.

Involve individuals from these groups to identify, recruit, and manage volunteers. If recruitment overtures, for example, are carried out exclusively by white or able-bodied members of your organization, these may be met with skepticism by those you are hoping to involve.

Make use of culturally specific media, organizations, and other resources in recruitment.

Internship Programs

Internships are structured volunteer experiences which offer formal training and are designed as focused learning opportunities. Some arts organizations have developed internship programs, typically attracting college students wanting practical experience, but often times drawing adults who may be in career transition or recently retired and looking for meaningful experiences. Many college programs encourage—and even require—students to do internships as field training. Graduate degree programs in arts administration often require students to do full-semester, full-time internships to fulfill their degree requirements. In these cases, students are usually paid by the arts organization. In the case of internships, expectations on both the volunteer's and the agency's part are high, so special care must be taken in assessing needs, making placements, and providing specific training and formal evaluation.

RECRUITMENT

Recruiting volunteers is not as simple as posting flyers saying that you need help. Effective recruitment first targets the people you believe offer what you're looking for and who might be interested in volunteering with you. Then you find the best way to connect with them. A positive impression will convince discriminating people that you can provide an interesting, well-organized, and personally meaningful experience with your organization.

Recruitment, whatever form it takes, should answer basic questions a volunteer may ask.

What is the purpose of your organization?

Why do you need volunteers?

What will a volunteer get out of working with you?

You should be able to demonstrate to a potential volunteer that:

- your organization is a worthy, credible one;
- you are well-organized, take volunteers seriously, and won't waste the volunteer's time;
- your organization can provide a meaningful, fulfilling, and challenging experience while being flexible given the volunteer's time limitations and need for appropriate training;
- you have specific opportunities in the form of job descriptions; and
- others with similar experiences have been involved in a productive way in the organization.

Recruitment Techniques

The same range of publicity and promotion opportunities that you use to market programs and services can be employed to announce volunteer opportunities as well.

Print and electronic media. Through press releases, public service announcements, and calendar listings in the general media, you can reach broad segments of your community. More specialized media (an African-American newspaper, a radio station with a large teen following) are effective in reaching certain segments.

Classified advertisements. Help wanted or opportunities placements might catch the eye of someone in career transition or interested in job training.

Feature articles and television and radio talk shows. These are great ways to recognize a particular volunteer's efforts or a recent major accomplishment, and to promote the program at the same time.

Newsletters. Organizational bulletins, newsletters, and listservs are effective at targeting individuals affiliated with groups, such as service organizations and clubs..

Brochures, flyers, mailing inserts. To satisfy ongoing or specific volunteer needs, a promotional brochure or information sheet can provide immediate information and be used to reach targeted groups.

Internet. Your website can give ongoing visibility to your volunteer program as well as promote recruitment periods.

Personal contact. Because volunteering is a people affair, the most effective recruitment techniques are those enabling prospective volunteers to meet face-to-face with people involved in the organization. According to a 2001 Independent Sector national survey, 71 percent of Americans who agreed to volunteer did so after being asked in person.[3] Volunteers who have had a good experience with your organization are often the most effective recruiters.

Person-to-person recruitment may take the form of:

- presentations to clubs, corporations, senior groups, and schools;
- presentations before or after performances when people are excited about what you do;
- door-to-door or neighborhood meetings;
- open house; or
- word of mouth.

The most effective recruitment techniques are those enabling prospective volunteers to meet face-to-face with people involved in the organization.

To recruit large numbers of volunteers for one purpose, the pyramid approach can be effective. Each board, staff, and key volunteer is responsible for recruiting a certain number of volunteers (say five), who in turn must each recruit additional volunteers (say two). By beginning with 20 individuals, you can recruit 300.

Volunteer agencies. Explore how national volunteer organizations, perhaps with branches in or near your community, can promote your arts organization to prospective volunteers.

> **City Cares of America** is a national umbrella organization for more than 24 local City Cares organizations across the country. It seeks to promote a heightened understanding of community needs and service and to improve the quality of life in the communities.
> www.CityCares.org

Points of Light Foundation works in partnership with the **Volunteer Center National Network** to help mobilize people and resources to find creative solutions to community problems. Volunteer Centers are conveners for the community, catalysts for social action, and key local resources for volunteer involvement.
www.pointsoflight.org/centers

RSVP (Retired and Senior Volunteer Program) is a component of the **Senior Corp program of the Corporation for National and Community Service.** It connects volunteers age 55 and over with service opportunities in their communities that match their skills and availability.
www.seniorcorps.org

Youth Service America (YSA) is a resource center that partners with thousands of organizations committed to increasing the quality and quantity of volunteer opportunities for young people ages 5-25 to serve locally, nationally, and globally.
www.ysa.org

VolunteerMatch offers a variety of online services to support a community of nonprofit, volunteer, and business leaders committed to civic engagement.
www.volunteermatch.org

Other resources which may operate volunteer placement services include local volunteer liaisons, chambers of commerce, community development agencies, libraries, councils on aging, and other community-based organizations.

Consider the following to determine which techniques to employ.

Are your volunteer needs ongoing or sporadic? Recruiting 500 festival volunteers for a three-day event requires different strategies than recruiting five volunteers who will share receptionist duties year-round.

How much time and resource do you have for the recruitment process itself? What are your capabilities for handling response to the recruitment process?

What technique(s) will be most effective in eliciting the response you would like?

When communicating with prospective volunteers, make it easy to say yes. Avoid cumbersome and protracted application procedures.

Above all, when communicating with prospective volunteers, make it easy to say yes. Avoid cumbersome and protracted application procedures. Be honest. Don't minimize challenges, time commitments, or other factors which you fear might discourage a volunteer. Whenever possible, send recruiters whose backgrounds reflect the types you are recruiting (i.e., send teens to recruit teens). Finally, stress the potential benefits to the volunteer and the people you serve rather than how your organization benefits from volunteers.

SELECTING AND PLACING VOLUNTEERS

For responsible volunteer positions, especially longer-term or ongoing ones, it's important to choose volunteers who can be the best match for the job. Four steps are helpful in assuring appropriate selections.

1. Involve the person who will work most closely with the volunteer in the selection process.

2. Use a written application, but make it simple and suitable to the responders; use it to gain basic information about the person and his or her interests and qualifications.
3. Interview applicants to get to know each other's aspirations, goals, and interests, and to assess if a mutually beneficial match can be made.
4. Check references for volunteers who will be placed in highly responsible positions.

Ask yourself these questions when making final selections.

What is the individual seeking from a volunteer experience?

Can your needs be met given the skills, interests, and capabilities of the applicant?

What are the applicant's personal qualities and how would she or he fit in the office?

What is the applicant's availability?

Rejecting and Confirming Volunteers

It's not easy to reject an applicant for a volunteer position. The reason may be that you cannot make the right match of skills and job so that both the volunteer and your organization benefit. It's a good idea to state at the outset that sometimes more people are interested than you can accommodate. Even so, honestly assess an individual's skills and suitability. Suggest skill areas to strengthen. And provide alternatives, referring the applicant to local volunteer agencies or other arts groups with whom the applicant may find a more suitable opportunity.

Whether or not you accept an applicant, make decisions expeditiously and notify candidates on the status of their applications. Too much elapsed time leads good people to lose interest and pursue other opportunities.

GETTING A GOOD START

Once a volunteer is on board, a number of practical steps can be taken to ensure a successful experience for both the volunteer and the organization. Primary among them are a memo of agreement, orientation, and training.

Memo of Agreement

At the outset clarify expectations about the volunteer's role on a project or in the organization. For a volunteer assigned to your fundraising auction, simply explaining expectations before the volunteer goes on duty, perhaps with a written information sheet for referral during the job, may suffice. If the volunteer position is long-term—for example, a semester-long student internship or a yearlong festival chairmanship, a memo of agreement can formalize the understanding of expectations for both parties. Such an agreement is generally similar to a job description and specifies:

- the volunteer's responsibilities and tasks;
- the volunteer's personal goals for the job; and
- the organization's obligations (travel reimbursement, training opportunities, evaluation procedures, etc.).

A memo of agreement fosters a sense of commitment by both parties to meet their obligations to each other. It may establish a trial period during which both volunteer and organization can assess if things are working out. It is also a reference tool as the volunteer's experience is periodically evaluated. At the same time, a memo of agreement should remain flexible and open to revision as the job needs to change or as a volunteer grows into new responsibilities.

Orientation

Orientation integrates volunteers into your organization's activity. It should address needs on three levels: individual, group, and task.

Team building creates a sense of belonging, of place, and helps to establish work and social relationships.

Individual Needs

Individual needs are most basic and should be addressed first. Take care to make new volunteers feel welcome, comfortable, and a part of your organization. This may be accomplished by developing a buddy system where seasoned volunteers can help new volunteers get started, learning individual interests of volunteers and engaging in nonwork conversation, providing the volunteer with a space to work, giving sufficient attention and training in the early stages, and, most importantly, monitoring how the individual's own motivating factors are being met.

Group Needs

Orient new volunteers to your organization. Cover the background, history, achievements, and aspirations of the organization, its programs, procedures, timelines, staff structure, and relevant policies. This may be done by inviting a new volunteer to a staff meeting, holding a special orientation meeting for several new volunteers, or making available annual reports, newsletters, and other written materials that convey a picture of the group. Volunteers should feel like they can get to know staff members even if they may not work directly with all of them.

Make sure that staff and board members introduce themselves and their roles to new volunteers individually or at an orientation meeting or reception so that volunteers connect to the people of your organization. Show how each member works toward and contributes to the larger picture. This team building creates a sense of belonging, of place, and helps to establish work and social relationships.

Task Needs

Even the most experienced professional or savvy board member may benefit from orientation to the steps and mechanics of the tasks at hand. Struggling with the quirks of the office copy machine can be as frustrating to completing a task efficiently as composing a fundraising letter for the first time. For any new undertaking, stop and remember that this may be a new skill for the volunteer—newcomer or veteran volunteer.

Orientation to tasks is most often accomplished one-on-one between a supervisor and a volunteer. Procedure manuals and instruction sheets are useful written tools. More extensive training may be critical for more demanding activities, such as making fundraising calls or coordinating an artist residency program.

Training

Training is an investment in your organization. It helps a volunteer to acquire knowledge and skills beyond specific individual tasks. Through training, volunteers understand their jobs better, take initiative, and therefore contribute in a deeper, more meaningful way. It is also an expression of your belief in volunteers' capabilities and value to the organization.

Training is an investment in your organization... It is also an expression of your belief in volunteers' capabilities and value to the organization.

Training may take a variety of forms, depending on the nature of the job and the skills being taught. These might include:

- one-on-one training, provided by a staff or board member or a senior volunteer;
- in-house workshops, presentations, discussions, practice, or role play; or
- attendance at conferences or workshops, or enrollment in continuing education or college courses.

VOLUNTEER MANAGEMENT

In rewarding relationships, there is a balance reflecting what both parties are getting from the association. If one party stands to gain disproportionately and this is apparent to the other, productivity sometimes diminishes. Everyone deserves to gain the satisfaction they expect.

Volunteer management is simultaneously the management of human relations and the management of work that needs to get done effectively. To be most productive and fulfilled, volunteers need to be supervised and nurtured on an ongoing basis, with special attention given to keeping each person motivated. Central to this process is effective communication. This means setting up regular opportunities to check on one's progress on specific tasks, to work out problems which arise, and to talk about how the volunteer is feeling about her work. It also involves ongoing evaluation and a willingness to make changes as the volunteer adjusts to the position.

Volunteer management is simultaneously the management of human relations and the management of work that needs to get done effectively.

Leadership

Effective volunteer managers recognize potential in people and maximize opportunities to develop and utilize talents while keeping their eyes on the goals of the organization or project at hand. To accomplish this, those overseeing volunteers need to recognize that different situations call for different approaches or styles of leadership and problem solving. Good leadership utilizes the potential and resources of the individual or group. When a volunteer is involved in and buys into pertinent decisions, confidence is built and commitment is reinforced.

Effective leaders:

- develop trust among those who work together;
- introduce challenges at appropriate times and accept risk;
- balance learning by mistake with averting mistakes;
- demonstrate confidence in volunteers, once it's earned;
- share individual and collective achievements with the entire group;
- model professional behavior and standards;

- project a positive view of the organization, its work, and people;
- perceive unspoken needs and foster a communicative environment;
- keep focused on the vision and the goals, and keep the work in context of its significance and impact;
- help unravel and break down tasks;
- provide information tools;
- help solve problems effectively; and
- empower volunteers with decision-making opportunities when they are ready.

See the Volunteer Coordinator sidebar for the roles embodied in this position.

Those overseeing volunteers need to recognize that different situations call for different approaches or styles of leadership and problem solving.

Retaining Volunteers

Some organizations have taken into account the changing conditions described at the beginning of this chapter and restructured their volunteer programs to accommodate flexible opportunities for people with demanding lives. They have, for example, shifted their expectations from longer- to shorter-term commitments.

Yet organizations still need long-term commitments from board members or other key volunteers where continuity is an advantage. So it is frustrating when a board member resigns prematurely, a key volunteer leaves due to burnout, or a promising volunteer mysteriously quits midstream. Problems of volunteer retention can often be traced to ineffective recruitment, placement, orientation, training, or management. Many of these experiences can be averted by following some of the advice provided throughout this chapter.

Below are common reasons organizations lose volunteers, and suggested approaches for prevention.

Burnout

Recruit enough volunteers.

Divide labor to reduce the work load.

Allow longer lead time to accomplish the work.

Encourage delegation among volunteers.

Provide leaves of absence.

Respect people's limits.

Make time for fun!

Loss of interest

Make sure the position matches the volunteer's interests and expectations.

Provide enough to do.

Offer more challenge.

Make clear the ways that the position makes a difference—the reasons for routine or clerical tasks—and provide support.

Recognize accomplishments on a regular basis and when a volunteer's efforts have helped to meet project/organizational goals.

THE VOLUNTEER COORDINATOR

Recruiting, training, and managing volunteers requires time, energy, and planning. For an organization intending to work regularly with volunteers, a coordinator to oversee volunteers and to work with staff is essential. The coordinator could be a staff member, a board member, or even a volunteer. In any case, the volunteer coordinator's job includes many responsibilities.

Planning
Guide staff to define volunteer positions.

Identify volunteer needs for various projects.

Develop timelines for recruitment and training.

Research potential volunteer sources.

Recruitment, Placement, and Orientation
Recruit volunteers.

Oversee or implement the review and selection process.

Orient volunteers.

Train and monitor training by others.

Lead by outlining organizational goals, modeling professional behavior, and providing direction, guidance, and assistance.

Management
Organize meetings.

Monitor morale, work load, quality, and quantity of work, the learning experience, and additional volunteer needs.

Replace volunteers who leave.

Keep records on the volunteer program, including volunteer contact information, letters of recommendation, and quantifiable information such as the number of volunteer hours contributed per year and the economic value of program.

Facilitate information flow among staff and volunteers through meetings, email announcements, etc.

Provide support and recognition.

Evaluation
Provide mechanisms for assessment of volunteer work through meeting and discussion, and for volunteer assessment of the project, organization, and volunteer program.

Recognition
Monitor staff or others who are overseeing volunteers' work to ensure ongoing recognition.

Provide meaningful recognition, suitable to the volunteer's job, tenure, and accomplishments.

Offer outside opportunities for new learning or ways to understand the big picture of the organization.

Rotate responsibilities to offer variety.

Lighten up and have fun!

Lack of motivation
Match assignments with interests and motivations.

Equip the volunteer with the information, tools, and support to tackle the job.

Steer activity toward clear-cut successes.

Offer more challenge.

Provide opportunities for advancement and participation in decision-making or new programs.

Validate positive effort through recognition and appreciation, both formal (events, certification, awards) and informal.

Low energy

Check the work conditions—space, supplies, scheduling, transportation—for possible problems.

Keep an eye on the work load, providing a balance between work and play. Have fun!

Be sensitive to personal or other factors competing for a volunteer's attention.

Interpersonal difficulties

Keep lines of communication open.

Detect problems before they flare up; anticipate trouble spots.

Check organizational attitudes toward volunteers.

Reassign a volunteer to a new staff person.

Recognition and Thanks

However you show appreciation, tailor it to the individual as much as possible.

Volunteers need ongoing recognition and thanks for their contributions. Most important, recognize and thank an individual volunteer in a way that is meaningful to him or her. If a volunteer is motivated to learn new skills, then sending him to a weekend workshop may be exactly the recognition needed: It says that you believe in his capabilities enough to invest in his training. A corporate executive who has volunteered time to put your books in order may be best served by a letter of thanks praising his help and sent to his employer as evidence of community service. For another volunteer seeking to make a difference in the lives of disadvantaged children, seeing the play produced in an artist residency may be the greatest possible reward.

Arts organizations have approached this important aspect of volunteerism in a variety of creative ways.

Training opportunities

Promotion to increased responsibility

Involvement in decision-making

Certificates of appreciation

Complimentary or reduced price tickets to programs

Recognition in the media through feature articles, thank you ads, letters to the editor, or newsletter features

Birthday celebrations

T-shirts, pins, etc.

Parties

Special opportunities, such as meeting guest artists

Contemporary Volunteer Organization Case Study: The Arts Commandos of St. Louis

Since 1991 the Regional Arts Commission of St. Louis, Missouri, has successfully organized a volunteer program that serves the short-term needs of the region's various arts organizations. Modeled after the Arts Commandos program created by the Oklahoma City Arts Council in 1982, the program is structured to take into account the busy lifestyles of business professionals who would like to help arts groups but who want finite and fun opportunities to lend a hand. Following is a description of the program. Examples of recruitment and management tools from the Arts Commandos are provided throughout the chapter.

Arts Commandos

The Arts Commandos program cultivates a corps of energetic volunteers who work as individuals or as a team to complete specific short-term or one-shot projects for nonprofit arts and cultural organizations in St. Louis. Comprising both professionals and community volunteers, Arts Commandos have the opportunity to experience the arts intimately, with a hands-on, task-oriented approach to serving the arts community. In 2005, there were more than 250 active members of the Arts Commandos.

To date, the Commandos have worked on more than 650 projects for a total of nearly 36,000 volunteer hours for the arts community! In 2004 alone, the Arts Commandos donated more than 2,000 hours.

> The mission of the Arts Commandos volunteer program is to provide a flexible, innovative, and personally rewarding way for individuals to benefit the St. Louis arts community by donating their time and energy to further the mission of each organization that seeks their support.

Arts Commandos do not promise to run an organization or to be fundraisers. They do promise to commit their muscle, brains, or any combination thereof to solve problems for arts organizations. The program is an innovative source of volunteers that addresses the needs of the arts community and provides personally rewarding experiences in a flexible format for volunteers.

How Arts Commandos Works

Arts and cultural organizations in the St. Louis area submit proposals to the Arts Commandos for short-term projects. Most projects are less than one day in length, and work shifts generally range from four to six hours. Tasks carried out by the Arts Commandos may include but are not limited to painting, carpentry, decorating, project planning, staffing events, waiting tables, light moving, etc.

Prospective Arts Commandos are invited to a biannual gathering where they can register and learn about upcoming projects for the year, including descriptions of the work that has to be done and the dates needed. Individuals sign up as a project manager or volunteer and have fun meeting other Arts Commandos in a social setting. Arts Commandos can choose to volunteer for as many or as few projects as they like.

Four chairpersons (typically two male, two female) head up the Arts Commandos efforts each year. The chairpersons are aided by teams of project managers (also paired in male–female teams) who coordinate each project. Some projects require only a small Commando workforce; others require many teams working simultaneously.

The arts organizations utilizing Arts Commandos volunteers supply all materials needed for a project, as well as refreshments and tokens of appreciation.

However you show appreciation, tailor it to the individual as much as possible. Both individual and team recognition can help people feel good about their work and their contributions to the organization.

Evaluation

Supervision and evaluation also should be appropriate to the job and the volunteer. A new ticket seller may need to be monitored by a veteran volunteer during her first shift or two. Volunteers involved in more extensive roles benefit from regular feedback on their work. Ongoing monitoring and feedback helps ensure quality and detects problems before they flare up. It is helpful when a new volunteer comes on board to discuss how you plan to monitor and evaluate work and to ask what will be the most helpful way to provide feedback.

Evaluation is a two-way street. It is as important for you to know how the volunteer experience is working for the volunteer as it is for the volunteer to know how he is doing. Evaluation questionnaires are useful for collecting information from volunteers about their own experience and about the volunteer program, both midstream and at the end of a volunteer experience. Organizations should also consider some deliberate way of learning volunteers' opinions about and recommendations for the job they did—an evaluation form, an exit interview, a lunchtime debriefing, or a project staff meeting.

IN CLOSING

A successful volunteer program meets the needs of both the organization and the volunteer. This shows in the achievement of your organization's goals and in the personal and professional growth of your volunteers. Strive to create an environment in which people are encouraged to give their best and to grow in qualities such as commitment, confidence, productivity, initiative, cooperation, imagination, self-esteem, and pride in work well done.

ENDNOTES

1 Independent Sector. (2001). *Engaging Youth in Lifelong Service.* Washington, DC: Author. www.independentsector.org

2 Rodriguez, S. (1997, Spring). Diversity and Volunteerism: Deriving Advantage from Difference. *The Journal of Volunteer Administration.* Richmond, VA: Association for Volunteer Administration, (XV)3, pp. 18-20.

3 Independent Sector. (2001). *Giving and Volunteering in the United States 2001.* Washington, DC: Author. www.independentsector.org

RESOURCES

The Association for Volunteer Administration advances volunteerism and enhances quality of life locally and globally by engaging leaders of volunteers through professional development, networking, and quality products and services. In *The Journal of Volunteer Administration*, it offers in-depth articles on program management, model projects, and tested techniques for successful volunteer involvement; articles representing a wide diversity of volunteer program types, settings, and locations; research; and a better understanding of volunteer administration. www.avaintl.org

Business Volunteers for the Arts (BVA), a network of 23 regional organizations around the country, links business professionals with arts organizations in their communities. Since its inception in 1975, BVA has generated over $100 million in donated services, cash, and other in-kind resources.
www.artsandbusiness.org/bvahome.htm

Energize Online Bookstore offers an extensive selection of volunteer management books and resources in print and electronic format.
www.energizeinc.com

e-Volunteerism: The Electronic Journal of the Volunteer Community is an interactive online journal spearheaded by internationally-known volunteerism consultants Steve McCurley and Susan J. Ellis. It includes practical and scholarly articles as well as extensive current and archived information.
www.e-volunteerism.com

Independent Sector is the leadership forum for charities, foundations, and corporate giving programs committed to advancing the common good in America and around the world. It publishes biennially a report, *Giving and Volunteering in the United States.*
www.independentsector.org

CHAPTER 10

Financial Management in the Arts

10

CHRISTINE BURDETT
WITH CONTRIBUTING EDITORS
SALLY ZINNO AND MAREN BROWN

Many volunteers and staff of community arts organizations are intimidated by the prospect of managing the financial aspects of their organizations or programs. Preparing and analyzing budgets is often delegated to an accountant or banker on the board—or assigned to a staff member who lacks training in financial management. In many cases, people bring their personal financial habits to their work environments, which can be potentially devastating for the organization if one is accustomed to routinely overspending their income (accumulating credit card debt) or failing to balance their checking accounts.

Financial responsibility, by law, rests with every member of the board, who are "fiduciaries" caring for the nonprofit organization (nonprofit) as a public trust for the rest of the community. Financial management is such a fundamental aspect of organizational sustainability that every board and staff member should understand the basics. The good news is that the principles of financial management are easy to understand and well within the grasp of every key member of the organization.

Good financial management can provide vital support to arts programs and important evidence of organizational stability to funding sources. Keeping accurate, up-to-date financial records guarantees that you will be ready any time those records are requested by the Internal Revenue Service (IRS), donors, loan officers, or members. Those records are proof that the organization has upheld its fiscal responsibility. If an organization's programs and budget are significant, the board and staff need qualified financial advice to ensure that the financial operations and data are appropriate.

Most importantly, financial management helps board members govern effectively and staff members operate efficiently, and it assures your constituency that your organization is run responsibly.

This chapter will help you to understand the terminology and practices of financial management, so that your organization can prosper in good times and bad. It covers how to:

- designate responsibility for financial planning and evaluation;
- set financial objectives;
- develop and use a budget effectively;
- apply basic principles of accounting that affect nonprofits;
- prepare and read financial statements;
- meet reporting requirements common to most nonprofits;

- evaluate options for computerization;
- foresee financial problems and opportunities; and
- analyze an organization's financial health.

THE MANAGEMENT CONTROL CYCLE

First, set objectives in measurable, financial terms, using a budget. Second, carry out programs according to that financial plan. At regular monthly or quarterly intervals, measure financial performance against the objectives using operating statements. Lastly, comparing actual revenues and expenses to those predicted in the budget and projecting end-of-fiscal-year results provides a basis to take corrective actions so that overall objectives may be met or revised.

In essence, the financial management cycle consists of three activities constituting basic management controls. First, set objectives in measurable, financial terms, using a budget. Second, carry out programs according to that financial plan. At regular monthly or quarterly intervals, measure financial performance against the objectives using operating statements. Lastly, comparing actual revenues and expenses to those predicted in the budget and projecting end-of-fiscal-year results provides a basis to take corrective actions so that overall objectives may be met or revised. In this way, problems may be uncovered before they become unmanageable crises. The plan also facilitates the process of evaluating opportunities that may arise.

BOARD RESPONSIBILITY

When it comes to financial management, the buck stops with the board of directors. Financial management is the board's fiduciary responsibility, both as individuals and as a group. When board members take their financial responsibility seriously, they can feel confident that they are fulfilling the public trust, and it is much less likely that they will encounter legal difficulties from mismanagement or debt. (See the Board Development chapter for more information about the role of boards of directors.)

Specifically, the board is responsible for ensuring that the organization has the resources available to achieve its mission. That responsibility includes approving the budget and monitoring actual performance, as well as setting and enforcing fiscal policy. Ordinarily the board is advised by a treasurer, a finance committee, and professional staff (when there is one). It is each board member's responsibility, however, to understand financial information that is reviewed and to make informed decisions.

Board and staff members need adequate time to review financial information before discussing or voting on it. Financial statements, budgets, and written explanations of the impact of the financial status on the organization should be available in advance of meetings to allow for examination and questions.

The Treasurer's Role

The treasurer is the board's chief financial representative. In smaller organizations with no director or finance staff, the treasurer may be responsible for signing legal financial documents (including checks), loan applications, or grant reports. The treasurer is also responsible for key functions, which may include bookkeeping, writing checks, reconciling bank statements, monitoring petty cash, preparing financial statements, and filing state and federal tax forms. When paid or volunteer staff members are assigned some or all of these tasks, the treasurer oversees their activities so that financial operations are performed in a responsible and ethical manner.

The treasurer is the primary communicator to the board concerning the organization's financial position, and helps the board to understand the organization's finances. Most meeting agendas include a treasurer's report to update the board on financial activity.

Finance Committee

The finance committee plays a key role in overseeing the financial operations of the organization and building public confidence in the organization's fiscal management. The finance committee advises the board on financial matters and typically exercises the following responsibilities:

- recommends an annual operating and capital budget and the multiyear budgets needed for long-term planning;
- monitors income and expenditures against budget and projections during the year and recommends changes to meet established goals;
- reviews and recommends financial policy and ensures compliance with legal reporting requirements; and
- oversees investments.

SET FINANCIAL OBJECTIVES WITH A BUDGET

A budget is a financial plan expressed in quantitative, monetary terms over a specific time period. It is the central instrument of financial planning and control. If a budget is prepared correctly and evaluated throughout the year, an organization can prevent or be forewarned of financial difficulty.

Budgets may be presented in various formats, but they always reflect revenues and expenses and the difference between them. A bit on nomenclature here: In financial management, the term *revenues* is used interchangeably with the word *income*, and the word *expenses* is sometimes substituted by the word *costs*. The difference between revenues and expenses is either termed a *surplus* (when revenues exceed expenses) or, if the figure is negative, a *deficit* (when expenses exceed revenues).

Why Prepare a Budget?

A budget is the means by which arts managers allocate resources to fulfill organizational goals. A budget:

- provides a plan that helps guide management decisions;
- guides subsequent spending decisions and serves as a yardstick to measure actual performance;
- spurs the keeping and maintaining of adequate financial records;
- clarifies the need to expend scarce resources effectively;
- supports grant applications and fundraising campaigns; and
- provides an objective standard for evaluation.

Who Develops the Budget?

A budget projects anticipated revenues and expenses based on the organization's operational plan for the year. In all but the smallest organizations, the budget should be generated from the bottom up. People who make the day-to-day spending decisions and must live within a budget should have key roles in creating the budget. The program managers are closest to the action and understand best what expenses are incurred and what revenues are likely to be generated. If the board has a related committee, the program manager often works with that committee chair or the committee as a whole to review the budget recommendations. The arts education manager, for example, would work with a board education committee on the budget for education programs and services.

Types of Budgets

There are three basic types of budgets.

Organizational budget—a financial plan developed for an overall operation

Program budget—a financial plan developed for a single project

Cash flow budget—a projection of available cash over a specified time period

An organizational budget can be created by combining all of the individual program budgets and adding general administrative revenues and expenses.

The Budget Process

Each organization's budget process must be developed to fit its governing procedures and mix of board and staff members. Some boards will expect a treasurer or finance committee to take the lead on budgeting, while others will entrust budget development to professional staff. Boards that meet quarterly are likely to plan their budgets earlier in the fiscal year than will boards that meet monthly.

An annual budget is based on the program and operational plan determined by the board and staff. The board and staff must first agree on the annual program goals and priorities and the administrative and operating objectives required to achieve them. The budget process, then, attaches expenses and revenues to the strategies required to implement the plan.

Eight Steps to Budgeting

Preparing a budget is a dynamic process and follows eight key process steps. Beginning here with budget preparation and continuing throughout the chapter we'll be using the numbers and actions of a hypothetical case, the City Center for the Arts (CCFA).

1. **Establish budget guidelines.** The board determines budget guidelines, including fiscal year (accounting period covering 12 consecutive months over which an organization determines earnings and profits), the percent for salary increases or anticipated inflationary increases; the target for the bottom line surplus; dates by which budget drafts and final version must be prepared; and general budgeting guidelines (for example, all programs must break even or no major capital expenses may be incurred).

   CCFA's budget covers one fiscal year, July 1 to June 30. Its general guidelines are that the total budget must generate a surplus in the range of $5,000 and that salaries and general overhead will be presented separately (rather than prorated to programs).

2. **Develop program budgets.** Program managers, working with committee chairs as appropriate, create a revenue and expense budget for each program area and earned income service, such as a retail store. (See the shaded Artist in Residence column in Figure 1.) Costs must be researched and revenues conservatively estimated for each program. Individual programmatic budgets serve as a tentative budget until the organizational budget is approved by the board.

Figure 1: City Center for the Arts Organizational Budget

Figure 1: City Center for the Arts Organization Budget
EXPENSE WORKSHEET

			PROGRAMS				FUNDRAISING			SERVICES		
DESCRIPTION	Total	General Admin.	Artist in Residence	Jazz Concert	Arts Festival	Dance Performance	Member Ship	Special Events	Other	News-letter	Other	Other
Salaries/Benefits	60,000	60,000										
Outside Fees/Services	1,000	1,000										
Office Supplies	500	500										
Phone/FAX	2,000	2,000										
Travel	2,500	1,000		1,000		500						
Memberships	600	600										
Professional Development	1,200	1,200										
Space Rental	3,600	3,600										
Utilities	0											
Insurance	250	250										
Printing/Copying	14,600	600	1,500	1,000	2,500	1,000	2,000			6,000		
Postage/Shipping	1,200									1,200		
Artist Fees	25,000		7,500	10,000	2,500	5,000						
Art Materials	5,000		2,000		3,000							
Equipment	0											
Purchase	6,000	6,000										
Repair	0											
Rental	5,500				5,000	500						
Hospitality	3,000				500			2,500				
Other	1,000				1,000							
Cash Reserve	10,000	10,000										
Total	**142,950**	**86,750**	**11,000**	**12,000**	**14,500**	**7,000**	**2,000**	**2,500**	**0**	**7,200**	**0**	**0**

Figure 1: City Center for the Arts Organization Budget
REVENUES WORKSHEET

		PROGRAMS/PROJECTS						
DESCRIPTION	Total	Artist in Residence	Jazz Concert	Arts Festival	Dance Performance	Fundraising	Services	Other
Corporate Grants	19,000	5,000	4,000		5,000	5,000		
Foundation Grants	25,000		5,000	5,000	5,000	10,000		
Government Grants	0							
Federal								
State	11,000	3,000	5,000	500	2,500			
Local								
Business Contributions	22,500			7,500		15,000		
Membership Drive	25,000					25,000		
Other Private Donations	3,000			3,000				
Fundraising Events	10,000					10,000		
Program Admissions	11,400		7,800		3,600			
Fees/Tuitions	6,500			6,500				
Advertising	5,000		2,500		2,500			
Sales	1,050			1,050				
Interest	0							
Other-School District	3,500	3,500						
TOTAL	**142,950**	**11,500**	**24,300**	**23,550**	**18,600**	**65,000**	**0**	**0**

3. **Draft organizational budget.** The chief executive or finance committee adds together the program budgets with overall administrative expenses into a single organizational budget for the year, as illustrated in Figure 1.

4. **Refine budget.** The board reviews the total picture to see if it meets budget guidelines and is realistic and achievable. It then negotiates potentially conflicting uses of resources, eliminates costs, and combines resources to prevent deficits. Grant and contribution projections are discussed by the fundraising committee and development staff.

Figure 2:
CCFA Annual Budget

Figure 2: City Center for the Arts ANNUAL BUDGET
July 1, 2007–June 30, 2008
Approved May 15, 2007

REVENUE	Proposed 2008 Budget	FY 2007 Actual	FY 2006 Budget
Contributed Revenue			
Corporate Grants	$19,000	$15,000	$13,000
Foundation Grants	25,000	23,000	30,000
Government Grants			
Federal			
State	11,000	13,000	13,000
Local			
Business Contributions	22,500	22,000	20,000
Membership Drive	25,000	22,750	22,000
Other Private Donations	3,000	3,000	
Fundraising Events	10,000	12,000	10,000
Earned Revenue			
Program Admissions	13,000	12,798	13,000
Fees/Tuition	6,500	5,575	5,500
Advertising	5,000	5,000	5,000
Sales	1,050	1,037	1,000
Investments		475	
Other	3,500		
TOTAL REVENUE	**144,550**	**135,635**	**132,500**

EXPENSES	Proposed 2008	FY 2007	FY 2006
Salaries/Benefits	60,000	56,392	56,500
Outside Fees/Services	1,000	1,000	1,000
Office Supplies	500	428	500
Phone/FAX	2,000	1,837	1,500
Travel	2,500	2,500	2,500
Memberships	600	600	600
Professional Development	1,200	1,000	1,200
Space Rental	3,600	3,600	3,600
Utilities			
Insurance	250	250	250
Printing/Copying	14,600	13,798	13,350
Postage/Shipping	1,200	1,223	1,000
Artist Fees	25,000	22,500	22,500
Art Materials	5,000	4,782	4,500
Equipment:			
Purchase	6,000		
Repair			
Rental	5,500	5,000	5,000
Hospitality	3,000	2,467	2,500
Other	1,000	1,000	1,000
Cash Reserve	10,000	15,000	15,000
TOTAL EXPENSES	**142,950**	**133,377**	**132,500**
Net Surplus (Deficit)	**1,600**	**2,258**	**0**

5. **Present, consider, and approve final budget.** The board presents, considers, and approves the final budget. Though one cannot underestimate the importance of program-level budgeting, the budget presented to the board is typically made available in a *program summary format*, in which individual program revenues and expenses are combined into a single annual budget. This enables the board to more easily focus on the mission and operating activities needed to support the organization. An example is presented in Figure 2, the CCFA Annual Budget.

   The figures in the "proposed budget" column correspond to the totals from the worksheets completed in Step 2 and 3. The board compares these to the previous year's actual figures and budget. Unusual deviations, higher or lower, are explained through accompanying notes.

If the program summary format is used, this same presentation of income and expenses should also be used in the *statement of activities* report that compares budget to actual performance throughout the year (see page 256 for an explanation of statement of activities). The budget for the following fiscal year should be approved before the start of that year.

6. **Share final budget with others in organization.** The board or chief executive communicates the approved budget back to the committee or staff responsible for each program.

7. **Monitor budget.** The staff, the treasurer, and finance committee monitor revenues and spending throughout the fiscal year, generally at regular intervals, such as quarterly or monthly. The organization compares the equivalent time period for the budget compared to actual revenues and expenses for that period.

8. **Make financial adjustments.** Staff and committee chairs adjust programs and spending decisions to keep the budget on target. If there is a significant *variance* (see Figure 8) between revenues and expenses, the organization will adjust its financial plan. For instance, one might have included income from a grant that was not received, or ticket revenues for a performance were overly optimistic. Before taking corrective action, the board will need to assess if these losses can be offset with higher revenues in other areas of the operation.

Additional Budget Concepts

Zero-based budgeting is a popular approach to developing a budget. Each revenue and expense line item is justified by current programs and conditions without regard to previous years' figures. The budget is built from scratch, zero.

Historical-based budgets are developed by reviewing the organization's recent expense and revenue history and adjusting last year's budget by a factor that compensates for new conditions—inflation, economic trends, new programs. In practice, most planners use a combination of the historical and zero-based approaches.

Fixed and variable costs are useful for distinguishing costs during budgeting. Some costs—like administrative salaries, rent, insurance, or utilities—will not be affected by the number or kinds of programs that are presented or by audience turnout. These are fixed costs. Variable costs depend upon the kinds and numbers of programs and include artist salaries, printing, advertising, technical staff, concessions, etc.

Relevant costs are those that planners consider as they decide whether or not to continue an existing program or develop a new program. Planners consider program costs and revenue among the issues that determine program value. The costs directly related to the program—including, for example, artist fees and marketing expenses—are clearly relevant costs in a decision about whether or not to expand a concert series. The mortgage payments on the theater are not relevant to making such a decision. Usually only the variable and direct costs for that program are significant in making the decision.

METHOD 1: Average overall ticket sales

Seating Capacity		800
Usual Paid Attendance	x	70% (.70)
Total Tickets Sold		560

METHOD 2: Modify Model 1 according to anticipated popularity of program

JAZZ CONCERT (predicted to draw larger than average audiences)		800
Average Ticket Price	x	$12
Total Anticipated Income		$7,800
DANCE PERFORMANCE (predicted to draw smaller than average audiences)		400
Average Ticket Price	x	$9
Total Anticipated Income		$3,600

How to Build a Budget

Building a budget is the most fundamental step in the financial management process.

Estimating Income

Always calculate income first. The anticipated level of revenue will guide the change in expenses that you can afford. If you calculate expenses of $1,000 first, it is too easy to predict that you'll sell 100 tickets at $10 each even if your experience makes this number unrealistic. So protect yourself from optimistically inflating revenues to match the expenses you want to meet by realistically estimating revenues first.

Estimate the amount you can conservatively expect to collect from each of the proposed activities. Don't guess. Consider past sales records, the economic climate, changes in your planned promotions, how competitors are doing, how peer organizations did with similar programs, and other related factors. Based on this information, develop models that help you to predict results and reduce guesswork.

To estimate performance revenues from ticket sales, for example, you could multiply the seating capacity for each performance times your usual percentage from previous sales (Method 1 above). If you have historical information about ticket sales for that type of performance, it is best to modify this base figure according to the anticipated popularity of each of the proposed performances, the attractiveness of the price, and the likely success of your marketing campaign (Method 2, above). Variably priced seats must also be accounted for in your estimates. Take the same approach for calculating likely registration fees for a workshop or sales in a gift shop.

For the City Center for the Arts, note the method for computing ticket income for the jazz concert and dance performance.

The program manager first determined the average number of tickets sold per performance in the past. She then reviewed sales history for past jazz concerts and determined that they had routinely sold out in the past, allowing her to reliably estimate an above-average audience. Conversely, the dance performance is a newer event that has not yet built as large an audience, and its budget is below the average.

Revenue forecasting should be made in conjunction with a marketing plan. A program that has a strong publicity and promotions plan is more likely to realize earned income objectives than one that has minimal promotion. See the Marketing the Arts chapter for more information about how to develop a marketing plan.

Although it is tempting to inflate revenue projections, always utilize the most conservative figures to protect the organization from deficits. List grant funds as revenue only if you are certain you will receive it. Base estimated fundraising revenue on previous successes and this year's planned campaign. As with the ticket sales example above, use your average membership renewal rate and your own past experience with a mail membership solicitation campaign to predict revenue. Be wary of dramatically increased fundraising goals, and exercise caution in estimating a big increase in any revenue figure unless there is a specific, achievable plan for realizing the increase, including the expenses needed to carry out the plan.

Estimating Expenses

The sample expense worksheet (see Figure 1) lists possible areas in which you may incur expense. Add to it any categories that apply specifically to your organization. Expenses should relate directly to the programs in which you expect to generate income. You may choose to list general administrative or fixed expenses first and then the variable expenses necessary to create the programs.

Take time to consider what it will actually cost to run each program. Base estimates on your own experience or the related experience of others. Call printers, insurance agents, and suppliers to get estimates. Consider the effects of the rate of inflation on last year's expenses and the impact of increased activity in a program or administrative area.

Be conservative. If in doubt about which of several likely values to assign for an expense, select the most expensive. In developing draft budgets you may use ranges of expense and related revenue to determine what you can do with the available funds. You may also wish to allow an amount in the budget for contingencies—unexpected or miscellaneous expenses.

Some planners allocate administrative expenses for each program. Staff salaries, rent, utility bills, insurance, postage, and other overhead expenses are charged to each program according to the amount of time or space that each one requires. This method more accurately projects the resources and costs necessary to conduct each program, but is more complicated to calculate. One must estimate how much time the staff expends on each program. Then one can calculate the percentage of floor space each occupies to determine its share of the rent, its portion of postage costs, etc. Some choose to allocate the obvious expenses—such as printing bills—to each program; they then come up with a rule of thumb to allocate other overhead expenses. For example, the proportion of staff time devoted to each program can be used to determine the share of other overhead expenses.

In most organizations that have more than one paid staff person, the chief executive submits a total amount for salaries and benefits for inclusion in the budget rather than line items for each position.

A budget's expenses should reflect an organization's priorities. For example, an arts organization committed to an education program that spends less and less of its money on its education program should take a closer look at the program.

Cash Flow Budget

Cash management is a critical issue for most nonprofits. Cash must be available when the organization needs it to pay bills, salaries, and other obligations; however, the annual business cycle usually results in an uneven flow of cash through the year. A cash flow forecast can help predict cash shortfalls or times of surplus. Knowing in advance of an impending cash shortage or surplus allows the nonprofit to manage cash flow rather than be managed by it.

If a shortage is predicted, the organization can ask a donor to advance a planned gift, negotiate a short-term bank loan, or make spending decisions that minimize or eliminate the temporary shortage. Similarly, the prediction of a temporary cash surplus can allow the financial manager to make short-term certificate-of-deposit investments to realize a higher interest return.

A cash flow budget begins by determining the opening cash balance for the period, then adding anticipated revenues received and deducting expenses that will be paid for each month. The ending cash balance for January becomes the opening cash balance for February and so on. Projections are based on past experience, anticipated activities and events, and anticipated obligations. All staff that has responsibility for program revenue and authorizing expenses should provide ongoing information for the cash flow budget.

Cash flow projections are useful only if they are compared to actual performance. At the end of each month, when the actual cash results are known, the future cash flow projection should be revised.

The figures in the cash flow projection (see Figure 3) correspond to the revenues and expenses in the City Center for the Arts' organizational budget.

OPERATE AND MEASURE PERFORMANCE

Since nonprofits hold assets in trust for the public good, they must establish and maintain financial operations and controls that ensure that they function in a responsible and ethical manner. In addition, the board and staff need to rely on systems and reports that allow them to monitor results and measure performance against expectations established in the budget.

The management control cycle explained earlier shows how the interdependent elements of financial management intersect. The projections are budgets, the measurement is done through accounting record keeping, and the comparison and monitoring are made possible with financial statements. The previous section considered budgets. Now we look at some fundamental principles of accounting—what you need to account for with bookkeeping, how to track cash, and then how to summarize the many daily transactions into summary financial statements.

Figure 3: City Center for the Arts Cash Flow Projection

Cash Flow	July	August	September	October	November	December	January	Febrauary	March	April	May	June
Beginning Balance	40,000	40,142	32,984	32,158	35,049	33,291	31,533	27,207	33,299	48,741	67,583	57,758
EXPENSES												
Gen. Admin.	11,558	6,558	5,559	5,559	6,158	6,158	5,559	5,808	5,558	5,558	5,558	17,158
Project A			3,667				3,667				3,667	
Project B	12,000											
Project C				14,500								
Project D									7,000			
Membership							2,000					
Special Events			2,500									
Other												
Newsletter	600	600	600	600	600	600	600	600	600	600	600	600
Other												
Other												
142,950	24,158	7,158	12,326	20,659	6,758	6,758	11,826	6,408	13,158	6,158	9,825	17,758
Balance	15,842	32,984	20,658	11,499	28,291	26,533	19,707	20,799	20,141	42,583	57,758	40,000
REVENUES												
Program A			11,500									
Program B	24,300											
Program C				23,550								
Program D									18,600			
Fundraising					5,000	5,000				25,000		
Contributions							7,500	7,500				
Grants								5,000	10,000			
Other												
142,950	24,300	0	11,500	23,550	5,000	5,000	7,500	12,500	28,600	25,000	0	0
Closing Balance	40,142	32,984	32,158	35,049	33,291	31,533	27,207	33,299	48,741	67,583	57,758	40,000

Nonprofit financial systems records, like those of all businesses, provide critical data needed by board and key staff and are subject to monitoring by outside authorities. As a result, they should be set up and maintained carefully and reviewed periodically by a person with accounting expertise so that the nonprofit is run according to generally accepted accounting principles (GAAP). GAAP, which are defined by the American Institute of Certified Public Accountants (AICPA) and the Financial Accounting Standards Board (FASB), provide the basis for sound accounting policies and procedures. Due to recent scandals in the corporate community, nonprofits are under increasing scrutiny, which has added to the complexity of doing business (see sidebar on Sarbannes-Oxley).

Financial records should be maintained by a qualified bookkeeper or a person with specific training. Reasonably priced and user-friendly accounting software is available to nonprofits and this accounting software should serve as the cornerstone of your *accounting system*, which is both the manual and electronic processes that you use to record your financial transactions and information. Using such software facilitates the process of managing financial information and producing financial reports.

GAAP groups the assets of a nonprofit into three classifications: unrestricted, temporarily restricted, and permanently restricted net assets. These indicate whether the funds have any donor-imposed restrictions on how they may be used.

Unrestricted net assets have no donor-imposed restrictions and can be used for any operating and programmatic expenses authorized by the board. Restrictions placed on funds by the board, but not by the donor, are considered unrestricted. Examples of unrestricted funds include revenue from ticket sales, membership, and retail operations, and an annual appeal for general operations.

Temporarily restricted net assets have donor-imposed purpose or time restrictions. Once the restrictions are met, the funds may be used. A grant for a school program is temporarily restricted until the program is complete, at which point the funds are released from restrictions.

Sarbanes-Oxley Act

Few legislative acts have had such widespread implications for the financial management of nonprofits as the American Competitiveness and Corporate Accountability Act of 2002, known more commonly as the Sarbanes-Oxley Act. After the 2001–2002 accounting scandals of Arthur Anderson and Enron, Congress took decisive action to improve corporate accountability through enhanced board oversight and auditing procedures. While the Act is aimed primarily at publicly-traded companies, many of its provisions that have broad application to nonprofits are only now beginning to emerge. State legislatures are passing or introducing legislation that adapts the spirit of the Act to improve nonprofit accountability and board oversight.

According to the *Sarbanes-Oxley Act and Implications for Nonprofit Organizations*, a 2003 report by BoardSource and Independent sector, the Act has the following implications for nonprofits:

Independent and Competent Audit Committee. The authors of this report contend that nonprofits must assess the costs and benefits of an audit (though an audit is usually required for organizations with budgets in excess of $500,000 that receive federal funds, audits can be useful for smaller nonprofits), and ensure that board members are able to interpret financial statements. The boards of larger organizations should separate the audit and finance committees so that there is no conflict of interest.

Responsibilities of Auditors. Though not mandated by the Act, BoardSource and Independent Sector recommend that nonprofits rotate auditors every five years and select different firms to performing auditing and nonauditing financial services, such as bookkeeping. In addition, the authors recommend that auditors disclose "critical accounting procedures and practices" to the audit committee.

Certified Financial Statements. While not required under the Act, the report recommends that both the executive director (president, CEO) of the nonprofit and its chief financial officer sign off on all financial statements to signal that they are accurate and complete.

Insider Transactions and Conflict of Interest. The Act specifically prohibits providing private loans to insiders, and though this is a rarity in nonprofits, the authors strongly recommend against nonprofits providing loans to their executives, even if it is not prohibited in the state in which the nonprofit operates.

Disclosure. The Act specifically regulates a number of disclosures that are common in publicly-traded companies, and although most are not required for nonprofit organizations, the authors advocate that nonprofits make their Forms 990 and audited financial statements readily available to the public.

Whistle-Blower Protection. The Act has a number of protections, which have implications for nonprofits, for whistle blowers who report the criminal actions of companies. The authors recommend that nonprofits proactively conduct internal audits to uncover areas of potential fraud and install procedures and policies to help prevent illegal activity.

Document Destruction. Sarbanes-Oxley regulates the destruction of documents that could be used in official proceedings. The authors recommend clear, written guidelines that mandate "document retention and periodic destruction," as well as how to handle electronic files and voicemail. If an official investigation is under way or in consideration, "nonprofit management must stop any document purging in order to avoid criminal obstruction."

For a more comprehensive discussion of the Sarbanes-Oxley Act and its implications for the financial management of nonprofits, consult the full report compiled by BoardSource and Independent Sector posted in the publications area of GuideStar.org at www.guidestar.org/news/features/sarbanes_oxley.jsp.

Permanently-restricted net assets are made up of contributions for which the donors require the funds be used in a specific way indefinitely. A gift to an endowment usually has a permanent restriction.

Such restricted funds must be tracked separately from funds donated for use in general operations. Regardless of how funds are designated, management has the obligation to use these various funds for the purposes for which they were intended and not use restricted funds inappropriately.

Collectively, the unrestricted, temporarily restricted, and permanently restricted assets comprise your organization's *net assets*, which are the residual amount of your revenues less your expenses from the inception of your nonprofit.

Accounting Methods

The process of financial record keeping is called accounting. A nonprofit chooses a "method of accounting" to show when revenues or expenses are recorded.

Cash basis accounting records when revenues are received, expenses are paid, and noncash transactions (such as credit cards) occur (recording a transaction means entering it in your ledger or accounting system). Neither accounts receivable nor payable are recorded in a cash basis system. *Accounts receivable* are monies owed to you but which you have not yet received (such as donations that have been pledged but not received). *Accounts payable* are bills that you have received but have not yet paid. While this method is easy to understand and implement, it often results in misleading financial information because it does not reflect financial obligations that may have been incurred but have not been recorded.

Accrual method accounting is a method in which all committed income and expenses, whether or not they have been actually received or paid, are entered in the books. Promised income—such as a grant or written pledge—are entered as income (account receivable); a promise to pay (for example, a purchase of art supplies) is entered as an expense (account payable).

In contrast to cash basis accounting, the accrual method aims to accurately reflect all of the activities and obligations made during the current accounting period, not just cash transactions.

Modified cash basis accounting is often used by nonprofits. Under this method, bookkeeping entries are made strictly on a cash basis throughout the accounting period. At the end of the period, entries are made at one time to adjust the financial records to an accrual basis form. This is usually done so that summarizing financial statements may be later presented in accrual form. Many nonprofits have their auditors make these journal adjustments for them, so that the organization need only be concerned with maintaining accurate cash basis records.

Accounting Procedures

The following briefly identifies and explains the steps to be followed in setting up a bookkeeping system. It is usually wise to seek the help of an experienced accountant or bookkeeper. When an organization's financial activities are substantial, the ongoing services of a bookkeeper or accountant are essential.

Internal control. This refers to procedures and policies that an organization can implement to improve security and avoid mismanagement of funds. A primary control measure is *separation of duties*, which requires that different people be responsible for aspects of the financial process such as check approval, check signing, and bookkeeping. However, in an all-volunteer organization or when there is only one staff member, this is nearly impossible. In these cases, the minimum safeguard is to require two signatures on checks. Often board members become involved in check signing and approval, especially for expenses over a specified dollar amount. An experienced bookkeeper or certified public accountant (CPA) should review your internal control practices periodically and make recommendations for improvement.

Bookkeeping. A well-designed bookkeeping system enables an organization to track income and expenses, produce financial statements, monitor the budget, and provide a "trail" of transactions for future workers to review. As such, it provides the basis from which an audit is completed.

Chart of accounts. A chart of accounts assigns a number or code to each type of transaction, using five categories: revenue, expense, assets, liabilities, and net assets. This makes it easier to keep track of transactions and produce reports in a consistent manner.

In recent years, several nonprofit support organizations joined to develop a Unified Chart of Accounts for Nonprofit Organizations (UCOA). The system is designed so that nonprofits can quickly and reliably translate their financial statements into the categories required by the IRS Form 990 and Form 990EZ, and other government reporting formats. UCOA is extensive, but any nonprofit could select the categories that apply to their own operations. A copy of UCOA is available from the National Center for Charitable Statistics at the Urban Institute (www.nccs.urban.org/ucoa). Some UCOA sample account categories are listed in Figure 4.

Recording cash transactions. For small organizations with few transactions, the simplest way to record cash transactions is with the checkbook, check register, and deposit slips. Use a chart of accounts to determine which transactions should be assigned to which sources, and use the codes when entering information in cash journals.

Cash receipts journal. A cash receipts journal is a source document for all income listed in an organization's financial reports. It records all checks and cash received, and identifies the source of the money received and the type of income it represents. The information in the cash receipts journal is transferred to the general ledger at the end of each month. It also provides a way to reconcile cash income with bank statements and the general ledger's cash control account. (See Figure 5.)

Entries in the cash receipts journal originate from bank deposit slips. The authors suggest using deposit books with duplicate sheets and stapling each deposit receipt to its page in the deposit book. Cash receipts must be deposited intact. Currency income should be deposited along with checks, not used to pay expenses directly. The same controls which apply to cash also apply to credit card receipts, for which procedures should be established for submission, verification, and reconciliation.

Figure 4: Chart of Accounts Example

Excerpted from Unified Chart of Accounts, version 3.0

1 Assets

1000	Cash
1040	Petty cash
1100	Accounts receivable
1200	Contributions receivable—pledges, grants, etc.
1210	Pledges and grants receivable
1300	Other receivables—notes, loans, etc.
1420	Inventory for use
1600	Fixed operating assets—land, buildings, fixtures, vehicles, etc.

2 Liabilities

2010	Accounts payable
2020	Grants and allocations payable
2100	Accrued liabilities—payroll, paid leave, taxes, etc.
2500	Short-term notes and loans payable
2700	Long-term notes and loans payable

3 Equity—unrestricted and temporarily or permanently restricted net assets

4 Contributions/Support

4000	Direct contributions—individuals, corporate, small business, etc.
4010	Individual and small business contributions
4100	Donated goods and services
4150	Donated art, etc.
4200	Nongovernment grants—corporate, foundation, etc.
4230	Foundation and trust grants
4410	United Way or CFC contributions
4500	Government grants—federal, state, local
4520	Federal grants
4530	State grants

5 Earned Revenues

5000	Contracts/fees—federal, state, local, etc.
5100	Program-related sales—service fees, etc.
5210	Dues—individual and organizational members
5800	Special events

6 Other Revenue—unrealized gain (loss), net assets released from restriction

7 Expenses (personnel related)

7000	Grants, contracts, and direct assistance
7200	Salaries and related expenses
7240	Employee benefits (not pension)
7500	Contract services—fundraising, accounting, legal, etc.

8 Expenses (nonpersonnel related)

8100	Nonpersonnel—supplies, postage, printing, etc.
8200	Facility and equipment
8300	Travel and meetings
8500	Other—list rental, contingency provision, etc.
8600	Business—taxes, bad debt expense, etc.

9 Non-GAAP Expenses—fixed asset purchases, additions to reserves, etc.

Figure 5: Cash Receipts Journal

DATE	CHECK NO.	SOURCE	AMOUNT	MEMBERSHIP	GRANTS	TICKET SALES	DONATIONS	OTHER
3/12	5762	e.e. Cummings	$500.00	$500.00				
3/12	148	John Smith	$ 30.00			$30.00		
3/13	A5487	Acme Foundation	$2,000.00		$2,000.00			
3/13		**Total Deposit**	**$2,530.00**					

Figure 6: Cash Disbursements Journal

DATE	CHECK NO.	DESCRIPTION/PAID TO	AMOUNT	GENERAL ADMIN.	PROGRAM A	PROGRAM B	FUNDRAISING	SERVICES
4/15	1174	AT&T	$85.00	$85.00				
4/15	1175	Acme Systems (rent)	$475.00	$475.00				
4/15	1176	Glory Productions (artist fee)	$3,500.00	$3,500.00				
4/15	1177	John Smith (refund)*	($30.00*)					

**The refund to John Smith must be recorded in the general ledger as a reduction in revenue rather than as an expense.*

FASB-defined separate accounting standards for contributions. When recording grants and contributions, the actual payments and formal written pledge should be checked to determine if the donor restricted the funds. Restricted funds should be coded accordingly. Tax deduction acknowledgement forms may need to be sent to the donor to comply with applicable regulations. In-kind contributions and donated services, including volunteer hours, are also recorded in the accounting system.

Cash disbursements journal. A cash disbursements journal records all cash disbursed by an organization, either in petty cash or by check. (See Figure 6.)

For organizations with few transactions and only one bank account, the check register can be used as both the cash receipts and cash disbursements journal. Notations should still be made in the register regarding the source of cash and the appropriate accounts for expenses and income. The chart of accounts code number should be written on checks, in the check register, and on deposit slips.

Bank reconciliation. The monthly bank statements must be reconciled with the cash journals. The reconciliation is the primary control over cash accounts and should be completed as soon as the bank statement is received to verify that the recorded information is correct. It should be completed before amounts are entered into the general ledger to avoid having to make correcting entries related to cash.

Other Financial Record Keeping

The accounting system should establish specific procedures for recording and reporting payroll expenses in accordance with procedures mandated by the federal government and each state. Organizations can receive guidance in setting up procedures and preparing reports from the IRS and designated state government agencies. Since organizations that fail to comply with the requirements are subject to penalties, the board and staff must ensure that the proper procedures are always followed.

Fixed assets are the property and equipment owned by an organization and valued over a certain amount. Accounting guidelines define how the purchase or donation of fixed assets is recorded. Because equipment and property lose value over time as they are used, their value is reduced over time according to guidelines for "useful life." The process of reducing the value is called *depreciation* and is recorded in the accounting system.

Financial Statements

Financial statements provide the information that the board and staff need to measure the financial status of the organization. The two core financial statements are the *statement of position* (SOP), formerly called the balance sheet, and the *statement of activities* (SOA), also called an income or operating statement and used for accrual accounting. Data for both reports are compiled from the accounting system. Boards also may wish to consult the *cash flow statement* to understand how well their organization is managing its day-to-day financial transactions.

Generally accepted accounting principles (GAAP) set guidelines for financial statements, and those guidelines are always followed when an auditor conducts a financial audit. For internal reporting, a board may modify the formats to provide data they need for decision making. Note that cash basis accounting is held to different standards.

The SOP records an organization's financial health at one point in time, such as the end of a month or fiscal year. It shows what an organization owns and owes, and the difference between the two. That difference, or total net assets, is similar to the net worth of for-profit organizations. The SOA summarizes an organization's financial activity over a period of time and allows comparisons between time periods.

Statement of Position (Balance Sheet)

The *statement of position* (balance sheet) is a snapshot of an organization's financial position as of a specific date. A SOP has three key sections.

Total assets are what an organization owns and is owed. Assets are divided into current assets or those available within the year, and long term or fixed assets.

Total liabilities are what the organization owes. Liabilities are divided into current liabilities or those due within the year, and long term liabilities due beyond the year, such as a mortgage.

Total net assets are the value of the assets minus the liabilities. Net assets are unrestricted, temporarily restricted, or permanently restricted.

The total assets presented on an SOP will equal the total liabilities plus the total net assets—hence the term *balance sheet.*

Many organizations compare the statement of position on the same date over several years to examine organizational change over time. An annual audit compares the end of the fiscal year audited to the end of the previous fiscal year.

Figure 7: City Center for the Arts Statement of Position

City Center for the Arts STATEMENT OF POSITION as of July 31, 2008 *ASSETS*				
Current Assets				
Cash		$48,000		
Accounts Receivable				
Grants Receivable		7,000		
Other Current Assets		150		
	Total Current Assets		$55,150	
Fixed Assets				
Equipment				
	Office Furniture	$6,500		
	Less: Accumulated Depreciation	1,200		
	Total Fixed Assets		5300	
TOTAL ASSETS			$60,450	
LIABILITIES AND Net Assets				
Liabilities				
Current Liabilities				
	Accounts Payable	$8,132		
Long Term Liabilities				
	Notes Payable	3,300		
	Total Liabilities		$11,432	
Net Assets				
Unrestricted				
	Beginning Balance	$31,760		
	Net Income	$2,258		
	Balance at July 31, 2008	$34,018		
Temporarily Restricted		$15,000		
	Total Net Assets		49,018	
TOTAL LIABILITIES AND NET ASSETS			$60,450	

The SOP is an essential tool for board and staff to monitor on a regular basis in order to determine whether the organization is financially healthy or at risk. Each organization should set a target for the level of assets it needs in order to support its mission for the long term. Board and staff also need to identify key indicators that they will use to monitor change. Note that organizations embedded in larger institutions (such as art centers in colleges or universities or departments in a municipality) will find a SOP somewhat meaningless for their department, since the actual owner of assets (such as the auditorium or gallery) is the parent institution. In this case, should such an organization be requested to provide a SOP for a grant application, it should, for instance, submit its parent institution's SOP instead.

Statement of Activities (Income Statement)

The statement of activities (SOA) summarizes revenues received and expenses incurred throughout an accounting period. The SOA uses the same format as the budget so that board and staff can compare actual financial performance with that projected in the budget.

Differences between what the budget projected and what actually occurred are noted as *variances*. Negative income variances mean that revenue is less than expected. *Negative expense variances* indicate that spending is less in a category than was forecast. In either case, a variance means that the leaders need to look more closely at that income or expense item to learn what has happened. Lower-than-forecast contributions could suggest that donors are not responding to the annual appeal as usual. Or lower figures could simply reflect that the annual benefit auction will not take place until the next month. For clarification, the SOA should include a column with the projection for the end of the fiscal year so the annual budget can be compared to the expected results for the year.

The SOA should be prepared monthly, quarterly, and at year's end. The monthly report should be reviewed by the staff and treasurer; the finance committee should review the SOA at least quarterly. Regularly scheduled reviews will enable board and staff to observe discrepancies and take steps to protect the organization from spending more money than it receives. This allows an organization's leaders to manage, not merely report the group's finances. (See Figure 8 on the next page.)

The SOA also relates directly to the statement of position. The net revenue, the excess or deficiency of revenues over expenses, is added to the net assets on the statement of position. If the net revenue is positive (surplus), the net asset amount is increased. If the net revenue is negative (deficit), the net asset amount is decreased. Thus, all revenues and expenses flow to the SOP. For the City Center for the Arts, the net revenue from the SOA amounted to $2,258. This amount was added to the net assets as shown on the SOP.

Compare total revenues to total costs to determine if the surplus will be maintained. Compare administrative expenses to program expenses, and direct the majority of your resources to mission-directed activities. Be alert to an increase in the percentage you spend on administration, especially if it is a trend over several years. You may also compare your results with those of similar organizations to determine if your trends are similar; however, such comparisons should be used only to indicate that added research is needed since each organization's circumstances are different.

Express each program's revenues and expenses as a percentage of total revenues and expenses. Look for programs that consume more than their share of expenses and contribute less than their share of revenues. If such a program is also peripheral to the fulfillment of your mission, it is a likely candidate for cost-saving measures or elimination. Look for significant changes in a revenue or expense category by comparing several years of operating statements. A drop in sales, grants, or fundraising should cue a close examination of the cause.

Financial Ratios

An additional way to test an organization's financial health is to use financial ratio tools, which reformulate financial statements into quick indicators of fiscal stability. Financial

Figure 8: City Center for the Arts Statement of Activities

City Center for the Arts, Statement of Activities for year ending July 31, 2008			
Budget INCOME	**Actual to Date from Actual**	**Total Annual**	**Variance**
Corporate Grants	$15,000	$13,000	$2,000
Foundation Grants	23,000	30,000	(7,000)
Government Grants			
Federal			
State	13,000	13,000	0
Local			
Business Contributions	22,000	20,000	2,000
Membership Drive	22,750	22,000	750
Other Private Donations	3,000		3,000
Fundraising Events	12,000	10,000	2,000
Program Admissions	12,798	13,000	(202)
Fees/Tuition	5,575	5,500	75
Advertising	5,000	5,000	0
Sales	1,037	1,000	37
Interest	475		475
Other			
TOTAL INCOME	135,635	132,500	3,135
EXPENSES			
Salaries & Benefits	56,392	56,500	(108)
Outside Fees & Services	1,000	1,000	0
Office Supplies	428	500	(72)
Phone/FAX	1,837	1,500	337
Travel	2,500	2,500	0
Memberships	600	600	0
Professional Development	1,000	1,200	(200)
Space Rental	3,600	3,600	0
Utilities			
Insurance	250	250	0
Printing & Copying	13,798	13,350	448
Postage/Shipping	1,223	1,000	223
Artists' Fees	22,500	22,500	0
Art Materials	4,782	4,500	282
Equipment:			
Purchase			
Repair			
Rental	5,000	5,000	0
Hospitality	2,467	2,500	(33)
Other	1,000	1,000	0
Cash Reserve	15,000	15,000	0
TOTAL EXPENSES	133,377	132,500	877
Net Surplus (Deficit)	2,258	0	2,258

ratios should only be used to diagnose potential problems, and not become the sole indicator of fiscal health. Further investigation can help to uncover problem areas. Here are some examples.

Current ratio determines an organization's ability to meet its debts. Current Assets (unrestricted cash and other current assets that can be converted into cash) ÷ Current Liabilities (debts payable within one year) = Current Ratio. A ratio of two to one is consider sufficient for an organization to pay its current obligations and have funds in reserve.

Current unrestricted net assets determine an organization's ability to meet its current obligations and also assist with cash flow management. (Current Unrestricted Assets – Current Liabilities) ÷ Annual Operating Expenses = Current Unrestricted Net Assets (as percentage of operating expenses). Generally, an unrestricted net asset level of ten to 30 percent of annual operating expenses is adequate to support current obligations and manage cash flow. Less than ten percent means that the organization will often experience financial crisis.

Quick ratio determines how well an organization can meet its immediate obligations. (Cash + Accounts Receivable) ÷ Current Liabilities = Quick Ratio. A quick ratio of two to one is considered to be good; less than one to one means an organization will encounter a cash shortfall.

Audits

An independent accountant can review an organization's various financial statements and operations and produce a full audit, a review, or a compilation.

Audit. An auditor renders an opinion that the financial statements are free of material misstatement, based on an examination in accordance with generally accepted auditing standards (GAAP).

Compilation. An auditor compiles financial data for the accounting period and prepares financial statements without expressing assurances that the statements comply with GAAP.

Review. An auditor reviews the organization's financial statements on a limited scope and provides limited assurance that the statements conform with GAAP.

An auditor tests transactions to evaluate the accuracy of accounting records and the degree of reliance he or she can place on the organization's internal controls. Not every transaction that has been recorded is examined. The end result of an audit is the expression of an opinion.

The compilation and financial review are most common for smaller organizations. Audits are usually performed only when required by funding sources or where dictated by the size and complexity of an organization. While there are no federal audit requirements for submitting a Form 990, in some states larger income organization must submit audited financial statements.

Audit Opinions

The auditor may render one of four basic opinions.

Unqualified. The financial statements are considered to be fairly presented in conformity with GAAP.

Qualified. The auditor takes exception to some specific part of the financial statements as presented or is unable to form an unqualified opinion because of some contingency which might affect the financial statements.

Adverse. In the auditor's opinion, the financial statements do not present fairly the financial position in conformity with GAAP.

Disclaimer. The auditor is unable to form an opinion due to limitations of scope, uncertainties in the future, or poor bookkeeping by the client.

Audit Benefits

Credibility of financial statements. The purpose of financial statements is to communicate in a direct manner what has transpired during the fiscal period. An auditor's opinion helps in this communication, because an independent expert has examined and determined that the financial statements are presented fairly. If an organization can tell its financial story accurately and completely, and it is accepted at face value, the potential contributor is more likely to feel that the organization is well managed. A certified public accountant (CPA) can provide key assistance in this process.

Meaningful statements. A CPA helps organizations prepare financial statements in a format that will be clear and understandable to the reader.

Advice on internal control and other matters. A CPA is in a position to advise the board on how to strengthen internal control or simplify bookkeeping procedures.

Assistance in tax reporting and compliance requirements. A CPA can help submit reports to regulatory agencies or the IRS.

Reports to the Internal Revenue Service

Annual tax return. Organizations with 501(c)(3) nonprofit status must file a yearly tax return, IRS Form 990 or 990EZ. If gross receipts are normally not more than $25,000 (check 990 regulations for changes), an organization is exempt and does not have to file a completed return with the IRS. However, even if an organization is exempt, if it receives a Form 990 package in the mail, it should file a return without financial data. In addition, some states require a completed return regardless of federal exemption.

Salaries and wages. Several forms are required when an organization has employees.

Form W-4 Employee's Withholding Allowance Certificate. This enables an employee to define the correct amount of federal income tax to be withheld from pay.

Form 941 Employer's Quarterly Federal Tax Return. These quarterly statements submitted to the IRS report tax liability.

Form W-2 Wage and Tax Statement. This annual statement is provided by an employer to an employee to summarize gross wages and deductions.

Form W-3 Transmittal of Income and Tax Statements. This cover sheet must accompany W-2 forms sent from an employer to the IRS.

Organizations also must submit forms when employing contractors.

Form W-9 Request for Taxpayer Identification Number and Certification. This is given to the employer by the contractor. When the contractor is an individual, this form is used to report his or her social security number.

Form 1099–Miscellaneous. This is the contractor's equivalent of a W-2 form.

Form 1096. This cover sheet must accompany 1099–Miscellaneous forms sent from an employer to the IRS.

Computerizing Your Financial System

A computerized accounting system may prove beneficial to an organization if any of the following apply:

- you write many checks each month or at certain times of the year;
- you track a number of programs or grants;
- you must create specific kinds of reports (such as multiyear comparisons) that your current system cannot produce; or
- your accountant recommends it.

The transition process from a manual system (or no system) to a computerized system will be easier if sufficient time is allocated for research, software testing, installation, and practice. Even the most proficient bookkeeper may make mistakes when using a new computer system.

Accounting Software

User-friendly and affordable accounting software packages are readily available at computer retailers. As a result, most nonprofits now use computerized accounting systems to maintain the ledgers and report financial transactions. Computerized systems ease the work of the bookkeeper and enable managers to get reports more quickly. Most commercial software packages allow modifications necessary for a nonprofit.

The most popular basic systems—QuickBooks from Intuit Inc. and Peachtree from Sage Software, Inc.—include basic ledgers and the ability to prepare budgets, cash flow reports, check writing, and payroll. While basic systems will work for many nonprofits, larger or more complex organizations may choose systems designed for nonprofits that provide additional system features, such as links to ticketing and fundraising components.

Each organization should first evaluate its existing system and determine what features it wants in the new system, compare the features of several software packages, talk to other nonprofits using the software, and compare prices before making a decision. Key considerations should be ease of use and the availability of training for staff.

Spreadsheets

Spreadsheet programs computerize the simplest mathematical functions and provide the ability to prepare specialized reports and graphs. Microsoft Excel and QuatroPro are two of the most common. Basic software packages that come with most computers include spreadsheet software. Microsoft Office, for example, includes Excel. The accounting software packages provide links to spreadsheets; some versions are able to download data directly from the accounting system into a spreadsheet so a specialized report can be created without re-entering all the data.

New software packages continually appear on the market. Ask your computer vendor about accounting and spreadsheet programs currently available.

Additional Internet Resources

Nonprofits Assistance Fund offers an excellent glossary of financial terms for nonprofits in the articles and publications area of their website.
www.communityloantech.org

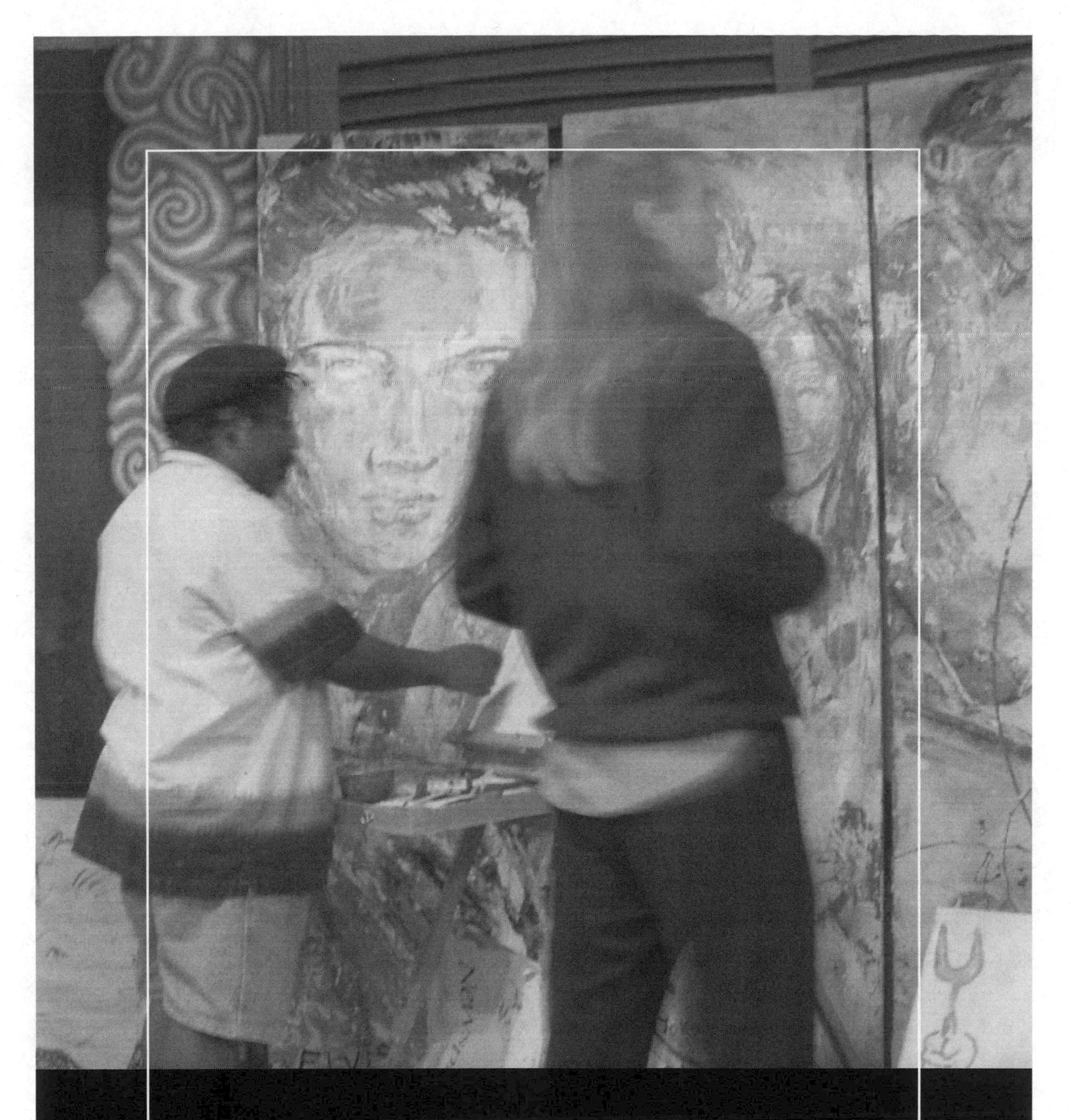

PART THREE
Programming and Participation

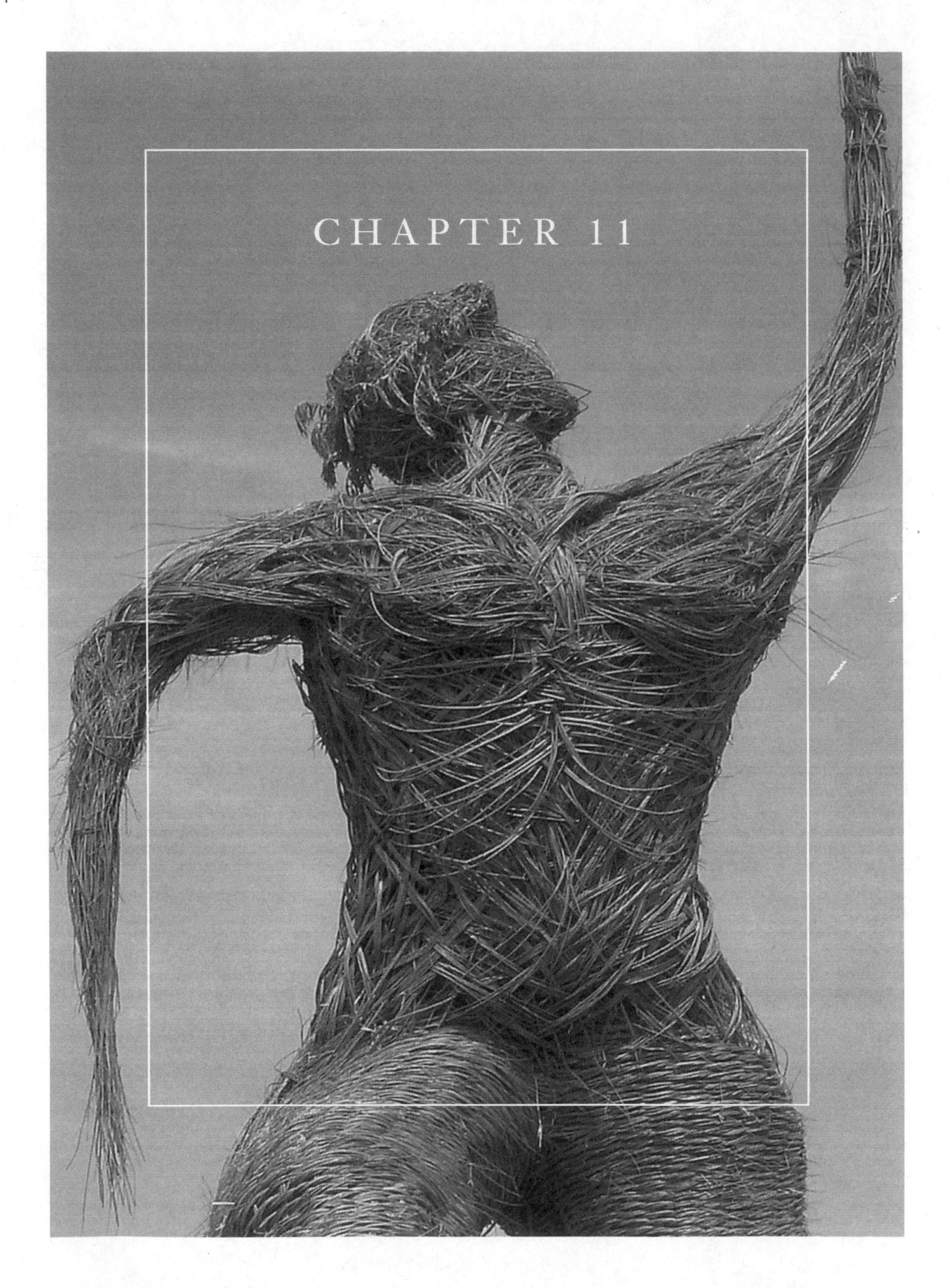

CHAPTER 11

Program Development

11

PAM KORZA

WITH CONTRIBUTING EDITOR DENISE BOSTON-MOORE

> In today's environment, we are going to have to do more than simply provide the work that will draw adult audiences back to our stages and museums: we are going to have to help them value, connect with, and engage in the arts. In this respect, we need to view our task not as a matter of an educational structure, but as a function of human experience, interaction, growth, and learning.
>
> —Nello McDaniel and George Thorn, Learning Audiences: Adult Arts Participation and the Learning Consciousness[1]

Many arts managers would say that programming is the most creative function of arts organizations. Curators, artistic directors, and program coordinators have the core and exciting responsibility to develop creative and meaningful programs that connect art with people. The way that arts organizations conceive and implement their programs has evolved tremendously in the last few decades in response to a variety of factors. Many adults lack grounding in the arts as a result of limited arts education in school. The commercial entertainment industry has influenced consumer habits. Demands of daily life restrict leisure time, and new and affordable technologies make it easier and easier to have whatever form of entertainment you want in the comfort of your own home. The demographics of communities are rapidly shifting as newcomers arrive and the baby boomer generation ages.

These trends, however, have flip sides. They present opportunities to use the power of arts and culture to fulfill human needs for connection, have meaningful leisure experiences, and build community. Increasingly, arts agencies of all types and sizes—from local arts agencies to major museums—are seeking inspiration and leadership from artists, audiences, their neighborhoods, and social and civic leaders in redefining programs to be relevant to community needs and interests. They are taking advantage of new technologies—using the Internet, low frequency radio, and iPods—to expand education and access to art itself. They are programming less as independent producers of arts and more as collaborators with school systems, tourism and economic development agencies, urban planners, and a host of other community groups and institutions to ensure that arts and culture are integrated elements of broader community ventures. In these ways, arts organizations are encouraging a community-wide recognition and celebration of cultural diversity, social change, youth advocacy, elder appreciation, and neighborhood vitality.

The arts are but one aspect of cultural life, which encompasses history and heritage, culinary traditions, lifestyles, and religion—all expressions of the creative human spirit. Programs which embrace these various creative expressions may include presenting or producing activities, community-based arts endeavors, residencies, festivals, thematic series, educational programs in the arts, and public art, to name a few.

As you read this chapter, imagine your own arts, culture, and programmatic frames of reference to make it relevant to your own work. The chapter provides a structure for conceiving, planning, and implementing programs that will help meet the needs of artists and the community, fulfill organizational mission, and aim to advance the arts themselves. These key questions are addressed:

What values and philosophy underlie your program directions and choices?

What difference do you want to make through your programs?

Who should be involved in program planning? How might you involve representatives of your target audience(s) and stakeholders?

What are some key considerations in designing programs to achieve organizational, artist, partner, and audience goals?

Is your program feasible? Does it have the necessary resources to meet its full potential for success?

How will you know if your program has succeeded?

PROGRAM PHILOSOPHY

An arts organization's program philosophy encompasses the values, principles, and creative point of view that guide its decisions and approach to artistic work as well as the way it connects that work to audiences and community. Your program philosophy should take into account the following considerations.

Organization mission. Programs should reflect the organization's purpose and whom it serves. A local arts agency may leave arts programming to the wide range of cultural organizations in the community and focus instead on services, grantmaking, and advocacy in order to build the capacity for local arts organizations to thrive and for citizens to have access to a breadth of cultural programs.. However, new opportunities often emerge as contexts change or as an organization strives to serve the needs of particular communities or audiences. Developing a public art program, for example, may be a compelling new direction for a local arts agency when new public buildings are being constructed in a community, and no other agency is poised to lead such a program. Analyzing such new opportunity in relation to how it may support the organization's mission can keep it performing in a vital way while ensuring that it stays focused.

Concept of "audience" or "community." Some organizations are expressly committed to serving youth or elders, a specific cultural community, or a community of circumstance (such as inmates in the prison system). Others may serve artists in a particular discipline or the full range of artists in a region. Still others may broadly define the residents of a defined county as its community.

In the 21st century, changing demographics in the United States should prompt an assessment of how current or new programs can effectively serve new members of a community, however it is defined. A community concert association in a rural Midwestern town, for example, used to serve a fairly homogenous white, middle class community. Today its programming considers a growing elderly population, a declining population of young adults who don't return to their hometown after college for lack of job opportunity, and an immigrant population, attracted by jobs to local vegetable packing plants.

Commitment to making programs accessible. To what degree can you make programs accessible to audiences and artists with disabilities or special needs? Can you commit the resources necessary to do so? See the chapter on Cultural Access for more on program accessibility.

Sources of program ideas. How are board, staff, volunteers, members, citizens, and stakeholders such as artists or youth or culturally-specific populations involved in defining your programs? How successfully do you balance being responsive with being proactive vis–à–vis artists and the community in developing new program directions?

Relationship to the world of art and ideas. Art is at the core of what we do, whether your organization is a producing organization that creates new work, presents the work of contemporary artists or those of the past, or works collaboratively with schools to develop arts education programs. Are you abreast of what is current in your part of the arts and culture world? Arts organizations, particularly those that preserve art of the past, are increasingly challenged to find creative ways to make their offerings relevant to social or civic concerns, community or economic development priorities, or broader quality of life goals.

Risk-taking threshold. How much does your organization challenge itself and its audiences, versus relying upon certain comfortable and cautious program choices? Reasoned risk that meets audiences at new and appropriate learning points can stretch them toward new interests in their engagement with the arts. Artists continually explore new art forms and are often at the vanguard of excavating the meaning of difficult contemporary issues. To what extent does your organization embrace artistic investigations and programs that may be controversial, and is it prepared to defend such choices if controversy arises?

Definition of success. What difference are you trying to make through your programs? How will you evaluate the impact of your programs and who will do the evaluating? What criteria will you use? A new music series that presents adventurous programming may need to take a long view to build audiences over time. The measures of success may be repeated audience attendance and modest audience growth over a longer time period than an established program, or how the program is serving artists' creative investigations. Notions of success and failure may need to be reconsidered to see the big picture; in other words, some programs may not immediately and fully meet artistic, audience, or community goals, but the cumulative effect over time shows advancement.

If your programming aims to meet educational, community development, or economic development goals, partners and stakeholders may have different definitions of success which must be considered. See the Program Evaluation chapter for additional information.

PROGRAM PLANNING

Arts organizations are continually presented with opportunities to develop new programs. They also face circumstances that suggest modifying, and sometimes terminating, existing programs. Program planning may be prompted by constituent need; artistic initiative; new or reduced funding opportunities; influences of a changing social, political, or cultural environment; or simply someone's great idea!

Examples

Modifying an existing program. An arts council staff member believes that expanding the successful holiday season craft sale to a year-round craft shop can better serve the region's craftspeople and provide additional revenue.

The arts agency's grantmaking program has withstood two consecutive years of severely diminished funds from state and local government sources. The trend will likely continue. The agency's current granting programs must be reevaluated and revised to reflect diminished resources and community need.

Developing new programs. A social service organization serving several neighborhoods has approached your arts center to help develop afterschool programs which would build respect between teens and elders.

Eliminating programs. "The Cutting Edge" roster of music presented by the performing arts center has lost money each of the last two seasons. The board of directors is suggesting to the program director that these types of programs be dropped in favor of the more profitable folk, classical, and world music offerings.

The program planning process helps an organization choose intelligently from various options and test their feasibility. Specifically, the process:

- gauges support for the idea and identifies potential partners;
- assesses and plans for the financial viability of the program, including financial risk;
- avoids overtaxing human and other resources; and
- formulates a workable plan of action.

The planning stage could take weeks, months, or longer depending on the complexity of the program. The program stands the best chance of smooth implementation and success in serving its participants and audience if you invest the time to plan.

Six Steps to Determine Program Feasibility

This section discusses six steps which will help you gauge the feasibility of a program opportunity and create a program plan.

1. Test assumptions inherent in the program idea.
2. Agree on the program's purpose, goals, and objectives.
3. Define the program specifically—who, what, when, and where.
4. Examine resources you need, have, and can get.
5. Identify and evaluate critical issues, obstacles, and opportunities.
6. Finalize the plan.

Step 1. Test Assumptions

Talk with program beneficiaries, artists, partners, and other players to determine if you are making assumptions, and if these assumptions are valid. In doing so, the organization begins to clarify:

- perceptions of the needs and interests held by various collaborators and participants;
- who can benefit from the program and how;
- what support systems are available; and
- whether your organization is the best one to implement the program.

Example
A neighborhood center staff member suggests that a Salsa dance project would offer community youth an afterschool activity that's fun and connected to their cultural heritage. She invites a locally-based Latino dance company to become a partner to help design the program and offer dance classes. Possible assumptions are: dance is the most effective art form to achieve the goal; the dance company has experience working with youth; a partnership is needed versus contracting with the dance company to simply offer a class; and such a project is a better use of scarce resources than other options.

Step 2. Agree on Program Goals and Objectives

What difference do you want to make with this program? Who do you hope to serve with this program? This step:

- ensures that everyone is working from a common understanding of shared goals as well as any that are distinct to participating artists, partners, and stakeholders;
- guides decisions in program development and implementation and keeps you on course;
- provides a clear and consistent message to your community, members, funding sources, volunteer, and the media about why you are doing what you're doing; and
- forms the basis for evaluating the impact of the program.

To arrive at clear program goals, some level of audience or community assessment—such as public meetings, focus groups, or surveys—may be important. The Strategic Planning chapter discusses various assessment processes, as well as how to write purpose, goals, and objectives statements for your programs. See the Arts and the Economy chapter if you want to address community or economic development goals.

Step 3. Define the Program

Visions are amorphous by nature. It is difficult to project a budget, technical needs, or the terms of a partnership based solely on the vision you may have for a program. Eventually a specific program concept (or a few variations on it) needs to be nailed down in order to evaluate its feasibility. To bring your program idea from that initial fluid vision to a clear and more specific concept, determine who, what, when, and where.

Who. Define who the program will benefit. An organization's programming may be grounded, first and foremost, in a commitment to support artistic investigation and advancement. Other organizations may define community or audience interests as the

Heather Gary's design for Countywide Community Arts in Arlington, Virginia, exemplifies a project developed with a clear sense of goals. As a visual artist working with pregnant and postpartum women in a residential treatment program, Gary found that her art projects could assist in their healing process. Cognizant of rehabilitation goals, Gary designed a project in which women constructed three-dimensional multimedia portable altars. The process of transforming cigar boxes into altars encouraged them to tell personal stories in unique and expressive ways and helped the women make relevant life connections and explore healthy options.

driving force in their program choices and directions. They may develop programs to attract targeted community populations, broaden audiences, or serve current audiences. Whether you start with art or the desired audience, carefully consider the relationship between the two. One may emerge as primary, and therefore shape the program in a certain way.

> **Example**
> When the Indianapolis Children's Museum mounted a major exhibition of Alexander Calder's work, the city's cultural organizations saw an opportunity to build local audiences as well as attract regional tourist audiences. With coordination and marketing from the Indianapolis Arts Council, they mounted a city-wide festival celebrating Calder and creativity. The event succeeded in drawing local audiences, but made limited advances with a regional market. Organizers assessed that, if a future event were designed to attract a regional market, it would need to produce one or more major attractions to entice audiences and capture media attention, offer incentives such as family packages, and be more concentrated in time to allow visitors to attend several activities during their visit to Indianapolis.

Estimate the numbers of people to be served. Clear audience estimates will help you to design programs that best meet the interests of your audiences; attract artists; raise money; secure sponsors; negotiate a facility or setting for the program; determine ticket prices; and develop a marketing strategy. If your program relies on fee-based income from ticket sales or registration fees, making a considered attendance estimate to develop a realistic budget is crucial.

Estimating the number of people may hinge on such factors as:

- capacity limits of the space;
- drawing power of the program or artist;
- availability of the targeted audience or community;
- what it will take to effectively promote to this audience;
- competition for the targeted audience; and
- what is considered reasonable and appropriate for the scale of the activity and its goals.

Clarify who will be involved in program planning and implementation. In what ways are the board, staff, program director, or executive director responsible? It must be clear who advises and who has final authority to make artistic decisions. In all volunteer organizations, board members may serve on various program committees and choose and work directly with artists. Generally, if an organization has paid staff, the board helps to define overall program philosophy and policies but staff implements programs, including choice of artists. Determine if and how artists should advise or be involved in program design and planning. When community advisory boards or committees are formed to help plan or implement programs, their roles should be clear as well. In public art programs, for example, sometimes community advisory groups help to define the criteria for public art projects in a particular place and may meet and speak with prospective artists, but may or may not be charged with actual artist selection.

Will you work with partner organizations? As arts organizations extend the reach of their programs to various populations and toward civic, social, or economic goals, they find it necessary to work in partnership with other organizations. Partners can help cultural organizations better understand the needs and interests of these participants and frame goals that reflect their concerns. They can provide access and help build trust navigate systems. Consider thoughtfully what will be meaningful benefits for partners as well as what they can contribute to planning and implementation.

See the People Resources under Step 4 for further discussion.

What. At the planning stage, outline specifics about content, scope, and format or structure of the program to give shape to your vision. For simple programs, it may be easy to define details. For more complex or extended programs, frameworks for key elements may be defined. Many community-based and public art projects define the goals and shape of a project only after a period of activity with community members, making it impossible to map out the entire program at the outset. In any case, enough sense of the program elements and their technical, time, and other requirements is needed in order to create a plan, understand resources needed, etc.

Where. The real estate industry sums everything up as "location, location, location!" For arts and cultural programs, as well, location is one of several important factors that can make or break a program. The choice of location can emphasize particular goals of the program. For example, alternating a weekday lunchtime concert series between the downtown business district, neighborhood parks, and soup kitchens helps to meet the goal of providing access to art for all citizens. Undesirable locations are sometimes deliberately targeted for transformation by arts and cultural activity.

Arts organizations with a goal of serving culturally diverse populations need to consider how various segments of the community perceive different settings. The art center or museum may not be perceived as a welcoming space. Practical issues of transportation may make it difficult for some people to get to certain facilities. Present programs in locations where people feel comfortable.

An organization should consider the following in determining where to hold its program:

Suitability. Will the facility do justice to the art form? Does it have suitable technical support?

Capacity. Can it accommodate the expected number of people?

Aesthetics. What can the space or setting lend aesthetically or conceptually to the program?

Accessibility. Is the location physically accessible to people with disabilities? Is the location close to public transportation? What psychological perceptions may exist concerning accessibility to the location?

Availability. Is the space available on the date(s) you want? Much cogitation is wasted if your dream location is already booked. Get to know the booking patterns of various facilities so that you can plan well enough in advance.

Cost. Are rental costs or costs of adapting the location feasible in terms of your budget?

When. Choosing a program date can involve as much strategy as choosing location. Factors to check on include:

- how long it will take to plan and promote the program;
- funding application deadlines;
- availability of the target audience or competing programs or diversions;
- complementary programs that may expand your audience and theirs;
- possibility to block–book an artist with another organization;
- availability of desired space(s);
- possibility of inclement weather for outdoor programs; and
- desire to establish an annual date.

Step 4. Examine Resources

Having defined your program concept in greater detail, test its feasibility against the money, time, and people needed to make it a reality. This step requires some objective assessment.

Financial resources. Only by developing a specific, research-based budget can you assess the financial feasibility of your program. Define expense and income limitations and potential, how much money needs to be raised, and what's needed to raise it.

The budgeting process is usually one that requires a give-and-take between the expense and income sides until the bottom line is what you want it to be. Do not approach this as an exercise in creative arithmetic, however. Each shaving of an expense or increase in an income projection must be honestly and realistically assessed, considering its implications to the program.

See the Financial Management chapter for more detailed discussion of budget development.

Financial objectives. Here are some pointers for developing program budgets.

Estimate income conservatively.

Maximize earned income potential.

Save money wherever possible by getting in-kind donations.

Don't give away too much. Determine complimentary ticket policies thoughtfully. Should corporate contributors be given a free ad in your program book or should they be asked to pay for advertising beyond their other contribution?

Don't spend too much money raising money. Carefully evaluate the costs involved in certain fundraising activities. The United Way keeps fundraising expenses within 15 percent of anticipated income.

Spend money where it counts. Ensure respectful compensation for artists. Consider terms of agreement with significant partners to ensure there is appropriate balance regarding investment and return.

Understand what your cash flow needs are and how you will accommodate them.

Minimize the chance for surprise expenses. Think specifically about what you will need. Don't base projected costs on ballpark estimates or old information. Research as exhaustively as possible to determine expense lines. If you have no way to determine costs, ask others in similar organizations to share their experiences with you.

Include a contingency expense figure. Three to five percent of total direct expenses (other than salaries and overhead) is common.

Be careful about developing programs in response to a specific grant or funding initiative, without considering grant requirements, such as matching funds, in your overall budget. More than one programmer has received funding for a project and is then heard to groan, "oh no, now I have to do it!" when they receive a grant.

If expenses are greater than income, evaluate the possible courses of action.

Can the program be scaled back? Can certain expenses be cut? Consider the implications of these actions in relation to your programmatic goals and maintaining the integrity of the art.

Can expenses be shared with collaborative partners or other community organizations?

Can certain expenses be amortized? A festival purchasing tents, a theater company creating portable sets for a tour, an art center purchasing display cases for an exhibition—these costs can be amortized on the organization's balance sheet (see Financial Management chapter) or spread across a certain period beyond the program at hand since they will support other programs in the future.

Can income be increased? Estimate cautiously.

Play out different budget scenarios. It is useful to develop two or three budget scenarios that anticipate varying degrees of income.

The ideal scenario. Your dream program achieves its income potential.

The compromise scenario. A modified program can be mounted with anticipated lower income. This scenario should reflect acceptable programmatic compromises.

The no program or delayed program scenario. This assumes that adequate income cannot be secured or earned to support program variations which still meet your programmatic goals. This may also suggest that an alternate timeline should be considered which allows for sufficient fundraising or the setting of a deadline by which a decision must be made to go forward or not.

In the fundraising stage, organizations often generate a budget for funders which reflects the ideal program, and a fallback internal budget which reflects the compromise program the organization is willing to present with a defined minimum assured raised or earned income.

The appropriate staff, board, and, perhaps, advisers in the community should review the financial picture drawn in this feasibility stage. At this point the review should test the validity of the figures. Did you project realistically? Are all potential expenses outlined? Have incomes been reasonably projected? Are there any that have not been identified?

People resources. Arts organizations are notorious for greeting every exciting program idea with a resounding, "Yes, let's do it!" Such passion has also launched many an arts organization's staff or board into a state of perpetual overdrive. Whether a single event or an ongoing program, the ebb and flow of work should be carefully considered, as well as the specific skills and expertise required.

> Do the necessary skills, expertise, and connections exist within the organization?
>
> Is it feasible for staff or board members to devote time and energy to the program? If so, can other regular activities be sustained without compromising quality?
>
> Will volunteers or new staff be required? Will training be necessary? Do you have the time and money to make this happen?

If you must seek expertise outside the organization, consider a friends group or existing volunteer corps, an ad hoc advisory group, contracted staff or a consultant, or partnerships with other organizations.

Partnerships require:

- building trust and an appreciation of each other's expertise and unique identity and contributions;
- familiarity with each other's language, ways of working, and the system within which each partner works;
- mutual understanding of the program goals and a commitment to help achieve them;
- understanding of each partner's particular goals and a program design which aims to satisfy them;
- delineation of authority, accountability, and responsibilities;
- agreement on financial risk–taking and gain; and
- a written agreement outlining the above.

See the Arts Extension Services' Learning Partnerships workbook online in the Resources area at www.umass.edu/aes.

The program should be based on a realistic assessment of the time it will take to plan, raise funds, and implement the plan. Identify critical deadlines, including:

- research (program components, community involvement, artists' availability, market potential, costs, funding sources, potential partners, technical concerns);
- fundraising (grant application deadlines and notification dates, and other fundraising efforts);
- staffing (recruitment, hiring, and training of paid oror volunteer personnel to staff the program);
- a finalized program when artists, artwork, and program participants are all secured and other components and design are set;

- final dates for bidding out contracts for services (if applicable); and
- key promotion opportunities and printing deadlines.

Timeline. A suggested timeline format looks like a grid with one axis for the months or weeks leading up to (and throughout) the program and the other axis for specific tracks of activities—such as administration, fundraising, program development and implementation, marketing, and technical support. These tracks may correspond to specific committees working on the program, and such a master timeline shows the relationship between activities. For example, in order for the marketing committee to send a press kit to the media six weeks before the concert series, the program committee must submit to the publicity committee a final lineup of artists with descriptions and photos four weeks before the press kit deadline, allowing time for the marketing committee to develop the kits. See the sample timeline in the Online Companion to this chapter. (See the last page of this book for the Internet address.)

In addition, the timeline helps everyone to visualize the plan's progress, the interdependence of various committees, and periods when staff or board may be in greatest demand. An agency timeline showing all of the organization's programs and services also helps place this program activity in a context of the total demand on the board, staff, and volunteers. For more complex projects, you may wish to use a software program like Microsoft Project, which helps to deal with multiple interdependent variables.

Step 5. Identify and Evaluate Issues, Obstacles, and Opportunities

Defining program and resource needs will undoubtedly identify issues and obstacles, as well as opportunities, which your organization must analyze and evaluate. For example, a consultant conducting a feasibility study for a national festival to take place in a major city discovered that local cultural organizations were fearful that county arts council funds would be significantly diverted to support the new festival, reducing allocations that were an important part of the arts groups' revenue base. The county arts council had to determine how it could support the new event without unfairly stressing its ongoing constituents.

Some useful questions to ask are:

> What do we lose if the program does not meet our criteria for success? What are the implications of losing these things?
>
> What can we and others—such as artists and audiences—learn by doing this program?
>
> What relationships might be built?
>
> Can we sort out certain short-term activities from those that require long-term planning?
>
> What internal or external conditions must be met before we can proceed?

Step 6. Finalize the Plan

At this point you should have the information you need to decide the likelihood of achieving your goals and objectives. Your options may be:

Go ahead with the program with a better understanding of what you need to do to make it a success.

Refine the program concept to bring it in line with resources you can reasonably secure.

Delay until you are able to secure the resources you need.

Stop if the program poses too great a financial risk, you don't have the time or personnel to carry it off, you don't have adequate community support, or it's outside your scope.

PROGRAM DESIGN

Regardless of the type of program or service you offer, its design should consider policies to guide actions and decisions; finding, selecting, and working effectively with the right artists; ensuring access, and creating a meaningful artistic experience for participants or audience members. This section explores these concerns.

Program Policies

Policies are guidelines that help an organization act consistently and in keeping with its values, principles, and mission.

Examples

An artist market that values originality and authenticity prohibits exhibitors whose work is made from kits or is not the original design of the exhibiting artist.

A presenter concerned that programs are accessible to economically disadvantaged community members creates policies which ensure child care and sliding scale ticket pricing.

A theater company committed to cultural equity institutes a policy of color–blind casting, ensuring that people of color can perform any role where color is not integral to the character.

An art museum only offers educational programs that relate to its permanent collections or temporary exhibitions.

Board and staff should create policies with input from the people who are most directly affected by the policies. While policies may require revision over time, because they are based in the principles and values of an organization, they should be somewhat enduring.

Quality: A Multidimensional View

Most arts organizations would agree that they strive to support the highest quality in the art they present, produce, or support. Mediocre or poor artistic content, form, or execution will negatively affect a community's view of the arts and its value, and betrays audience trust.

Absolute standards of excellence are found to be limiting, though, when other social, civic, or educational goals are linked to the creative endeavor. The conventional paradigm that focuses solely on the artistic product is making way for an expanded framework that considers the quality and impact of process and the value or meaning of the artistic experience for participants or audience members, in addition to artistic excellence. Here are some general guidelines about defining and fostering quality.

Consider who defines criteria and standards. Involve people with expertise in the discipline, genre, and language to articulate standards of excellence. Hip-hop artist Rennie Harris observes that critics who write about his work without a historical understanding of hip-hop tend to perceive the pieces only as acrobatic spectacle, and often reinforces cultural stereotypes about the exotic black male body.[2] Artists themselves should be involved in articulating criteria and standards as well as knowledgeable critics. Others involved in community-based cultural work advocate that community members affected by the work have valuable contributions to make in defining what is artistically excellent and meaningful.

Articulate criteria specifically. It is important to be as specific as possible when communicating with artists who might apply to participate in a program, grant review panelists, or staff or judges who are making decisions. Aesthetic criteria might relate to artistic-cultural vision, accepted discipline- or genre-based criteria, craftsmanship and skill in execution, and risk-taking. Criteria sometimes can be effectively expressed in terms of what is *not* desirable. For example, the town of Amherst, Massachusetts, values its historic architecture and personages, such as poets Emily Dickinson and Robert Frost. As community members discussed aesthetic standards for environmental changes, they advocated for design standards that maintain the integrity of the historic district, but also cautioned against the potential to overdo historic references, trivializing Amherst's history. By describing what was not acceptable, townspeople further clarified the originally stated design goal.

Understand and employ culturally-specific criteriawhen presenting forms of a particular culture. Artwork that is created outside of the dominant culture is often judged according to European or Western standards. As a result, its formal qualities, meaning, and the nuances of aesthetics are misunderstood or misrepresented. People who are of the cultural community being evaluated should be a part of the system assessing quality. See the African in Maine sidebar.

Uphold artistic integrity in presenting art. Adapting a traditional ethnic dance form that is rooted in ritual to Western stage presentation, for example, might render it inauthentic. Presenting an artist's laser art event on a foggy night to keep to schedule could so diminish the intended visual effects that the artist's reputation and yours could be hurt. Involve the artists or specialists to determine if and how reasonable adaptations can be made without compromising integrity.

Develop methods of evaluating quality that are fair, accountable, and enable the work to be assessed in its best light. Such methods might include review of work through conventional slides, tapes, CDs, DVDs, or other reproductions of an artist's work. However, some work does not translate well in reproduced formats and may best be viewed in person. In addition, some work may only demonstrate its full meaning with the benefit of audience interaction or in the setting for which it is originally intended, for example, sacred spaces, natural environment, or the city street.

African in Maine: What Constitutes "Quality"?

African in Maine was a two-year programmatic effort by the Center for Cultural Exchange (CCE) to respond to the cultural needs of refugee Sudanese, Somalian, and Congolese communities in Portland, Maine. CCE supported these three communities to define and implement cultural programs, drawing upon contemporary and traditional African music and other art forms, to represent themselves to each other and the wider Maine community. Below, former CCE Artistic Director Bau Graves offers his views on the question of what constitutes quality:

> American arts professionals often decry the lack of "professionalism" and "quality" in community-based art. However, communities themselves rarely make such distinctions. *African in Maine* offered moments of extreme artistic virtuosity, such as the performances by Papa Wemba or Kanda Bongo Man. It included events that held special significance for the insider communities, such as the performances by Emanuel Kembe and Shego Band. But it also included many events that were amateur attempts by local community members to represent themselves.
>
> From the perspectives of the participants and their communities, this is irrelevant. Indeed, the events that featured community members acting, singing, and dancing onstage had an emotional resonance with their audiences that exceeded the response to the stars. This does not imply that community members lack insight into aesthetic nuance; they know very well what constitutes quality within their own cultural sphere, and they want that, too. It does state that issues of quality are often secondary considerations in the value of cultural events to insiders. Who is onstage can be far more important than what is onstage. The imposition of outsiders' views of what constitutes "quality," puts a frame around ethnic performance that is foreign to the experience of most community members. This particular, often-voiced preoccupation with "quality" within the American public arts community (especially among funders) is a red herring, itself a reflection of the elitism that still prevails in too much public cultural work.

—Bau Graves[3]

Defining Quality of Experience

The most outstanding performance of La Traviata may not be rewarding for a viewer who is unfamiliar with opera or who does not understand Italian. Preexisting perceptions of the arts or of your programs must also be addressed. Elements that may contribute to quality of the artistic experience include:

- **meaning** that audience or participants derive from the work, their participation in its development, or educational or interpretive tools which provide context and new insight (interpretive strategies are further discussed later in this chapter);
- **accessibility** of language through presentation of the artistic work in the first language of non-English speaking participants or sign interpretation for people who are deaf or hard of hearing;
- **relationship made with artists** through informal opportunities to talk with the artist;
- **media coverage and criticism** which is thoughtfully developed in tandem with the arts organization or relevant partners; and
- **overall tone and feeling of the program** established by the demeanor, respect, helpfulness, and energy of staff and volunteers.

Finding and Selecting Artists

Many arts organizations develop rosters of artists as a result of their own research, services, and programming. They also contact colleagues and solicit artists to be included in rosters, artist directories, and slide registries. The Internet has opened up vast informational resources as well, with artists' own websites as well as arts service organizations which list or link to member artists or other listings. See the Ways to Identify Artists sidebar for additional ideas.

Generally, there are three ways to select artists for your programs: direct invitation, application or a call for proposals, and first come, first served.

Direct invitation. When you know what you want and which artist can satisfy your goals, make a direct invitation to that artist.

First come, first served. This process obviously requires the least amount of effort but also provides the least opportunity for quality control or programmatic design. You might employ some basic parameters to define who can submit work. A first-come, first-served approach may be quite suitable for a broad-based community event which celebrates everyone's creativity, or where balance or differing levels of quality are not a concern in the work presented.

Application or call for proposals. Applications or proposals are often solicited when the organization does not have a preconceived idea about which artist to choose, wants to give many artists equal opportunity to participate in a project, or simply wants to make choices from a wide range of possibilities. Artists are commonly solicited for festivals, public art projects, or to apply to granting organizations for funding. Applicants are evaluated according to preestablished criteria. An advantage of an application process is that it can uncover talent unfamiliar. Therefore, it is important to get the word out in as many ways as possible.

Applications or calls for proposals should include:

- a description of the program or project (mission, format, location, anticipated audience, schedule);
- eligibility requirements;
- selection criteria;
- documentation required to represent the artist's work, such as slides, CD, DVD, or videotape;
- description of the review process;
- application deadlines; and
- dates by which artists will be notified of decisions.

Administering a call for proposals or applications and then conducting a review or jurying process to evaluate what has been submitted involves time, staff resources, and expense to promote the opportunity.

Selection by jury. A jury or peer panel involves one or more individuals with relevant expertise who select artists by reviewing examples of work (usually slides, video, CDs, or DVDs) or proposals. While staff or volunteers might serve as jurors, outsiders can lend a fresh perspective and may, if notable, lend credibility and attract artists to participate. Composing a selection jury or committee is an art in itself. Consider these variables for the right balance of expertise and perspective:

- knowledge of the art form(s) being reviewed;
- other important knowledge or expertise, such as an educator would bring to an artist–in–residence selection committee;
- belief in your program goals;
- representation of diverse cultures or, for culturally-specific programs significant representation by members of that culture;
- gender balance; and
- appropriate geographic representation.

It is important to determine how important reviewers' familiarity with the locale or region might be to achieving decisions that support the program goals. For example, an urban neighborhood arts program whose goal is to stimulate dialogue on issues important to residents warrants strong local representation. In any case, it is important to orient jurors to program goals and policies in order to make decisions that meet your interests.

Working with Artists

Artists are your most valuable partners, and treating them and their work with respect is important to the end result and to your organization's reputation. Once again, the specifics will vary from program to program, but some common guiding principles can help ensure good artist relations and a quality program.

Include artists as program advisers and in planning. Artists' experience and insights are particularly important when venturing into new or unfamiliar areas of programming, or when program goals warrant that artists become familiar with the context for their work, such as residencies or public art projects. Artists can:

- help frame the goals of a program;
- help design the specific content or format of a program;
- serve on selection committees and juries;
- determine possible educational or interpretive activities;
- advise on technical aspects of presenting their work most effectively; and
- help identify audience segments who might be attracted to their work and suggest promotion strategies.

Pay artists professional fees. Artists are professionals and deserve professional rates of compensation. Cultural groups should not ask for donated services or artwork from artists who are trying to make their living from their work. When estimating artists' fees, consult with artists or agents before you prepare a budget. Research fees for a variety of artists to become aware of the going rate. It is common practice, particularly when dealing with agents, to negotiate fees. You may be able to reduce the cost of a performance by block booking with other presenters in your region. Some artists will

WAYS TO IDENTIFY ARTISTS

Scout artists through direct contact.

Attend festivals, exhibitions, performances, and other events. Make note of and contact artists of interest.Visit artists' studios during open house events or by appointment.

Tie into networks.

Get recommendations from other programmers.

Ask artists for recommendations.

Talk to folklorists in your region or state (ask your state arts or humanities council or historical commission).

Explore the talents of local college or university faculty or students through art departments, outreach programs, and speaker bureaus.

Contact your local arts agency, statewide assembly of local arts agencies, or discipline-specific arts service organizations in your region.

Connect with national service organizations that represent your interests, such as the Association of Performing Arts Presenters, Meet the Composer, or National Performance Network.Attend booking conferences and showcases that allow you to view artists' work first hand and talk directly with artists and agents.

Connect with local libraries or other non-arts entities which work with artists.

Identify sources of artist lists.

Artist agencies and representatives

State arts agencies (applicants and recipients of fellowships, project and artist residency grants, slide registries, artist survey lists, or lists developed to promote artists in the state)

Regional arts organizations (New England Foundation for the Arts, Southern Arts Federation, Arts Midwest, Mid-America Arts Alliance, Western States Arts Federation) for performing arts touring rosters and touring exhibitions

Artist organizations (Contact the National Association of Artist Organizations, Washington, DC, for its directory.)

Young Audiences, Very Special Arts, and other national organizations with state affiliates whose services include linking artists

Find traditional or community-based artists.

Churches

Music stores

Community schools of the arts

Local newspaper, radio, or television

Ethnic clubs or associations

Senior citizen clubs or homes

Civic organizations

reduce their fees if there are other clear advantages which you can offer, such as the sale of artwork. If you ask artists to do something not anticipated in the scope of the original contract, respect that the artist is providing additional service and is due additional compensation. Depending on what is requested, the artist may choose to do it at no cost, but this should never be assumed.

Consider the fairness of artist entry fees and of asking artists to donate work. Entry fees are commonly charged in competition programs, festival markets, and other situations, often to offset costs of processing entries, provide return shipping of entry materials, insure work, etc. There is debate about the fairness of charging artists to "take a chance" since there is usually no guarantee that an artist will be accepted, win a prize, or make money by participating. Many artist organizations have lobbied against such fees. In general, organizations should make every effort to earn revenue from other sources first.

Likewise, artists are often asked to donate a performance or artwork for a fundraising event or auction. Arts organizations should examine the fairness to artists of such requests. If you choose to make a request, ask what is something "concrete and valuable" to offer the artist in exchange for his or her donation.

Develop a contract. Contracts protect the artist's and your rights by spelling out precisely the responsibilities and requirements of each party. Contracts need not be formidable documents but should clearly outline the terms of the relationship. The complexity of the contract depends upon the complexity of the artistic service and on certain institutional requirements. Major artistic productions, public art commissions, or extended residencies may have voluminous contracts. Remember that all contracts are negotiable and, if it is your first time entering into such an agreement, it is wise to seek help from an experienced arts administrator or legal counsel. For help on legal issues, contact your nearest Volunteer Lawyers for the Arts.

Work the system to support artists' interests. Arts organizations which are part of local government or state institutions sometimes face challenges working within bureaucratic systems never designed to accommodate artists' needs and timelines. It often becomes necessary to advocate that the system operate more flexibly to support artists' needs. This is particularly true when hiring international artists, who are under greater scrutiny with the advent of Homeland Security regulations. This can greatly extend the contracting time for artists, especially in governmental agencies, and it is wise to work with officials to ameliorate any potential difficulties before they arise.

Examples

Contracts may need to be adapted to include a planning as well as implementation phase for projects that cannot be fully defined until planning efforts are completed.

Provide advance or midpoint payments. Paying artists and reimbursing expenses after "services are rendered," typical in public agencies, can put an undue burden on artists, particularly with projects where there is significant development work or up front costs. Artists, unlike a commercial construction company, do not usually have the cash reserves to cover up-front costs for a major public art project.

Prepare artists with what they need to know. Artists will do their best job if they are informed in advance about the program goals and theme, the kind and size of audience to expect, the nature and limitations of the space in which their work will be presented, and that you care about their well-being, their work, and their success.

Logistical information such as the following should be summarized in a preprogram letter or in the contract for the artist's reference:

- travel and hotel arrangements made for the artist;
- information, including directions, on where the artist needs to go;

- the time the artist is expected to arrive onsite and the time needed for setup;
- hospitality that will be provided to the artist, whether through individuals to greet and escort the artist or meals offered during the artist's stay;
- assistance that will be provided to the artist to help unload equipment, set up, or support during rehearsals, exhibitions, or workshops; and
- the technical specifications and dimensions of the stage or exhibition space and the audiovisual equipment available (many performing arts spaces offer this in downloadable form on their websites, which can be particularly helpful for traveling shows).

Treat artists as professionals and as people. If artists feel well treated, they will want to work with you again. Consideration, respect, and enthusiasm should extend through staff and volunteers in their interactions with artists, even in the most difficult moments. Ask artists their preferences. While it may be true, for instance, that local hosts could provide home-cooked meals and the comforts of home to artists staying in your community (not to mention saving you hotel and per diem costs), the artist may need and prefer the privacy and down time of a hotel. Recognizing the work of artists after an event or exhibition with a handwritten letter and small personalized gifts can make your organization stand out from other venues when you are seeking to hire the artist in the future.

STRATEGIES TO CONNECT ART AND AUDIENCES

Keeping core audiences is essential to survival. However, for many reasons, arts organizations are constantly working to develop new audiences and to stretch current audiences to try new things. Practically speaking, new and more adventurous audiences can mean more revenue. More importantly, though, engaging more and varied segments of the community mutually supports their needs and interests and an organization's mission and goals. In addition, thoughtful efforts to build audiences for art, be it conceptual music or independent film, supports artists' desire to connect their work with open and appreciative audiences.

Here are some strategies that have been used successfully by artists, arts educators, and arts organizations to sustain old audiences as well as engage new people. For more information about audience participation, please see the Marketing chapter.

Sequential Programming

Sequential arts programming is based on the same premise as any sequential learning—meeting learners at their current level of skill or familiarity and challenging them to engage on a deeper level of discovery. For years, arts presenters and museum educators, among others, have looked to learning such theories to understand how adults learn and what motivates them to do so.

Sequential programming first defines *entry points* for adults to have a meaningful encounter with art. Either through the choice of art or the interpretive strategies that accompany it, a programmer creates a way for the participant or audience member to find relevant personal or cultural associations between the art's content and his or her own ideas, experience, knowledge, or understanding.[4] Over time, other artwork or experiences are offered that build on this encounter, and the work may become more complex, challenging, or adventurous as participants or audience members gain familiarity, confidence, and deeper appreciation.

Example
Some orchestras have used a sequential programming strategy to move current audiences from the expected repertoire of works from the classical canon to lesser-known works of the past as well as work by contemporary composers. A "new" work might be presented in each program of the season, with commentary by the conductor and an opportunity for the audience to engage each other in questions that help make personal connections, such as: Did this work make you think of any other music with which you're familiar? or Knowing that this work was influenced by sounds of nature and concerns for environmental preservation, is there anything that you heard within it that suggested such interests? As audiences gain more exposure and understanding, the orchestra may begin to expand the kinds of offerings within a program or create programs focused on new work.

Making Connections

We may talk about audience development or building community, but art is experienced first and foremost on an individual level. A successful experience may be an emotional, visceral, or intellectual connection, but it is always a personal connection.

Making connections between the arts and other subjects or fields with which people are familiar and interested is a prime strategy for making the arts more accessible and meaningful. Programs might explore the physics of dance or the religious purposes of stone carving in history to interest science buffs or faith-based communities, respectively.

Frequency

Providing audiences with multiple opportunities to experiment with and get used to unfamiliar forms of art can enhance their interest in and understanding of that art form.

Example
Hancher Auditorium at the University of Iowa has built an enthusiastic audience for dance over three decades. Through a combination of frequent dance performances in the auditorium, community residencies by visiting dance companies, and a long–term relationship established with the Joffrey Ballet, Hancher has seen some amazing demonstrations of its audience's commitment. For example, 2,000 children attended a matinee performance of the David Parsons Company, despite the fact that it was held on a school holiday. The Hubbard Street Dance Company's performance was postponed after the community experienced a devastating flood. Despite the delay and the fact that the company hadn't performed at Hancher for ten years, 1,900 seats were sold.

Extended or Return Engagements

Multiple encounters with the same artists and their work help people to gradually understand and appreciate them on deeper levels than a single encounter might allow. Residencies are a common form of extended engagement. They typically involve some mix of presentation of the artist's work, education or training about the work, and participatory art making. Residencies can last from a couple of days to many months.

Many artists whose community-based work addresses social or civic goals work over a period of time with a particular group of community members.

Such extended engagements enable artists to get to know their audience and to develop specific experiences in response to the needs and interests of the audience. Likewise, the audience gets to know the artist as both a professional and as a human being.

> **Example**
> Project 2050, a youth program of New WORLD Theater at the University of Massachusetts Amherst, began in 2000 as an ongoing exploration of the year when it is projected that people of color will become the majority in the United States. Addressing the issues compelled by these changing demographics, the project engages professional artists, youth, scholars, and community activists in artistic creation and civic dialogue. The program's core is a summer retreat in which youth participate in a series of daily workshops led by leading artists in areas such as playwriting and poetry, breakdancing, beatboxing and lyricism, singing and songwriting, stepping, and visual art. Central to the depth of young people's exploration of issues and the quality of their artistic work has been the return year after year of a core of professional artists. Through their repeated presence, they have fostered artistic and personal growth among youth, many of whom participate in the program for two to four years.[5]

Interpretation

Interpretation of artists' work can help audiences to gain deeper understanding and greater appreciation of the work. Some artists conduct audience discussions before or after people experience the work. Program books or exhibition catalogues and labels may include artistic intent statements, contextual information, artist biographies, and insight about creative process. Interactive computer kiosks have exponentially expanded the way that museum visitors can access information. In advance, feature articles, radio and television interviews, or podcasts can provide insight into the work and the personality behind it. Demonstrations give perspective on the process of art making, especially for more complex or esoteric art forms.

Some artists resist interpreting their work for their audiences, preferring instead that the work speak for itself. The programmer's role is to balance the artist's wishes with the needs of the audience.

Developing Interpretive Materials

Determine when to introduce information. In viewing exceptionally challenging work, audience members might benefit from information before a presentation. At other times, it might be the artist's or programmer's preference to wait until the presentation concludes in order not to influence the viewer's own interpretation.

Use user-friendly language. Develop information that is engagingly written and free of art jargon or terms. Whenever feasible, offer translations for non–English speaking audience.

Be creative in providing information. Old conventions of art interpretation take a didactic approach, emphasizing dates and chronologies, movements, and formal analysis. A newer approach instead offers questions for viewers to reflect on, alternative views on the work, and prompts which help establish relevant connections between the work and the audience.

Make interpretive information accessible. Use accessible fonts and type sizes, and make information available in a variety of forms for people with different needs. See the Cultural Access chapter for more information.

PROGRAMMING CONSIDERATIONS

When offering work that may be provocative, controversial, or outside of what is familiar or accepted, arts organizations need to venture knowledgeably and with forethought regarding how various constituents or audiences may respond. They need to be aware of political, cultural, and economic contexts that can affect how work will be perceived and received. The challenges of such opportunities shouldn't be avoided. They may actually offer a chance for important dialogue to occur and an opportunity for building alliances and bridging ideological differences. Following are some pointers on two programming considerations deserving thoughtful approaches: managing controversy and presenting culturally-specific work.

Controversial Work

Many factors in contemporary times—competition between the arts and other sectors for decreasing public dollars, ongoing and newly emerging social concerns, vigorously wielded political and religious agendas—have made the environment for the arts more volatile and scrutinizing. Sometimes predictably and sometimes not, arts organizations need to act thoughtfully to try to avert controversy, as well as deal constructively with it when it does arise. Here are some measures that might effectively prevent or help deal with controversy.

Be accountable in making program choices. Involve community people on the selection committee, hold community focus groups to discuss new program directions, or involve arts professionals who can substantiate the artistic merit of a project. Working closely with community partner organizations can help you understand how the work may be perceived and received by different community segments. This, in turn, can help frame and present the project with concern for the values and interests of those who might find the work controversial.

Prepare project and organization leaders. Discuss the work within the organization so that board and staff members at all levels understand its intent, how it relates to the organization's mission, and how the organization will publicly support this choice. Clarify in advance of the program with board, staff, and other key partners the process to deal with controversy in the event that it arises. What kinds and degree of negative response warrant action?

Be clear and consistent about your organization's position. It is important for everyone associated with the controversial program to be able to articulate why it was undertaken and to be supportive of it and the artist, even if the work is personally not their cup of tea. Designate one person to speak to the press and concerned parties on behalf of your organization in order to be consistent with statements and responses.

Educate the media in advance. Draw upon positive relationships with feature writers, editors, and producers to try to secure advance media coverage that will prepare the community about the project. Offer the press a private preview with the artist present to provide them background information and a clear statement of artistic intent.

Provide interpretive materials. Sometimes people are just confused by the underlying meaning of a work of art or performance. Interpretive materials can help to clear up any misunderstandings and objections by clearly stating the artist's intent behind the work.

Respect differing opinions. Provide opportunity for opinions different than your organization's position to be expressed and dialogue to take place. Allowing for different opinions in your interpretive materials can also help to advance understanding and stave off negative reactions.

Muster supporters. Invite them to write letters to the editor or make calls to city council members or other leaders who should know that community members support your organization's program.

Conflict and challenge are not necessarily bad things. They can uncover issues beyond those at face value that, if addressed, can lead to new understanding—and even to healing within communities. Although easier said than done, arts leaders can transform controversy into constructive results. Find ways to educate and engage before, during, and after a controversial program has happened. Finding ongoing opportunities to engage the community in discussion about your program objectives and highlighting positive attention to your programs from other places and professionals can help create inroads toward constructive exchange.

Culturally Specific Work

Culture comprises a set of practices and expressions—language, behavior, ritual, values, food, and art—shared by a group of people. Cultural groups can encompass an ethnic community; youth; gay, lesbian, bisexual, and transgendered people; people who are deaf or hard of hearing; and newcomers to the United States. Supporting and presenting the creative expressions of specific cultures well requires knowledge and sensitivity about those cultures and their creative forms. Ideally, a culturally diverse staff and board can lend relevant cultural perspectives, expertise, and oversight to offering and supporting culturally specific work. Absent that, working closely with partners, artists, advisors, or community members helps ensure that the integrity of the work is upheld. Many cultural organizations form advisory committees to advise on the faithful presentation of culturally specific work.

Cultural representation is a complex matter that deserves attention beyond what this chapter can address. Concerns regarding self-determination, authenticity, appropriation, or exploitation can arise, even with the best of intentions. In addition, strategies for audience education and cross-cultural audience development are often needed to help understand meaning embedded in the work. Here are some fundamental considerations in developing culturally specific programs.

Aim for authenticity. Authenticity is most commonly thought of in relation to *origins* or *authorship*—for example, whether a painting is an authentic Rembrandt. However, authenticity also relates more broadly to whether the art is a true expression of a culture's values and beliefs. When working with traditional or folk art, authenticity is typically defined in terms of *continuous tradition*, that is, aesthetic forms and practices that are passed down through families or members within a culture. When folklorists or traditional artists look for authenticity, they not only look for continuity in the materials, form or style, function, and craftsmanship, but also in the spiritual, social, or cultural meaning of that work.

Questions that may arise around authenticity of work include: Can an artist of one culture effectively interpret art of another culture? How far can traditional artists exercise personal creative freedom before the work is no longer *authentic* or true to the tradition?

Consider appropriate presentation modes. Meaning and authenticity can be lost or compromised in presenting work out of its intended social, religious, or environmental context. Arts programmers need to ask such questions as: Can an African ancestor ritual be performed in a concert hall without stripping it of its meaning and authenticity? or What essential defining qualities are lost when hip-hop is taken out of the context of urban streets and put on stage? Evaluate these opportunities with the advice of the artists, and provide the artists with additional orientation to the project and its goals, a description of the audience, space, language, format, etc.

Recognize cultural norms. Not everyone who is used to clapping along with the music would know that folk fiddlers find audience clapping disruptive to the rhythm and to the way the music should be heard. Presenting the traditions of a culture unfamiliar to your audience often warrants informing audience members about what to expect and about appropriate behavior. For more on presenting folk culture, see *Folk Festivals: A Handbook on Organization and Management.* (See in the book's References section.)

Discourage the commodification of traditional culture. In the American Southwest, Native American cultures seek to protect the integrity, privacy, and spirituality of religious dances. To safeguard sacred ceremonies from being denegrated to the status of tourist attractions, many are not performed publicly. Through your own program choices, as well as advocacy among other local presenters, local arts agencies should take care to avoid romanticizing, commercializing, or otherwise commodifying cultural traditions.

Understand the needs of artists of contemporary and traditional art forms. Many artists of a particular culture create work that makes little or no reference to their cultural traditions. Others may combine traditional and contemporary sensibilities. Still others may draw upon cultural references but evolve an altogether new, contemporary style. Do not assume that artists who are of a particular culture are traditional or folk artists.

Accessibility

Involving artists with special needs and making programs accessible to people with disabilities are important concerns for programmers. It requires forethought and resources to address how people who are deaf or hard of hearing might experience a theater production or how people who use wheelchairs can view artwork. See the Cultural Access chapter for a full discussion of this issue.

LOGISTICS

Whether you are producing a weeklong outdoor festival in a city park, running a grant program, or transforming a solid waste management plant into a community environmental educational facility through public art, the vast volume of technical and logistical considerations never ceases to amaze and sometimes poses significant obstacles to programmers.

For most programs, there are common areas of concern. These include: site design regulations; permits, and licenses; signage; equipment, supplies, and services; insurance; and security. Develop an operations manual for repeated programs to help streamline the planning and implementation of future programs.

Site Design

How you use your space and situate various elements within it affects the quality of the experience that artists, audience, and organizers have. Before making decisions, consult with appropriate individuals—such as the manager of the facility or property, police and fire marshals, and others who have used the space—to learn about any overriding rules and concerns regarding the site. Following are some questions to answer in designing your site.

How can the site design support effective presentation of the art? What relationship to the art and what experience do you want people to have? What characteristics of the location support this? Are there relationships between various program components that need to be reinforced through their proximity to each other?

What will be the flow of people through the space? What are givens and how can you manipulate traffic flow to serve artistic goals as well as to ensure safety, security, etc.? How will such concerns affect the location of program components, such as directional signs? How can you encourage or discourage people in and out of certain areas?

> **Example**
>
> An annual outdoor sculpture exhibition on the grounds of an historic estate displays sculpture on the lawn adjacent to the main house and along the walking trails in a more remote wooded area. While the woods offer a beautiful setting for the work, many artists have complained that visitors often overlook those pieces. The organizers improved signs and stationed volunteer tour guides at certain locations to encourage more people to venture beyond the lawn display.

How might weather conditions affect outdoor program sites? Check historical data and consider alternative dates for inclement weather or plan for dealing with weather issues during an event.

Regulations, Permits, and Licenses

Rules governing required licenses and permits vary from place to place. To learn exactly what you need, check with the license commission, liquor commission, police and fire departments, building and electrical inspectors, and the board of health. This section addresses those areas for which permits or licenses are usually required.

Alcohol. If the facility you are using doesn't already have required licenses, you will need to get a liquor or beer and wine license as well as liquor liability insurance.

Food. Unless you are in a facility which has a food operation and is already approved by the board of health, all food vendors are required to get food permits from the local board of health to ensure sanitary food preparation, proper refrigeration, etc.

Gambling or raffles. Raffles, casino nights, and other pay–for–a–chance kinds of activities require a permit. Find out who authorizes such permits in your town by calling the city clerk's office.

Electrical. For significant modifications made to accommodate your electrical needs, a special electrical permit may be required.

Building permits. Attachments to buildings, such as signs or banners, or construction or erection of permanent or temporary art works or other structures may require permits from your local building commission.

Street closure or assembly permits. In some communities, festivals, parades, and other special events that take place in public settings require permission to close off or assemble in public ways.

Fire code compliance. Local fire marshals will want to evaluate the safety of your site in terms of maximum capacity, ingress and egress (where people enter and exit the location), and to ensure that standard fire lanes are adhered to for access by fire trucks. In addition, certain materials and objects—such as tents, projection screens, or curtains that you might bring to a location—must meet fire retardancy standards. In the latter case, the supplier might have such guarantee in writing from the manufacturer, or the fire marshal may require a sample of the material for testing.

Signage. Signs should help people get to and navigate within the program site. Find out from local officials if permission is needed to post temporary signs and at what point in time they may go up.

Equipment, Supplies, and Services

The vocalist and her voice should be the center of attention…not the sound system.

Nothing is too big or too small to be considered in this area of logistics: from masking tape to videotape, podiums to portable dance floors, rented tables to tents, track lighting to theatrical lighting, sound systems and assistive listening systems, backhoes and bucket trucks. Here is where your detail-oriented people must think thoroughly about what is needed. The costs of renting or purchasing goods, equipment, or services can easily consume a budget, so it is best to determine early which of these might be donated or borrowed, orwhat can be secured in-kind or purchased at a reduced price.

Artistic integrity could be easily compromised to save a few dollars. Providing dancers with an inadequate floor on which to perform may not only affect the quality of the performance, it could cause injury. Determine artists' needs very specifically. Talk honestly about shortcomings related to your site or technical support before you contract with an artist and review carefully the technical needs outlined in the artist's own contract rider.

The Devil's in the Details! Visualizing What You Need

Identifying all of the logistical needs can seem like an overwhelming task. One effective technique for anticipating a program's logistical needs is called visualizing. It involves putting yourself in the shoes of the various key individuals involved in the program—an audience member, artists, VIPs, volunteers, etc.—and imagining yourself moving through the program moment by moment.

Set aside ample quiet time and have what you need to begin to make lists. You might do this alone or with one or two others who are working with you. Picture how the program will look. Be very detailed in this visualization. Imagine yourself attending the event. How you will get to the program? Where will you park? Where are you entering? What signs do you need to find your way? Who is greeting you? Imagine the artist's arrival. What equipment will she or he need to set up? What kind of volunteer or technical staff will be there to help? Imagine the concession stand. How many tables and chairs do you need to display the merchandise and seat the sales staff? What signs are needed to indicate prices? How will purchases be accepted (cash, credit)?Is seating needed for the program? What configuration will work best, and how many chairs will be needed?

The objective is to give yourself the time and space to imagine every detail. Don't censor any part of your visualization; the point is to reveal items or processes that you might not think about without the benefit of time and space. If program planners do this for their area, in addition to requesting logistical needs from artists, community partners, and others involved, they can begin to put together the master list of logistical needs.

Insurance

There are many kinds of insurance that can protect you, artists, artwork, and the public. Consider what your programs might require among these basic insurance types.

Personal liability insurance. Your organization may already be insured for personal injury for your own facility. If you present programs in other locations, understand who is responsible for liability coverage. Some facilities will insure rental users. Others will require you to purchase liability insurance. Ask for proof of liability coverage through a policy currently covering your organization or agree to a hold harmless clause in a contract.

Liquor liability insurance. At many arts festivals, concert intermissions, and fundraising events, alcohol sale is a reliable revenue generator. If you sell alcohol, you must do so responsibly.

1. Evaluate the potential for abuse. Is the audience you expect likely to consume excessively and put themselves and others at risk?
2. Ask the site management if there are any rules or laws prohibiting the sale or serving of alcohol. Some places, for example, have open container laws that prohibit individuals from walking around with alcohol in open containers. This can affect festivals, outdoor concerts, etc.
3. Consult with police or the local liquor board regarding specific rules about who can serve alcohol and what kind of training may be required.
4. Determine the coverage and cost of securing liquor liability insurance. Weigh the enhancements alcohol offers to your program and profit margin against the

added cost of insurance. Many arts organizations present alcohol-free programs in order to be socially responsible and because the legal and financial risks are too great.

Inclement weather insurance. Weather insurance protects against loss of profit or extra expenses caused by inclement weather conditions. This may be especially attractive to outdoor festivals or concerts which stand to lose significant admission or concession revenues if crowds are kept away by bad weather. The costs are generally quite high, and you must evaluate the fine print carefully. Cost and coverage of rain insurance are determined by complicated definitions of what constitutes damaging rain or other attendance–prohibiting weather.

Rain insurance premiums are typically calculated by mixing ingredients from the following recipe:

- the probability of rain as determined by the insurance company's weather maps;
- the projected revenue lost by the insured if it does rain; and
- the deductible as expressed by the amount of rain in inches that you can tolerate over a given time period.

So, for example, an event might pay a certain amount for rain insurance only for the most lucrative hours of the festival. Another might purchase rain insurance to cover a defined dollar amount of loss in the instance of "five continuous hours of rain" as specified in the policy.

Insurance for theft, damage, or loss. Valuable artwork, cultural artifacts, artist's equipment, and any other valuable objects should be insured for theft, damage, or loss. Insurance companies require the exact value of each item and specific information about security measures to be taken.

Security, Safety, and Emergencies

Security encompasses the protection of people, art, the facility, equipment, onsite cash, and other valuables. Volunteers may be suitable to perform certain security functions—such as guarding artists' equipment or seeing that the fire lane on your festival grounds is kept free of vehicles. However, official police security may be a necessary precaution for guarding the ticket office where cash is handled, a major celebrity who might pose a crowd control problem, a beer concession, or valuable artwork.

Some emergencies can be averted. A prolonged heat wave, for example, prompted one festival organizer to purchase huge quantities of water to help visitors and participating artists stave off heat prostration. Staff at a partnering juvenile detention center should orient artists-in-residence to potential behavioral problems in advance of their onsite work and may need to attend and oversee residency workshops.

By nature, however, most emergencies are unpredictable. No matter what the program, you should be prepared for medical emergencies. Staff and volunteers should know:

- who has training in CPR;
- if there are onsite medical professionals, where they are located, and how they can be contacted quickly;

- where telephones are for calling 911;
- where first aid for minor accidents can be received; and
- what the plan is for halting or continuing program activities in the event of a disruptive emergency.

Other kinds of emergencies include severe weather for outdoor events, lost children, fire, or crowd control problems. Emergency procedures should be prominently displayed in program materials to inform the public how and where to get help. If you are running programs for young people—such as classes or camps—carefully define what staff can and cannot do in informational materials sent to parents. For instance, many parents may expect staff to administer injections or other medications, yet doing so could open your organization to lawsuits if improperly administered. Similarly, you must be careful about screening artists and staff members who work with young children in unsupervised settings. All of these precautions help to ensure the safety and security of your program participants.

AFTER THE PROGRAM

Program wrap-up should be done with the same care and attention given to program planning. There is a range of post-program activity.

Follow-through and Thanks

Agreements made before the program should be dutifully kept in a timely way. Return borrowed items. Pay bills promptly. Write and send final reports to funding sources and partners.

Everyone affiliated with the program should receive a thanks as personalized as is possible. Involve various volunteers or staff who had contact with participants, volunteers, etc., to take responsibility for drafting letters. To let people know their role has been important, it is a good idea to have letters cosigned not only by those who had most direct contact with them but also by the executive director, president of the board, or the director of the program.

Program Documentation and Evaluation

The Program Evaluation chapter provides an in-depth discussion of program evaluation principles and practices, including documentation that supports your evaluation interests. A couple of notes are worth reinforcing.

Plan for documentation and evaluation from the beginning. Be sure staff and volunteer organizers know what information and documents they should be collecting and organizing as the program is developed and implemented as well as after the fact.

Encourage an expeditious closure to the program. Hold wrap-up and evaluation meetings very soon after the program has concluded while ideas and impressions are fresh, and before people begin to move on to other things. Set a deadline by which final summary reports should be completed.

The types of information that should be documented or compiled are listed in Program Documentation: Things to Collect, found in the Online Companion for this chapter (see the last page of this book for the Internet address).

IN CLOSING

Many arts programmers say that developing arts programs draws equally upon the left and right sides of the brain. From the right side, they exercise vision, knowledge, and creativity to conceive and design exciting arts and cultural activity and to support and champion artists and their aesthetic investigations. They develop educational, interpretive, and participatory ways to link art with people and communities which leave a lasting impression and a desire for more. The left side of the brain figures out how to make it real—how to organize and execute the myriad of details in order to support the art and people's experience of it. This chapter has introduced how to muster the whole brain to develop meaningful and successful arts programs from the mundane elements to the sublime!

As do other *Fundamentals* chapters, this chapter underscores the increasingly integrated ways in which arts organizations are working in their communities. Innovative program collaborations have enabled cultural organizations to connect with community members in new and meaningful ways. The program development process has become as much about the process, exchange, and learning that results from making programs together as it is about the envisioned outcome.

ENDNOTES

1. McDaniel, N. & Thorn, G. (1997). *Learning Audiences: Adult Arts Participation and the Learning Consciousness.* Washington, DC: The John F. Kennedy Center for the Performing Arts and the Association of Performing Arts Presenters.
2. Kuftinec, S. (2002). *Critical Relations in Community-Based Performance: The Artist and Writer in Conversation.* Retrieved at http://www.americansforthearts.org/AnimatingDemocracy
3. Graves, B. & Juan Lado, M. (2005). Áfrican in Maine. *Cultural Perspectives in Civic Dialogue: Case Studies from Animating Democracy.* Washington, DC: Americans for the Arts, 55–56.
4. Ibid, 41.
5. For more on Project 2050, see the case study chronicling the project's participation in Animating Democracy at: http://www.americansforthearts.org/animatingdemocracy/reading_room/reading_002.asp

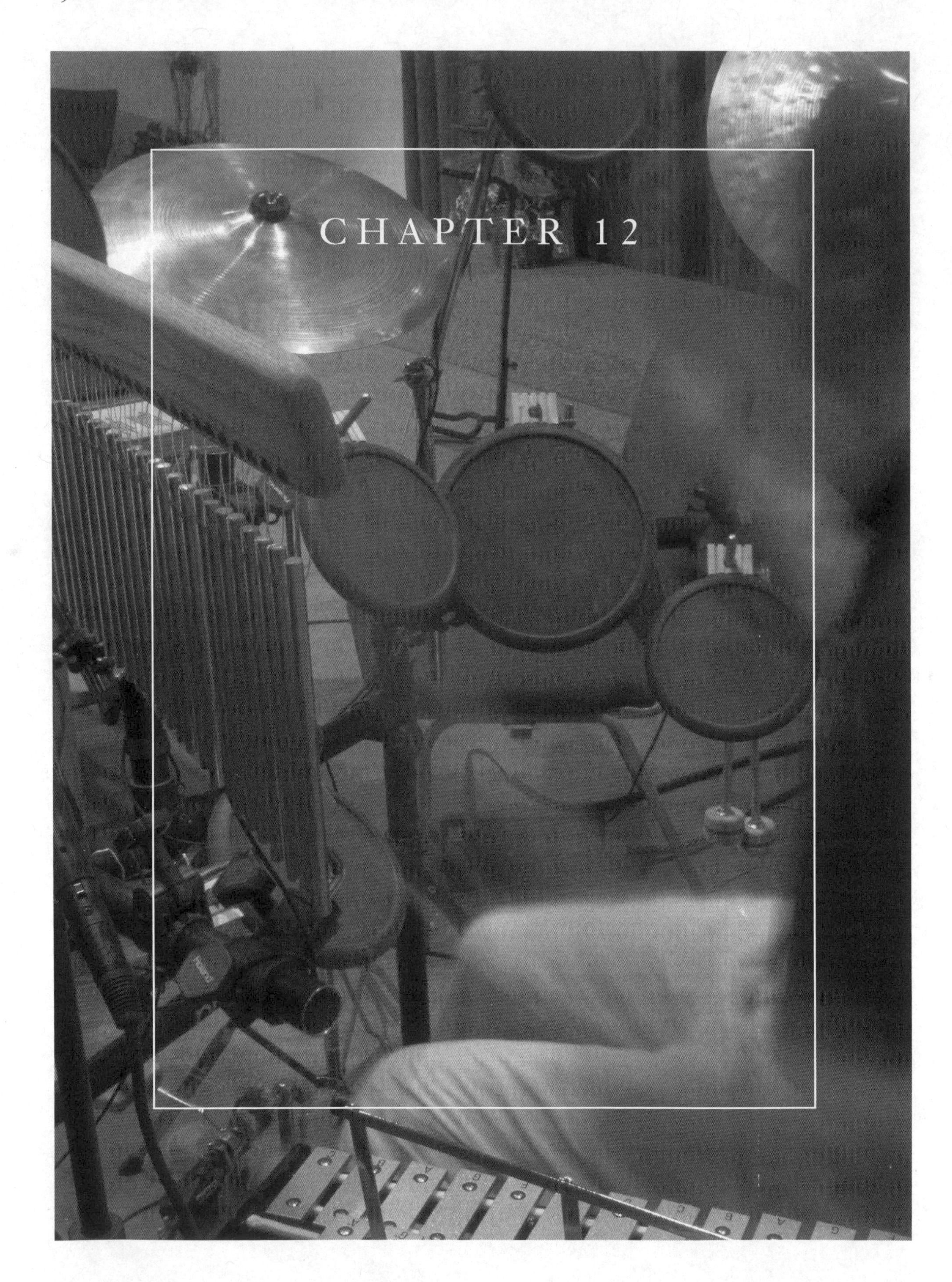

CHAPTER 12

Marketing the Arts

12

BARBARA SCHAFFER BACON

WITH CONTRIBUTING EDITORS
MAREN BROWN, DOROTHY CHEN-COURTIN,
AND SHIRLEY SNEVE

Americans are making more money, are working harder and longer, and want to make the most of their lives. As a result, they are very guarded of their leisure time and want their children to get a good education.

The competition for that free time is intense. From 200-plus channels to watch on television to professional sports events and community activities, choices even in the smallest rural communities are overwhelming. With comfortable, fast, and efficient transportation, it's easier than ever to see professional theater or symphonies in major metropolitan areas all across the country. And with today's audio technology, one can listen to high quality recordings in the comfort of home, rather than drive across town to hear a live performance.

Arts organizations face tremendous competition for an individual's attention. Because of this, cultural groups need to deliver a clear message that engages participation from its community. Delivering the organization's message to the community and the individual is at the heart of marketing.

We are challenged, through marketing, to extend a complete and meaningful invitation to all Americans to seek the arts as a means of expression and celebration. Multiple strategies are needed to make the arts more central to the lives of more citizens.

Promotional tools are also changing. Powerful personal computers can extend an organization's marketing capacity through the Internet, desktop publishing, statistical and financial analysis, and database management. Email, high-speed Internet connections, cable television, and Geographic Information Systems (GIS) are becoming, if not already, indispensable tools for increasing the capacity for effective communication. It is within this environment that we consider marketing.

Marketing is communication. Whether you represent a cultural group or a local arts agency, marketing is central to the fulfillment of your goals. Marketing is a means of telling the public who you are, what you do, and how they can be involved. Marketing strategies can accomplish key tasks, such as:

- attracting donors, volunteers, and members;
- developing audiences and ticket sales;
- promoting events, artists, and cultural resources; and
- advocating policies that support arts and cultural development.

Despite changes in technology, the core marketing principles remain constant. This chapter introduces foundational marketing concepts and explores their application to the many marketing challenges faced by cultural organizations and local arts agencies. It also shows how to apply these various tools that connect arts and community.

THE ROLE OF MARKETING

Many people equate marketing with selling a product. While the promotion of specific programs and services is the most visible aspect of an organization's marketing efforts, marketing is much more than selling and includes a full range of communication activities.

Image Building

Ongoing efforts to establish a positive image and build a good reputation in the community will enhance your agency's ability to market programs and services. If the public image you create is consistent and credible, the community will trust your agency when making decisions about supporting and attending arts and cultural activities.

Education

The majority of people are familiar with only the most popular artists and traditions. Most arts presenters seek a balance between more recognizable and more challenging arts programming. Marketing, therefore, also educates audiences in order to make programs more accessible and familiar to them. Your promotional strategies should work to inform, excite, or motivate the public about events or issues they may perceive as intimidating, dull, or "not for them."

> **Example**
>
> At one art center, a volunteer publicist prepared some standard press releases for an upcoming exhibit of collage works by an older woman. Her releases focused on the look, style, and materials of the art, as well as the awards and recognition the artist had received. Three weeks into the show, a reporter interviewed the artist and published a profile that revealed how the woman had come to create art late in life after many bouts with depression. The story noted how the artist's work helped her to express her ideas and feelings. After the article, the center received calls from many seniors groups wishing to arrange tours.

In order to educate the public, arts promoters need to educate themselves. Although it isn't necessary to be an expert on every art form and tradition, you should learn enough about the art, the artists, and programs to describe the experiences they might offer and help your intended audiences find connections.

Building Participation

Most of the literature on audience participation uses the term *audience development* to describe the efforts of arts organizations to better understand and serve their patrons. More recently, there has been a shift to the term *building participation* because it avoids the connotation that people experience the arts exclusively by attending live performances or visiting a museum. The arts are an interactive experience, and participation can be enhanced in ways other than merely increasing audience size. A landmark 2001 study, *A New Framework for Building Participation in the Arts*,[1] dramatically changed the way that cultural organizations think about their audiences.

Institutions must determine how participation-building efforts fit with their overall purpose and mission, available resources, and the community environment in which they operate. In other words, arts organization must take an integrative approach to building participation, one that:

- links the organization's participation-building activities to its core values, purpose, and goals;
- identifies clear target groups and bases its tactics on good information about those groups;
- clearly understands both internal and external resources that can be committed to building participation; and
- establishes a process for feedback and self-evaluation.

The study states that a central strategic issue involves deciding what an institution means when it says it wants to increase participation. An institution can increase participation in three basic ways.

1. **Broaden** it by through the capture of a larger share of the existing market by attracting individuals who constitute a natural audience for the arts but are not currently participants.
2. **Deepen** it through intensifying its current participants' level of involvement.
3. **Diversify** it by attracting new markets comprised of individuals who typically would not entertain the idea of participating in the arts.

An institution that decides to pursue all three ways at once faces a difficult challenge, because each of these markets requires a different engagement strategy.

This framework helps us to understand that audience development goes beyond simply increasing attendance. It occurs when new groups of people are attracted to a program or organization and develop an interest, connection, or commitment. By combining program development and promotional strategies, arts marketers can provide bridges to connect new audiences with opportunities for expression and enrichment.

Audience development occurs when new groups of people are attracted to a program or organization and develop an interest, connection, or commitment.

According to Brad G. Morison and Julie Gordon Dalgleish, authors of *Waiting in the Wings*,[2] audience development involves first creating *points of entry*—opportunities for new groups to discover the benefits of arts participation in cordial settings that are "comfortable and least intimidating." They recommend then offering *stepping stones*—program options and variations that allow new audiences to "gradually increase their interest, understanding, and adventurousness."

The demand and potential for audience development is great. The traditional arts audience is limited and graying. Now, with art more broadly defined, we can offer new audiences more forms, more traditions, more places, and more ways to experience the arts. Market research can provide insight into the needs and habits of potential audiences and enable arts organizations to design desirable programs, services, and convincing promotions.

Example

A theater has been offering contemporary works by artists of color for ten years. Through its programming, the theater has explored both the human and American condition from a diverse range of cultural viewpoints and theatrical styles. The theater is hosted by a presenting institution that offers primarily mainstream touring programs. The theater, through its own independent marketing efforts, attracts an audience that is racially and ethnically diverse. White people are attracted to the theater's cultural and political content, while the name recognition and spectacle of some of the presenting institution's programming creates a point of entry for Asian, African-American, and Hispanic audiences. Recognizing the potential for crossover between the theater's and the presenting institution's audiences, the theater began to promote its season through the concert hall's general season brochure as well as independently. Concert hall audiences are expected to try the theater's programs, and the theater's audiences may explore the wider selection of the concert hall's offerings. Each provides a stepping stone for the other's audiences to explore new cultural territory.

Assessment and Planning

When used as an integral part of an organization's planning and evaluation strategies, feedback from marketing efforts—whether successful or failed—can tell you more than how well your promotion worked. Market research activities such as focus groups, surveys, and participant evaluations can also reveal:

- how the agency is perceived in the community;
- what a community or a specific group expects or wants from your agency;
- how well programs work for targeted audiences; and
- whether the marketing message was heard.

See the Strategic Planning and the Program Evaluation chapters for more on conducting focus groups and designing and administering surveys.

In commercial environments, market research is used as a tool to minimize risk when developing new products and services. In nonprofit settings, market research helps organizations allocate scarce resources to build on program successes, respond to audience and education needs, and increase the role arts and cultural organizations have in building strong communities.

Organizations that understand marketing as more than selling can use it as an assessment tool and a means of engaging in an ongoing dialogue with the public. See the Online Companion for an outline of an organizational marketing plan that uses the principles found in this chapter. (See last page of this book for the Internet address.)

MARKETING CONCEPTS

The definitions of marketing offered in The Many Definitions of Marketing sidebar incorporate three key marketing concepts: management, exchange, and markets.

Management

Marketing is not just the random use of press releases, posters, or advertising; it is a managed process involving analysis, planning, implementation, and control. Marketing is the implementation of a carefully formulated campaign using selected promotional tools designed and timed to achieve desired results.

The Many Definitions of Marketing

While there is no single definition of marketing, those offered below share common themes. Though the classic principles of marketing are employed in the same professional manner in both the commercial and the nonprofit sectors, nonprofit arts organizations recognize the important educational role their product plays in a creative society.

The American Marketing Association defines marketing as "the process of planning and executing the conception, pricing, promotion, and distribution of ideas, goods, and services to create exchanges that satisfy individual and organizational objective."

Philip Kotler notes that "marketing is the analysis, planning, implementation, and control of carefully formulated programs designed to bring about voluntary exchanges of values with target markets for the purpose of achieving the organizational objectives. It relies heavily on designing the organization's offerings in terms of the target market's needs and desires, and on using effective pricing, communication, and distribution to inform, motivate, and service the markets."[3]

K. Diggles places the artist in the foreground of marketing the arts. "The primary aim of arts marketing it to bring an appropriate number of people into an appropriate form of contact with the artist, and in so doing to arrive at the best financial outcome that is compatible with the achievement of that aim."

Exchange

Marketing brings about voluntary exchanges of things of value that are mutually beneficial. In an exchange, all parties benefit—the patron enjoys the benefits of purchasing an artwork and the artist enjoys remuneration for his or her work. A business sponsor's financial investment advances its public relations objective, and the local arts agency uses the sponsor's funds wisely to advance its artistic goals.

We ask audiences to exchange time or money for the experience of the arts. Often, time is the more valuable of the two. While price can be a critical factor, consumers also ask themselves how they want to spend their time. If they consider investing time, they ask if the experience will be worth it. In promotions, featuring *added values*—such as easy parking, parties, or educational events—can enhance the value of the exchange. A promotion that speaks directly to consumers' interest in getting the most for their time might sound like this.

Example

On the Downtown Walking Tour:

See where history was made.

Discover our architectural treasures.

Hear the stories of our community makers.

All this in 90 minutes…and exercise, too!

Join us, weekdays and Saturdays at noon, for a walking tour of downtown. This program is sponsored by the Arts Council, the Chamber of Commerce, and the Historical Society.

Markets

Marketing involves identifying, selecting, and cultivating targeted audiences. It is not an attempt to entice the general public. In market *segmentation*, specific groups are identified and research conducted to understand their attitudes about the arts and gain insight into their lifestyles. Marketing campaigns are then directly targeted to capture their attention and elicit a response.

Target marketing is effective for drawing more of the kinds of audiences already supporting you and for developing new audience segments. It can be key in discovering how to overcome barriers to participation for previously excluded populations.

Example

As a music presenter in a suburban area, you learn from national research that young singles and couples are good audience prospects for jazz performances. The program committee wants to offer a short series of Saturday night concerts that will appeal to a younger audience. Before investing in this new venture, however, you conduct two focus groups and get some surprising feedback about the attitudes, beliefs, leisure activity patterns, and media habits of the target population.

Many affluent singles and young couples frequently go away on weekends.

Weeknight performances are more likely to draw singles because they have no family obligations or childcare needs.

Many singles are as interested in the social aspect of cultural events as in the artistic content.

People think of jazz as "serious."

Everyone goes to the Wednesday night two-for-one deal at the local cinema.

A widespread perception exists that "there is nothing to do on weeknights."

You bring this information to the program committee, which uses it to design a Thursday night series featuring cabaret-style performers, sale of refreshments, and plenty of intermissions during which audience members can socialize. You promote it as a relaxed "jazz coffeehouse" evening and develop a joint promotion with the local cinema. By the third month, your performances are the thing to do for this market segment.

THE MARKETING MIX

Many factors that could impact audience turnout—weather, local economics, and personal obligations—are outside of your control. However, as the above example illustrates, there are four marketing elements that you can control: product, price, place, and promotion. Known as the "four Ps," all are necessary and mutually dependent ingredients in the marketing mix and should be considered when you aim to meet the needs of a particular audience. Recent work in the marketing profession considers the importance of three more factors: physical evidence, people, and process.

Product

Product is the mix of programs, products, and services an organization offers to the public—such as concerts, exhibitions, residencies, publications, or grants. Often an artistic director or program committee has sole responsibility to develop or select programs. However, programs should be selected with target markets in mind, and marketing issues should be considered when designing programs. Communication between those responsible for programs and those responsible for marketing is key. See the Program Development chapter for approaches to developing programs.

Many consumers think about spending the evening out or at home with their families when they consider attending a cultural event. They do not necessarily focus on the specific artists or works in a program. Amenities such as parking, refreshments, opportunities for socializing, and activities for children may all contribute to the quality of the consumer's experience. Therefore, such amenities should be designed and promoted with the program.

Price

Price is the value—expressed in terms of money and time—placed on the programs, products, and services offered for exchange. A concept central to pricing programs is determining what the market will bear. The price should be not so high as to prohibit participation and not so low as to shortchange income (or profit) potential. The cost of going to a local movie house is often a good indication of what many in the community consider an accessible price.

> **Example**
> The Baltimore Symphony Orchestra, trying to turn around an elitist image, developed a new product, Casual Concerts. A shortened, hour-long version of evening concerts is performed, and includes friendly and informative discussion from the director. A reduced admission price reflects the shortened program. Orchestra members dress casually and audiences are encouraged to do the same. Presented on Saturday mornings, the series offers an alternative to the lengthy programs and costly tickets typical of classical music concerts.

When setting prices, consider who is excluded at what price levels and how you can keep programs open to those less able to pay. Some approaches to keeping price affordable are:

- free or low-cost admission or registration, subsidized through grants or sponsorships;
- sliding scale, permitting the consumer to pay according to ability;
- early-bird incentives offering a lower price before a certain date, or other special incentives, such as buy one, get one free;
- complimentary tickets; and
- premium price tickets that subsidize tickets sold at more affordable prices and which might include admission to an artist reception.

Pricing a program or organizational membership should be based, in part, on a budget analysis that identifies real costs and a baseline per seat or person cost. By running the numbers, you can compare various pricing scenarios to determine which is most likely to attract audiences or generate a profit. This kind of review will help you avoid under pricing and financial losses, and will also prepare you to seek program sponsorships.

Most cultural organizations cannot sacrifice earned income. Often programs that begin as free events eventually charge admission in order to survive, but not without some degree of consumer dissatisfaction. An educational process can help audiences appreciate the cost of presenting the arts as well as their responsibility to help support them. Public radio and television have become particularly adept (and bold!) at this in their periodic fund drives.

Example

An arts council produced a popular folk festival. Offered free at first, the event attracted thousands of people. The arts council, however, anticipated the financial reality that it would have to begin charging admission. In order to retain its audience, paid admission was phased in gradually. First they set up unattended donation boxes; the next year people were personally invited by volunteers to make a donation at an attended donation box; then they suggested a specified donation amount; finally, they charged a ticket price of that same amount. The council was able to sustain attendance throughout the transition.

Place

Place refers to program locations. Convenience, desirability, and emotional obstacles associated with a location can affect the marketability of a program. Place also refers to distribution, that is, the means of making programs and services available and accessible to buyers. Does the theater program tour the region or promote regionally to attract audiences to a downtown hall? Are tickets available by telephone, Internet, and mail order or only at the box office? Is programming offered only in one art center, or are churches, business lobbies, and recreational sites also used? Honestly assess any barriers that prevent visitors from patronizing programs and events, and devise ways to overcome these obstacles.

Example

As cities and towns recognize the value of the arts and culture to attract tourists and revitalize the economy of a region, they are also grappling with the issue of place. Because art venues are often situated in historic districts or within multiuse structures, they are frequently difficult to find. Recognizing a need to make the arts more accessible, the city of Worcester, Massachusetts, devised new wayfinding systems to enable arts patrons to more easily locate the cultural attractions in the city.

Promotion

Promotion is communication to target audiences that create an interest in or desire for programs and services. This includes use of advertising, posters, direct mail, telemarketing, press releases, and a host of other tools to inform the public about your program. The Marketing Tools section in this chapter focuses on this area.

Physical Evidence

Cultural organizations share a similar problem with the service industry, according to arts marketing consultant Dorothy Chen-Courtin. The arts represent an *intangible* product. The potential user cannot "kick the tires" prior to purchase, and the product or experience will never be the same for each individual, or even to the same person over time. Even when watching a movie for the second time, the viewers may have a different reaction to it based on previous experience and the audience watching it with them.

How Do I Set Ticket Prices?

A common conundrum facing arts managers is how to set ticket prices. While pricing theories abound, most experts agree that one should take into consideration the following factors when setting prices: market, cost, and capacity. For nonprofit cultural organizations, the issue of pricing is complicated by the educational mission of the agency. When establishing prices for cultural events, consider the following variables:

- Cost to produce or create the program or service
- Seating capacity or maximum number of units you can produce
- Anticipated audience attendance for the event or the anticipated number of units you expect to sell (Consult the history of prior events or sales or survey patrons to gauge their reaction to different ticket prices.)
- Price charged by competitors in the market (such as nearby community art centers, museums, galleries, and the like) that offer similar events or services
- Corporate sponsorships, grant subsidies, and other income raised to underwrite the program costs
- Gut instinct.

Remember that marketing plans must support the level of attendance sales that you project!

Let's look at an example. An arts organization is planning to offer a jazz concert at its community art center. The cost to produce the event (artist fees, sound equipment, space rental, marketing, staffing, and other costs) is $1,000.

The performance venue has 200 seats. The organization usually gives away ten complimentary tickets at each performance to VIPs and friends of the artist, so the highest number of tickets it could sell at each event would be 190. Based on substantial prior experience offering similar performances, the organization anticipates that it will sell 80 percent of the total seats, or 160 tickets.

Ticket sales are the organization's sole source of revenue. It has found that other performances in its region are generally priced at $10 to $20 per ticket. The organization thinks its own audience will pay no more than $12 per ticket, as the artist is less well-known and a few loyal patrons indicated that this is what they would pay to see the artist. Gut instinct is an important factor in setting prices, especially as one gains experience in presenting events. Never overlook that feeling in the back of your mind that is warning you that a price may be too high or low. Often it is correct!

Now let's look at the numbers. Below is a chart that summarizes the potential income from pricing the jazz concert at $10 per ticket or $12 per ticket. In either scenario, the organization will come out ahead, based on costs of $1,000 and its history of attendance. In general, it is best to set prices at the highest levels you think your audience can afford. Remember the income can be used to support other programs that may be more experimental in nature or help to subsidize seats for those who are not able to pay the full price (such as students, for instance).

	Minimum # seats needed to cover costs of $1,000		**Average # seats**		**Maximum # seats**	
Ticket price	# Seats	Revenues	# Seats	Revenues	# Seats	Revenues
$10	100	$1,000	160	$1,600	190	$1,900
$12	84	$1,008	160	$1,920	190	$2,280

Customers of an *intangible* product, such as a concert or visual arts exhibit, often rely on *tangible* cues or *physical evidence* to evaluate the service before its purchase and to assess their satisfaction with the service during and after the experience. The proper management of the physical evidence surrounding the visual and performing arts experience will assure or reassure the audience of the mission and objectives of the organization.

Two principal categories of physical evidence are marketing communication tools and onsite physical projection.

Marketing communications materials. Marketing tools that provide tangible evidence of how an organization implements its mission and positions itself include its logo and corporate identity, fliers and brochures, onsite signage, publications in which the organization places its advertisements, email, and the organization's website.

Onsite physical projection. The outside appearance, architecture, and interior décor of the arts organization; onsite amenities; and the appearance and communications quality of front-line personnel all work in concert to assure and reassure the audience. The choice and management of these site-specific elements serve as physical evidence of how an organization carries out its mission. Does the message delivered through communications materials match that of actual physical site? Customers will be able to recognize a logo if it is used consistently in print, on the website, and at the cultural venue.

Outside signage that clearly indicates the program venue, where to park, and where to enter may be the deciding factor to someone considering a visit to your organization. Is the entrance accessible to all, including persons with disabilities? Are outside smoking areas well marked, kept clean, and away from main entrances?

People

Success, for an arts organization, depends on the seamless delivery of a great experience, be it an exhibition, a concert, a play, or a dance performance. Who and what can ensure this seamless delivery? People do, through a good process—the last two Ps of the marketing mix.

The people referred to here include audience-contact personnel and volunteers—such as the receptionist, box office personnel, guards, performers, specialists (artists, musicians, and curators, etc.), as well as the board of directors, management, and staff. Audience-contact personnel create an instantaneous and lasting impression on the public. Board, management, and staff build, nurture, and sustain the ongoing rapport with the public. Performers and specialists produce and deliver the experience that the public comes to see, hear, and enjoy.

The implication here is clear; the selection, training, and empowerment of people for the arts organization must be thoughtfully executed. Every individual has a specific functional responsibility. Collectively, everyone also is responsible for quality, service, and delivery. Cross-functional cooperation is critical.

Process

In this context of marketing, process refers to the smooth integration of all aspects of the marketing mix. By now it should be clear that arts organizations are essentially service organizations delivering pleasurable experiences while catering to human-comfort needs. Those that succeed have effective processes in place to ensure that customers are well served and satisfied from the time they first hear about a program until they leave the program.

Creature comfort needs include the auxiliary product benefits discussed earlier. They may be basics such as well-lighted parking, properly air-conditioned and ventilated spaces, tasteful decor, handy water fountains, and clean restrooms. Additional benefits can include well-stocked gift shops, snack bars, and quality restaurants. All these basics and extras, as well as the core product offering, need planning, scheduling, and managing of capacity and logistics. The seamless delivery of the experience depends on effective operations management.

In marketing terms, products need to be designed as *product bundles*, which include the core product, the extended product, and auxiliary product offerings. Now we know that the core, extended, and auxiliary product offerings all depend on good process.

Traditionally, organizations view program operations and marketing as separate functions; however, managers today see that arts marketing and operations are interdependent functions. Success depends on cooperation, where administration, operations, facilities, and marketing all plan, schedule, and deliver as a team.

All seven elements—product, price, place, promotion, physical evidence, people, and process—are necessary and mutually dependent ingredients in the marketing mix. Neither an excellent program nor a bargain price nor a massive promotion will, in and of itself, attract audiences. In order for a marketing campaign to succeed, all seven elements must be designed in relation to one another and with specific target markets in mind. Fortunately, this is easier than it sounds. For regularly offered programs, you may discover the right mix by trial and error. A deliberate examination of the seven Ps is particularly useful when designing new programs, reaching out to new market segments, or evaluating a past campaign. If something didn't quite work, consider whether you offered the right mix of product, price, place, and promotion, as well as physical evidence, people, and process for your intended markets.

In order for a marketing campaign to succeed, all seven elements must be designed in relation to one another and with specific target markets in mind.

MARKET RESEARCH

Market research is a process of finding out more information about existing or prospective markets to help you make better program and marketing decisions, and to help minimize the risk of developing new programs and services. The goal of market research is to gain insight into the interests and behavioral patterns of these markets. For many organizations, however, the idea of conducting market research seems overwhelming. The research process can, in truth, be as simple as observing who is attending programs and reviewing existing box office records and program evaluation forms, or it can involve more complicated data analysis and survey methods.

Offering new programs or promoting to new audiences on a limited basis is a viable means of testing a market's response if these activities are accompanied by preplanned evaluations. For example, a festival wishing to assess an audience's appetite for various arts offerings might station volunteers to ask exiting audience members which performances and exhibitions they look forward to seeing more of in the future.

Market research methods might be employed to:

- test interest in a new program direction;
- understand why membership is dwindling;
- learn about the interests of potential new audiences;
- identify a disinclined group's barriers to participation;
- gather market profile information needed to identify and secure media or corporate sponsors; or
- determine the best placement for publicity, promotion, and advertising.

The time and energy invested in gathering market information pays off with the ability to pinpoint the most effective marketing resources and make expenditures in the most productive places.

If you know where to look, good information already exists and free or low-cost expertise in conducting market research is close at hand.

Market Research Information

The following outline indicates the kinds of information, input, and feedback which can be solicited through interviews, focus groups (a group interview with several carefully selected representatives of a constituency with common interests or affinities), and surveys. A researcher should select carefully and tailor the questions to meet specific needs.

To get to know a market segment, you might gather some of the following types of information:

Values and Beliefs

Impressions of cultural life in the community

Beliefs about the importance of the arts

Feelings about the arts and culture that are currently available

Perceptions of cultural activities lacking in the community

Arts Participation

Attendance at cultural events or institutions—including kinds of events and how often

Obstacles to attending cultural events

Impressions of particular events, organizations, or institutions

Leisure Activity

Available leisure time

Current ways of spending leisure time

Most preferred leisure pursuits

Feelings about the amount and kinds of activities available for adults and children

Media Habits

Sources used to obtain information about cultural and leisure activities

Typical advance planning time to participate in cultural activities

Feedback on Completed Programs and Events
Inclination to attend (support) the program again

Suggested improvements to make the program better serve interests or needs

Other programs that would be of interest to patrons

Price
Opinion about fair price for the program

Feeling about investment of time required to participate in the program

Promotion
Response to the marketing campaign message and image

Recommendation about different or additional information for marketing materials

Place
Opinion about convenience and desirability of the location

Opinion about the date and time of the program

Accessibility of registration or ticket purchase

Recommendations for improvement

Feedback on Ongoing Activities (for example, membership)
How members first became aware of the organization

Benefits that convinced members to join

Most positive experience(s) since joining

Negative experience(s) with this organization

Most important benefits of belonging

Suggested other offerings

Reasons for renewing or not renewing membership

Internal Information

Constituent data. Your own records are an important starting point for market research. For example, analysis of membership, subscriber, or class registration mailing lists by ZIP code indicates from where your participants are coming. How does your general mailing list compare with your membership? Is the audience for every program coming from the same location or does it vary?

Some agencies work to collect more specific data on their constituents and supporters—age, family status, occupation, media habits, and even preferences and opinions regarding programs. This information is solicited at various points of contact—such as registration, membership recruitment, the agency's website, or ticket purchase. With it you can construct demographic profiles of your market segments. If this information is charted over time, you may see where you are gaining or losing constituents, and discover other relevant trends.

Example
A community music school learned that 65 percent of its students under 12 years old came from the inner-city neighborhoods surrounding the school; 75 percent of

Market Research at Work

An art center noticed a small but steady increase in participation from senior citizens in its art classes. The program coordinator convened two focus groups of participants to learn if this market segment could be expanded, and what would help the center design programs and promotion. The two focus groups were asked to respond to a series of questions.

Why do you participate in the center's programs?

What do you get out of your participation in the center's programs?

When is the best time for you to participate?

What else do you do with your leisure time?

Where do you get information about leisure/educational/arts activities?

The focus groups revealed that, while a few seniors had studied art in college or practiced handcrafts as hobbies, the arts had not played a big part in their lives. Several noted that they thought they might feel uncomfortable at the art center. Many noted that they liked the exposure to "serious art" in contrast with the arts and crafts programs sponsored by the senior center. The quality of instruction was commended frequently.

Most enjoyed the social contact provided by the classes but emphasized that doing their own creative work was the primary motivation for enrolling.

While the groups ranged from people on fixed incomes to those with significant discretionary funds, all reported careful spending habits and concern for getting good value for their money.

Though there was no consensus, mornings were the most popular time for classes. The majority were reluctant to sign up for classes that stretch out over too many weeks because they could interfere with holiday or travel plans.

Participants mentioned the newspaper, senior events calendar, and church newsletters as their most frequently used information sources. Two radio stations were noted for their programming and news. Few were aware of cable television activity listings. Many noted that they frequently attended free arts festivals and other cultural events. Few consulted the Internet for information.

Based on these responses, the program coordinator set as an objective an increase in senior participation by 20 percent over the next year. Specific efforts to meet that objective in the first year would be to:

- reconfigure the classes to run for fewer weeks but with longer sessions;
- increase morning offerings;
- design a promotional campaign around the message, "It's not too late to start with the arts!";
- give more emphasis in publicity and promotion to the quality of instruction and opportunity for serious art study; and
- offer a program of studio art, gift shop tours, and short lectures on "what to look for in fine art and craft" to senior groups.

the students 12 and over were from other city neighborhoods, with 50 percent of these coming from suburban communities. Based on these statistics the school sought to discover why the neighborhood children were dropping out and why more students from distant neighborhoods and communities tended to be enrolled at 12 and older.

Make it a priority to create systems to collect data and to regularly review constituent profiles.

Program evaluations. Many arts groups hold debriefing meetings or distribute and collect questionnaires at the conclusion of a program. These are a means to gain valuable feedback for future program design and promotion. Formulate evaluation questioning to best serve your marketing needs. Questions should generally address each element of the marketing mix—product (the value and quality of the program); price (the fairness of the price, the value for time or money spent); place (the convenience of the site and other logistical details); promotion (the effectiveness of message, image, and distribution of publicity and promotions); physical evidence (cleanliness and signage); people (helpful and courteous staff); and process (admission and ticketing).

Tracking. You can calculate the response rate to certain marketing efforts, and evaluate and compare cost-effectiveness. See the Marketing as Management sidebar for a description of the wealth of tracking options made possible with new technologies.

Here are some simple techniques for monitoring the results of specific promotions.

Ask callers and visitors how they heard about the program. Keep a tally of responses. A daily log of inquiries and registrations received can provide a useful comparison to monitor program registration in subsequent years. More mid- to large-sized cultural institutions are tracking their calls in Customer Relationship Management systems, which help to further refine the information.

Insert different code names in newspaper, radio, Internet, and television advertisements, as well as email campaigns. When callers respond to the ad by asking for "Nancy" or "George," it can be recorded and tallied. Code names can be assigned to certain stations or publications, or they can be more specifically associated with the time of day or day of the week the promotion is scheduled to appear.

Code mailing lists used for direct mail. When creating the graphic piece, design it so that the registration or subscription form, which is returned to you, is on the backside of the mailer panel. Keep track of the different mailing lists you have used by coding them in some visible way—such as a code number, a colored marker stripe down the edge of purchased mailing labels, or a bar code. By counting the coded forms when they are returned, you will know which of your mailing lists are producing the best results. Data capture can be done manually (code number or colored stripe), with a bar code reader (which visually scans coding), or with a RFID reader (which scans embedded computer chips that broadcast information). Bar code readers are dropping quickly in price, and are likely to become more commonplace (and less time intensive). RFID (radio frequency identification) is becoming the new technology of choice and, as its price drops, will become more available to nonprofit marketers.

Use short audience surveys at events, on your website, or through email correspondence to collect demographics or assess media effectiveness and reach. Incentives, such as ticket giveaways and free beverages, are often used to encourage cooperation and increase the rate of return.

Provide incentives for people to respond to a promotion. Offer a discount or free item through coupons located in ads, direct mail, website, email, or flyers. This is especially useful for promotions that don't require a specific response, such as a general brochure about your organization. When people trade in their coupons for their discount or freebie, you get some idea of the impact. If coupons are coded according to their source, you can compare the return from each source. Requesting that coupons are returned with that person's home ZIP code is another way to learn the geographic draw of your program.

Financial data. Documentation of marketing expenditures can provide a basis for comparative analysis and valuable data for tracking the effectiveness of specific marketing campaigns and projecting future marketing costs. A spreadsheet that allows comparisons of marketing expenditures over several years could help establish a baseline for future marketing budgets. In *Waiting in the Wings*, Morison and Dalgleish recommend calculating the cost per dollar of income (all related direct marketing expenses divided by the total ticket, membership, or fundraising income) as the simplest way to compare the relative cost-effectiveness of various marketing strategies. You can obtain more specific data about the success of specific marketing efforts by examining the data in online advertising and email campaigns, website tracking services, and other options now made available through technology.

External Information

Census data. The first place to check for demographic facts and trends about communities of interest is to visit the U.S. Census Bureau at www.census.gov. Due to the infrequency of U.S. Census sampling (the official population census is conducted once every ten years, though there are more frequent small samplings taken), this information can be augmented with more recent data from local, regional, county, and state sources—such as town or regional planning officials, marketing specialists, or a nearby university or college. Population breakdowns, education and income levels, employment patterns, housing and community growth trends, and much more are all available from census data. The same information that your municipality uses to predict the need for sewers, schools, and roads can help you with your programming and marketing decisions. For example, if the per capita income in a region has dropped, it may be affecting citizens' ability or willingness to pay for cultural activities. A growing number of single-working-parent households might suggest the need for a before-school program to assist parents who must leave for work before school officially opens.

Demographic analysis systems. More detailed demographic information is also available. One well-known system is called PRIZM, developed by Claritas Corporation. It combines ZIP code data with information about people's age, income, and education —including spending habits and dozens of other factors—to identify *clusters* of consumer characteristics. Other systems can combine your database with census data to see at a glance where your audience comes from and where other similar consumer clusters might be found. Organizations can use the information to aim mailings and other promotions at specific target markets or to identify target markets they want to learn more about through further research.

The competition. An important part of market research is to be aware of what arts colleagues and competitors are doing. Observe what programs are offered at what prices. Study promotions for clues as to what audience segments are being targeted. See if you can determine what their marketing strategy seems to be. Such information will help you define your organization's own image and position, or niche, in the market.

Direct constituent contact. Just as word of mouth is the best way to communicate your message, it is also a great way to hear what current or prospective constituents have to say. By seeking the opinions and responses of consumers, you can begin to view your organization and its programs from their perspectives and, therefore, more objectively.

Other data sources

The police or courts may be able to provide statistics on at-risk youth populations.

The United Way and GuideStar.org record information on nonprofit organizations, philanthropic trends, and human service issues.

Real-estate agents track who is moving into town and know their concerns for recreation, education, community services, and cultural activities.

The public school system profiles its student population, especially with the advent of No Child Left Behind, which requires districts to keep detailed profiles of its study body. This information is usually accessible online.

Local newspapers and radio and television stations profile their own readers, listeners, and viewers.

National arts service organizations—such as the American Symphony Orchestra League, Dance USA, Chamber Music America, and Americans for the Arts—have profiles of constituents and audiences.

Trade publications, like the *Chronicle of Philanthropy* and *American Demographics*, can provide useful statistics and information on audience, fundraising, and marketing trends.

Interviews, Focus Groups, and Surveys. The typical methods of market research through direct audience or constituent contact are personal interviews, focus groups, and surveys. All three are useful as market research tools that allow you to:

- get to know new market segments (at an introductory or assessment stage);
- solicit input as programs and marketing campaigns are being designed (at a formative or planning stage); and
- receive feedback on programs after they have taken place (at the evaluation stage).

See the Strategic Planning and the Program Evaluation chapters for more information on designing effective interviews, focus groups, and surveys.

MARKETING TOOLS

Marketing campaigns typically utilize four communication strategies: public relations, publicity, promotion, and advertising. Within each there are specific tools that you can employ to accomplish different things. A press release, for example, presents the facts about an upcoming concert—the dates, location, price, and nature of the program—while a radio interview with the musician offers listeners a chance to hear what the music sounds like and to become familiar with the artist and her approach. Both are useful but each does a specific job.

Public Relations

Public relations are those activities that build goodwill within a community or audience. Public relations concerns how the public perceives and regards your work. Aims of public relations efforts might be to enhance visibility or credibility for your organization, to build trust with a particular market segment (often a new one), to develop a particular image (defining a niche or character), to inform audiences of recent accomplishments, or to counteract general misperceptions, such as the effects of a particular controversy. Public relations involve several key components.

Networking can be accomplished by participating in professional and civic organizations; hosting periodic breakfast or lunch engagements for community leaders, government officials, or members of the media; and participating in civic activities initiated by the chamber of commerce or service organizations.

Marketing as Management

Each year, a museum strategically coordinates marketing efforts for its annual fund drive.

Six weeks prior to the start of the campaign, staff create an "annual fund drive" section on the museum's website to promote the fund drive, including online pledge opportunities. Board members are asked to make their "first in" donations, and 100 percent board participation is used in all marketing messages. An email newsletter is designed to update patrons on the progress of the campaign, and all advertisements are designed.

Five weeks before the campaign, ideas for human interest stories are offered to the local newspaper editor and two radio talk-show hosts. These generate feature stories and radio interviews that appear **two weeks before** the fund drive is launched and serve to develop general awareness that the museum's fund drive is about to begin.

Direct mail solicitations (referring to the website's online pledge area) are mailed to previous and prospective supporters **the day before a press conference** that kicks off the marketing campaign. The press conference generates television news stories that night and paper coverage the next morning. The direct mail immediately reinforces these media messages.

A telephone solicitation to those who received the mailing is implemented over **five weeks following the press conference.**

Press releases and email newsletters are issued at regular intervals during the fund drive to update the public about campaign progress. Prerecorded radio spots, featuring local leaders discussing the benefits of the arts in the community, are aired for **five weeks beginning with the press conference.** Postcards are sent as a follow-up to the earlier direct mailing to remind people how to make a donation and of the deadline by which to pledge.

Midway through the campaign a show of student work from local schools opens in the museum lobby, attracting parents, teachers, and friends in addition to community leaders. The annual drive is promoted during the awards ceremony. Also during this time, a series of short lunchtime concerts is offered downtown to maintain visibility for the museum and the fund drive. Regionally-targeted advertisements are established on search engines.

The six-week campaign ends publicly when the campaign chair accepts a check from the head of a local publishing firm that pushes the campaign over the top. A picture appears in the evening paper and the fund drive's success is reported on morning newscasts.

Board and key staff can advance an organization's mission through active involvement in the community. Attending city commission meetings and participating in community events—including events put on by your competitors—increases the credibility and importance of the arts in your region.

Community relations can be built through friendly, helpful treatment of the public through frontline volunteers and staff; letters to the editor giving thanks or praise; offers of resources, such as space, for other community purposes; or word-of-mouth recommendations.

Reliability, professionalism, and businesslike operations, which all contribute to an organization's reputation in the community, can be cultivated by maintaining a stable address (post office box for organizations without an office), investing in a quality phone answering system and replying to messages promptly, and paying bills on time.

Visibility can be enhanced through public speaking engagements, brief videos introducing your organization played at community events and meetings, regular programs on cable television, or volunteer participation by staff or board in public television auctions or fundraising phonathons.

Publications communicate an organization's aims, scope, and quality, and offer opportunities to stay in touch with supporters and discover new ones. Invest time and effort to ensure high-quality publications, which present a consistent, professional graphic image.

In the event of negative publicity, such as a publicized mismanagement problem or a controversy surrounding the content of an art exhibit, a proactive public relations effort grounded by a clear position statement may be necessary to reestablish credibility or to reinforce the organization's commitment to community interests while sticking to its principles.

Publicity

Publicity is the backbone of marketing for most arts organizations. It involves the dissemination of newsworthy information free of charge by newspapers, magazines, radio, and television. While the media is required by federal communications law to provide free service through which news of local and community interest is communicated, they have limited print space or airtime to accommodate all the potential requests for coverage. There is no guarantee that your press release will be printed or your public service announcement aired. Therefore, knowing how to present your information clearly, concisely, and in standard formats increases your chances of having your information used.

There are many publicity tools at your disposal.

- Press releases and public service announcements
- Calendar and event listings on cable television, radio, Internet, phone systems, and in print media
- Feature stories, reviews, captioned photographs, and press packets
- Press conferences

- Letters to the editor and editorials
- Radio and television talk shows
- Newsletters and other printed publications
- Websites, email newsletters, and blogs

Publicity coverage depends on effective relations with key media contacts. This section offers guidelines on how to prepare and present publicity communications; however, it is wise to find out from editors with whom you will have frequent contact—especially local ones—what their particular style and format preferences are. Each editor has different requirements. One may welcome your email offer of several ideas for feature stories on your annual concert series. Another might regard this as an annoyance and prefer to receive a full press packet, develop his or her own ideas, and then call you for feedback. Maintain an updated file (using a spreadsheet like Excel, for instance) with information on deadlines, editors, and preferences. This will prove a valuable resource, especially if staff or volunteer publicity coordinators change often. Try to deliver your first article personally so that you can introduce yourself and begin to establish a relationship. Acknowledge assistance with thank-you notes.

Press (or news) releases present factual, timely, newsworthy information. Not a sales pitch, they answer the questions: who, what, where, why, when, and how. The opening sentence should be compelling, and the first paragraph should include all the essential information. This makes it easier for the editor to shorten copy if space is limited while still providing the reader with the most valuable and pertinent information. The media are not in business to provide you with free publicity. Your press releases will be used more often if they contain news, are presented in usable form and do not require research or revisions (more information, spelling corrections), and are not filled with the writer's opinions and glowing remarks regarding the event. Give 'em the facts!

Public service announcements (PSAs) on radio or television provide the essential information in standardized lengths of usually ten, 30, or 60 seconds. PSAs may take the form of written announcements that broadcasters read on air (or scroll on television), or they may be recorded on tape with music, sound effects, or visuals added for television. Make sure your copy takes into account the difference between the written and spoken word. The spoken word can sound more informal, so sentences should be kept simple and short. Before launching into producing your own prerecorded PSAs, determine from broadcasters if they will actually use your announcements. Enlist the help of professionals in conceiving and producing recorded PSAs or ask for donated or reduced-rate assistance from the stations themselves. Although each station is required by law to provide free time for PSAs, there is no guarantee that your announcement will be aired. Providing concise, usable copy increases the likelihood of frequent use. PSAs are often broadcast during less than prime time slots (late night, early morning, midday), with primetime slots reserved for paying advertisers.

Calendar listings of daily events provide basic information: event name, times, location, price, ticket availability, or registration instructions. Some newspapers run calendar highlights offering descriptive listings and photos as well as the basics. Find out who the arts calendar editor is. Many websites allow you to post low resolution digital images (in jpeg format) along with your calendar listings.

Feature stories highlight background and human elements behind the news, lending color and meaning to facts and events. Because features provide a sense of immediacy and depth of coverage, they can attract attention, offering readers substantial information and insight that may convince them to take action. A feature story can be timely—that is, related to a program you are mounting, a grant you recently received, or another newsworthy occurrence—or it can cover subjects not tied to any particular event, such as ongoing arts education or a special, long-term volunteer program.

Because features provide a sense of immediacy and depth of coverage, they can attract attention, offering readers substantial information and insight that may convince them to take action.

Feature articles are most often written by a publication's staff writer or frequent contributor. Suggest story ideas and try to persuade the editor or writer to develop them into features.

Effectively pitching an idea for a feature article involves the following steps:

1. Develop the idea(s) or angle you want to propose based on the publisher's interests.
2. Determine to whom to pitch your idea (arts, city, or business editor, or a particular writer who might be interested in writing the story).
3. Mail or email a press release providing basic information, along with a cover letter suggesting your idea. Background materials can be helpful but should be kept to a minimum. Follow up with a phone call to discuss your idea and any responses that the editor might have. Be prepared to provide contact information on people who might be featured in the article.

Monthly magazines typically require several months lead time prior to publication; newspapers require several weeks prior depending on the nature of the article.

Captioned photos, even without an accompanying article, can be extremely effective in catching the reader's interest. Always try to obtain high-quality photographs (in both digital and print forms) from your participating artists and plan to take professional quality photos at your own programs for future publicity use. Type photo captions on a separate sheet, succinctly describing what or who is portrayed and the other pertinent facts—when, where, and how. Accompany the photo with a note providing contact information and, ideally, a press release with more details. Email or mail it to publications, according to their preferences.

Press packets combine several of the above elements. They allow you to present to the print and electronic media the full picture of a special program and perhaps to plan multiple opportunities for coverage. A press packet for an arts festival, for example, might include:

- a cover letter introducing the packet and any special comments on its contents;
- a press release providing an overview of the entire event;
- one or more additional press releases focusing on particular programs, highlighted artists, or aspects of mounting the event, conceived with the idea that the media might develop a feature story around a particular subject or run a series of releases building up to the event;
- a calendar listing;
- photos with captions;

- background description of the festival, its history, and highlights; and
- background information on particular artists or subjects about which you are pitching a feature story idea.

Press packets should be sent out six to eight weeks in advance to a select group of writers or editors (they can be costly). While planning, consult with key media to determine when and to what extent they might cover the program so that the press packet can be timed to meet their needs.

Press conferences are gatherings of the media to provide comprehensive information, discuss an issue, launch a campaign, or field questions. Press conferences are reserved for important or major occasions. Invitations are sent to key editors, writers, news directors, and anchors, and follow-up calls are made to encourage attendance. Often an appearance by one or more of the artists in your program, a spokesperson for the program, or other celebrity is built into the press conference to make it more enticing. Press packets may also be distributed.

In the case of a press conference called to clarify an organization's stand on an immediate issue, a controversy, or a city arts budget debate, prepare a written statement to announce at the conference and distribute to the press.

Guest editorials in your local newspaper allow contributors to express points of view on topics or issues of local, national, or global interest.

Letters to the editor and editorials are another way to express your views through print and electronic media. They are widely read and create an opportunity to influence public opinion. Guest editorials in your local newspaper allow contributors to express points of view on topics or issues of local, national, or global interest. Consider carefully what you want to express before you call the editor to propose it. If the issue is timely, be prepared to respond quickly.

Radio or television talk shows can publicize featured artists or organizational affiliates and provide thorough, insightful coverage. Talk show producers book six or more weeks in advance. It is important to research the interests and styles of particular programs in order to determine if they reach your market and provide an appropriate vehicle to discuss the subject. Local cable access stations are a great resource for interview programs; some local arts agencies have even created their own weekly program featuring local artists, organizations, and subjects.

Websites, email newsletters, and blogs are all excellent ways to reach audiences with information about programs and services. The assumption here is that you will be submitting information to others who are publishing these materials virtually (see below for your own website promotion). This might include state arts agency newsletters, regional websites, or blogs.

Promotion

Promotion typically augments the publicity plan by providing supporting material that helps the consumer gain information, form an opinion, or make a decision to act. While the media cannot guarantee the use of your publicity materials, promotional methods are completely within your control. You can control what is said, where promotion is done, and who and how many people you will reach. For this reason, promotional strategies often target specific markets.

Types of Promotions

- Graphic items—brochures, flyers, posters, and postcards
- Information pieces—newsletters, reports, slide shows, and videos
- Signage—signs, marquees, banners, table tent cards, and displays
- Telephone and computer resources—telemarketing, fax transmission cover sheets, email, websites, podcasts, bulletin boards, and phone information lines
- Promotional events—preview performances, presentations, or ceremonies
- Specialty items—buttons, bumper stickers, mugs, T-shirts, and caps

Example
One rural arts council utilized buttons as a main promotional vehicle. With a button machine they owned, they produced two sets of buttons for every event. The first button used a word or image to tease the viewer into asking what it meant. These were distributed to merchants in town five to six weeks before the event. Store clerks everywhere wore them, generating interest by word of mouth. Later, a second button and related flyers and posters sporting full information were released.

Pointers on Writing Promotional Copy

Before you begin, remember that copy should answer these essential questions:

Who are you?

What is the aim of your promotion?

To whom are you talking?

Who are you? Establish your organization's image (family-friendly, cutting-edge, contemporary, an art oasis) through choice of language, tone, and writing style.

What is the aim of your promotion? Be clear on what the promotion should accomplish and what action you want the reader to take. For example, do you want to bring attention to your message, provide insights about the art, inform about an issue, or elicit action? Don't forget to include the who, what, when, where, and how information in all your promotions! When writing for the Web or email, begin with an action phrase like "click here" or "visit this link."

To whom are you talking? Communicate with a person who represents the market segment you intend to reach with your message. Consider age, sex, income, education, occupation, social status, and area in which your audience lives. Imagine what would make that person respond to your messages. What benefits would move them?

As you write, keep these tips in mind:

Be specific, clear, and concise.

Use active verbs and vivid language.

Avoid jargon.

Motivate and stimulate. Emphasize the benefits of the program:
don't over promise.

Emphasize unique aspects of your program—what sets it apart from similar programs.

Be consistent in editorial style.

Edit more than once.

Get feedback before finalizing copy. This is especially true with emails, where you have no opportunity to revise your message after you hit the "send" button!

Image and message. Successful promotional efforts combine image and message to capture the target market's attention. Whether the promotion is a direct mail brochure, website, or banner over Main Street, it should create a vivid impression in order to compete with the hundreds of other promotions and advertisements an individual encounters on a daily basis.

Image communicates how you want to be recognized and perceived by your market; message is what must be communicated.

Image is conveyed through both the choice of visual elements and the tone, content, and language of written copy. Image communicates how you want to be recognized and perceived by your market; message is what must be communicated. Unlike most publicity efforts, the information conveyed in promotion need not be newsworthy; it is often educational or informational—a brochure about your organization or an annual report, for example. Your message emphasizes the benefits the consumer seeks (discovered through your market research) and should be tailored to the specific targeted market.

It is a good idea to acknowledge and directly address obstacles perceived by your potential audiences. For instance, if you think some people are worried that they don't have the proper attire, be sure to stress that they don't need a black tie to appreciate your symphony.

Distribution

Print promotions—such as direct mail, posters, or flyers—require careful distribution to achieve the best results. Random postings, for example, will not be as effective as strategically identifying locations that desired audiences frequent. Similarly, email campaigns should be targeted for maximum impact.

The timing of promotions must be carefully considered in relation to when people should, or are inclined to, take action and in coordination with other publicity and promotion efforts. For example, an attractive, well-written brochure enticing people to a fundraising dinner and concert loses its effectiveness if it reaches people too late (or too early) for them to plan to attend.

The effectiveness of a promotion also relates to other activities built around it.

Example

A mini-preview performance in the mall by a visiting performer may reach hundreds of passersby. However, thousands of people may potentially be reached if the preview is announced in the local newspaper ahead of time and on the loudspeaker at the mall, an inexpensive flyer with the specifics of the full performance is distributed to mall audiences, and the final performance is well promoted in local newspapers.

Advertising

Advertising is the purchase of space in print media, airtime on radio and television, and the placement of online advertisements. Its advantage is that, unlike a press release or PSA, it is guaranteed to appear and you can control when and where it does. Advertising is a sure way to reach a market if you determine that it responds to a particular publication, radio or television station, website, or search engine. Effective advertisements reinforce messages and information with related graphic images and soundtracks. Because of its expense, professional production is critical to the success of an advertising campaign. Advertising may take the following forms:

- Display ads in newspapers, magazines, and trade journals
- Display ads in newsletters, playbills
- Classified ads
- Transit placards
- Billboards
- Radio or television ads
- Banner ads, improved search engine rankings, and other Web-based promotions

The effectiveness of advertising is enhanced by frequency. A message must be repeated to be reinforced, especially amid the clutter of commercial advertising. Rarely will a single ad placement have a significant effect.

Advertising can require a hefty financial investment to make an impact. Many arts organizations have a limited ability to accommodate the costs of multiple ads, but resourceful ones take advantage of some of the following cost-saving ideas.

Consider asking an advertising agency to assist you with media advertising purchases (there's no cost to you).

Ask the media for ways to save money. Many offer special rates for nonprofits or reduced costs for multiple placements, camera-ready copy, or advance payment.

Purchase advertising space with other arts groups or complementary businesses, like restaurants or hotel chains. A quarter- or half-page ad promoting four to eight events will catch the reader's eye more effectively than smaller ads scattered throughout the paper. Further, ad rates usually decrease as the amount of space purchased increases.

Arrange media sponsorships, including donated advertising, with newspapers and radio television stations that reach compatible or desirable markets.

Ask your regional and state tourism departments to assist funding advertising in order to attract visitors to your area.

Ask businesses to let you use their regular advertising space or to add a line about your event to their ads (piggyback advertising). Find other creative ways to advertise cooperatively with the local business community.

Example

An arts center negotiates a special arrangement with its local newspaper. On the third Friday of each month, the center runs a full-page ad featuring its upcoming monthly calendar of events. The center makes an annual contract with local businesses, guaranteeing them a small ad surrounding the center's ad. The businesses receive 12 placements, one per month. The center not only pays for its monthly ad but also makes a profit by selling to the businesses ad space at slightly above the newspaper's usual rate.

PLANNING A MARKETING CAMPAIGN

Effective marketing is accomplished through a planned campaign that draws on all four communication methods—public relations, publicity, promotion, and advertising—and utilizes a variety of tools. To recap, public relations strategies build on an organization's image and contacts in the community. Publicity, because it involves free access to the media, is usually at the core of a nonprofit arts organization's marketing campaign. Promotional tools reach targeted audiences and can attract participation through images and messages that you control. Advertising reinforces messages and encourages the market to act.

The elements and design of a campaign derive from the goals you want to achieve. Marketing goals could be increased attendance for your poetry series, greater visibility for your organization within the Latino community, a new image for the organization based on a redefined mission, or public education about your programs and their impact in preparation for an annual fund drive. With even more specific objectives in mind (for example, to increase by 15 percent the number of first-time donors to the annual fund drive), you can distinguish specific potential markets and design a strategic framework of activities to reach those markets.

A marketing campaign is an integrated set of activities involving three interrelated factors.

1. **The message and image you want to communicate.** What do you want to say or project? How do you want to distinguish yourself from the "competition"? What language and tone will you use? What visual image do you want to establish?
2. **The strategic timing of those messages.** When will you put your various marketing strategies into play? When should the public receive information?
3. **The means** (newspapers, magazines, cable television, radio, bulletin boards, posters, flyers, buttons, websites, email) you will use to reach the desired markets. Where will you be noticed by the market(s) or public(s) you want to reach? How do they get their information? What will be the most effective means to use to reach those markets?

Successive publicity activities and promotions can stress each of these stages in turn. However, each press release, brochure, or advertisement should also guide the reader or listener through each stage. The four stages comprise a basic outline for writing promotional copy.

Make sure your *offline* presence is coordinated well with your *online* presence: in fact, think carefully about how you plan to link all of your marketing messages to be sure you are creating the strongest brand (see sidebar).

Criteria for Evaluating Marketing Strategies

There are many possibilities for marketing your program, but you cannot accomplish them all effectively and not all will serve you equally well. Even though you may be able to afford advertising, it may not be the best way to reach a particular market segment. The availability of money, time, and labor also forces you to choose methods within your means that will bring you closest to your objectives. Each specific marketing objective should be approached by making deliberate strategic choices relative to particular markets you want to reach and the message you want to send. The essence of a campaign is that its individual elements work together to achieve the desired objectives.

Criteria for choosing among the various promotion alternatives include money, skills and resources, and time.

Money. How much money is available or should be budgeted to achieve the desired results?

Ideally, beyond maximizing use of free media, a budget is built based on the choice of campaign elements that will most effectively reach specific audiences. More frequently, however, organizations start off with a set amount in the budget for marketing. While some organizations allocate ten percent of their programming budget for marketing expenses, there are no rules of thumb. Organizational resources differ, and diligent use of in-kind services, volume or nonprofit discounts, and partnerships can all affect the need for cash.

Often the toughest marketing decisions concern whether or not to spend money on high-cost promotions. If these hold real promise for reaching target market(s), you must evaluate the potential reach (how many people will see the promotion) and effectiveness (how many people may respond) in relation to the cash cost.

To promote an annual event, a multicolor poster, despite its expense, may work more effectively than an inexpensive flyer. The poster not only calls the community's attention to the upcoming event but also may have a lasting impact if the image is popular and posters are collected and displayed afterward. At other times, less costly promotions, such as email, may be more than adequate. You cannot apply the same marketing formula to every activity and event.

Many organizations develop a marketing plan centered around their own budget capacity but solicit partners or underwriters to support special, more costly promotional strategies that advance the marketing objectives in significant ways. Media and business sponsorships and donations of goods and services can extend the impact of limited marketing dollars.

Skills and resources. Marketing campaigns require skills, information, and equipment. These may include writing, editing, photography, design, and access to printers, mailing lists, and poster distribution systems. Your members or staff may have many of the required skills and resources and can acquire more through training. Sometimes you must recruit experienced professionals as volunteers or pay them to help design or implement a marketing plan.

What's in a Brand?

More and more arts professionals appreciate the value of branding as a critical component of their overall marketing strategy. A brand is the symbolic expression of your cultural organization, as expressed in the images and messages you convey. The power of branding is that these messages and images combine to elicit an emotional response on the part of your audiences, such as a feeling of excitement, trust, fun, and so forth. Practically speaking, your brand is expressed in your logo, the colors and images you use in marketing materials, the look and feel of your website and email communications, even the name badges and uniforms that staff members wear. The more consistent you are with your messages and images, the stronger your brand. Before you embark on a branding campaign, think strategically about what ideas you want to fix in the minds of your audiences: Do you want to be seen as a cutting edge museum? Do you wish to be known as an elegant "night out" performing arts center? Or are you most interested in communicating family-friendly art experiences? All of these ideas suggest different strategies, and you will need to think how best to express your core mission in the marketing materials you develop. Market research can help to test the success of these ideas before you " go live" and create a consistent brand.

If you are trying to tap a new market, use media with which you may have no previous experience or rapport, or develop a graphic image, it may make sense to hire a publicist or public relations firm. If embarking upon an extensive regional or national program that involves marketing on a significant scale, your organization might also benefit from hiring a professional firm that knows your markets and can devote the attention necessary to ensure success. However, those who are involved with your organization and programs on a day-to-day basis are ultimately the most knowledgeable and enthusiastic promoters and can make the most genuine impression with the media.

Time. The timing and interrelationship of different marketing components is a key part of a campaign strategy. The most critical deadline is when you want people to act, but you must also consider when particular markets are likely to act. For example, by what date must the total number of advance ticket sales to your fund raising event be known in order to give caterers a head count? If your local market makes decisions to attend an outdoor festival within three to five days of the event, then advertising and feature stories in the local paper should be planned to culminate during that period. A direct mail effort might be planned to reach people three weeks before the event to prepare target markets with the information they need to act.

By determining these key audience *action points*, you can then project backwards to give them enough time to get information and yourself enough time to implement marketing activities. Allow adequate time for distribution of promotional materials. Other timing factors to consider include:

- demands on staff or volunteer time to coordinate various marketing efforts;
- deadlines for program details to be set in order to include them in materials;
- service timelines, such as for graphic designers or printers; and
- media deadlines.

Comparing Effectiveness

Ultimately, the potential effectiveness of different marketing strategies must be weighed against your potential to meet your marketing objectives and value per dollar spent.

Potential to meet your marketing objectives

Example

The Glimmerglass Opera of Cooperstown, New York, hoped to expand its audience from the five surrounding towns to those within a two-hour driving radius but had never promoted significantly beyond the local area. By evaluating the media habits of its market and the potential reach of various media and promotion methods, the company decided to invest $5,000 in television advertising for one season. Television, while costly, ensured the reach needed to the right market. The results were a 65 percent increase in subscription sales.

Value per dollar spent. To evaluate cost-effectiveness, a break-even analysis is often useful. Ask yourself these questions.

How many responses do you need to cover costs and to generate a surplus?

What is the likelihood that you will succeed in recovering costs?

How many people will you reach with this effort?

The value of promotions sometimes reaches far beyond the audiences actually drawn. An exhibit may draw 12,000 visitors, but promotion and publicity may reach 35,000 homes and 60,000 people. This reach may prove valuable to corporate or media sponsors interested in increasing their own visibility. A high-quality, professional look for a particular promotion may make a more lasting impression and serve as a better investment in long-term public relations.

Labor Intensiveness

Carefully weigh the labor intensiveness of each promotional method to assess its effectiveness. New technologies have significantly reduced the time it takes nonprofits to market programs and services. For instance, some organizations have all but abandoned huge mailings in favor of email campaigns, which are far less labor intensive and costly.

A promotional video about an organization's programs might require significant time, focus, and energy to produce but ultimately reduce preparation time and enhance presentations to civic and other community groups. An added benefit is that it can be offered as streaming video on the arts organization's website.

Follow-through to promote the results of a program will also contribute to general community awareness and extend the program's impact as an investment for the future. For example, your organization may wish to:

- generate follow-up features;
- sell posters;
- encourage letters to the editor;
- create photo displays;
- send thank yous;
- use video for local cable programming or websites; and
- release a summary report.

Campaigns are not necessarily designed from scratch every time. Comparisons are easier to make if you track the effectiveness of specific marketing efforts. Through experience, organizations can observe what works, get the timing down, and devise a checklist of standard activities that can be incorporated into most every campaign.

Rules for Marketing Success

While marketing has many variables, it need not be a complex endeavor. Seven basic principles can help guide your decision making.

1. **Know your organization.** Good marketers must be familiar with all aspects of their organization and its mission. They must also believe in and be knowledgeable about the programs and services they promote.
2. **Know your audiences.** Market segmentation and targeting can net big returns if coupled with effective research, audience involvement in program planning, and record keeping. These activities can be a key to addressing audience development challenges in our culturally diverse society.

3. **Know your tools.** There are many promotional tools to choose from, each effective in its own way. Don't limit your repertoire to the same bag of tricks. Your publics and programs will demand a varied, creative approach. Explore the opportunities provided by newer technologies.
4. **Fight the urge to spend money.** Allow plenty of time for planning and implementing marketing campaigns so that you can locate and secure the resources to do more with less.
5. **Plan every move.** Use your market research to make decisions and use a timeline to design and manage your campaign.
6. **Follow through.** Once you devise a marketing plan, be sure to follow through with all commitments. Remember that in an effective campaign, each element is enhanced and reinforced by the others. If one falls short, the impact of the whole campaign may be lessened. Be alert also for unforeseen opportunities or problems that require changes in the plan.
7. **Be creative.** Creativity is the last and most important element of your marketing strategy. After all, you are marketing the arts! Fortunately, arts organizations attract creative people, and the same imagination that is applied to programming can also be applied to marketing.

THE INTERNET AND MARKETING

According to the Pew Internet & American Life Project, 72 percent of American adults use the Internet, or 145 million people. Of these, 91 percent use email, and 90 percent use search engines to find information on the Web. Of those who use search engines, about 59 million use them on a daily basis, and the numbers are growing exponentially.[4] Google consistently ranks at the top of search engine usage by Americans, with 89.8 million unique users a day. Yahoo, MSN Search, Ask Jeeves, and AOL rank in the top five search engines with Google.

Today, people expect organizations to have a website that is current and easy to navigate. Constituents use the Internet to keep informed, purchase tickets, and even pay their membership online. It is becoming so common to purchase tickets online that even audiences of small community arts organizations are expecting this service. Small presenters may choose to partner with a larger presenter or a commercial ticket vendor in order to respond to this audience demand.

Planning Your Website

Color printing is "free" on the Internet, so make your site as colorful as you want. Your website should be a carefully planned part of your overall technology plan. It is easy to learn how to use a website editor or the tools that come with any word processing program, but difficult to learn good design and function without proper training. Your board member's daughter may be able to design your website for free, but you may end up with a disastrous looking site. One of the most difficult aspects of website design is that visitors can enter at any point in your site. You can't design it like a book, but instead have to think about how all the parts interrelate.

Online content. An organization's website should include information that helps meet customers' needs and advances the arts organization's mission. It should be logically organized and easy to access.

Who?

Your address, phone and fax numbers, copyright notice, and contact emails

Staff and board

Major donors

What?

Mission statement

Programs

A "press room" will assist public relations by posting press releases and images online.

Where?

A map and directions to your location

Parking information

Accessibility information

When?

List updated calendar information, including ticket prices

List hours of operation and duration of specific programs

How?

Provide membership information

Explain how to donate or purchase tickets online

List volunteer opportunities and job openings

Online usage. Design your site so that important information falls "above the fold"—that is, have important text fit when viewed from the smallest computer monitor. In general, writing for the Web is a different skill altogether, since visitors typically scan information.

When appropriate, make use of streaming video, digital images, podcasts, and other multimedia content to enhance visitors' experience and provide more opportunities for them to engage with your organization.

Track your website users through online contact forms, quick polls, and "behind the scenes" tracking software, such as Web Trends.

Use your website to update constituents, board members, and patrons about the arts. Provide downloadable information about the impact of arts and education, legislation that affects how your organization and other nonprofits operate, or information about your community that can help advance your mission.

Link to your partners and funders. Travelers who seek out cultural tourism events and attractions are likely to be interested in other aspects of the community and region.

Link to local restaurants, the chamber of commerce, state and regional tourism bureaus, other cultural attractions, or any service that you think may increase visits.

Customer service. Like any interaction your organization has with the public, your website should reflect the seven Ps of the marketing mix. Good customer service is just as important on the Web as it is in person.

Don't overuse large graphic files that make your site slow to load.

Make your site accessible. Guidelines that assist the blind and people with low vision are being developed constantly, along with the assistive technology. See the Cultural Access chapter for more information.

Allow the public to sign up for an online newsletter or to donate money, and respond to them quickly.

Keep calendar information current. If your hours change, if road construction slows traffic down in front of your facility, or if a performance is sold out, let the public know through your regular channels of communications, including your website.

Promoting Your Website

Design your site to be "search engine friendly" through devices such as writing content that reflect search engine phrases that visitors are likely to use to find your site, hidden keywords, and meta tags. Register your site with search engines and other arts organizations to increase the ranking of your site.

List your website address on everything! Email signature files, brochures, business cards, stationery, merchandise, advertisements, and press releases should all list your Web address.

Encourage your partners to link to your website from their websites.

CONCLUSION

Due to the nature of nonprofit work, far too often the approach to marketing tends to be overly tactical and characterized by fragmented actions. Quick, symptomatic fixes are often used while underlying strategic causes are ignored. Since nonprofits are increasingly required to be accountable for both the short and long term, a well-thought out marketing plan is an important step in that direction.

The Online Companion for this chapter outlines an approach to developing a marketing plan for your organization or for individual programs. In brief, a marketing plan will be developed with as much whole-organization participation as possible and will provide action items and responsibilities for different programs and functions. The plan will become a common road map for the fiscal year, serving to unite the shared vision of the organization as it moves toward a common goal.

ENDNOTES

1. McCarthy, K. F., & Jinnett, K. (2001). *A New Framework for Building Participation in the Arts.* Rand Corporation.

2. Morison, B. G., & Dalgleish, J. G. (1992). *Waiting in the Wings: A Larger Audience for the Arts and How to Develop It.* Washington, DC: Americans for the Arts.

3. Kotler, P. (1996). *Marketing for Nonprofit Organizations* [5th edition], Englewood Cliffs, NJ: Prentice Hall, Inc.

4. Travel Industry of America. (2005). U.S. Consumer Travel Data TIA Travelscope Survey. Retrieved at http://www.tia.org/researchpubs/custom_usconsumer_traveldata.html

CHAPTER 13

video • internet • phone
$29.95
a month for 6 months plus taxes and fees*
of Starz® & Encore®
of Family Cable on all televisions

Cultural Access: Extend the Complete Invitation

13

GAY HANNA
WITH LISA KAMMEL

Shifting demographics are affecting communities and institutions. These changes are reflected in the composition of our public and private organizations—schools, healthcare and social service agencies, businesses, cultural organizations, etc.—and underscore concerns for inclusion and equal access. According to Elaine Ostroff, founder of Adaptive Environments,[1] "our expectations have changed: we expect to have choices about what we do and where we go without regard to age or ability."

However, ancient taboos still exist regarding disabilities, perpetuating forms of discrimination. Some cultural organizations simply ignore access issues due to other priorities. The results can be thoughtless acts of exclusion in the planning, implementation, and evaluation of cultural facilities and programs.

There are many opportunities for growth by reaching out and opening up programs to older Americans and people with disabilities. For-profit businesses across the country recognize this and attend to the concerns and needs of these burgeoning populations through advertising and realistic, positive images of the targeted populations. Cultural organizations stand to gain a new and larger audience from those who want to become involved in making and appreciating the arts.

The Ordinariness of Difference in Ability

Twenty-seven million Americans report some difficulty with walking (less than three million use wheelchairs).

One in six Americans (17 percent), 45 years of age or older, reports some form of vision impairment even when wearing glasses or contact lenses.

Twenty-two million Americans have some level of hearing impairment, most with some residual hearing.

The Arthritis Foundation estimates that 40 million Americans have arthritis.

Aging in America

There are 78 million baby boomers in America (those born between 1946-1964).

Between 2010 and 2030, the 65-and-over population will rise over 70 percent.

Of all the human beings who have ever lived past 65, half are currently alive.

Throughout most of history, only one in ten people lived past 65; now 80 percent do.

Three-quarters of all assets in the United States are controlled by people 60 years of age and older.

—Adaptive Environments

'Nothing about us, without us' was the theme that emerged from the 1970s disability rights movement and continues to be echoed today by individuals with disabilities and even by older adults. *Inclusion* is the essential word in making the arts fully accessible. Make sure that you involve these targeted populations not only in planning for inclusive programming, but as staff, board members, panelists, creators, volunteers, and as audiences.

—Paula Terry, director, AccessAbility Office,National Endowment for the Arts

The most important thing to remember when interacting with people with disabilities is exactly that—they're people.

—Rose Marie McCaffrey, former program director, The Associated Blind, Inc.

Accessibility is a work in progress because there are always new technologies and developments that advance inclusive programming. It is essential to review and evaluate—on a regular basis—policies and procedures, facilities and programs, print materials and websites, and to include an accessibility component in all board, staff, volunteer, and constituent training.

Cultural organizations that are not actively concerned with accessibility and inclusion for staff, board, volunteers, and constituents not only risk the loss of funds and invite law suits, but are missing the opportunity to grow and learn about this country's 54 million citizens with disabilities who represent potential patrons, artists, teachers, students, administrators, and audiences.

Inclusion is a key issue to create cultural accessibility. All organizations need to extend a complete invitation to people regardless of their age, race, religion, or disability. Cultural organizations should do more than just invite people that have been excluded in the past to attend their programs. They must also work with their communities to remove the physical and attitudinal barriers that prevent a diverse population from participating in their organizations.

This chapter discusses accessibility through an introduction to basic philosophy, terms, best practices and model programs, tools, and resources. In learning ways to adapt existing facilities and programs readers will bring the community into the organization and the organization into the community. This, in turn, can create exciting institutional changes.

Extending a full invitation to participate in your organization requires more common sense than funding. Attitude is of greater importance than the latest adaptive technology. Connections are made person to person with dignity and respect.

CULTURAL ACCESS IS SOCIAL JUSTICE

The basic premise of cultural access is one of social justice. It is an ongoing process that assumes diversity of users and that a broad spectrum of abilities is ordinary, not special. Sharon Sutton, Ph.D., professor of architecture, urban design, and planning, University of Washington, refers to a community as "the great public theatre where all can perform their part." In order to attain inclusion and the gradual democratization of society, cultural accessibility seeks to give a voice to disempowered persons in shaping their social and physical environments.

Designing the Great Public Theater: Access for All Ages

Cultural access, the process of creating "the great public theatre," links physical and attitudinal changes with individual and community empowerment. All players want to participate in society and find their way independently. Based on professional literature and practical examples from *Access for All Ages*,[2] the following points describe a philosophy of cultural access:

People are the measure of all things. The user should not have to adapt to the environment and service: the environment or service should adapt to the user.

The average person does not exist. The fact that everyone is different does not mean that separate accommodations should be made for each person in each group.

People's varying and differing needs should be translated into provisions usable by everyone.

Realize the relation between age and accessibility. To serve children and older adults, accommodations should be designed to support their differences in size, physical endurance, and perceptual changes. Issues regarding safety and independence should be addressed as well.

Design for all. The maximum number of people must be physically and mentally able to have access to the services they want to use.

Start with services that are frequently used. Achieving cultural access for all requires great effort with scarce resources. First, analyze the services most frequently used.

Connect form and content. Accessibility means more than a good building: more important is the organization's welcome attitude at all levels and phases of service.

Communication is key to cultural access. The realization of cultural accessibility is good communication with the user, both during the design phase of a certain service or accommodation and its use.

There is no end point, but a continuous process. Because each situation is different, new questions are constantly raised. Cultural access as a stream of experiences with challenges and opportunities has no end point, but is a continuous process of attention and communications.

From public parks to the private rooms of hospice patients, cultural programs are providing new avenues for community service. Case studies and best practices are available in each arts discipline—music, dance, drama, visual arts, and literature—as well as a listing of artists and arts organizations which are considered leaders in the field of cultural access. For more information on cultural access, refer to the National Endowment for the Arts (NEA) Office for AccessAbility entry located in the Government and Nonprofit Resources section of the Online Companion for this chapter. (See the last page of this book for the Internet address.)

Though the disability rights movement grew up along side other identity-based movements in the 1960s and 70s, the particular discrimination disabled people have suffered—attitudinal, employment, and architectural barriers; educational and social segregation; institutionalization; even forced sterilization—kept many isolated from one another. This made the formation of the disability subculture difficult, if not impossible. Only after several decades of disability activism—which has brought about landmark civil rights legislation, independent living centers, and the formation of a distinct community—has the disabled American voice begun to reach a wider audience, both on and off stage. A growing number of playwrights and performance artists have given artistic expression to the experience and culture of disability from an insider's perspective.

KNOWING THE LANGUAGE OF CULTURAL ACCESS: TERMS AND TYPES

Accessibility means different things to different people. Barriers to access can be based upon economic disadvantages, cultural or ethnic bias, ageism, and physical or mental disability. This section outlines the public mandate for access in the United States and provides a vocabulary to stimulate individual conversations and community partnerships to establish a space that is accessible to everyone.

Accessibility

According to *Everyone's Welcome: The Americans with Disabilities Act and Museums*,[4] accessibility means making the site's exhibits and programs available to all visitors. The goal is to eliminate physical, communication, and attitudinal barriers.

Physical access means removing barriers to allow all people to move independently throughout a facility.

Communication access means providing graphic information along with alternative formats such as assistive listening devices and visual aids, such as a raised line map of the space, to help all people receive and communicate information effectively.

Attitudinal access means being sensitive to human diversity, so that all people feel respected and included.

Providing access not only helps people with disabilities but also make life easier and more convenient for everyone involved. It also is not just a choice; it is a law. The Americans with Disabilities Act (ADA) was passed in 1990 as a comprehensive civil rights act enforced by the U.S. Department of Justice.

Americans with Disabilities Act

The ADA is a federal civil rights law created to ensure equal access for people with disabilities to employment, government programs and services, and privately owned places with public accommodations, transportation and communications. It is modeled after earlier civil rights laws that protect individuals from discrimination based on race, color, sex, national origin, age, and religion. Unlike other civil rights legislation, non-discrimination laws for people with disabilities have specific design and technical provisions and requirements in order to provide equal opportunities for participation.

> Accessibility begins as a mandate to serve people who have been discriminated against for centuries; it prevails as a tool that serves diverse audiences for a lifetime.
>
> —Janice Majewski, former accessibility program coordinator, Smithsonian Institution

According to the ADA, an individual is considered to have a disability if he or she:

- has a physical or mental impairment that substantially limits one or more major life activities (such as people with paralysis, hearing or visual impairments, seizure disorders, HIV infections or AIDS, mental retardation, or specific learning disabilities);
- has a record of such an impairment (such as cancer survivors or people who have recovered from a mental illness); or
- is regarded as having such an impairment (such as people who have severe facial or other disfigurements that are substantially limiting only because of the attitudes of others).

The ADA also covers a person on the basis of a known association or relationship with a person with a disability, such as a family member, friend, or acquaintance.

The ADA has five sections that address a specific category of coverage:

Title I. Employment

Title II. Programs, services, and activities of state and local governments, including public transportation

Title III. For-profit and nonprofit organizations that operate places of public accommodation or commercial facilities, or which offer certain types of examinations and courses

Title IV. Telecommunications access

Title V. Miscellaneous provisions which are applicable to all other titles.

The ADA and other laws like it must have a system of implementing regulations that establish enforceable requirements. For example, the ADA requires the Department of Justice to establish regulations for Titles II and III, including cultural organizations such as museums and performing arts centers. The Department of Transportation also issues implementing regulations for Titles II and III. Title I has implementing regulations issued by the Equal Employment Opportunity Commission. Most cultural organizations, whether public or private, must adhere to the employment provisions of Title I.

Further, temporary events, rented facilities, and contracted program services must be accessible and in compliance with the ADA.

Notify visitors regarding access services. Every event, activity, and program should be accessible to people with disabilities. If the event is publicized, cultural organizations should provide people with disabilities the opportunity to request accommodations. To find out if accommodations are needed, list the following statement on all notices about the program, e.g., website, newspaper ads, and flyers.

> For individuals with disabilities requiring access accommodations, please contact [insert name of contact] within a minimum of [insert number] hours prior to the program so that proper consideration may be given to the request.

The recommended notice is a minimum of 72 hours. This provides plenty of time to make the necessary arrangements. A more advance notice can be requested.

> The disability community is coming of age with the advent of technology, changing social/political attitudes, and a growing understanding of abilities over disabilities. Like in the case of other minority groups, arts are an area that can give this previously stifled community a stage on which to present its issues, aspirations, and triumphs.
>
> —Douglas Towne, executive liaison, Disability Relations Group

Making All Guests Feel Welcome

The following steps, used to make visitors with disabilities feel welcome and comfortable, may be included as part of an organization's plan for providing effective communication:

- provide orientation brochures and guide maps (including raised line maps) that identify accessible features with disability symbols of accessibility;
- provide orientation and information brochures in large type so that all users can use the same brochure;
- provide an advertised incoming TTY (text telephone) line so visitors with hearing or speech impairments may contact the organization;
- offer sign language interpreted tours for visitors with hearing disabilities; and
- provide captioned and audio-described orientation videos.

—*Everyone's Welcome: The Americans with Disabilities Act and Museums*

BUILDING INCLUSIVE COMMUNITIES

This section describes *universal design*, a planning strategy that goes beyond minimum access standards. Universal design and targeted program development serve as the building blocks for an inclusive community.

Cultural organizations that go beyond the minimum standards to design programs and places for all ages and populations create bridges from access to unlimited opportunities. *People First* language is an excellent first step in building inclusive arts environments. It costs nothing yet changes attitudes while opening the door to broadening opportunities for everyone.

The Principles of Universal Design

Universal design is the design of products and environments to be usable by all people, with disabilities and without, to the greatest extent possible, without adaptation or

TECHNICAL LOCAL AND STATE ACCESSIBILITY ASSISTANCE REQUIREMENTS

Many state and local governments have more stringent accessibility requirements than the ADA. For further assistance on local accessibility requirements, contact your state and local governments or refer to the Disability and Business Technical Assistance Center (DBTAC) found in the Disability Resources section of the Online Companion to this chapter. (See the last page of this book for the Internet address.) Information below is excerpted from *Everyone's Welcome: The Americans with Disabilities Act and Museums.*

Which Title Should I Follow, Title II or Title III?
If your cultural organization is owned and operated by a state or local government, you must follow Title II. If your cultural organization is privately owned and operated or a nonprofit, you must follow Title III. If you are privately owned but receive funds from a state or local government, then you will follow Title III. However, the government funding source may, as a means of meeting its Title II obligations, require you to comply with certain Title II provisions.

Title II. Local and State Government Cultural Organizations
Cultural organizations...

- must ensure that individuals with disabilities are not excluded from services, programs, and activities because buildings are inaccessible or because of policies or practices, unless to do so would result in a fundamental alteration;
- are not required to take any action that would result in a fundamental alteration in the nature of the service, program, or activity, or in undue financial and administrative burdens;
- must ensure equally effective communication with individuals with disabilities; and
- must maintain accessible features of facilities and equipment.

Existing Facilities
State and local government cultural organizations must conduct a self-evaluation of all programs and activities to identify any physical or policy barriers that may limit or exclude participation by people with disabilities.

Cultural organizations must choose to modify the facility, relocate the program or activity, or provide the activity, service, or benefit in another manner that meets other ADA requirements. If modifications are done, physical changes must comply with the ADA Standards for Accessible Design (ADA Standards) or the Uniform Accessibility Standards (UFAS).

Alterations
Any alteration that affects the usability of the facility must comply with the requirements of the ADA Standards (without the elevator exemption) or the UFAS to the greatest extent feasible.

New Construction
New construction must comply with relevant requirements of the ADA Standards (without the elevator exemption) or the UFAS.

Administrative Requirements
In addition to self-evaluation, entities with 50 or more employees must:

- develop a grievance procedure;
- designate an individual to oversee ADA compliance;
- develop a transition plan that catalogs the physical changes that will be made to achieve program accessibility; and
- retain the self-evaluation for three years.

Title III. For-profit and Nonprofit Cultural Organizations

Cultural organizations...

- must provide goods and services in an integrated setting, unless separate or different measures are necessary to ensure equal opportunity;
- must eliminate unnecessary eligibility standards or rules that deny individuals with disabilities an equal opportunity to enjoy the goods and services provided;

- must make reasonable modifications in policies, practices, and procedures that deny equal access to individuals with disabilities, unless a fundamental alteration would result; and
- must maintain accessible features of facilities and equipment.

Existing Facilities Open to the Public
Cultural organizations must remove architectural and structural communication barriers in existing facilities where it is readily achievable to do so.

Cultural organizations must provide readily achievable alternative measures when removal of barriers is not readily achievable.

Alterations
Any alteration that affects the usability of the facility must comply with the requirements of the ADA Standards to the greatest extent feasible.

New Construction
Cultural organizations must design and construct new facilities to comply with the ADA Standards.

What are the Meanings of *Readily Achievable* and *Undue Burden*?

Readily achievable indicates whether an action is easily accomplished and able to be carried out without much difficulty or expense. An *undue burden* is a significant difficulty or expense. Cultural organizations should consider the following factors when considering whether an action, such as barrier removal, is readily achievable or poses an undue burden:

1. nature and cost of removal;
2. the cultural organization's overall financial resources, number of employees, effect the action will have on expenses and resources, legitimate safety requirements necessary for safe operation (including crime prevention measures and necessary steps for protecting the integrity of art work), artifacts and historical structures on display, or any other impact on the organization's operation;
3. the geographic separateness and administrative or fiscal relationship of the cultural organization to any other associated cultural organizations or parent entities;
4. if applicable, the overall financial resources and size with respect to the number of employees of any associated cultural organizations or parent entities, as well the number, type, and location of their facilities; and
5. if applicable, the type of operation or operations of any associated cultural organizations or parent entities, including the composition, structure, and functions of their work forces.

A greater level of effort is required to meet the undue burden standard than the readily achievable standard for removing barriers in existing Title III cultural organizations.

Meeting Ongoing Obligations of the ADA

Monitoring ADA obligations is an ongoing process. Title II cultural organizations must continually provide accessible programs and communications. Title III cultural organizations must, when readily achievable, remove barriers. Alterations, reconstructions, additions, or new construction for all cultural organizations must meet ADA requirements.

Cultural organizations should also understand how their local, state, and federal laws affect each other. All cultural organizations must comply with the ADA Standards; however, additional steps may need to be taken to comply with state or local laws.

ADA Resources
Information about specific ADA requirements for Title II or Title III cultural organizations is available online at www.usdoj.gov/crt/ada or through the ADA Information Line at 800-514-0301 (voice) or 800-514-0383 (TTY).

specialized design. According to Adaptive Environments, the seven principles listed below may be applied to evaluate existing designs, guide the design process, and educate both designers and consumers about the characteristics of more usable products and environments.

Equitable use. The design is usable and marketable to people with diverse abilities. For example, provide stair and smooth surface options for people.

Flexibility in use. The design accommodates a wide range of individual preferences and abilities. For example, provide different forms of vertical access such as stairs and an elevator.

Simple and intuitive use. Use of the design is easy to understand, regardless of the user's experience, knowledge, language skills, or current concentration level. For example, use clear parking zone signage that includes way-finding arrows.

Perceptible information. The design communicates necessary information effectively to the user, regardless of ambient conditions or the user's sensory abilities. For example, provide maps for orientation in different sensory forms such as tactile and visual models.

Tolerance for error. The design minimizes hazards and the adverse consequences of accidental or unintended actions. For example, provide lighted shapes that begin at the front door and continue to the reception desk so the path of entry is clear to all.

Low physical effort. The design can be used efficiently and comfortably and with a minimum of fatigue. For example, provide a door that requires a low physical effort to open, such as a sliding door with an automatic eye.

Size and space for approach and use. Appropriate size and space is provided for approach, reach, manipulation, and use regardless of user's body size, posture, or mobility. For example, provide water fountains that are the appropriate size and space for the approach and use by all.

Tips for Program Development for Five Target Populations

Requests for on- and off-site arts programs and services provide opportunities for new partnerships that serve target populations with unique individual needs. Universal design can be partnered with adaptive or assistive technology to meet unique individual needs and be the foundation upon which broad-based community cultural access is built.

An organization's first priority should be basic facility and program accessibility. However, it is important to explore potential relationships with community partners to develop outreach programs that meet specific individual and group needs. There are basic protocols and best practices to follow for outreach programs to serve target populations with a high level of staff and environmental support.

Below are descriptions of program considerations for five major target areas of arts outreach: arts education that includes students with disabilities; health care; juvenile justice and corrections; lifelong learning in the arts and aging, which includes intergenerational activities; and art centers for adults with disabilities.

***People First* Terminology**

Place the person before the disability. For example, say "person with a disability" rather than "disabled person."

Avoid referring to people by their disability, for example, "an epileptic," "blind people," or "a deaf person." A person is not a condition. Instead, refer to people with disabilities as "a person with epilepsy," "people who are blind," or "a person with a hearing loss."

People are not "bound" or "confined" to wheelchairs. They use them to increase their mobility and enhance their freedom. It is more accurate to refer to a person in a wheelchair as a "wheelchair user" or "a person who uses a wheelchair."

—Adaptive Environments

Arts Education for Students with Disabilities

The inclusion of students with disabilities in school and community arts education programs is a reality that often catches educators unprepared. The prospect of adjusting teaching styles, instructional strategies, and classroom management is a daunting task. The dynamics of arts education welcome such innovations. In *Strategies for Inclusive Classroom Environments,*[5] VSA arts emphasizes the compatibility between the arts and a diverse student population.

I'm not someone who just sits in a wheelchair all day. Singing has changed the way people perceive me.

—Jenna Feci, VSA youth performer

The arts appeal to diverse learning styles, creating greater opportunities for students and teachers to connect in productive ways.

The arts make learning more interesting by correlating learning experiences to life experiences.

The arts provide a forum for creating innovative teaching strategies.

Multicultural aspects of the arts foster appreciation and acceptance of diversity.

The arts educator should keep the following list of tips and strategies in mind while creating an inclusive classroom environment.

Capitalize on students' individual interests and suggestions for both content and strategy.

Utilize content to reach or interdisciplinary lesson plans to stimulate interest and dialogue.

Tap the network (exceptional student or special educator specialists, parents and other support staff) for moral, instructional, and financial support.

Discuss appropriate roles for teaching assistants or student aides beforehand in order to prevent potentially uncomfortable or goal-defeating situations.

Understand the Individual Educational Plan (IEP) process and incorporate arts education as a means to accomplish important goals.

Modify the classroom environment to promote inclusive principles.

Welcome ongoing evaluations, modification, and reinforcement.

All arts education programs, including artist residencies and performances, must provide accommodations for students with disabilities. Including all students in arts education is not only the right thing to do, but is also a powerful way to effect positive change in the academic and social life of students with disabilities.

For further information regarding best practices, model programs, and technical assistance for developing inclusive arts programs, explore the resources available through Very Special Arts, www.vsarts.org.

Throughout the ages the arts have been used to uplift the human spirit, provide expression for feelings, and create a sense of community. Increasingly, these strengths of the arts are becoming ever more valued for their contributions to the health and welfare of our communities and to individuals. As a consequence, the arts are flourishing in hospitals, hospice, clinics, and nursing homes for their ability to reduce stress, enhance the healing environment, improve doctor-patient relations, communicate information, and provide patients with dignity, self expression, and release from pain.

—Naj Wikoff, director, Healing and the Arts, C. Everett Koop Institute, and president, Society of the Arts in Healthcare

Arts in Health Care

John Graham-Pole, MD, founder of Arts and Medicine at Shands Hospital at the University of Florida in Gainesville, acknowledges the coming of a second renaissance—one that celebrates the marriage of art and science in medicine. No longer confined to the orchestra pit and the gallery wall, the arts are infiltrating the hallowed halls of hospitals nationwide. Modern scientific evidence supports this direction. The list below provides examples of controlled studies on the effect of art in health care in diverse settings.

Aesthetic environments shorten postoperative recovery and hospital stay.

Artmaking reduces anxiety in patients with cancer and blood diseases.

Artmaking raises circulating endorphin and natural killer cell levels.

Cooperative play-acting and theater games raise pain thresholds and mood.

Creative writing lessens the physical symptoms of asthma and arthritis.

Creative writing reduces anxiety, depression, and doctor visits.

Dancing improves circulation, coordination, and alertness in elders.

Music enhances sleep patterns, alertness, and growth of newborns.

Music lowers state and trait anxiety in patients after myocardial infarctions.

Music raises pain thresholds and reduces postoperative pain medications.

Sharing stories regularly lengthens lifespan of advanced cancer patients.

Sustained laughter lowers blood pressure and stress hormone levels.

World-class art collections and performances inhabit the public spaces of major health care centers from Seattle, Washington and Iowa City, Iowa to Gainesville, Florida. Artist residencies bring the arts to bedsides while impromptu dance and play-back theater groups can engage patients, families, and their caregivers outside of hospital rooms. The opportunities for community cultural organizations to enrich the lives of their constituents in hospitals, hospices, and long-term care facilities are expansive. For further information about arts in health care, visit the Society for Arts in Healthcare's website, www.thesah.org.

Arts for Juvenile Offenders in Retention and Corrections

Adult crime is decreasing, but juvenile crime is on the rise. States pass bond issues to build more prisons and begin to imprison youths as adults at younger and younger ages. The cost of lost youth and the societal burden of fully maintaining incarcerated youth are staggering. Grady Hillman, an award-winning poet and technical assistance director for the arts partnership program sponsored by the NEA and the U.S. Department of Justice's Office of Juvenile Justice and Delinquency Prevention, writes that evidence from adult and juvenile correctional arts programs have clearly determined that reduced recidivism rates occur among participants. Some states like California, with its Brewster Report, have quantified institutional benefits into cost savings for taxpayers.

Correctional arts programs take place in three unique settings, according to Hillman: school alternative learning centers, community probation programs, and detention facilities (county jails, prisons, or juvenile detention). Each has its own set of specific considerations for artists and arts administrations similar to other partnership programs. It is important to note that 50 percent to 75 percent of the youth involved in juvenile crime have an identified disability, such as a learning disability, severe emotional disturbance, or a form of mental retardation compounded by cycles of poverty, neglect, and abuse.

Many at-risk youth need accommodations of special education with supporting therapy. The arts offer youth involved in juvenile offenses a positive alternative to finding self-expression, increased self-esteem, and windows of opportunity to achieve academic success. Artists become important role models as well. Hillman offers the following advice regarding artists working in juvenile and corrections environments.

Artists need to be prepared for restrictions on art supplies and space.

Artists should not try to "rescue" students.

Artists should ensure that students' artwork is protected between sessions.

Artists should never make promises they cannot keep.

Experience is critical to longevity and to gaining acceptance within the correctional system. Accountability is key, as well as clear and ongoing communications within the arts and juvenile justice partnerships. According to the Office of Juvenile Justice and Delinquency Prevention and the NEA, the results of arts programs in the lives of youth involved in juvenile crime are shown in reduced disciplinary infractions in alternative education and correctional facilities, improved attendance in alternative education settings, and reduced recidivism upon release from correctional facilities. The arts offer at-risk youth ways to re-enter community life and contribute successfully to it.

For further information, contact the U.S. Department of Justice, Office of Justice Programs, www.ojp.usdoj.gov.

Arts and Older Americans

Betty Friedan suggested that age allows us to pioneer and explore new horizons for society and our communities. In regard to the current "age wave," creativity is becoming an emerging metaphor with new possibilities for aging with integrity. It is an unprecedented time for America with:

- 70 million baby boomers aging;
- Americans living longer, with life-expectancies rising from 45 to 75 years of age; and
- a declining birthrate juxtaposed against an aging culture.

To Andrea Sherman, Ph.D., an intergenerational specialist at the Mill Street Loft, this population revolution presents an extraordinary opportunity and challenge for arts

Arts programs for healthcare environments are no longer optional amenities; they are an important characteristic that distinguishes facilities in their communities and attracts patients, staff, and donors.

—Annette Ridenour, president, Aesthetics, Inc.

The arts programs helped to set our girls free from the constraints placed on them by the lives they have led, the crimes they committed, and the consequences they are now dealing with. They learned to think and express themselves by setting words and dance to the music within themselves.

—Jacque Coyne, executive director, Florida Institute for Girls organizations, artists, and aging communities. In the Americans for the Arts *Monograph*, The Arts and Older Americans, Sherman identifies specific ways in which the arts can be involved in this age shift.[6]

1. The arts can be used as a vehicle to help us understand and define aging, through conversations created through writing workshops, forums, theatre, and dance.
2. The arts offer the opportunity for self-expression amidst loss, for achievement, and in reengagement amidst voids and uncertainty. Many older adults face frequent loss in their lives—jobs, spouses, health, friends, or income.
3. The arts can provide ample opportunities for lifelong learning and service to others.
4. Arts organizations can expect older adults to participate and need arts programming.
5. The arts can benefit from people's contributions and resources. Older adults can be creators, mentors, teachers, tutors, and advisors, sharing the wisdom they have gained through a lifetime of experience.

> We are on the threshold of a powerful and challenging time—an 'age wave'—where new paradigms for creative aging continue to be developed.
>
> —Susan Perlstein, executive director, The National Center for Creative Aging

Arts programs unite generations to develop mutual understanding—young and old celebrating culture and rebuilding communities together. Opportunities to enter this new paradigm of program service and resource development have the potential to reinvigorate cultural activities community wide. However, cultural organizations must remember to address the "age wave" as it relates to the ADA accommodations in order to provide accessible and inclusive programs and services. For further information regarding best practices and model programs for services for older Americans, explore The National Center for Creative Aging, www.creativeaging.org.

Arts Centers and Community Day Programs for Adults with Disabilities

Many arts centers offer programs developed primarily to meet the needs of adults with disabilities through creative expression in the arts. These centers, now established nationwide, also provide pre-vocational and vocational training in the arts and arts-related fields, thanks to the leadership of Florence Ludins-Katz, MA, and Dr. Elias Katz, Ph.D. at the National Institute of Art and Disabilities. Due to the large-scale transfer of people with profound mental and physical disabilities out of large dismal state institutions to community residential facilities, the number of day programs for adults has greatly increased. According to Ludins-Katz and Katz in *Art and Disabilities: Establishing the Creative Art Center for People with Disabilities:*[7]

> In contrast to earlier beliefs, there is widespread agreement that disabled people not only belong in the community but should be active members of the community, and should not be forced to exist in state institutions isolated from their fellow-citizens. As a consequence, large numbers of people with disabled persons [can] now live in the community. But the question remains—how can they lead normal lives? Certainly, it is not normal to wander about the streets or to remain isolated in one's room at home. Therefore it is necessary to provide many different types of community activities and facilities to meet their special needs and desires...[by] the establishment of an art center which has many similarities to an

> art studio or an art school, disabled persons come of their own volition. They work as artists and regard themselves as art students or as artists. They have an opportunity to exhibit their work and share it with others and in turn the community is enriched by their strength and creative power.

Such arts centers may include a gallery, performing arts areas, educational and vocational programs, and arts-related community outings. Among the many goals of the creative arts center model developed by Ludins-Katz are artistic development, enhancement of self-image and self-esteem, improvement of communication skills, marketing of artwork, and active participation in the community. The centers link professional artists and arts organizations to an underserved population of people with profound disabilities, their families, and social service providers. ARCs (formerly known as the Association for Retarded Centers) adopted this innovative approach to day programming across the nation. For further information, visit the National Institute of Art and Disabilities website, www.niadart.org.

A team approach is essential to developing high quality, sustainable arts and community service partnerships. The artist plays a key role in to the development of program content with educators and health and social service providers. The artist contributes to creating a context in which dynamic relationships can form that and effectively serve populations in highly structured environments.

THE PROCESS FOR CULTURAL ACCESSIBILITY

Strategies to create cultural access should begin with making the difficult easier. For example, ask the questions: What change can be made to enhance communications for all users? and Who should be involved? The Global Universal Design Educator's Network then recommends drafting strategies to make it happen.

The American Association of Museums, in *Everyone's Welcome: The Americans with Disabilities Act and Museums,*[8] presents a process that cultural organizations, particularly museums, can use to plan, implement, evaluate, and advertise accessibility at their sites. The short-term goal is compliance with the ADA minimum requirements. The universal design long-term goal is to achieve totally accessible programs and facilities at every level.

Comprehensive Accessibility Plan

The American Association of Museums suggests nine building blocks to achieve accessibility. Some of the steps provided below are required by the ADA, while others provide guidance in improving accessibility of programs, goods, services, and facilities. Section 504/ADA coordinators are designated within each state arts agency to monitor and assist cultural organizations with accessibility compliance and planning.[9]

Nine Building Blocks to Accessibility

Include a statement of commitment. A commitment to accessibility should be included in the institution's general policy or mission statement. The statement should affirm that the institution welcomes people with disabilities and strives to provide access for all to the institution's programs, goods, services, and facilities. This is similar to the ADA Title II requirement for providing notice to the public. Embracing the concept of accessibility is essential and should have full support of the director, board, and all staff.

Our policy at the Ohio Arts Council is to ensure everyone has access to the arts. People with disabilities are included on every grant review panel. Their expertise is invaluable in creating a universal environment for the arts in Ohio. We supply ongoing technical assistance and resources specially to support cultural access. Arts organizations must comply with the ADA and are encouraged to go beyond. We withhold state arts funding from any organization that is not in full compliance with this important civil rights law.

—Phyllis Hairston, 504/ADA coordinator, Ohio Arts Council

Designate an accessibility coordinator. The overall responsibility of the accessibility coordinator is to oversee the implementation of the institution's accessibility plan. This plan should be institution-wide from facilities, programs, and public relations to financial, volunteer, and staff development. The accessibility coordinator could be a single individual or a group of employees. Facilitating access within the institution could be the individual's sole responsibility or, in smaller organizations, it could be one of several duties the individual carries out. Training should be provided to individuals who do not have knowledge and experience with disability and accessibility issues. Local centers for independent living are excellent resources for training and ongoing technical assistance support. If a group of employees serves as the accessibility coordinator, then each employee should serve as a resident expert for a particular accessibility goal, and one person should be responsible for the overall coordination.

Obtain input from people with disabilities. An effective way to achieve this is to organize an accessibility advisory council, which typically consists of staff members, at least one board member, people with disabilities, and those who represent people with disabilities. Individuals should be chosen to participate because of their experience, knowledge, or interest in issues affecting how people with disabilities use cultural institutions, and they should reflect varied points of view on disabilities other than their own. The institution should have clear procedures for reviewing and implementing recommendations of the council.

Train staff on accessibility. All personnel—staff, volunteers, board members, and outside consultants—should become familiar with accessibility issues, including the ADA and relevant state laws. In order to achieve this, institutions should train staff on a regular basis. Training should include an initial orientation to educate existing staff about disability issues, and assistance with the evaluation process and ongoing support. Accessibility training should include, but not be limited to meeting and hearing from individuals with disabilities as a first step in providing specific and accurate information on the needs of people with disabilities; the institution's legal responsibility concerning non-discrimination of people with disabilities and compliance with accessibility laws; and development of staff expertise on various-accessibility related solutions. Local training can be conducted by your local Center for Independent Living Center. Nationally, the Very Special Arts of Massachusetts' Cultural Access Institute provides annual national training.

Review facilities and programs. Cultural institutions should examine all of their activities, programs, communications, services, policies, and facilities to identify existing barriers and discriminatory policies or practices. This is considered self-evaluation and is required by the ADA Title II. An accessibility study should review: language of the institution's policies and practices; accessibility of programs, activities, events, website, and publications from a communications standpoint; accessibility of buildings where programs, activities, and events take place or where goods or services are provided; and adequacy of staff training for visitor and volunteer access. The review process should incorporate discussions by staff, volunteers, board members, the accessibility advisory council, and specialists or consultants.

Implement short and long term accessibility efforts. After an institution has conducted an accessibility self-evaluation, it should begin planning for needed accessibility modifications in areas including programming, barrier removal, effective communications, and new construction or alterations. Short-term modifications should be determined and handled immediately. Long-term modifications should be identified, and a transition plan should be developed to help institutions implement the transformation to accessible programs and facilities in a realistic and cost-effective way.

Promote and advertise accessibility. All promotional ads, institutional literature, postings, and announcements should be accompanied by accessibility symbols where appropriate. Accessibility symbols include the following types of access: wheelchair accessibility, sign language-interpreted programs and text telephone (TTY) availability. Institutions should also use other means of standard communications such as targeting specific media and contacting disability related organizations, services, and social groups. Visit the Graphic Artists Guild Foundation web site for downloadable accessibility symbols at www.gag.org/resources/das.php.

Establish a grievance process. The ADA Title II law requires that entities with 50 or more employees have a grievance procedure. As the ADA does not establish a specific process, many institutions use the same procedures as with other civil rights complaints. Under the ADA, visitors and volunteers have the legal right to file complaints and lawsuits against cultural institutions that do not provide accessible programs and facilities. Institutions may be able to resolve potential disputes before formal complaints are filed by providing a grievance policy. By working with a complainant to identify and correct access problems, experience has shown that institutions can resolve most informal and verbal complaints.

Conduct an ongoing review of accessibility efforts. The ADA requires cultural institutions to continually evaluate remaining barriers to determine whether or not their removal has become readily achievable. Institutions should develop long-term policies and systems to incorporate accessibility into all new projects, programs, and activities. Because accessibility is a work-in-progress, institutions should also periodically reevaluate themselves to make sure they are meeting the needs of staff and visitors in the most cost-effective ways possible.

Disability Issues

Organizations should consider people with disabilities as persons with *varying* abilities as this is how many people with disabilities see themselves within communities. Nine Building Blocks to Accessibility[10] addresses the issues of sensitivity training and developing an ongoing community advisory group to guide the creation of a universal environment for the arts. In the following section, Douglas Towne, from the Disability Relations Group, describes three key issues that determine the level of participation from people with disabilities—economy, transportation, and cultural identity.

Economy. Although there are increasing numbers of highly successful professionals with disabilities in every area of employment, among the disabled population in America, there is a 75 percent average unemployment rate. Many survive on the limited Social Security income or Supplemental Security income payments they receive from the government. This cash benefit can only amount to $400 to $700 per month. Cultural organizations should consider these factors when involving people with

Process Checkpoint List

Use the following list of checkpoints to help you achieve universal accessibility.

- ☐ Form an advisory committee on accessibility.
- ☐ Make an institutional commitment to universal accessibility.
- ☐ Do an accessibility survey.
- ☐ Develop a long-range plan with input from board, staff, and the advisory committee.
- ☐ Develop a fundraising plan with input from board, staff, and the advisory committee.
- ☐ Develop a marketing plan that includes outreach to new audiences.
- ☐ Make sure your goals are clear to everyone and that staff and volunteers are aware of how they are expected to participate in achieving them.
- ☐ Employ architects and other professionals to work with your staff, board, and advisory committee to achieve facility accessibility.
- ☐ Review programming choices.
- ☐ Review the way-finding plan.
- ☐ Review marketing and advertising promotions.
- ☐ Reevaluate on a regular basis.

—*Beyond Access to Opportunity: A Guide to Planning a Universal Environment for the Arts*

varying abilities as volunteers or participants. The cost of cab fare alone could keep them from participating in your organization. A ticket price of $20 could quite literally be five percent of their monthly income.

Transportation. Transportation is one of the most difficult barriers that block people with varying abilities from full community inclusion. You will find that transportation systems available depend on your community. If you have a local transportation authority that provides mass transit, under the ADA they are required to provide access to their system for people with disabilities. This includes *paratransit* services for those who cannot use the fixed route system. Check with your state and local government to determine what other resources may be available. It maybe necessary to partner with other community nonprofits that have the ability to offer accessible transportation. It is important to remember that moving people in wheelchairs around is costly. A partnership with your local Center for Independent Living is recommended so that you avoid any misstep and get the necessary support from the disability community. It also can tell you the state of accessible transportation in your community, so that you can include people with varying abilities from the onset of your program.

Cultural identity. When identifying different disability cultures, the deaf and blind communities often times may be best accessed through other local organizations such as the Deaf Service Bureaus or the local chapters of the American Council of the Blind and the National Federation of the Blind. These groups, in some cases, consider themselves separate cultures but still can be contacted through your local Center for Independent Living. Should you have any difficulty in accessing assistance locally, you can also connect with the Disability Relations Group, www.drgglobal.com.

What is a Universal Environment for the Arts?

A universal or inclusive environment for the arts is one that is usable by everyone, people with and without disabilities and people of all ages. It is an environment with a physical plant (buildings and grounds) and communication systems that go beyond minimum access standards to serve the broadest public. It is an environment where the choice of programs and exhibits reflects a commitment to being part of an inclusive community.

In response to the passage of federal legislation requiring public institutions to make it possible for people with disabilities to use their programs and services, we saw the development of what are now commonplace architectural design features, curb cuts and ramps being the most familiar. Interestingly, the design elements originally developed for people with disabilities were adopted by people without disabilities. For instance, ramps are used by people pushing strollers, people making deliveries, and many others without disabilities.

The way people choose to use so called accessibility adaptations makes an important point: places and products can be designed that work better for everyone. We shouldn't be asking ourselves how to construct a ramp for one group of people and a staircase for another. We should ask ourselves how to create an entrance that everyone can use. The same is true of non-space issues. A tactile model can enhance everyone's enjoyment of a work of art. A readable print presentation is just that: more easily readable for all.

Using the model of universal planning moves the discussion beyond separate accommodations for people with and without disabilities to a discussion of how to create an environment that works for and is respectful of the independence and culture of everyone. Universal planning makes choices that recognize that we are all different, that we have different ways of doing things, and that we have different preferences about how we access information and how we communicate. Universal planning makes choices that create flexibility so that, as the designer Satoshi Kose suggests, "we modify the environment, instead of modifying people to adapt to the environment."

—*A Universal Environment: Beyond Access to Opportunity*
New York State Council on the Arts

TOOLS FOR CREATING A UNIVERSAL ENVIRONMENT FOR THE ARTS

Universal Environment=Usability=Opportunity

Recently, studies have shown that architectural and other accessible adaptations that have been developed to serve people with disabilities are being used by people without disabilities as much if not more than people with disabilities. *Everyone's Welcome: The Americans with Disabilities Act and Museums* presents the following example for a universally designed museum exhibit:

> Suppose [a museum exhibit] was designed for use by a visitor in a wheelchair, labeled with large-print text, offered with tactile alternatives, and included an audio-description tour. This case now offers greater access and convenience to families with babies in strollers, visitors at the back of a large group, and small children not yet able to read.[11]

It is evident that people with disabilities, as well as the general public, are being served better by organizations that offer an environment that is usable by all. It is in an organization's best interest not only to address the ADA standards, but to reach out to all audiences with an environment that can be utilized by everyone. There are many important factors to consider when creating such an environment.

Developing an Accessible Facility: Enhancing Mobility, Vision, and Hearing

Staff, volunteers, and visitors should first and foremost be able to safely and successfully find, enter, and move through a public facility and its designated visitor areas.

Provide a safe and independent route of travel for the site and its buildings that is accessible by all people, especially those who use wheelchairs, walking aids, walk with difficulty, or have a visual impairment. Everyone, including people with disabilities, must be able to move about the site with safety and ease.

- A single, continuous, accessible pedestrian path should be provided that is at least 36 inches wide, firm, stable, and slip resistant without low or overhanging hazards or obstructions, and not require the use of stairs.
- All circulation paths provided must be free of protruding objects.
- The accessible route should provide a direct path from parking, bus stops, drop-off areas, and sidewalks into a primary building entrance that links or joins all designated visitor areas, such as exhibits, program spaces, gift shops, drinking fountains, and restrooms.

Provide an accessible route to the entrance of the facility.

- The route provided should be free of steps or have a ramp, elevator, or a gently sloped walkway to change levels.
- Another entrance can be provided or converted into an accessible entrance if the existing main entrance is inaccessible, difficult to modify, or modification would destroy historic significance.
- Signage should be installed at the accessible entrance if multiple entrances are available.
- If all entrances are not wheelchair accessible, signage should be installed at the inaccessible entrances directing people to the accessible entrance(s).

Provide an accessible ticket booth or information front desk, center, or area.

- The ticket booth or main information desk, center, or area should be on the accessible route that connects the parking and the accessible entrance.
- If there is an information desk or ticket booth, there should be sufficient space that allows a person using a wheelchair to approach and maneuver into a position to receive information or pay for a ticket.
- To be wheelchair accessible, a section of the desk or counter must be no higher than 36 inches.
- The information desk should provide a brochure that explains the facility's overall layout. The ADA requires directional information found in brochures to be available in alternative formats such as tactile or audible.
- A raised line-map or tactile model of the floor plan, with raised lines and Braille labeling, is helpful to all visitors.

Provide an accessible circulation route throughout the facility.

- The circulation route should be well lighted, clearly defined, and have a simple geometric layout that is easy to follow.

- The accessible route should be smooth, level, slip-resistant, and not have stairs or steps.
- Avoid highly glazed ceramic tile because its surface is slippery and makes it difficult for a person in a wheelchair to get sufficient traction.
- Sufficient room should be provided so a person in a wheelchair can maneuver throughout the space.

Eliminate protruding objects.

- Protruding objects must not infringe on any interior or exterior pathway.
- Building elements such as fire extinguishers, signs, drinking fountains, or plants may not protrude from walls or hang down from the ceiling in any way that a person with a visual impairment could run into the element and be injured.

Provide adequate signage, lighting, and other way-finding cues.

- Signage should be located in standard, logical, and predictable places that are perpendicular to the visitor pathway.
- Signage required to be accessible by the ADA Standards is divided into two categories: signage that identifies permanent rooms and spaces must be tactile and visually accessible; and signage that provides information about or directions to functional spaces must only meet the visual criteria.
- Directional signage must be high contrast and have a nonglare finish.
- Lighting of at least five to ten foot-candles should be provided along the accessible route.
- Changes in illumination can be provided to indicate changes in direction.
- Pathways or accessible routes can be indicated by different surface texture.
- Signage should refer to the direction or accommodation and not to the users, i.e. "ramped entrance" or "accessible parking."

Use a consistent system of control barriers throughout the facility.

- Barriers, so as not to be a hazard themselves, should be cane detectable. A barrier's leading edge or detectable element must be no higher than 27 inches above the floor to be cane detectable.
- Barriers should not prevent a visitor from seeing, hearing, or interacting with a program, performance, or exhibit.

Provide an accessible emergency system.

- Provide as many accessible emergency exits as the number of fire exits required by the National Fire Protection Association's Life Safety Code (NFPA 101).
- Provide emergency exits that lead to the main accessible entry route or another accessible route.
- Provide notification about accessible emergency exits at key points in the facility.
- Provide both visual and audible fire alarm systems.

Developing Accessible Communications in Public Programs

It is equally important to ensure that people are provided with accessible information and services while visiting a cultural organization.

Readable print. Provide legible printed materials—such as publications, brochures, programs, and signage—that address the needs of people with disabilities, older adults, those learning English as a second language, those trying to read materials in low lighting, and those in groups reading to children.

- Use a simple serif or sans serif font for printed material and labeling. Helvetica, New Century Schoolbook, Arial, and Times Roman are among the most legible fonts.
- All publications should use a minimum 12-point type size.
- Use upper and lower case type. Type set in all caps is difficult to read and should be limited to titles and headlines.
- Avoid very condensed, extended, extremely bold or light typefaces, and underlined text.
- Type should exhibit a high degree of contrast from its background. Text and visuals should be at least 70 percent darker or lighter than their background.
- Illustrations and text should not be printed over each other.
- Make margins justified on the left and ragged on the right.
- A matte or non-shiny paper or background that will not produce a glare is recommended for printing.
- The size and shape of a publication should be manageable by someone with a hand or motor disability.
- Spiral binding is recommended for large publications so the piece will lie flat if someone is using a reading machine.

For additional information regarding graphics for signage, refer to the Communication Accessibility Resources section of the Online Companion for this chapter. (See the last page of this book for the Internet address.)

Exhibition Labels

- Avoid the use of complex English, jargon, and technical language in text panels unless such language is explained within the text or in supplementary handouts.
- Use the active voice in text panels; limit sentence length.
- Use a maximum of 55 characters per line in exhibit text because text containing too many characters on a line is difficult to read.
- Provide a short overview paragraph set in clear, large print at the beginning of introductory and thematic label panels which allows visitors to gather key information without having to read all of the text.
- Carefully link sentences and paragraphs and try to limit a sentence or paragraph to one idea.

- Provide line drawings, silhouettes, and photographs that complement label text to aid comprehension for those with reading difficulties.
- Main exhibition label information must be available within the galleries in alternative formats—such as Braille or audio—for people who cannot read print.
- Do not set text in all caps and avoid the use of script and italic type for essential information. Alternatives to italic type—such as underlining, boldface, quotation marks, or another color—should be used for book citations, artwork titles, foreign words, and quotations whenever possible.
- If an exhibition title is presented in an ornate or decorative type, it should be repeated in a clearer type at an accessible location near the exhibition entrance.
- Select type size appropriate to the viewing distance. Keep in mind the effects of crowds on actual viewing distance when calculating distance. At any distance, people who have low vision will need larger type than other visitors.
- Print only on a solid background. Print on imaged backgrounds, textured surfaces, or backgrounds with differing colors and tones are unreadable for people with low vision and perceptual difficulties.
- Mount labels so visitors can get very close to read them. People with low vision often must be within 75 mm (three inches) of a label to read it. Label and location should be situated so that the reader does not block his own light and should be out of the way of barriers, protruding objects, stairs, or the swing of a door.
- Keep in mind the natural line of sight when mounting labels. Labels mounted at 45 degree angles to the front of an exhibition case or vitrine are more accessible to people who have low vision than those that are mounted flat on the floor of the case.
- Mount wall labels at a height comfortable for both those seated and standing. Wall labels mounted with a centerline at 1370 mm (54 inches) above the floor are at an optimum height for everyone.
- Locate labels in consistent locations throughout an exhibition.
- Provide sufficient light to read labels. For text to be readable by people with low vision, lighting on the label must be between 0 to 30 foot-candles.

Audio description. Audio description, a narration service that allows people to hear what cannot be seen, allows people with vision loss to experience theater performances, film presentations, and museum exhibitions. Audio describers capture the essence of a scene and provide detailed information in clear, concise statements; see all of the visual elements of an image or an event; determine and convey the images most necessary to an understanding and appreciation of the event or program being viewed in as few words and in as little time as possible; and complement the program or exhibition with descriptions, not interfere with it.

Samples of audio description from Audio Description Associates can be found online at www.audiodescribe.com.

Conveying audible information. Provide appropriate services to convey audible information effectively. Methods offered that allow people with hearing loss to experience programs will vary depending on the complexity of the program, the information being conveyed, and an institution's budget.

Captioning. Captioning translates the spoken word into simultaneously displayed text in programs such as films and video productions. There are several different captioning methods that may be used.

Open captioning is a useful method for displaying spoken portions of video programs because the captions always appear on the screen. It is important to consider the placement of the captions so they do not obstruct the screen and viewing of the program. Open captioning is preferred by many and is an excellent example of universal design as it improves reading skills, allows the audio volume to be turned down, and is used by many to learn English as a second language.

Closed captioning is similar to open captioning except it allows captioning to be turned on or off. For television, it requires a special decoder or a television with a decoder chip to display the captions and control buttons for video displays.

Rear Window Captioning System® displays captions in reverse on a light-emitting diode (LED) text display mounted in the rear of a theater. People who wish to view the captions have a transparent acrylic panel attached to their seats to reflect the captions so they are superimposed on the movie screen.

Assistive listening devices and other assists for people with hearing loss

Assistive listening devices (ALD) increase the volume of sound. They can be used in live performances, films, lectures, and guided tours. The three types of ALDs are: (1) inductive loop, which transmits sound using an electromagnetic field; (2) infrared systems, which transmit sound via light waves; and (3) FM systems, which transmit sound via radio waves. The equipment needed for ALDs depends on how they will be used; however, a transmitter and several receivers will be needed. Provide ALDs that increase the volume of *desired* sound without increasing the loudness of background noises.

Signaling systems such as flashing lights or vibrating receivers alert visitors with hearing loss that a program or performance is beginning, going into intermission, or ending.

Sign language interpretation by certified interpreters should be available by request for meetings, special events, and programs. The most common form of sign language interpretation is American Sign Language (ASL), though Signed English is another form of interpretation that is used. Note in all publications, advertisements, registration forms, and at information desks who visitors should contact and by what deadline to arrange for an interpreter.

Tactile presentations. Provide tactile opportunities whenever possible. Touch allows people with vision loss to experience programs such as visual art exhibitions.

Use original art and artifacts whenever possible for tactile exploration. Since most original art cannot be touched, casts and reproductions should be added, ideally for everyone to touch.

TIPS FOR DEVELOPING DISABILITY AWARENESS

These tips are to be used as a starting point to develop a better understanding of disability issues and the disability community as a whole.

General Suggestions to Improve Access and Positive Interactions

- Offer assistance, but do not insist. Always ask before you assist someone and do not help without permission. If you do not know what to do then ask the person what would be helpful.
- Focus on what the person is able to do, rather than on their disability. Be aware that alternative ways of doing things can be equally effective.
- Be aware of limitations specific to a disability, but do not be overprotective. Do not exclude someone from an activity because you think his or her disability would be a problem. People with disabilities need to be able to take risks and make their own decisions.

Suggestions to Improve Access and Positive Interactions for Major Disabilities

Blindness and Visual Impairments

- When guiding a person who is blind, let him or her take your arm. If you encounter any obstacles, such as steps or curbs, pause briefly and identify them.
- Speak directly to the person in a normal tone and speed.
- Do not pet or play with a working service animal.
- Inform him or her that you are entering or leaving a room.
- When a person with vision loss is meeting many people, introduce them one at a time.

Deafness and Hearing Loss

- It is important to remember that the major issues for people who are deaf are the challenges they experience in trying to communicate with people, not their inability to hear, and gaining information from the hearing society.
- When talking to people with hearing loss, use a normal tone and speak clearly and distinctly.
- Use facial expressions, body language, and pantomime.
- If there is a sign language interpreter, speak directly to the person who is deaf, not the interpreter.
- If you do not understand a person with hearing loss, ask them to repeat themselves.

Learning Disabilities

- It is important to remember that learning disabilities do not mean inferior intelligence.
- Be aware that periodic inattentiveness, distraction, or loss of eye contact by a person with a learning disability is not unusual.
- Discuss openly with a person with a learning disability the preferred way to communicate.
- Be aware and sensitive that some information-processing problems may affect the social skills of someone with a learning disability.

Mental Illness

- It is important to remember that people with mental illness do not have lower intelligence.
- Be aware that people with more serious forms of mental illness may have difficulty processing or expressing emotions.
- Be aware and sensitive to the fact that a person with a mental illness may overreact to emotionally charged topics or discussions.
- It is helpful to learn more about the nature of a person's diagnosed mental illness.

***Developmental Disabilities* (which can include autism, cerebral palsy, brain injuries, and other neurological impairments)**

- Interact with a person with a developmental disability as a person first.
- Avoid talking around or about a person with a developmental disability when they are present.
- Break down concepts into small and easy to understand components.
- If necessary, involve an advocate when communicating with a person with a developmental disability.

Mobility Impairments

- Do not be afraid to shake hands with someone who has very little grasping ability.
- Do not hold onto a person's wheelchair because it is seen as part of the person's body space. Holding on to, touching, or leaning on a person's wheelchair is both inappropriate and can be dangerous.
- Talk directly to a person in a wheelchair, not someone who is attending to them.
- Consider sitting down when talking to a person in a wheelchair to share eye level.
- Use people-first terminology such as "person with a physical disability." Avoid using inappropriate terms such as "cripple," deformed," or "wheelchair bound."

—*Access and Opportunities: A Guide to Disability Awareness*

Provide clear and concise verbal descriptions of works of art being touched to enhance the experience.

Provide tactile pictures and hands-on art activities to supplement information about the artwork.

For very large sculpture, small replicas may be mounted adjacent to the original at an appropriate height that allows people seated in a chair or children to explore it through touch.

Developing Accessible Communications in Promotions

People generally find out about cultural programs and events from newspapers, radio, mailings, posters, newsletters, television, and websites. In order to effectively inform people with disabilities about accessible programs and events, alternative approaches to providing public information should be practiced.

Simple statements. Provide simple, low-key statements regarding accessibility in all publicity—for instance, "This facility is accessible to all people." Do not use the word "handicapped" or the phrase "accessible to the handicapped."

Disability access symbols. Use disability access symbols in publicity and promotional materials to indicate what type of accessibility the facility offers. The most recognized symbol is a stylized wheelchair, the International Symbol of Accessibility. Other common ones denote availability of TTY, sign language, live audio description, large print, and access for people who are blind or have low vision such as guided tour or tactile description. Disability access symbols can be downloaded free of charge from The Graphic Artists Guild at www.gag.org.

Broadcast media. Use broadcast media when possible, particularly to reach people with visual and cognitive disabilities. Television can potentially be the ideal way to communicate to people with disabilities because it provides audio and visual elements as well as many programs that are audio described or captioned.

Accessible website. Specific steps must be taken to ensure that your website is usable by everyone, including people with sensory loss. Use navigation that is simple, intuitive, and easy to follow. Make the text scalable to allow visitors to view the text at whatever size is comfortable for them to read. Use text-based browsers as well as conventional graphical browsers, and add audio to visual information whenever possible. Some specific features to make websites accessible are:

- **alt-text tag** (audio descriptions of the content of an image which interface with voice activated computers);
- **D-link** (provides a longer, more complete description of what an image looks like);
- **captions** (multimedia captions can be used to make video or audio clips in websites accessible); and
- **descriptions** (descriptions of static images or more in-depth narration of a video clip to describe what is taking place).

Telecommunications. Publicity and promotional materials should provide and promote accessible telecommunication devices, such as TTY numbers.

Local disability organizations. Notify local disability organizations and groups about accessible activities, programs, or services. They can usually be found in the resource pages of the telephone book. Additional information can be found through centers for independent living, school systems, health care organizations, and local government.

Further information is provided in the Online Companion for this chapter. (See the last page of this book for the Internet address.)

FUNDING ACCESSIBILITY

Usually, one of the first concerns of accessible adaptations is the cost. Since the development of universal design, however, designs and renovations are no longer considered as costly, disruptive, or unsightly as they were before the ADA. It is estimated that for a new building, universal design elements amount to less than one percent of total construction costs. Universal design was developed to eliminate the need for costly special features that benefit only a small group, and instead creates structures that are more easily adapted to the changing needs of all building occupants and visitors.

Examples of Funding Sources for Disability-related Programs and Services

> **Department of Housing and Urban Development** offers Community Development Block Grants which provide funds each year to state, county, and city governments for projects that remove barriers in both public and private cultural facilities and programs.
>
> **NEC Foundation of America** provides grants that focus on science and technology education and the application of assistive technology for people with disabilities.
>
> **Mitsubishi Electric America Foundation** funds projects and organizations that advance the independence, productivity, and community inclusion of young people with disabilities through technology.
>
> **MetLife Foundation** supports various educational, health and welfare, and civic and cultural organizations. MetLife's initiative, Access to the Arts, funds innovative programs that encourage organizations to make the arts more inclusive and accessible for the special-needs community.
>
> **The Foundation Center** provides resources by geographic region and subject area to private and corporate foundations.

For contact information, see the Funding Resources section of this chapter's Online Companion. (See the last page of this book for the Internet address.)

When applying for funding and writing grants, the Association of Science and Technology Centers (ASTC) recommends the following:

> **Include target audience statistics** when describing the need for an accessibility project. For example, about 20 percent of the U.S. population is classified as having a disability, with nearly half considered to have a severe disability.
>
> **Use demographics** of the cultural organization's surrounding community. Visit the Census Bureau website (www.census.gov) for population data in your particular

area. Local government and organizations that serve people with disabilities also maintain current statistics.

Use input from focus groups, visitor surveys, or advisory committees in writing grant proposals to make sure the project responds to its target audience.

Include costs of program accommodations—sign language interpretation, audio description, or large print programs—in your project budget when applying to a federal agency, such as the National Endowment for the Arts.

CONCLUSION

The "design for all" principal is an advantage for all ages. A complete invitation can and should be extended for the great public theater where everyone is a player.

To paraphrase *Access for All Ages*, providing cultural access to all creates these advantages.

- The arts become accessible to more people.
- The arts remain accessible in each phase of people's lives, especially for children and older adults.
- Everyone profits from an accessible society because sooner or later everyone will belong to a special category.
- Fewer additions and provisions will be needed for targeted populations, which will make arts facilities and program operations more durable and, in the end, cheaper.
- An accessible arts environment contributes to the realizations of other policy objectives related to social justice, safety, and quality of life, such as independent living for all including young people with disabilities as well as older adults.
- Arts programs and productions will profit from a larger circle of employees, volunteers, and patrons.

Creating cultural accessibility through a universal environment where all can participate may require systemic change within the organization, but the rewards will launch your programs and make your facility a vibrant part of community life.

ENDNOTES

1. Adaptive Environments is an educational nonprofit committed to advancing the role of design and enhancing experience for people of all ages and abilities. Its work balances expertise in legally required accessibility with promotion of best practices in human centered or universal design. For further information on Adaptive Environments, refer to the Government and Nonprofit Resources section in the Online Companion for this chapter. (See the last page of this book for the Internet address.)
2. *Access for All Ages!* (2000). Utneet, Netherlands: National Age Discrimination and National Bureau for Accessibility.
3. Sandahl, C. (2001, April). Access, Activism & Art, *American Theatre*, 18(4).
4. Salmen, J. P. S. (1998). *Everyone's Welcome: The Americans with Disabilities Act and Museums.* Washington, DC: American Association of Museums.
5. VSA Arts. (1998). Strategies for Inclusive Classroom Environments. Washington, DC: Author.
6. Sherman, A. P, (1996, November). The Arts and Older Americans. *Americans for the Arts Monographs*, 5(8). Retrieved at http://pubs.artsusa.org/library/ARTS033/html/1.html
7. Ludins-Katz, F. & Katz, E. (1990). *Art and Disabilities: Establishing the Creative Art Center for People with Disabilities.* Cambridge, MA: Brookline Books.
8. Salmen.
9. The Americans with Disabilities Act (ADA), passed in 1990, builds upon Section 504 of the Rehabilitation Act of 1973. Whereas Section 504 prohibits recipients of federal funds from discriminating on the basis of disability, the ADA expands this into a prohibition of discrimination on the basis of disability. For more information, visit http://www.usdoj.gov/crt/ada/cguide.htm or the Resources section of this chapter's Online Companion. (See the last page of this book for the Internet location.)
10. Salmen.
11. Ibid.

CHAPTER 14

Arts Education: Developing a Successful Program

14

MARETE WESTER
WITH CONTRIBUTING EDITOR DAVID O'FALLON

The work of state and local arts agencies and education agencies can intersect productively in numbers of ways. While there has been a surge in efforts to provide exemplars and "models" of good practice, there is no one plan, no one formula, no "magic bullet" that will ensure the success of arts education programs in all environments. The rationale underlying such joint efforts is the basic assumption that these endeavors are of mutual benefit. To the arts agency whose primary concern is for artists and arts organizations, education is the infrastructure that discovers the artistic talent, nurtures it, and develops the audiences that sustain it. To the education agency whose primary concern is to transmit knowledge and learning to new generations, the arts as they exist in society are concrete manifestations of one of the higher orders of human achievement. No art can thrive without education; no education can be complete without the arts.[1]

There is a growing awareness that the arts are one of the most powerful means we have to address issues that concern a very broad and diverse set of public interests. Increasingly through well-publicized research efforts, the arts have made the case for their role in the revitalization of neighborhoods and communities, as well as economic impact. When tragedy struck on September 11, 2001, a powerful city and country turned to the arts to help heal the wounded human spirit through song, poetry, murals, and tribute—a vivid demonstration of why the arts stand as the universal bridge to developing mutual understanding and collaboration among diverse cultures and ethnicities. The United States relies heavily on the creative spirit of its citizens; consequently, the arts occupy a fundamental role in the lifeblood of democracy.

Thus, the discussion of the arts as public policy cannot help but include the role of the arts in the many facets of education—one of the earliest fundamental rights established by our founders. Current and longitudinal research continues to demonstrate the impact of the arts on the development of young children and support of learning at any age. The inclusion of the arts in federal and state policy, including educational goals and standards, has encouraged more schools to incorporate the arts as a sequential component of a quality K-12 education and has challenged schools to find the resources to do so after decades of neglect. In the community at large, a greater number of adults are longing to participate in learning that allows them creative freedom and the ability to be expressive. And more arts organizations are taking seriously their role in educating the public in, through, and about the arts.

While these trends began to emerge at the end of the last century, we now are realizing a greater interest from all sectors in the critical role the arts are playing in our society.

In a school year that brought unthinkable tragedy and sudden horror into the lives and communities of so many we serve, it was gratifying to be in a position to be part of the healing process. Many schools turned to us for help through arts enrichment and residencies that dealt directly with the celebration of the American spirit and issues of diversity and moral courage. The same was true in our community arts initiatives as, through a variety of programs for caregivers as well as children and families, we had the opportunity to demonstrate the power of the arts to comfort, inspire, and empower.

—Caroline Ward, executive director, Arts Council of the Morris Area (NJ), April, 2002

In 2000, Alan Greenspan, former chairman of the Federal Reserve Board, called for the need to support an "economy of ideas," stating:

> Even the most significant advances in information and computer technology will produce little additional economic value without human creativity and intellect... Critical awareness and the abilities to hypothesize, to interpret, and to communicate are essential elements of successful innovation in a conceptual-based economy. As with many skills, such learning is most effective when it is begun at an early age. And most educators believe that exposure to a wide range of subjects—including literature, music, art, and languages—plays a considerable role in fostering the development of these skills.[2]

The world of arts education is an exciting one, delving into both the mysteries of the mind and the human condition. It is a subject that will invariably inspire debate, and strong feelings on behalf of its proponents, as well as its critics. Those working in arts education—whether in the schools, in the community, or in cultural institutions—must be prepared to be advocates, to understand the breadth and scope of a field in constant dynamic change, and to continually work towards achieving a common agenda that will help create a supportive environment in both the schools and the community.

Taken as a whole, this is an enormous task. Consequently, we have come to realize that only by working together can we as educators, artists, administrators, and supporters continue to move forward. As we gradually make the cultural shift from "making the case" for arts education to "making it happen," and as the demands on our already scarce resources continue to grow, we must explore and invent better ways to collaborate and deliver quality arts education experiences.

This chapter attempts to provide navigational tools to the new explorer making the journey into arts education. Each explorer will confront different terrain and environmental conditions: while some will be scaling cliffs, others may be taking a walk in the sun. For those of you swimming upstream in a driving rainstorm, take heart: the wisdom and advice of those who have crossed the river before you with no wind and a broken paddle are there to give you guidance and cheer you on.

ARTS EDUCATION: EVOLVING FROM FRILL TO FOCUS

The Arts in the Schools: A Brief History of (Almost) Everything

There is no such thing as a "brief" history of the evolving role of the arts in public education and their educational role in the community. This topic can (and does) fill volumes of books, articles, essays, as well as public policy documents and legislation—not to mention being at the heart of countless organizations and associations across the country founded for the purpose of either promoting or fulfilling quality education in and through the arts. Those entering the world of arts education for the first time may find themselves overwhelmed by its apparent complexity. However, understanding a bit of the history and events that have led us to the present can help alleviate some of those feelings and pave the way for future success.

This section provides a cursory overview of some of the trends and events that have shaped the status of arts education today. In doing so, it pays tribute to those writers, thinkers, and activists who have contributed so greatly to the field. The visionaries no longer with us, yet whose writings continue to illuminate—such as Ernest Boyer and Charles Fowler, are authors whose books, speeches, and articles are worth reading for their prescient understanding of the value of arts education to our future. Serious students of history, as well as those for whom arts education is or will become a lifelong calling, are encouraged to delve into the works of our living standard-bearers as well.

Prominent educators, psychologists, artists, and administrators—such as Howard Gardner, Elliott Eisner, Dennie Palmer Wolf, and Jane Remer—have provided the field with some of the best and most pivotal thinking in arts education. With the explosion of information now available on the Internet and through association websites, new thinking regarding arts education will continue to emerge and enrich the opportunities for ever increasing developments in this field.

Research into how we learn, along with the entrance of arts education into the pop self-help culture through research-based books such as *The Mozart Effect*, has stimulated a growing public acceptance and thirst for understanding and cultivating creativity. The environment for arts education is changing rapidly.

Early efforts in arts education. Since the late 1800s, the arts have been part of our public school consciousness. Art disciplines—most frequently music, but also dance, theater, and visual arts—have appeared in elementary and secondary curriculums in varying degrees and have experienced cycles of interest punctuated with neglect throughout the history of public education. Dependent on where we were in the cycle, partners outside of the school setting emerged to support, stimulate, or restore the loss of school arts programs. This has resulted in the expansion of the field of arts education to include school as well as community-based efforts, and those working in it to comprise arts specialists, generalists, artists, and arts groups.

Early federal role. Federal interest and support for arts education in the nonprofit world can be traced back to the founding of the National Endowment for the Arts (NEA) in 1965. Earliest examples of NEA support for arts education include the Arts and Education Laboratory Theater Project (1966), in cooperation with the U.S. Office of Education and state and local school boards, as well as the Artists-in-Schools Program (1969), which provided funds to state arts agencies to place professional artists in residency programs in both schools and in community settings. From the 1960s onward, the NEA focused more of its energies on supporting the work of artists and arts institutions in the education realm, and less on efforts that directed support toward improving the arts in K-12 education.

Early national movements. During the 1970s, the U.S. Department of Education and The John F. Kennedy Center for the Performing Arts, in seeking to strengthen state policy for arts education, created a network of state alliances for arts education. Now established as the Kennedy Center Alliance for Arts Education Network, this program created some of the first efforts in state planning for arts education and helped to lay the groundwork at the state level for the future education reform movements of the 1980s and 1990s.

During the early 1980s, the NEA rethought its role in relation to public education. The need for this reassessment was defined in large part by the NEA's 1982 survey of public participation in the arts, which revealed dramatic declines in public attendance at live performances, and pointed to a growing concern on the issue of the cultural literacy of America's population.

The move to strengthen arts education within the public schools was further catalyzed by the 1983 report, *A Nation at Risk*, which focused unprecedented attention on the state of American education as a whole. Concerned by the results of both the public participation survey and *A Nation at Risk*, Congress charged the NEA with preparing a study on the state of arts education nationwide. The NEA released *Toward Civilization: A Report on Arts Education* in 1985, creating new momentum to include the arts as an integral part of school reform.

Developments from the private foundation field. Nearly simultaneous to the increasing attention on arts education in the public sector, private foundations in the 1970s and 1980s began developing and promoting strategies and initiatives aimed at improving public school instruction in the arts. Most notable among these early efforts are those of the Getty Center for Education in the Arts and the (John D. Rockefeller III) JDR 3rd Fund.

The Getty Center early on dedicated a substantial component of its resources to improving the quality and status of visual arts education in the nation's public schools (K-12) by advocating an instructional strategy known as Discipline-Based Arts Education (DBAE). The program has worked with teachers throughout the country to develop curriculum and instructional methods based on disciplines it deemed central to creating and understanding art: art production, art history, art criticism, and aesthetics. Revolutionary in its time and a significant influence in the development of public sector arts education policy, the DBAE proposed that the most effective art education programs are based on working partnerships among teachers, school administrators, artists, museums, universities, parents, and the community.

In the 1960s, financier and philanthropist John D. Rockefeller III commented, "We need to expose all of the children in our schools to all of the arts, and to do so in a way that enriches the general curriculum rather than reinforcing the segregation of the arts." Unlike many radical new ideas that eventually languished due to lack of support, Rockefeller decided to invest in his idea and founded the JDR 3rd Fund's Arts in Education Program in 1967. In addition to its programs, the JDR 3rd Fund was one of the first major foundations to support the research of Howard Gardner and Dennie Palmer Wolf in Project Zero and the Arts PROPEL project, fund task force reports, and support the discussion of the arts as a central part of education reform. The JDR 3rd Fund also helped bring the influential writings of Charles Fowler to the forefront of the national debate and supported some of the earliest national gatherings that brought arts educators, artists, community arts leaders, state arts agencies, and state alliances for arts education together with federal officials and national leaders to discuss the case for arts education and to develop plans for comprehensive arts programs.

Though the program abruptly ended with the death of its founder in 1979, it was responsible for some of the most groundbreaking developments in presenting the arts as a catalyst for improving the school climate and environment. The Fund's quest to develop and support demonstration sites across the country to be used as models for changing schools through the arts helped form similar efforts conducted by state and local partnerships years later. In the 1990s, the federal impetus finally caught up through the reform model posed by the Goals 2000 Educate America Act, and the inclusion of the arts in the model. Profiled in *Changing Schools through the Arts: How to Build on the Power of an Idea,*[3] the Rockefeller Fund set a unique standard among private foundations by supporting the growth of systemic approaches to the arts in public education throughout the country, by promoting private/public sector partnerships, and by opening the door for more private foundations to join in these efforts.

Congressional expansion of the role of the arts and humanities. In the mid-1980s, Congress expanded the role of both the NEA and the National Endowment for the Humanities (NEH) in arts and humanities education in the schools. In 1986, acting on the new provisions and its own research, the NEA moved toward a greater focus on curriculum-based arts instruction through its arts education program, instituting the 1987 Arts in Schools Basic Education Grants (AISBEG) Program. Perhaps no other single effort since has created more opportunity for the development of infrastructure, partnerships, and support systems for improving arts education at the state level. AISBEG catalyzed the work of state arts agencies with state education agencies to help influence local schools in making the arts a priority within the school day. In creating new opportunities to support and strengthen the work of these state agencies with state alliances for arts education, it focused attention on advocacy and statewide programmatic efforts for improving curriculum and creating a greater partnership role for artists and arts organizations with the schools.

Giving way to the NEA's Arts Education Program, the AISBEG Program ended in 1991, after being widely credited with supporting statewide arts education programs and joint state agency planning processes in nearly two-thirds of the states in the country.[4] During the mid-1990s and in spite of a more than 50 percent reduction in its federal budget, the NEA continued to support arts education not only through its grant programs to state arts agencies and nonprofit arts organizations, but increasingly through its leadership initiatives, which have resulted in a strengthened support network for arts education throughout the country. One such example is the Goals 2000 Arts Education Partnership (now Arts Education Partnership). (For more information on such resources, visit this chapter's Online Companion. See the last page of this book for the Internet address.)

The growth of local arts agencies in arts education. The increasing level of support and attention to the growth and development of arts education in national and state policy has its parallel on the local level. Though less well-documented, community efforts to bring learning in the arts to children and citizens have their roots in the country's rich folk arts traditions, the community guild schools for the arts movement (a growing trend even today), and the emergence of children's theaters, as well as other arts and nonprofit organizations (such as National Young Audiences) which have worked for decades to further arts education.

The emergence of the local arts agency (LAA) movement as a major force in arts policy development has also impacted the arts education field in important ways. As the field has matured, the LAA's work in arts education has expanded, catalyzed by incentive funds from state arts agencies and the NEA, as well as community cultural planning efforts that pointed to a community desire for increased opportunities in arts education.

The recognition of LAAs' critical role in supporting state and federal initiatives to strengthen arts education and translating them to the local level has resulted in a burgeoning movement of community partnerships and advocacy efforts to influence local decision making. For no matter how strong the policy for arts education may be at the national or state level, the final decisions on what is taught and what is supported through funding, facilities, and staffing are made locally.

The 1995 LAA survey conducted by the National Assembly of Local Arts Agencies (NALAA) (now Americans for the Arts) reflected a growing number of LAAs participating in arts education activities in some way: 57 percent produced artists-in-the-schools programs; 42 percent conducted curriculum design in partnership with schools; and 71 percent were engaged in advocacy and lobbying efforts to strengthen the arts in the local school systems. In FY 2000, a more detailed survey revealed that more than 65 percent of LAAs produced arts education programs, with 58 percent partnering with other organizations to provide programs and services. On average, 45 percent provide teacher training; 50 percent operate artist residency programs; and nearly 75 percent engage in advocacy for arts education. According to the survey, arts education is the fourth largest funding category for grant-making LAAs, averaging approximately 83 percent of the grants made, surpassed only by music, visual arts, and theater (90, 88, and 84 percent respectively).[5]

In 1995, NALAA launched the Institute for Community Development and the Arts to promote greater government investment in the arts by educating state and local arts agencies, government officials, and funders about using the arts as community change agents for solutions to economic, social, and educational problems. Among its most important contributions to arts education is the chronicling of innovative local approaches to arts education and the "nontraditional" funding sources that support them—in large urban settings and suburban communities, as well as remote rural locations. The approaches reflect a growing diversity and maturing of the field, from family arts programs and job-training in the arts for young people to experiences in underrepresented art forms (such as dance and theater) in the schools or even in juvenile justice settings. As more diverse funding streams become open to the idea of the arts as a solution to societal problems, a growing number of communities are exploring new and ever-more sophisticated approaches to addressing local challenges through the arts.

With LAAs playing leading roles in arts education in their communities, arts education has emerged as a major policy area for Americans for the Arts. Americans for the Arts' focus on arts education includes critical programs and services in advocacy, visibility, research and information, and national partnerships.

Making the Arts Basic: Standards-based Education Reform

National standards. Perhaps no other single policy initiative in arts education has united the arts community more than the development of the National Standards for Arts Education in 1994. Borne out of the push by the National Governor's Conference in 1989 to establish National Education Goals and, subsequently, world-class education standards for all students in all "critical" subject areas, the development of the National Standards for Arts Education were, and continue to be, pivotal for several reasons.

Impact on policy. The inclusion of the arts in the national standards movement has embedded the arts in national education policy, which in turn impacts state education policy and, subsequently, local education policy.

Stimulus for systemic change. At the federal level alone, the inclusion of the arts as a core subject area in the National Education Goals and in the development of the national standards has triggered other major policy shifts, especially with regard to funding. Since 1994, the Elementary and Secondary Education Act (ESEA)—the most comprehensive piece of federal education legislation—has continued to broaden its funding opportunities for arts education, including: support for the development of state and local arts standards; assessments, research, and professional development programs for teachers; and opening competitive state and local grant initiatives to encourage the inclusion of arts education. These, in turn, have provided incentives for states to develop state standards and assessments in arts education, and to include the arts in the state's plan for standards-based education reform.

Catalyst for collective action. In the 30 plus years of the modern arts education movement, progress has always been impeded to a certain degree by the competing voices and sectors which hold differing views of arts education. The National Standards for the Arts were developed through a broad-based process that brought together arts specialists and arts leaders in the disciplines of dance, music, theater, and visual arts. Through the work of these committees, focus groups, and public commentary, the National Standards for Arts Education are the closest we have come to achieving consensus on what we believe a quality education in the arts is, can, and should be.

Common ground. By articulating a clear set of principles of what children should know and be able to do in all artistic disciplines, the National Standards for Arts Education have provided a valuable resource both to educators and to the arts community. The concept of *standards* is a principle that is readily accepted by educators, business leaders, parents, and politicians. Arts specialists, who are often banished to the fringe of the curriculum, are able to approach administrators and school boards armed with the language and demonstration of "academic rigor" in the arts. Artists and cultural groups use the arts standards to illustrate the connections between their work and the curricular goals of the school. Thus, the standards have become the banner under which arts education can collectively move forward, and the means by which the previously ephemeral has become concrete.

Even more enduring than the national standards was the coming together in the early 1990s of the various public, private, nonprofit, and education sectors around a national advocacy effort for arts education. While the governors succeeded in establishing National Education Goals and launching a major national effort in 1989 to improve education, they also galvanized the arts education community by initially leaving the arts out of the national goals altogether. Thus, the fact that we have national standards for the arts at all is testimony to the power of collective action in support of a common goal. That a new administration and Congress actually reaffirmed the inclusion of the arts as a core academic subject in 2001 with the "No Child Left Behind" legislation is evidence that even the most diverse groups, with at times conflicting agendas and priorities, can succeed in moving forward when enough voices make themselves heard.

Making the case. The efforts in the 1990s to make the case for arts education also drew attention to the fact that the arts were one of the least researched areas of the curriculums, placing arts advocates at a distinct disadvantage when confronted with school administrators or politicians asking for proof that it works.

The NEA was an early leader in efforts to stimulate longitudinal research that attempted to provide evidence of the impact of the arts in the curriculum, releasing *Schools, Communities, and the Arts: A Research Compendium*[6] in 1995.

The value of arts education is now firmly grounded in theory and research. Although the hard-nosed, scientific language used in studies is often lacking in literary eloquence, the evidence accumulated is eloquent testimony to the remarkable relationship between learning, knowing, and the arts.

—*Eloquent Evidence: Arts at the Core of Learning*[7]

Though independent studies on the impact of arts education on a variety of topics from student learning to drop-out prevention had been taking place, this was one of the first efforts to gather this information together in a single document for policy makers, community advocates, and schools. Shortly thereafter, the President's Committee on the Arts and Humanities and the National Assembly of State Arts Agencies, with support from The GE Fund, released *Eloquent Evidence: Arts at the Core of Learning*, which summarized the key research findings into a compelling document that would not only make the case for arts education locally but for help to fuel the dramatic shifts in federal support for arts education that were to come.

Champions of Change. In an effort to spur interest in improving the amount and quality of research available in arts education, the Arts Education Partnership's Research Task Force called for the federal government to support periodic compendia of the latest arts education research of importance to researchers, practitioners, and policy makers in its report, *Priorities for Arts Education Research*.[8]

In 1999, the major research compendium *Champions of Change: The Impact of the Arts on Learning*[9] was released. By examining a variety of arts education programs and using diverse methodologies, researchers developed seven major research studies that sought to explore why and how young people were changed through their arts experiences. They were able to demonstrate higher levels of overall achievement among students taking part in the arts, a leveling of the playing field for disadvantaged students, as well as evidence of a positive impact on behavior in both school and personal lives. Collectively, the research provided compelling evidence to strengthen the need to include the arts in the educational life of children—for both their intrinsic and their educative value. As the executive summary reports, "Another broad theme emerges from the individual *Champions of Change* research findings: the arts no longer need to be characterized solely by either their ability to promote learning in specific arts disciplines or by their ability to promote learning in other disciplines. These studies suggest a more dynamic, less either-or model for the arts and overall learning that has more of the appearance of a rotary with entrances and exits than of a linear one-way street."

Critical Links. In 1999, the NEA and the U.S. Department of Education provided grant support to the Arts Education Partnership to commission and manage the development of a second compendium, *Critical Links: Learning in the Arts and Student Academic and Social Development*.[10]

Released in 2002, *Critical Links* is an important step in centering the arts in the education reform debate. The compendium explores the arts as forms of cognition—ways of acquiring and expressing knowledge—which help every child reach the levels of achievement needed for academic and social success. Sixty-two studies of learning in dance, drama, music, visual arts, and multiarts are profiled. Comments are also made on the contribution of each study to the field of arts education research and practice, and on its implications, strengths, and weaknesses. Through this design, *Critical Links* focuses on the cognitive capacities used and developed in learning and practicing the arts, and the relationship of these capacities to students' academic performance and social interactions and development.

Community Involvement in Arts Education

Community involvement in arts education has transformed from program delivery to increasing levels of influence in local decision and policy making. As the field matures and the strategies for promulgating arts education in the community become more sophisticated, LAAs and nonprofit cultural organizations are being challenged to do more with the opportunities that have opened up as a result.

The 1988 publication *Arts and Education Handbook: A Guide to Productive Collaborations*[11] outlined the kinds of programs and services LAAs and nonprofit arts groups have typically sponsored or provided to schools and the community. By no means exhaustive, the list does define the broader arenas through which a LAA or nonprofit can engage in supporting arts education.

Resources for education. Provide such resources as curriculum development, artist residencies (schools and nontraditional settings), arts classes or workshops outside of schools, and help in organizing advocacy efforts on behalf of mandated K-12 arts curriculum in schools.

Information and technical assistance. Offer curriculum consulting, develop in-service workshops for teachers and other teacher training models, and connect the schools to cultural resources in the community.

Events. Sponsor events such as festivals for children and adults, performances, tours, exhibitions, workshops, and projects.

Artist listings. Provide directories of local artists and their contact information and artistic disciplines.

Artist rosters. List those local artists who do residencies and those who are part of official state, regional, or national residency programs that take place locally.

Preassembled exhibits. Offer a collection of a single artist's work, a regional show, or a thematic collection with information materials and presentations. Some LAAs belong to larger regional networks that connect with public, university, and private collections and educational programs.

Touring services. Help link schools with regional artist touring agencies or artist representatives, keep costs down by "block booking" a touring artist in a number of schools or communities, or even create touring educational programs.

Facilities, equipment, and space. Provide access to facilities which support schools without proper equipment or studio, rehearsal, or performing space, or which may wish to expand students' experience beyond the school setting.

Trips. Help schools and the community organize study groups or trips with an arts or cultural theme in local, regional, or even international settings.

Advocacy assistance. Train parents, teachers, and the arts community to be effective advocates, and help them to lobby for changes in local school curriculum or policy toward the arts.

Fundraising. Though most if not all nonprofits have had to struggle for financial survival, many use their fundraising experience to help support schools and educational programs. Private or publicly-funded arts-in-education programs support additional activities in the schools. LAAs may also cosponsor activities with other organizations, help identify an underwriter for a school program, or make key contacts with the private sector.

Since this list was compiled in 1998, two important areas in which LAAs play major roles in arts education have emerged.

Partnership building. More and more local organizations find that their programs—whether in schools or in various community settings—are more successful and have greater impact in the community when partnered with other cultural, civic, social, or governmental agencies that share similar goals.

Community cultural planning. Increasingly, the results of community cultural planning have revealed the community's desire for increased opportunities for youth and adults to engage in the arts. The sophistication of these plans has led to creative strategies, new partnerships with local government and education agencies, and a more prominent role for the LAA in the field of arts education.

FIRST THINGS FIRST: PREPARING TO TAKE THE PLUNGE

Is Arts Education the Right Thing to Do?

> To do well in the arts-in-education business, you must ground your organization's efforts in a clear understanding of education and of what you hope to accomplish. You must be able to articulate an education mission, strategy, and program to avoid criticism that your education program is just a marketing scheme to put bottoms in seats. To compete for funds to support education programs, you must excel in education, not just the arts.
>
> —David O'Fallon[12]

The decision to embark on a program in arts education should not be entered into lightly. In order to be effective, the program must be integral to the mission of the organization, affirmed by stakeholders, and well within the organization's capacity to sustain it. While more funders are increasing their support for arts education, they are in turn demanding a greater accountability for programs both to advance the national education agenda (through standards-based reform) and to demonstrate greater long-term impact rather than token exposure in one-shot programs. The costs—both human and financial—for any organization contemplating the development of an arts education program are substantial, and only sustainable if the capacity for which the program is undertaken is built on a sound philosophy and not merely as a potential fundraising strategy or marketing ploy.

Conducting a self-audit. With the myriad of opportunities available to address arts education needs from pre-K through senior citizen, it is essential for the LAA or nonprofit arts group to first determine on what its values towards education in the arts are based—that is, what is its mission? Without a clear sense of direction, it is easy to become overwhelmed by the multitude of directions to pursue in the world of education or fall victim to the various pitfalls that litter the path.

The number one "pitfall": following the money trail. Too often, the lure of potential funding is the primary catalyst for a nonprofit to decide to work in arts education. Over the past several years, federal and state arts agencies, foundations, and corporations have increased funding opportunities and provided other incentives to encourage more arts groups to adopt a philosophy and strategy for education. While most of these incentives emerged from recognition of the importance of arts education for the long-term health of children and the stability of the cultural community, it is also true that funders have sought refuge in arts education from the fall-out of the "culture wars" of the late 1980s and early 1990s. Then, many private entities stepped away from funding the arts "for art's sake" because of restrictions in federal funding to the arts and court battles over "obscenity" versus "art."

The role of arts education as the "safe port in the storm" for funders has more or less subsided and has evolved into an endorsement of arts education as an important national policy goal. There nevertheless remains a dynamic tension between trying to divide the scarce available dollars between support for artistic development and support for arts education. The arts in general are among the most underresourced of public obligations, whether examined as part of the nonprofit sector or as part of the educational system.

Impact of limited resources and competing pressures. Historically, schools, when faced with limited resources and competing pressures, often eliminate arts programs as a means to cut costs (and balance the budget). Conversely, the arts organization, when faced with limited resources and competing pressures (and in some cases, prompted by well-meaning funding sources), tend to view arts education as a means to acquire badly needed new funding (and balance the budget). To save a dollar, the schools eliminate a fundamental means by which they can educate the whole child, thus losing sight of the learner. To gain a dollar, the arts organization may feel pressured to embark on a program that is only tangential to its mission, and thus in the process may lose sight of the artistic vision.

If decisions on arts education are made for purely economic reasons, then ultimately it is the learner who loses. Arts education cannot exist as an afterthought—not in the schools, and not in the structure of the nonprofit. If it is to fulfill its true potential, arts education must be viewed as a core value within the system—no matter where that system operates. It must be planned for purposefully, ingrained within the vision and policies of the organization—and all those involved should be committed to it for the long run.

What are the Needs in Your Community?

Assessing the state of arts education in the community. As more LAAs have become involved in conducting community cultural planning, arts education has emerged as a central issue in the majority of these efforts. Many communities are engaging in additional planning efforts that focus specifically on the needs of education in the arts, for children as well as adults.

The Strategic Planning chapter explains many of the techniques and strategies applicable to a community cultural planning process. These will serve well the LAA interested in focusing on meeting community needs through arts education. Arts organizations will find Figure 1: Self Audit Worksheet helpful in determining to what extent arts education should be part of their planning and programs.

Working with schools in community planning. Schools present a special challenge for the community arts organization seeking to integrate issues of education into its community planning efforts. Often, the local education system occupies the largest local government expenditure—and subsequently wields significant political clout. The trends occurring on the national and state levels present a paradox in working with

Figure 1: Self-Audit Worksheet:

Deciding Whether Arts Education is for You

Reflection Exercises for Boards and Program Planners

Adapted from O'Fallon, D. (1996). The Arts Organization and Public Education: A Guide to Conducting a Self-Audit. In J. Remer (Ed.), *Beyond Enrichment: Building Effective Arts Partnerships with Schools and Your Community.* Washington, DC: Americans for the Arts.

FOCUS QUESTION 1

What is our philosophy of education?

What does "education" mean to our organization?

What does "education" mean to the people we serve?

Where are the arts in this philosophy? What is the role of the arts in the national education reform agenda? How is it playing out in our state? In our community?

PURPOSE OF EXERCISE: Developing a solid philosophy of education helps establish a strong sense of purpose and create an identity for the organization's role in arts education. It also lends credibility to the organization seeking to develop sustained relationships with educational institutions—especially in the public school system. The self-knowledge gained helps the organization clarify intent, and avoid being drawn into practices and activities that fall outside the agency's mission and strain the organization's capacity. The program will suffer if the educational goals become fragmented or are not clear from the start.

FOCUS QUESTION 2

How are our core values related to education and our education programs?

Is building knowledge or awareness *about* an art form or artist our primary educational goal?

Is building personal skills or creative abilities *in or through* the arts the primary goal?

Is it a combination of the two?

What role can we do best?

What role is in the best interests of the organization?

PURPOSE OF EXERCISE: The core values as defined by the organizational mission should form the foundation of the education program. For example, an organization founded with the mission of advancing American jazz as an art form would be ill-advised to decide to develop its education program around the American musical theater because that's what the middle school wants. While this seems self-explanatory, many organizations can get pulled in the wrong direction by trying to adapt themselves to fit a school's or funder's agenda that extends beyond the scope of their mission. By acting on its strengths, the organization will be better able to define the goals, purpose, and resources available to launch the program effectively, as well as develop the will and capacity to sustain it.

school systems: though the policies continue to emphasize the arts in core academic content areas and suggest the need for greater support for arts education in the school system, the new emphasis on testing and accountability drains potential resources that might have been applied to arts program development. Nevertheless, despite the challenges, the local education system is an important potential ally in a community's overall cultural plan, and key to any effort to improve K-12 sequential education in the arts.

Based on the seminal research reports released in 2000—*Gaining the Arts Advantage: Lessons from School Districts That Value Arts Education*[13] and *Champions of Change: The Impact of the Arts on Learning*—and its own guidelines for the *Creative Ticket to Student Success* and other awards programs, the Kennedy Center, through the Kennedy Center Alliance for Arts Education Network, developed a useful planning tool to guide efforts in community assessment of arts education. *A Community Audit for Arts Education: Better Schools, Better Skills, Better Communities*[14] is designed to assist local education, community, and cultural leaders in assessing the status of arts education in their schools and school districts, as well as to encourage community partnerships to strengthen and expand arts education for all students. Among the most practical applications of *A Community Audit for Arts Education* is its usefulness as a vehicle for encouraging conversation and community planning in support of arts education, and in helping members of the school and general community understand the ingredients needed to support and sustain an effective arts education program.

Conducting a community assessment. *A Community Audit for Arts Education* helps leaders assess the status of school district arts programs through the lens of 13 critical factors essential to implement and sustain comprehensive arts education programs. These factors are organized under three larger categories: Informed Leadership, Educational Content, and Community Connections.

The Six Factors of Informed Leadership

1. The school board provides a supportive policy framework and environment for the arts.
2. The superintendent regularly articulates a vision for arts education and works to ensure its successful implementation and stability.
3. A cadre of principals collectively supports the policy of arts education for all students and is often instrumental in the policy's successful district-wide implementation.
4. The district arts coordinator facilitates program implementation throughout a school system and maintains an environment of support for arts education.
5. Parent/public relations seize opportunities to make their programs known throughout the community in order to secure support and funding.
6. Continuity of school and community leadership is necessary to implement comprehensive arts education.

The Six Factors of Educational Content

1. Planning provides a comprehensive vision and proposal for arts education which is implemented incrementally.

2. A foundation during elementary school in arts education is the basis for strong system-wide programs.
3. Opportunities for higher levels of achievement—such as magnet schools and advanced placement programs—help secure and sustain community support for the district's overall educational goals.
4. The teacher as artist needs to be allowed and encouraged to continue to learn and grow in mastery of their art form as well as in their teaching competence.
5. National, state, and other outside forces are effectively employed to advance arts education.
6. Continuous improvement efforts promote reflective practices at all levels of the schools to improve the quality of arts education.

The One Factor of Community Connections

The community—broadly defined as parents and families, artists, arts organizations, businesses, local civic and cultural leaders, and institutions—is actively engaged in the arts politics and instructional programs of the district.

In almost every instance where this kind of audit is used, leaders learn more about 'what is being done right' than they knew before the process began. By using the audit as a tool to come to consensus about the status of arts education, leaders can then work together to identify priorities and "next steps" which are appropriate for their community.

A Community Audit for Arts Education: Better Skills, Better Schools, Better Communities

As with any community cultural planning process, the audit invites planners to expand their circle of *critical friends.* This not only helps gain the broadest and most complete perspective on the state of arts education in the community but strategically begins the process of building a group of school and community leaders with the power and influence to lead an improvement effort.

Spheres of influence: understanding the players and their needs. Successful arts education programs often operate in a complex system, balancing the needs of the target audience with the constantly changing environment. An important aspect of becoming adept at navigating the system is to develop a basic, working knowledge of the significant players—those who influence, support, manage, or are impacted by education.

Oftentimes, these various individuals unite under the mutual goal of providing the highest quality education possible for children or the adult community. However, the educational ideals that each group adopts can lead straight into some of the most challenging debates—and in some cases, all-out wars—which are more about politics than education. It is important, then, to attempt to understand the people who are involved and have an interest in education in the community, what their beliefs are, and what motivates them. This knowledge will help you better understand the environment in which you will be operating and identify your potential allies and helpers, as well as the potential obstacles you may have to overcome in order to achieve your goal. The major participants who impact arts education on the local level include:

Pre-K through 12, Public Elementary and Secondary Education
Students

Arts specialists

Arts and/or curriculum supervisors

Generalist teachers (who may or may not use the arts in the delivery of their subjects, or who are teaching some aspect of the arts in lieu of an arts specialist)

Principals

Superintendents

Parents (PTAs, PTOs, or other parent advisory groups)

Community education foundations (A growing trend of nonprofit education foundations, these are being established as a separate fundraising arm of public schools; a community-based board is established to set grantmaking policy for activities and programs that send additional funds into the school. Since many of these local education foundations support arts programs, these are important allies.)

Higher Education

Deans of fine and performing arts departments (who train artists/performers)

Deans of education departments (who train new teachers)

University or college art galleries or performing arts centers

Student arts groups, associations

Nonprofit Arts Groups

Arts education providers or service organizations (whose primary mission is to conduct arts education programs, artist residencies, and/or teacher training)

Performing or producing arts organizations, (which operate an educational program, or for which education is a goal within the larger mission)

Museums or cultural centers with education programs or divisions

Individual artists (independent or as part of an organization's artist roster)

Community schools of the arts (which operate training programs in the arts for students of all ages, outside the formal school setting)

Government and Private Funding Agencies

Town, city, or county councils or commissions (approve funds for the school district and the LAA)

State arts agency

State department of education

Businesses and corporations supportive of education and arts education

Chambers of commerce

Foundations supportive of education and arts education

Who is really calling the shots? Trying to decipher the process behind school decision making often requires the arts administrator to do some detective work. On the surface (or according to the organizational chart), the chain of command may seem obvious. However, the power structure active in local schools is very much an individualized phenomenon, based on how much school policy is being driven by state mandate, local initiative, or a mix of the two.

The school may be embroiled in bitter politics: for example, did the school board come into power on a platform of improving learning or of reducing the local property taxes? Are the teachers employed there happy or engaged in bitter contract disputes? Is the

Figure 2: Types of School Programs—Pre-K–12

CATEGORY	DESCRIPTION
Assembly/Exposure	An artist or performing group will be brought to the school to perform, usually for large numbers of students. This may take the form of lecture/demonstrations, abridged shows of classic or new works, or fully staged events. Even though the performance may be a single event, groups prepare curriculum guides for teachers and may be involved in pre- or post-event workshops to assist in extending learning objectives. The event is developed and produced by the arts organization and may or may not include developmental input from school.
Field Trips	Students are transported from school to a location to view exhibits or performances or to take part in workshops. Again, most organizations design curriculum guides and instructional events to enhance student learning and increase the relevance of the educational experience.
Artist Residency	Artist residencies can span one day to several weeks, and involve a professional teaching artist in a meaningful, hands-on interaction with students. Residencies can be targeted to a particular class or grade level, to the general school population, or to encourage the artistic growth of advanced art students. They can include in-depth work in a particular discipline (creating or refining skills, critique, or aesthetic awareness) or in using an artistic discipline or multiple artistic forms to connect to the study of another academic area. Most residencies now involve the active participation of both teachers and artists in defining residency goals and developing curricular outcomes. At minimum, residencies will include at least one orientation session with teachers prior to the start of the residency and involve teachers and artists in a feedback and reflection system to allow for program adjustments and continuous improvement during the course of the residency.
Teacher Training	Teaching artists or other specialists meet with school staff in workshops, meetings, or conferences aimed at improving their skills in delivering instruction in and through the arts.
Curriculum Development	A natural extension of the teacher training model, artists work alongside teachers to develop curricular strategies to extend the development of lesson plans, interdisciplinary instruction, and extended units of study in the arts, or in employing the arts throughout entire curricular areas.
Preschool/ Early Childhood Education	Through federal incentives and initiatives such as Head Start, preschool programs are an increasing concern of public schools. Preparing students to be ready to learn by the time they enter the K–12 system—especially for children in economically disadvantaged, urban, and rural areas—has also led states to support preschool programs in their communities. Partnerships with schools, social service agencies, Head Start programs, and private day-care centers provide additional resources to help arts-based learning become part of the preschool curriculum.
Afterschool: School-based	Afterschool programs can be operated by the school or in partnership with nonprofit community-based groups, government recreational divisions, or social service agencies. School-based afterschool programs do not replace quality arts instruction during the school day but are designed to provide activities for students that promote and reflect learning goals that complement school policies and curriculum.
Special Needs Students	The arts play a unique role in assisting children with special challenges to learn new ways of coping with their world. Artists in partnership with educators and healthcare providers can develop programs and strategies to reach children who may not respond in any other way. Activities may take place as part of school-based curriculum, onsite in cultural institutions, or in specialized schools and facilities. Pre-planning and interaction between artists and education specialists is essential to ensure developmentally appropriate activities and safe learning environments.

teachers' union more powerful than the administration? How active are the parents? How are the arts specialists viewed at the school? Are they considered full members of the academic faculty, or do students take arts classes so that the "real" teachers have adequate planning time? (Consider that in some communities, there have been examples where, as part of the teacher union contract, arts specialists were required to cover classes so that classroom teachers could have planning time. Such an agreement all but kills any effort to develop a team-teaching approach in the arts and limits the amount of thematic planning that can be accomplished between arts specialists and classroom teachers.)

Building a network of *critical friends*. While knowing the environment and the disposition of the players beforehand can help fend off future problems, it is almost impossible for one person to know everyone and all the dynamics at play in schools. One way to address this is to use the planning process to develop a network of *critical friends*. This network can, and should, include individuals who may never be directly involved in your program. Many key decision makers and leaders central to early planning efforts will be more than willing to serve as informal advisors, especially when you ask for their expertise in navigating through the public school system. Asking questions before making a proposal can help you avoid stepping into a potential minefield—and making enemies before you get a chance to make friends. It will also help you determine whether this is an environment that is conducive to ensuring a successful program—and ultimately worth the investment of precious time, energy, and resources in the first place. Maintaining open, ongoing, and positive relationships with the people involved in your planning strengthens the foundation for successful implementation later on. (For sample worksheets on learning partnerships, visit this chapter's Online Companion. See the last page of this book for the Internet address.)

Programs to suit the community's needs. Arts education programs taking place in the community tend to fall into two general categories: those that take place in the K–12 setting or are integrally connected to the school curriculum; and those that take place beyond the school setting. Each broad area has its particular benefits and challenges to the LAA or nonprofit arts group embarking on the development of a new program.

Figures 2 and 3 outline various types of arts education programs. The descriptions reflect the growing recognition of both the value of school-based programs that deliver effective standards-based education, and of community-based programs serving therapeutic, social, or recreational needs.

The afterschool movement. The late 1990s saw an increase in national attention and the direction of federal resources toward afterschool programs. Federal agencies, such as the U.S. Departments of Education and Justice, supported this movement not only through general funding but also by providing resources for groups interested in developing quality afterschool programs.

With the advent of the federal Twenty-first Century Community Learning Centers Program in 1998, hundreds of millions of dollars have been made available to schools in collaboration with nonprofit and public agencies, community-based and social service organizations, as well as businesses to support the development of quality afterschool programs in rural or inner city neighborhoods. While the administration of these federal funds devolved from federal grant programs to the state level in 2002, resources to develop strong education-based afterschool programs continue to be part of the federal government's national education strategy.

Through the work of several national organizations, the arts have become a visible part of afterschool efforts. In 2000, under the auspices of the Kennedy Center's Education Department, leaders from the Kennedy Center Alliance for Arts Education Network and the Kennedy Center's Partners in Education program were convened to create a protocol for the development of quality afterschool arts education programs. Its purpose was to guide groups in understanding what constitutes excellence in afterschool arts programs and how they can be designed to complement in-school programs. With potentially hundreds of millions of dollars to be awarded through competitive federal grants, the report, *The Arts beyond the School Day: Extending the Power*,[15] is in fact timeless in its recommendations for designing an effective afterschool arts education program.

Essential elements of quality afterschool arts programs. The Kennedy Center's After-School Protocol Task Force identified nine essential elements, which, when taken together, forge the framework for ensuring the development of a quality arts-based afterschool program. In this framework, successful, arts-based, student-centered afterschool programs:

- are focused on student needs;
- offer unique opportunities for imaginative learning and creative expression;
- employ and support quality personnel;
- are structured to maximize student learning;
- engage families with their children;
- are actively supported by school leadership;
- invite collaborations with community partners;
- are committed to ongoing planning and evaluation; and
- leverage a wide variety of resources.

The preschool movement. The National Goals for Education catalyzed an interest in improving the quality of early childhood education by establishing as the first goal that all students will start school ready to learn. Taking up this charge, several major national studies focused on identifying the state of early childhood education and making recommendations for improvement. *Preventing Reading Difficulties in Young Children*[16] was one of the first reports to highlight the arts' ability to provide language-building activities through the use of stories, games, songs, and poems that emphasize rhyming or manipulation of sounds.

In 1998, the Arts Education Partnership established the Task Force on Children's Learning and the Arts: Birth to Age Eight, charging it with developing a framework and resources to help guide arts organizations in creating arts-based, developmentally appropriate early childhood programs, and in linking the arts to the literacy of young children.

Figure 3: Types of Community-based Programs—Pre-K to Senior Citizens

CATEGORY	DESCRIPTION
Community and Cultural Centers	An local arts agency or nonprofit arts group may run daytime or evening arts classes for very young children through senior citizens as part of the management of a government or nonprofit facility. A cultural facility may also sponsor pre-performance lectures, gallery talks, or tours rather than formal instruction. The establishment of community schools for the arts is a growing national movement that allows affordable access to exceptional instruction in the arts for children and adults. The community schools' primary mission is to provide quality arts instruction and may or may not provide performance or exhibit opportunities.
Parks and Recreation	Many parks and recreation divisions provide concerts and sponsor festivals and ongoing programs for residents to take part in the arts. Some divisions sponsor arts classes for children and adults through summer recreation and training programs, community theater, or music programs; others contribute by offering their community space to local groups and clubs.
Health Facilities and Social Service Organizations	Programs in hospitals or care facilities that support children and adults dealing with physical or emotional challenges are an increasing part of LAAs' work in arts education. Artist residencies, art therapists, and arts partnerships respond to the arts' power to heal and greatly impact lives.
Juvenile Justice and Preventative Programs	Enlightened correctional facilities for youthful offenders and adults recognize the importance of rehabilitative programs. Many employ artists to conduct classes; others have formed partnerships with artists and arts groups to bring in a poet, writer, or theater artist to work with the prison population. These programs not only impact the development of marketable language skills but contribute to the emotional rehabilitation and social development of participants.
Community-based Afterschool Programs	Afterschool programs that are independently operated by nonprofit, community-based, local/government recreational divisions or social service agencies are designed to provide activities for students that are not formally linked to achieving school curricular goals.

The task force report, *Young Children and the Arts: Making Creative Connections,*[17] defined three guiding principles to be used and thoroughly integrated in the development of arts-based programs and resources for young children.

The Child

Children should be encouraged to learn in, through, and about the arts by actively engaging in the processes of creating, participating in, performing, and responding to quality arts experiences, adapted to their developmental levels and reflecting their own culture.

The Arts Experience

Arts activities and experiences, while maintaining the integrity of the artistic disciplines, should be meaningful to children, follow a scope and sequence, and connect to early childhood curriculum and appropriate practices. They also may contribute to literacy development.

Learning Environment and Adult Interactions
The development of early childhood arts programs (including resources and materials) should be shared among arts education specialists, practicing artists, early childhood educators, parents, and caregivers, and the process should connect with community resources.

PLANNING YOUR ARTS EDUCATION PROGRAM

There are many types of arts education programs that target different audiences, and may take place in a variety of settings. The chapters on Strategic Planning, Program Development, and Program Evaluation contain information that will help you structure program development in arts education in community settings and, in fact, contain many fine examples of how this can be accomplished. This section focuses on planning for arts education programs that either take place in schools or are designed to help support school learning and curricular goals.

Engaging the Schools in Planning

Starting off on the right foot. Many problems that can arise in building a relationship with schools can be avoided with careful preplanning. The first step in developing an effective arts education program involves asking critical questions.

What are the school's educational priorities? Ask for the school's mission statement. Is the school primarily focused on basic or higher-order thinking skills? Is there a focus on social skill development, cultural awareness, or technology? Understanding where the school is operating from allows you to assess whether the program goals are aligned with school goals.

What is the teaching philosophy? It is easier for arts groups to develop programs and activities that are aligned with the standards and intersect with curricular goals if they know ahead of time if the school is engaged in aligning its curriculum in standards-based reform or with other state or national directives.

Does the school have previous experience with bringing in artists and arts groups? If so, what worked? What didn't? Knowing of potential impediments can help an arts group avoid becoming embroiled in a problem situation not of its own making.

What facilities will be available for a residency? What performance or classroom space will be made available? If students will be transported to a cultural site, who will coordinate and pay for it? Most types of arts programs require adequate facilities in order to maintain the quality of the experience. If the school does not have appropriate space, transporting the students expands the available learning opportunities. If the school does have facilities but does not adequately account for scheduling and usage, the impact of the experience will be diminished.

What are the major events on the school calendar? Understanding when it's a good time for a residency (for instance, the week when the state conducts its assessment and testing program is definitely a bad time) helps ensure that the program will begin on a positive note. Teachers will have time to participate, and fewer distractions will be present.

Who will be the primary liaison from the school? It is essential to have a spokesperson/coordinator from within the school environment to help outsiders navigate through the culture and bureaucracy. It is also important to have a willing coordinator who has the respect of others in the school and can get things done.

Although these questions are presented in the context of a school environment, they are equally appropriate with some adaptations for other settings, such as social service, hospital, or community agencies.

History is not destiny, and timing is everything. Having a history of good working relationships with a school or district is no guarantee that your program can or will be sustained in the face of change. Change can be as profound as a complete overhaul of the policies and procedures governing the education system, or as simple as the loss of one or two key personnel who usually make things happen. Schools have notoriously experienced the dramatic loss of entire arts programs or long-term artist residencies when the arts teacher retires or the outside funding stream dries up.

Conversely, a history of bad experiences can be erased with either a change of leadership or a change in internal school policies. Programs that have in the past been blocked by a disinterested superintendent or principal can receive new consideration with a new administration. A dance residency in one year can spark interest in the creation of a dance program the following year and the hiring of a part-time dance teacher.

Expand your network of "eyes" and "ears." It is always important to monitor what is happening on the school level, but doing so requires time, energy, and access to information. Federal and state education policies and initiatives impact local schools, often in profound ways. Many groups develop relationships with a school district through a dynamic superintendent or district-wide curriculum coordinator, only to find the following year that the district has switched to site-based management—meaning that decision making at all curricular and program levels becomes the province of the principal and school-based site-management teams. Where the primary liaison was once a single individual in the central district office, contacts may now have to be made with each local leadership team.

Newer educational trends involve the inclusion of parents not only in the traditional supportive roles of raising money for isolated activities but also in committees that make decisions on curriculum, budget, and program offerings. Understanding how the school operates—where the spheres of influence really lie and what outside forces are at play—is key to a productive working relationship. Equally important is investing the time to develop multiple working relationships with a number of individuals in order to ensure the continuity of the program should the major players move on or transition into different roles.

Defining the Program

Targeting participants. As a result of planning, a nonprofit arts group or LAA should have a fairly good understanding of the participants for whom the program will be targeted. The more defined the constituent population for the program can be, the greater the ability to develop targeted and focused activities that can successfully meet program objectives.

Number of participants. This is one of the more difficult questions for an arts group to answer early on, because there may be views of what is possible versus what is preferable. Certainly, a start is to identify the programmatic strengths of the organization. A teaching artist who is brilliant with small groups of children may feel overwhelmed if the school insists on an assembly program for the whole fifth grade. Conversely, a fully staged production of Macbeth provided to a single seventh-grade English class would be an opportunity lost if not presented to the whole middle school.

Exposure versus immersion. In general, exposure-oriented programs tend to be more successful in reaching greater numbers of students—if that is part of the decided goal. Programs designed for a more in-depth investigation into the art form tend to be more successful with smaller numbers of students. However, these generalities are not absolute and can be influenced by a number of factors, including the length of a residency, the number of teaching artists and educators involved, the opportunities given for teacher training, or the extent of the collaborative planning that occurs throughout a school or grade level. Many groups balance the need to serve a large number of constituents with the ability to conduct an in-depth arts experience by utilizing both performance and hands-on events or by providing thematic learning opportunities in multiple settings (classroom, art class, assembly, afterschool, etc).

What do we hope to accomplish by doing this? This question lies at the core of a "backwards design" process—that is, beginning with the end in mind. Although the notion seems abstract, it helps focus clarity on the mission and goals of the program, set standards that define program content, and lead to the development of criteria that can be used to determine whether or not goals have been achieved. Continually asking how a program would look if it met your highest goals will lead you to ask what worked and what are the criteria for determining if you've been successful. If you view assessment as an ongoing element of the learning process, it can inform and improve the work or performance and also garner the facts and statements needed to satisfy funders and bureaucratic reporting requirements. See the Program Evaluation chapter for more information on how to set goals and evaluate programs.

Program documentation. If schools and arts groups as a whole are guilty of anything, it is spending too little time and energy documenting and telling "our stories." Yet these stories help others to understand arts education efforts in new ways and are essential to effective advocacy.

Decisions regarding what to document should be linked to program and evaluation objectives. In this way, documentation becomes a vital part of the learning and assessment process. It is much easier to collect images and products throughout the duration of the program than to scramble to find information at the end.

The uses of documentation are many: to display skills learned by participants, products developed, and processes used; to demonstrate program effectiveness to potential supporters; to train new program leaders; and to report back to granting agencies. When looking at various means of documenting a project, it is helpful to keep two questions in mind.

Why is this needed? Possible answers: *As a learning tool*—Students learning a dance are videotaped and shown it so that they can have immediate feedback.

Students also can use clips of themselves in a "video portfolio" to demonstrate their progress over time. *As a training tool*—A videotape of a master artist conducting a teacher training workshop is used as part of a workshop to train new teaching artists. *As a reporting tool*—A video montage of a school's artist residencies are taken by parents to a school board meeting to demonstrate the value of these programs.

Who is the audience for it? Possible answers: *funding sources*, *program planners*, *learners*, *internal board members*, or members of the *community*.

Developing a Student-centered Curriculum

A student-centered curriculum is based on the assumption that the learner, and not the event or artwork itself, is the primary focus within the learning experience and environment. To distinguish between the two focuses, consider the difference between these two learning tasks.

The educational goal of the first learning task is to help students know more about the choreography of Martha Graham. To support this goal, students may read a biography of Graham, view videotapes or films, or see a dance performance of Graham's work in a school assembly or at a performing arts center. At the end of the lesson, students should be able to answer basic questions about Martha Graham's life, her work, and various aspects of dance as it pertains to her artistic vision.

The educational goal of the second learning task is to help students make a personal statement by creating a dance in the style of Martha Graham. Obviously, many of the activities outlined above would still be appropriate—but as a means to an end rather than an end in itself. To learn about Graham's work, students will study how her concepts developed, what techniques she used, and what influenced her work. They would then apply this knowledge by creating a personal artistic statement through dance. In this example, the student is actively engaged in understanding a process—an understanding that extends beyond a single artist, performance, or event.

Understanding developmentally- and age-appropriate curriculum. The stages of artistic development in children are based in part on their overall cognitive and motor abilities and also on how much and what kinds of arts experiences have been available to them in their home, school, or community.

Very young children are naturally drawn to the arts, largely as a result of play. Children who have not yet fully developed verbal skills will still move their bodies to sounds, respond to singing, and try to imitate their parents' facial expressions. With appropriate adult facilitation, these basic forms of play can evolve into the acquisition of skills and frames of mind that we recognize as rudiments of the artistic process.

Children learn to observe, organize, and interpret information they receive from their environment. As they grow, these observations gain greater depth, more intricate patterns emerge, and interpretations grow more insightful.

Children learn to make decisions, even at the most basic level. By engaging in the arts, children must take action and can see, in the product or event they create, the results of their decisions.

> **Children learn that they can communicate in many ways**—with adults and with each other through words, sounds, movements, and pictures.

Compelling evidence exists that early arts experience has an impact on all aspects of a child's learning and development and that, in many ways, "earlier is better." Yet earlier must not mean rushed, or the projection of adult approaches onto younger abilities. A one-year old is different from a three-year old, who is different from a five-year old, and so are the strategies for engaging them appropriately, sensitively, and meaningfully in the arts. In fact, arts education that is not developmentally appropriate may be worse than no arts at all. For example, children should not be placed in high pressure programs which focus on product and performance, but rather placed in developmentally appropriate activities which engage them in process, experience, and exploration, and build on what they naturally do. The differing needs of children ages five and under from those ages six through eight are an example of one such important distinction.

Early childhood thus presents both a unique opportunity and a unique challenge, and a part of that challenge is to engage and support all those who care for and educate young children in making the arts an integrated and vital part of their earliest experiences. A major component of that challenge is to ensure that artists understand and adapt to the developmental needs of young children or work in partnership with early childhood professionals who do.

Arts education program planners should have a general understanding of the various stages of learning development, and how these stages play out in the learning environment. An art experience given to an eight year old with absolutely no background or frame of reference for the art form presented could prove overwhelming: the child is likely to become frustrated and shut off from the learning experience. The same experience given to an eight year old with an extensive background and grounding in the fundamentals of the art form might view it as remedial: this child is likely to be bored and disinterested. In both cases, the child will have a negative view of the arts experience. Whatever program is eventually developed, it should be adaptable, so that if the population encountered is either less prepared for the program than anticipated or more advanced in knowledge and abilities, the program can easily be adjusted. The more careful the preplanning, the less likely the artist or arts group is to step into a situation for which he or she is not prepared.

There are many resources to assist program planners in an examination of age-appropriate activities. The websites of the Kennedy Center's ArtsEdge and the Getty Center for Arts Education have curricular models and ideas based on actual field practice. For instance, consider the sequential model in Figure 4: Ideas for Art Making.[18]

Achievement standards. The National Standards for Arts Education (along with most state standards in the arts) define both content—what students should know and be able to do in the arts disciplines—and achievement standards—those specific competencies within each of the disciplines, according to grade clusters, that together demonstrate whether the student has mastered or is proficient in the content. Thus standards, whether state or national, are written in a form considered developmentally

ABILITY AREA	IDEAS FOR MAKING ART
Lower Elementary or Level 1	Students use observations of people, places, objects, and events as sources of ideas for art making.
Upper Elementary or Level 2	Students consider purposes of art such as communicating, persuading, recording, celebrating, embellishing, and designing in developing ideas for art making.
Middle School or Level 3	Students draw upon personal and cultural values and concerns as subjects and themes for art making.
High School or Level 4	Students critically examine trends in their choices of ideas for art making as a basis for future work.

Figure 4: Ideas for Art Making

Originally retrieved from ArtsEdNet, *Lesson Plans & Curriculum Ideas: Scope & Sequence,* © J. Paul Getty Trust, 1999.

appropriate for students in the respective grade clusters and represent a good starting point for program planners to learn more about where to start in developing a program for children.

The very best strategy an artist or arts group can follow when developing a curriculum for a particular age group is to involve experts. Education professionals—including arts specialists, classroom educators, educators who work with special populations, early childhood educators, child psychologists, curriculum developers, and administrators—undergo extensive training to understand how and when children develop different cognitive and motor skills. They can provide useful feedback as to whether a program is targeted to the appropriate age group.

What *essential questions* will the program answer? The essential questions conceptual framework is a useful planning and organizational tool for arts education program developers. It helps establish content themes; organize outcomes and activities for artists, teachers, organizers, and students; and stimulate inquiry-based learning. At the same time, it allows for thinking about how structure and sequence will play out in different time periods—such as a 45-minute workshop versus a two-week long artist residency—and establishes a basis from which to develop appropriate assessment measures.

Artists and arts groups can work with teachers as well as students to develop essential questions for the educational program. Essential questions can be derived from a number of different sources: from an exploration of a particular standard area (how dances are made); a specific part of the arts group's artistic season (the upcoming retrospective festival of the work of August Wilson); a critical issue for the students (bullying); or the identification of a specific theme (the year-long celebration of the 100th anniversary of the founding of the town).

Examples

Dance: How have different ethnic groups used dance in celebration?

Music: Where are "melodies" found in nature?

Visual Arts: How does color convey moods or feelings?

Theater: How can costumes tell a story?

See Essential Questions as a Tool for Program Development in the Online Companion for information on Carnegie Hall's LinkUP! Program. (See the last page of this book for the Internet address.)

Who Should Teach the Arts?

One of the most enduring, needlessly polarizing, and fundamental questions in arts education is: Who should teach the arts to children? If a program is to succeed, attention must be paid to the *excellence of the experience* as both a learning opportunity and an artistic event. This requires valuing the skills of both the trained arts specialist and the professional teaching artist for the strengths each brings to the learning process.

Too often this debate becomes oversimplified and rancorous for all the wrong reasons, degrading into those who believe that only certified arts specialists should teach the arts to children and those who believe that only practicing professional artists can deliver artistic quality. Such extreme positions serve only the self-interests of those perpetuating them. The end result of ideological or power-based quarrels is a weakening of the arts in the educational setting, and resources and attention deflected away from creating the best possible experience for students.

It therefore is incumbent upon the program planner to engage the most qualified specialist to deliver the program, always with an eye toward the end result.

Criteria for the "teaching" artist. One of the most important roles a LAA can play in regard to arts education is to help artists become partners in education programs. Consequently, an essential component of a successful arts education program is the selection of artists who excel not only in their art form but also in their ability to impart their knowledge and skills effectively. Not all great artists are effective teachers. It is the job of the arts organization to match the skills of the teaching artist with the needs of the learners.

Common Qualities of Effective Teaching Artists

Artistic quality and professional integrity. An effective teaching artist will possess exceptional skills in his or her discipline, present a body of professional work, and be able to demonstrate professional success in the art world.

Ability to communicate. An effective teaching artist will not only be able to verbalize ideas and concepts about the art form in an interesting way, but also will use multiple means of demonstrating, illustrating, and otherwise imparting understanding about the art form. Good communicators tailor their presentations to the age group and make an effort to understand special needs or challenges.

Ability to engage the learner. An effective teaching artist engages the learner in the discovery of new ways of thinking and doing. One of the most valued aspects of an artist residency is the high degree of hands-on activity. These activities should encourage the learner to unlock the creative skills within and not merely provide a carbon copy of the teaching artist's work. Effective teaching artists help the learner establish a creative identity by not fostering a "do what I do" environment.

Flexible working style. An effective teaching artist checks her or his artistic temperament at the door. The school environment is different from the studio:

artists must be prepared to take the good with the bad. Most schools are still run on the factory-model: the period ends when the bell rings; the students in the class are who you have to work with (you can't pick and choose); and the school functions on rules that more often than not conflict with being creative. A willingness to understand and work within the confines of the school structure is essential to fostering a strong working relationship.

Respect for educators. An effective teaching artist makes use of the teacher as a partner in the residency. Arts specialists are often practicing artists themselves but are generally not given credit for their work as artists in school. Teachers have expectations for what a residency can accomplish, and what experiences and activities could enhance educational objectives. By working together, the artist and the teacher can maximize their strengths for the benefit of the students.

Motivation for teaching. Above all, effective teaching artists *want* to teach—and love to do it. Teaching is an important part of who they are. Teachers and students will pick up on someone whose primary motivation for being in the classroom is to earn some extra cash.

Who Should Teach the Arts?

In essence, Who shall teach the arts? is a question undergoing redefinition. Within the context of the [National] Standards, the answer will become 'someone who is able to bring children to the knowledge and ability to do what the standards call for.' Regardless of what new credentialing processes may require, 'qualified' increasingly will mean someone who:

- can guide children through a balanced, sequential process of learning that achieves clearly stated outcomes;
- can instill in children an appreciation for the various art forms and the products of the arts disciplines in all their diversity;
- can bring children to clearly stated levels of performance in a given arts discipline; and
- can help children arrive at a knowledge of the cultural and historical context of the arts disciplines.

—Dr. John J. Mahlmann, executive director, Music Educators National Conference (MENC)

Partnerships

More often than not, arts education efforts involve multiple organizations that cross a variety of sectors with a vested interest in arts education: nonprofit, for-profit, and public arts and education agencies; schools; private funders; and parent, volunteer, and community groups. However, the general enthusiasm for starting a partnership is sometimes eclipsed by the challenges of sustaining one. Therefore, it is important for an organization to consider whether a partnership or collaboration is really the best strategy for meeting a need.

In 1999, at the request of the U.S. Department of Education and the NEA, the Arts Education Partnership produced a guide to developing successful arts education partnerships to address community needs. Entitled *Learning Partnerships: Improving Learning in Schools with Arts Partners in the Community*, the guide sought out leaders from the arts, education, business, civic, and government sectors to advise on effective approaches to partnership development. A companion workbook is available free for download on the Arts Extension Service's website at www.umass.edu/aes.

The guide identified 18 critical factors that will sustain an effective arts and education partnership over time.[19]

1. The partners understand shared goals that ultimately enhance student learning.
2. The individual partners' own goals are met within an effective partnership.
3. In sustained partnerships, leadership becomes shared.
4. Partners within effective partnerships assume a shared sense of ownership in the collaborative program.
5. Effective partnerships are creative.
6. The organization and structure of sustainable partnerships must be flexible.
7. Strong partnerships survive setbacks.
8. Effective partnerships engage multiple community sectors.

9. Good community arts and education partnerships involve multiple artistic and academic disciplines.
10. The arts are valued for themselves and for their capacity to enhance student learning.
11. Sustained partnerships are concerned comprehensively with education.
12. Partnerships are best sustained when there is support at all levels of partner organizations.
13. Effective partnerships invest in the professional development of their personnel.
14. Partner institutions learn and change.
15. Evaluation and documentation help achieve partnership goals.
16. Sustained partnerships create an infrastructure that supports community/school learning relations.
17. Effective partnerships attract sustained funding.
18. Good partnerships require persistence and patience.

Assessing Student Learning

Community arts organizations that sponsor educational programs should assess the effectiveness of their programs and determine ways to improve their delivery. The Program Evaluation chapter makes an effective case for why program planners need to develop an evaluation framework and describes concrete processes for setting up an effective outcome evaluation (What is the impact of the program? Has it met its goals?) This section more specifically discusses assessment of student learning. (For a sample program assessment and a Summary of Major Task Force Report Findings showing program impact, visit this chapter's Online Companion. See the last page of this book for the Internet address.)

Improving versus auditing performance. The primary purpose of assessment should ideally be to improve performance—not merely audit it. This is the fundamental premise espoused by leading assessment experts, most notably Grant Wiggins, of Authentic Education. Wiggins's work centers around moving schools, groups, and individuals away from the praise-and-blame paradigm of assessment to assessment as a means of growth.

Though one can make an argument that this should be true in all program endeavors, it is especially important within the context of arts education. As many educators are quick to point out, the Latin root of education is *educare*—to draw out. If this is the core meaning behind education, then it is essential to build in opportunities for continuous learner improvement, since it is in the act of doing, reflecting, critiquing, and correcting—and repeating this process again and again—that we grow as artists and individuals.

Assessing learning. When we begin a conversation regarding the assessment of student learning in the arts, too often the automatic reaction is that we are speaking about reducing an arts experience into a "true or false" standardized test. However, such assessments divert students' attention from understanding large ideas and processes to mastering facts.

In *Taking Full Measure: Rethinking Assessment through the Arts*,[20] Dennie Palmer Wolf and Nancy Pistone argue for the use of assessment as an "episode of learning," and lay out a framework of three "essential lessons" about monitoring or measuring student learning.

> **The *contents* of assessment** suggest assessments that address the full range of what is involved in making a work of art—a process of complex problem solving that is deliberately multidimensional. Within this framework, the contents of assessment are expanded beyond the quality of the final piece or performance to include early and ongoing processes, such as investigations into ideas, reflections, actions based on critique, and responses.
>
> **The *conduct* of assessment** suggests that assessment—as opposed to testing—is a process of ongoing monitoring of progress and quality, where students are active participants. Assessment is used for more than an occasion to assign grade or rank: it becomes an ongoing "episode of learning."
>
> **The *tools* of assessment** support assessment as an ongoing component of learning. Since learning is measured over a longitudinal time frame, tests that measure knowledge or recall at a particular moment—that is, multiple-choice or end-of-year exams—give way to "process portfolios," which are "longitudinal histories of themselves as people learning an art form." [21] Journals, critiques, and portfolios by their very nature are designed to provide evidence of knowledge of the processes and values, as well as sustained work and reflection.

Educative assessment requires a "known set of measurable goals, standards, and criteria that make the goals real and specific (via models and specifications), descriptive feedback against those standards, honest yet tactful evaluation, and useful guidance."

—Grant Wiggins[22]

Testing student learning has become a political tool, the result of taxpayers bearing the support for the public-school system and anti-tax movements at the federal, state, and local levels. The national emphasis on testing in reading and math at multiple grade levels—with a punitive linkage of federal funds to student performance as part of the education legislation—has proven challenging for school systems, and has stressed the fragile gains made by the arts over the past decade.

Good assessment is about good design. Designing a good assessment involves setting *performance standards*, and developing *criteria* by which to measure success. It is also a matter of beginning with the end in mind. You must have a clear idea of what "success" will look like for the learner to design a system that can retrieve the information you need, and provide the evidence that the goals have been achieved.

The feedback loop: analyze, adjust, improve, repeat. Feedback follows a continuous loop of fact–impact–commentary. *Facts* are presented about what did or did not happen related to the program goal, without interpretation or judgment. By analyzing the effects that occurred as an immediate result of the facts, students begin to understand the *impact* of their actions. The learning event comes full circle through *commentary* (the explanation of the facts and their impact in the context of the goal, given in a nonemotional manner), leading to an understanding of what adjustments must be made to the next performance to incorporate the feedback and subsequently improve the performance.

See the Online Companion for this chapter for examples which illustrate ways to assess student learning in the arts that achieve what most standardized tests cannot—that is, the improvement of student performance. (See the last page of this book for the Internet address.)

CONCLUSION

Advocacy for Arts Education: Whose Job is it Anyway?

Whose problem is the lack of quality arts education programs in schools? The answer is plain and simple—*ours.* It doesn't matter if we don't have a child in school; it doesn't matter if we don't "do" education programs. If we, as a community concerned about the arts as a whole, do not fight for it, it will not be there. Voicing support for arts education needs to be a part of every nonprofit arts organization, local arts agency, or cultural institution's mission—even if they are not directly involved in providing or supporting arts education programs. It is clearly in the best interests of children and the public good that the arts grow and flourish in lifelong learning opportunities both in school and beyond.

Advocacy for arts education is not necessarily easy; it involves bringing together a critical mass of individuals who may at times hold opposing views of the means and methods for making the arts a central part of the school and community. As discussed earlier, the enormous strides that have recently been undertaken and proven successful on the national and state levels indicate that reaching a common vision for arts education is achievable.

Local advocates need to be conscious of bringing all interested voices to the table. Engaging in local school politics can be messy, but it is necessary. Arts advocates can play a vital role by being active in school groups—such as parent committees or planning efforts—and, perhaps more importantly, by working to make sure supportive arts voices are elected to local school boards.

See the Arts Advocacy chapter for more information about arts advocacy processes.

Avoiding the Tiger Traps: Some Final Tips for Surviving the Jungle

The most difficult aspect of arts education program development—especially when creating programs that take place in, or in conjunction with, schools—is negotiating through the political realities present in public education. More new programs fail or are thwarted, not because of the lack of good ideas, because of a basic naiveté or dismissal of the school culture. Hopefully, the previous sections have provided enough food for thought and concrete strategies to prevent the newcomer from stepping into the pitfalls that will invariably dot the path.

In summary, the best way to survive the most dangerous beasts in the jungle without being eaten alive is to know where they lurk. The best intentions are imperiled if the following common traps aren't considered:

The organization is seen as a threat to teacher job security rather than as a partner in improving arts education.

The organization ignores or fails to respect the school culture or embarks on a competing rather than complimentary agenda.

The organization is not able to win enough widespread support from the major players or fails to establish a "win-win" relationship not only with school leadership but also with those who will most feel the impact of the program.

The organization loses sight of its commitment to quality in both artistic presentation and educational goals.

In the end, successful program development in arts education—whether for school students or the larger community—depends on building quality relationships, developing mutually supportive goals, and establishing a firm commitment to work toward achieving a greater good.

Practically speaking, this takes time and a willingness to prepare and nurture the soil before cranking up the plow and tilling the fields—especially if there isn't clear consensus on what it is you're being asked to plant. As with most good learning opportunities, however, in the long run there is more to be gained from the journey than from rushing to reach the destination.

ENDNOTES

1. Fowler, C. (1998). *Arts Education Handbook: A Guide to Productive Collaborations.* Washington, DC: National Assembly of State and Arts Agencies.
2. Greenspan, A. (2000, July 11). *Structural Change in the New Economy.* Remarks made at the 92nd Annual Meeting of the National Governors Association, State College, PA.
3. Remer, J. (1990). *Changing Schools Through the Arts: How to Build on the Power of an Idea.* Washington, DC: Americans for the Arts.
4. Welch, N., & Greene, A. (1995). *Schools, Communities, and the Arts: A Research Compendium.* Retrieved at http://www.asu.edu/copp/morrison/public/schools.pdf
5. Davidson, B. (2001, August). *Local Arts Agency Facts: Fiscal Year 2000* (Monograph). Washington, DC: Americans for the Arts.
6. Welch.
7. President's Committee on the Arts and Humanities & National Assembly of State Arts Agencies. (1995). *Eloquent Evidence: Arts at the Core of Learning* [Brochure]. Retrieved at http://www.nasaa-arts.org
8. Arts Education Partnership. (1997). *Priorities for Arts Education Research.* Washington, DC: Author.
9. Fiske, E.B. (Ed.). (1999). *Champions of Change: The Impact of the Arts on Learning.* Retrieved at http://www.aep-arts.org
10. Deasy, R.J. (Ed. (2002). *Critical Links: Learning in the Arts and Student Academic and Social Development.* Retrieved at http://www.aep-arts.org
11. Katz, J. (Ed.). (1988). *Arts and Education Handbook: A Guide to Productive Collaborations.* Washington, DC: National Assembly of State Arts Agencies.
12. O'Fallon, D. (1996). The Arts Organization and Public Education: A Guide to Conducting a Self-Audit. In J. Remer (Ed.), *Beyond Enrichment: Building Effective Arts Partnerships with Schools and Your Community.* Washington, DC: Americans for the Arts.
13. Longley, L. (Ed.). (1999). *Gaining the Arts Advantage: Lessons from School Districts That Value Arts Education.* Retrieved at http://www.pcah.gov
14. The John F. Kennedy Center for the Performing Arts Kennedy Center Alliance for Arts Education Network. (2000). *A Community Audit for Arts Education: Better Skills, Better Schools, Better Communities.* Washington, DC: Author.
15. Conk, J. (2000). *The Arts Beyond the School Day: Extending the Power.* Retrieved at http://www.kennedy-center.org/education/kcaaen/resources/afterschool.pdf
16. Snow, C.E., Burns, M.S., & Griffin, P. (Eds.). (1998) *Preventing Reading Difficulties in Young Children.* Committee on the Prevention of Reading Difficulties in Young Children, National Research Council. Retrieved at http://www.nap.edu/readingroom
17. Goldhawk, S., & The Task Force on Children's Learning and the Arts: Birth to Age Eight. (1998). *Young Children and the Arts: Making Creative Connections.* Bruce, C. (Ed.). Retrieved at http://www.aep-arts.org
18. J. Paul Getty Trust. (1999). Originally retrieved from ArtsEdNet, *Lesson Plans & Curriculum Ideas: Scope & Sequence.*
19. Dreeszen, C., Aprill, A., & Deasy, R. (1999). *Learning Partnerships: Improving Learning in Schools with Arts Partners in the Community.* Washington, DC: Arts Education Partnership.
20. Palmer Wolf, D., & Pistone, N. (1995). *Taking Full Measure: Rethinking Assessment through the Arts.* New York: College Entrance Examination Board.
21. Ibid.
22. Wiggins, G. (2002, May 6). Retrieved at http://www.relearning.org

CHAPTER 15

Program Evaluation: Looking For Results

15

CRAIG DREESZEN

"You want me to evaluate *what*?" The harried arts center director puts down the phone after a call from a foundation program officer and wonders where she will find the time to learn another management skill. It may be that you, too, have discovered that a basic understanding of program evaluation is becoming a high priority for arts managers.

While the incentive to evaluate is coming increasingly from funders interested in accountability, the real value of evaluation is the information it provides to improve programs. Fortunately, your programs and constituents will reap so many tangible benefits from evaluation that you will be very glad you learned to do it.

UNDERSTANDING THE PRINCIPLES OF PROGRAM EVALUATION

A New Era of Accountability

We are in an era of increased expectation for accountability. It is no longer sufficient to promise in a grant application that you'll change people's lives with your arts programs and then note in your final report that lots of people attended and seemed to have a good time. The paradigm is shifting. Now funders, partners, stakeholders, and others are asking that we demonstrate results. By understanding what they would consider success and integrating evaluation early into your planning, you can design a program that has a better chance to achieve its objectives. However, do not promise more than you can deliver. If your program ultimately has little influence over the outcome you're hoping to achieve, alter your target to one you can achieve.

Evaluation need not be shrouded in mystery or jargon. It need not be any more complicated than the task requires. This chapter will explain the concepts and language of evaluation, give you a simple, six-step process to define your hoped-for results, and outline how to ensure that these were achieved. The text, examples, glossaries, and worksheets will prepare you to plan and implement an evaluation of a program. They build upon the *Learning Partnerships Evaluation Workbooks*, found online at www.umass.edu/aes/learningpartners/index.htm.

While there are many methods of evaluation, this chapter takes a goal and outcome-based approach. Your evaluation design is a chain of logical reasoning that links assessed needs to program goals, intended outcomes, program activities, and finally to achieved outcomes.

A Brief History of Evaluation

The move to "reinvent government" led to the passage of the U.S. Government Performance and Results Act (1993), which required federal agencies to demonstrate precisely what they intend to accomplish with federal funds and then to report the extent to which intended results were achieved. State governments are also starting to "fund for results."

The United Way led the nonprofit movement toward outcome-based evaluations when, in 1995, it radically changed the way it evaluated its applicant programs. Previously, it asked if a program was well conceived. After 1995, it asked what a program's outcomes were, focusing on benefits or changes to individuals or populations after participating in program activities. Instead of asking how many students took the reading course provided by a literacy program, it asked how many students learned to read.

More private foundations, such as the W.K. Kellogg Foundation, followed suit, requiring outcome measurements of their grantees. This was a significant change. Before this, if we measured results at all, we usually observed and reported programs and activities but not the effects of those activities on our constituents. We counted heads but did not often attempt to measure changes in skills, knowledge, or attitudes. (See the resource list for United Way and Kellogg Foundation publications on evaluation.)

Three Kinds of Evaluation

Evaluation specialist Michael Sikes has summarized three broad kinds of evaluation: needs assessments, process evaluation, and outcome evaluation. (See Figure 1.) This chapter focuses on outcome evaluation because it is the prevailing paradigm in nonprofit funding.

Evaluation Terminology

Much of the mystery of evaluation relates to its terminology. Common words have specific meanings in evaluation and many similar terms have subtly distinctive differences. To complicate matters, evaluators sometimes disagree on what the words mean. If you consult another reference on evaluation, you may find different models and terminology.

Outcome. An *outcome* is a specific result that can be attributed to a program. Most evaluators insist that an outcome should describe specific benefits to program participants. The United Way says that "outcomes are benefits for participants during or after their involvement with a program. Outcomes may relate to knowledge, skills, attitude, values, behavior, condition, or status."

> **Short-term outcomes** are the immediate effects of your program. (Nearly all participants said they learned more than they had expected.)
>
> **Intermediate outcomes** are effects that linger over time. (Six months after the program, the majority of participants were using what they learned in their work.)
>
> **Long-term outcomes** are lasting impacts of your program. (Participants have incorporated what they learned into improved performance.)

Objective. Planners usually use the term *objective* to describe an *intended outcome.* An outcome is an achieved objective. These terms are virtually equivalent, although planners use *objective* to describe desired future results and evaluators use *outcome* to describe either future or actual results.

Activity. Programs are made of activities. You produce concerts or exhibitions, present performers, or send artists into schools or community centers to achieve various outcomes.

Purpose	Kind of Evaluation	Key Questions
Designing programs	Needs assessments and feasibility studies	Whom should the program serve? What are their needs? How can these needs be met?
Keeping programs on track	Process evaluation or program monitoring	Is the program being implemented as planned? What are its interim effects? What should be changed to improve the program?
Measuring results	Outcome evaluation	What is the impact of the program? Has it met its goals?

Figure 1: Evaluation Methods

Output. Outputs are the immediate products of program activities. Some use the term *process outcomes* instead of *outputs* to mean the immediate *results* of activities. To minimize confusion from equivalent terms, this chapter uses *output.*

Think of outputs as the results of activities that do not describe specific benefits or changes to participants. Outputs may be tangible (concert, book, or curriculum), but they are not measures of changed behaviors or environments (which would be outcomes). Evaluations of arts programs report tangible outputs more often than intangible participant outcomes, as these may vary with each audience member. In arts evaluations, outcomes and outputs are often reported without distinction.

> If you think of an outcome as the answer to the question, "What change will this program make in the world?," you can think of *indicators* as "what would you accept as evidence?"
>
> —Lynn Griesemer, University of Massachusetts Donahue Institute

Examples

We produced six concerts, attended by 2,800 people.

We developed a new curriculum guide that relates the museum's collection to the sixth-grade learning standards.

Indicator. Indicators, sometimes called *performance measures,* are measurable evidence that shows the extent to which an intended outcome has been achieved. As outcomes may not be directly observable and often are not measurable, indicators provide indirect evidence. They often are quantifiable so that evaluation results can express the number or percentage of program participants that achieved the intended outcome. Multiple indicators often can be identified for each outcome.

> As you look for indicators, ask yourself, what does the outcome look like when it occurs? How do you know it has happened? What do you see?
>
> —The United Way's *Measuring Program Outcomes*

Examples

We want children participating in the artists' residency program to improve their self esteem. As self-esteem cannot be observed directly, one indicator will be higher scores on the Coopersmith self-esteem test taken after the program compared with scores before the program.

Teachers observe children's changed behavior as reported on a final evaluation form.

Note that while the first indicator in the preceding example is readily quantifiable, the second is less so. With enough time, however, you could ask the teacher to reflect on the behavior of each child and then quantify how many children demonstrated behaviors consistent with higher self-esteem.

The United Way has additional useful definitions.

Outcome targets. These are numerical outcomes for a program's level of achievement on its outcomes.

Benchmarks. These are performance data that are used for comparative purposes, such as comparing results to a similar program or results from this year against last year.

The Logic of Evaluation

In evaluation, we explore a logical chain of expressed intentions, actions consistent with our intentions, and effects of those actions. To understand evaluation, you need to understand this logic. It isn't complicated, but if you don't grasp it you will struggle.

A logic model is simply a graphic representation of the if-then logic of your evaluation: If we implement a new arts-integrated curriculum, then children should learn how to analyze a painting. There are many different, and valid, logic models. The United Way and Kellogg Foundation portray their logic models as a causal chain that starts with resources and concludes with outcomes or impacts. Figure 2 illustrates a simple model. Figure 3 shows a more comprehensive logic model that specifies short-term, mid-term, and long-term outcomes.

Figure 2: Simple Logic Model

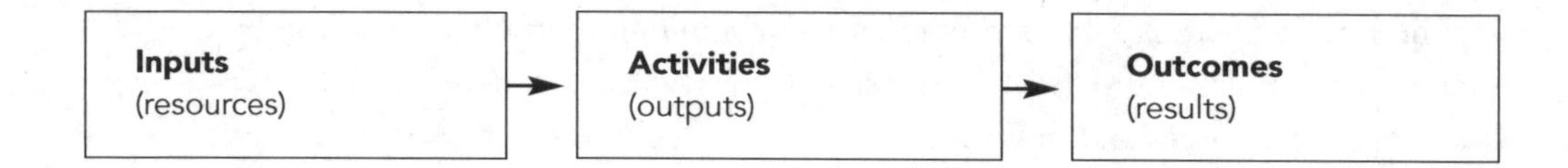

Figure 3: Logic Model

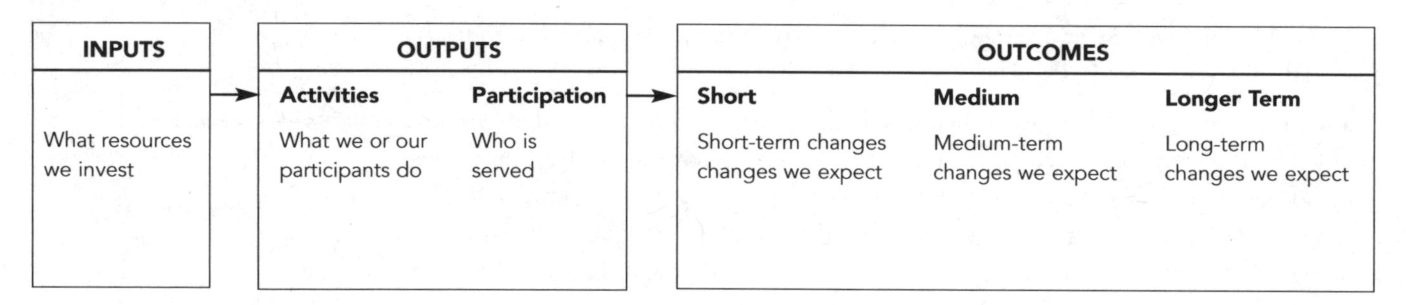

To use the simple logic model in Figure 2, start at the end with the outcomes you wish to achieve, determine what activities will produce those outcomes or results, and then what funding and other resources are required to implement the activities. Your plan should be logical. If you do planned activities, is it logical to expect your anticipated outcomes? Have you allowed for adequate resources to produce the planned activities?

An Outcome-based Program Evaluation Framework

This framework (see Figure 4) illustrates an approach to program evaluation that compares objectives (intended results) to outcomes (actual results). Outcomes should be consistent with and further organizational goals. In deliberately planned programs, the process starts with outlining long-range goals and continues with determining and evaluating short-term outcomes. Goals themselves are not evaluated since they usually

Figure 4: Outcome-based Evaluation Framework

Goals Long-term results (not subject to evaluation)	**Goal Example** Students will get a well-rounded education with arts integrated into the curriculum.
Objectives Intended results (tangible or not) projected in planning to help fulfill a long-term goal	**Objective Example** White and Latino eighth graders will learn improved mutual respect through theater project.
Indicators Predicted evidence that, if observed, will show the extent to which objectives are achieved	**Indicator Examples** 1. Fewer stereotypes will be mentioned in interviews. 2. Teachers will observe improvement in respectful behavior. 3. Fewer disciplinary reports will be filed. 4. Play will demonstrate excellent artistic standards, appropriate to eighth graders.
Program Activities Actions that implement planned arts education program (also called outputs)	**Program Activity Examples** Playwright will work with kids to produce their own play illustrating respect for other cultures.
Evaluation Questions Questions about activities or outcomes to be answered during evaluation	**Evaluation Question Examples** 1. Do kids describe each other with more respect? 2. Do kids demonstrate more respect? 3. Did the play demonstrate artistic merit?
Evaluation Measures Observation of indicators to document outcomes	**Evaluation Measure Examples** 1. Pre- and post-event student interviews 2. Teacher observations and reports 3. Vice principal report 4. Critic reviews 5. Visiting artist observations and reports
Outcomes Actual results that include achieved objectives and unanticipated consequences	**Outcome Examples** 1. Sixty percent of students report fewer stereotyped remarks after production. 2. Teachers report less harassment. 3. Race-based disciplinary actions are down 30 percent. 4. Play demonstrated artistic excellence.

envision very long term results. The best evaluations define indicators at the outset, which will be observed later for evidence that the intended outcomes were met or not. Evaluation can also discover unforeseen outcomes in programs. Work backward through the framework from achieved outcome to defined objectives (or desired outcomes) for the next program. This framework is used for the workbook section of this chapter.

When or How Often to Evaluate a Program

You don't have to measure everything all the time. A program doesn't need continuous scrutiny until something significant in the program, environment, or constituents changes. If conditions do not change dramatically you can use your evaluation results over time to seek funding and plan subsequent programs. You will know when things have changed enough that a re-evaluation is in order.

Apples and Oranges: Outputs and Outcomes in Basic and Applied Art

We might debate endlessly the distinction between art for art's sake and art used to achieve some specific benefit. It is not productive here to compare which of these is more valuable. It does, however, make a difference in how we evaluate.

When we present performances and exhibitions intended to delight or inspire the audience, we are challenged to measure such intrinsic outcomes. Outcome evaluation, as described in the United Way Logic Model, specifies initial, intermediate, and long-term outcomes. Changes, such as increasing understanding or ennobling the spirit, aren't often affected by a single exposure to art, and even if they were, they would be difficult to measure. So we measure how many people we serve and how well they think we serve them. We count heads and ask opinions. Although these short-term measures may be less satisfying than understanding long-term outcomes, they may be good enough to plan and improve our art programs.

In contrast, when we enter the realms of education, social service, juvenile justice, and health education with our art programs, we may be trying to influence readily observable behaviors like learning to read, staying drug-free, or getting a job. In such cases, our evaluations should align more closely with the norms of outcome evaluation. If we say that our poet in the school program will help kids learn to write, or that our AIDS education theater will raise AIDS awareness, then we have to demonstrate results. Schools and health educators have mostly embraced the need to be accountable for outcomes. In arts education or community action programs, we follow stricter standards of accountability. In these cases it is not sufficient to measure outputs. Our funders and partners want to know how many kids improved their reading (outcome), not how many kids studied with our poet (output).

Some program managers may conduct regular participant evaluations and then less frequently do more rigorous external evaluation. The Arts Extension Service asks students of each distance education class to rate their learning experience. Every 18 months it then commissions an external evaluator to do in-depth evaluation research.

Program Monitoring and Documentation

When funders request an evaluation, they sometimes get program documentation instead. This is a valuable function that can inform evaluations, but it does not measure results as does an outcome-based program evaluation.

Program documentation is the reporting of monitored program activities and outputs—what participants did in a program rather than the results. It can capture descriptions of program methods, activities, and tasks through descriptive narratives, anecdotes, testimonials, photographs, and other nontabulated data. Documentation also is important to transfer what has been learned to new partners.

PREPARE FOR THE EVALUATION

Before you start to evaluate a program you must make some decisions. Will you use an outcome-based or another form of evaluation? Who will evaluate? Will you evaluate during or at the conclusion of your project. Who has a stake in the evaluation and how will they be involved? Be clear about who the audience is for the evaluation.

Consider the Feasibility of Evaluating a Program

Evaluator David Karraker starts with an *evaluability assessment*—that is, what is involved in doing this evaluation? Karraker advises that "As you size up the evaluation task, consider what is involved in doing it. You don't want to evaluate a program if it's harder or more expensive to evaluate than to do the program itself! Be clear about the purpose of the evaluation. Ask where information already exists. Consider how easy it is to get and use the information. Do you have to reorganize the data? Would less-straightforward measures work as well? Is there some information that we can get at easily enough, well enough to make competent decisions about the program?"

What can be evaluated? Which of your intended results can be observed, and thus evaluated? In general, evaluate objectives (outcomes), but not goals.

You can plan to achieve profound or simple results. Many of these intentions can be readily evaluated and some cannot. In general, the more tangible the intended result, the more readily it can be observed. Intangible results, such as changed human attitudes, may also be assessed in evaluations. In this case, evidence, such as perceptions, suggesting that intended results have been achieved may be sought through interviews.

The United Way, in its *Measuring Program Outcomes: Training Kit,* offers three tests to determine if you have described outcomes that can be evaluated.

> Is it reasonable to believe the program can influence the outcome in a nontrivial way, even though it can't control it?
>
> Would measurement of the outcome help identify program successes and pinpoint and address problems or shortcomings?
>
> Will the program's various 'publics'—staff, volunteers, participants, collaborating organizations, funders, and the general community—accept this as valid outcome of the program?

For more information on how to assess objectives, read the United Way item, *More Difficult Outcomes to Measure,* found in this chapter's Online Companion (see the last page of this book for Internet address).

Whatever methods of data collection are used, the data collected must meet two conditions to be considered accurate: they must be valid and reliable. Respondents may be tempted to answer questions in ways that they think are expected of them or that does not place them in jeopardy. Evaluators will want to take steps to ensure that they have obtained the most accurate (i.e., valid and reliable) responses they can get. A data collection item (such as a question on a questionnaire) is valid to the degree that it actually measures what it claims to measure.

—U.S. Department of Education *Evaluation Primer*

Why Evaluate?

There are essentially two motivations to evaluate programs.

Evaluate to improve programs. Evaluation results can enable you to design a better program, manage a program, collect information to plan the next program, and provide feedback to program participants (artists, teachers, administrators, students, etc.).

Evaluate to be accountable. Your chief executive, board, program funders, constituents, or program advocates will also be able to see the outcomes of your program in reports written with evaluation results.

Note that the need to present outcome evidence of results and the need to demonstrate persuasive evidence to support advocacy and funding may sometimes be in conflict with each other. You have to be open to learn that you may not have obtained your outcomes. Funders should not (but may) expect that every funded program will work. Innovation entails risks. Learning what did not work through program evaluation is one of the benefits.

To Whom Will You Address Evaluation Results?

An evaluation may serve funders, stakeholders, and partners, in addition to your own interests. Different audiences may want to learn different things from evaluation and

Some Intangible Outcomes

Assume that you are doing an exhibition of contemporary Navajo rug weaving. You hope people will attend, enjoy the show, and learn to better appreciate Navajo culture. To evaluate the exhibition, you have developed two hoped-for outcomes.

Enjoyment. Gallery visitors enjoying the show is a worthy outcome, but difficult to measure. The best way is to ask them. A volunteer could ask visitors to comment in a guest book, hand exiting visitors a short form, or ask a few questions orally. To avoid bias, volunteers should be given a protocol to ask every nth visitor (every tenth for example). (Note that user satisfaction in social service program is not usually considered an outcome.)

Appreciation. For this outcome, it's easy to think of indicators. The question is whether it is feasible to collect the data. One good indicator would be that people score better on a test about the Navajo culture after seeing the exhibition than before. This is pre- and post-testing. It can be quite reliable, but may take more time, money, and visitor patience than you can muster. An alternative indicator is that people say they learned to appreciate the Navajo culture when asked as they exited the exhibition.

value different kinds of evidence. A parents' group may be moved by a compelling anecdote, and a foundation may require experimental test results. Sometimes the same data can be reorganized to respond to the interests of different constituents. Who are the primary audiences for your evaluation? Consider your board of directors, program participants (especially those who helped with the evaluation), funding agencies, public officials, partners and their governing boards, program staff and volunteers, constituents and stakeholders, or the general public.

When Will You Evaluate?

The best evaluations are done while programs are in progress (formative) and at the conclusion (summative).

Formative evaluations, often informal, are undertaken in order to improve programs while there is still an opportunity to affect the outcomes. Program staff or volunteers typically do formative evaluations.

Summative evaluations, often conducted by professional evaluators, tend to be more formal and rigorous and are undertaken in order to observe what outcomes were accomplished. They often are used to demonstrate results to funders or governing boards. They also can be used to improve programs that are reoccurring.

Who Conducts Evaluation? Staff versus Outside Evaluator

Often program managers implement evaluation of their programs. Internal evaluations have the advantages of economy, first-hand knowledge, and expedience. In addition, evaluation skills are cultivated within the organization, and lessons learned can be implemented immediately. A disadvantage is that self-evaluation presents the risk of bias. An evaluation consultant may be perceived by funders and other stakeholders as more reliable and unbiased. This is more costly, but may yield more credible results.

If you choose to work with an outside evaluator, you may need to write a request for proposal (RFP) to define what is to be evaluated and what you want from a consultant.

A Note about Proving Impact

Recognize that your programs are just part of the many forces that act upon your constituents and communities. It is difficult to prove that a program causes a specific result. If low-income kids in your arts education program do better in school, was it your art program that made the difference or was it a parallel supplemental reading program? Even when you can't cite proof that program A caused outcome B, you can say that there is a positive correlation between your program and an observed result. In other words, you ran an arts infusion program for disadvantaged youth and saw their grades, school attendance, and interest in learning go up. Explore alternative explanations for observed results, but if you see the outcome you intended, cite it even if you can't conclusively prove a cause-and-effect relationship.

You don't have to prove that there was no other cause of the improvement. Make your observations even more valid by comparing your outcome with another time or place. What were these kids like before your program and after? How did your group of participating kids compare with a similar group without your arts experience? The first question can be thought of as pre-and postintervention testing. The latter proof is what evaluation researchers call control group experimenting.

We know art does save lives, but can we prove it? You don't have to abandon your higher aspirations nor must you measure every hoped-for outcome. But don't hold yourself accountable to measure your progress on these higher goals. You can aim high for your goals and measure more modest outcomes in your evaluation. Did they enjoy the program and would they come again?

See the AES Online Companion to this chapter for Writing a Request for Proposals for Outside Evaluators (see the last page of this book for Internet address).

Evaluation Budget

Evaluators recommend allowing from ten to 15 percent of your overall program budget for expenses related to evaluation, depending upon the scope and rigor of your intended evaluation plan. If you use outside evaluators, this may be the single largest expense.

PREVIEW OF YOUR EVALUATION PLAN

You may summarize your evaluation plan with a sheet like the one illustrated in Figure 5 for each of your program's goals. Then plan how to collect the data. The illustrated evaluation framework is an example of what you may produce (adapted from a framework developed for the Arts Extension Service by David Karraker and Dyan Wiley).

THE STEPS OF THE EVALUATION PLANNING PROCESS

There are six steps to planning for evaluation.

1. State goals.
2. Write outcomes (tangible and intangible).
3. Write indicators (define kinds of indicators and refine).
4. Assemble the evaluation plan.
5. Define evaluation questions.
6. Assign evaluation tasks.

Figure 5: Evaluation Framework

Goal. Integrate the arts into JFK Middle School curricula.

Intended Outcomes	Indicators	Data Sources	Data Collection Methods
Teachers will learn to develop arts-infused lesson plans.	Plans will have more arts sections than before.	Teacher lesson plans	Meet with teachers and review lesson plans.
Two artists-in-residence will help students learn their local history unit through storytelling.	Scores for participating students on standard tests will be higher compared to similar classes.	Scores of tests designed to measure student learning for this curriculum standard	Gather scores from participating classes and from a comparable group without a residency.
Arts curriculum specialist will be hired by August.	Employment will occur, and a line item for position will be in budget.	Principal and school budget	Call the principal.

These steps are described in greater detail (complete with worksheets and guidelines) in the *Learning Partnerships Evaluation Workbooks.*

IMPLEMENT YOUR EVALUATION

Based on the evaluation plan developed with the aid of materials included in this chapter's Online Companion (see the last page of this book for the Internet address), consider how to implement the plan. The first step of implementation is to collect evaluation data.

Step 1: Collect Evaluation Data

Look for Existing Information

Make evaluation easier—and save time and money—by first identifying existing sources of information, such as those described below. This baseline data can be used to compare your results with the situation before your program existed, or compare your program constituents to a more general population. Program partners—such as schools and social service or health agencies—may also provide a ready source of data on their constituents.

Suggested sources of existing information

Your own records
Attendance
Annual reports
Community assessments done for strategic planning
Previous evaluation reports

Your grant records
Proposals

Interim and final reports
Grant-review panel scores and comments

School partner records
Attendance
Ticket or gallery sales
Scores for standardized tests
Grade averages
Disciplinary actions
Reports of assessments, studies, evaluations, or plans
Demographic reports

Community data
Community assessments done as part of community cultural planning
Census demographic data—available from city or regional planning agencies or library (online source)
Chamber of commerce or economic development agency community assessments and economic data
Health agency, community foundation, United Way, and human service agency community assessments
Various local data maintained by library
Demographic data from local news media
Police reports

Collect New Information

Even if you use existing information, it is likely that you will need more that relates to your specific outcomes. You have at least three options: 1) design experiments; 2) plan to observe directly; or 3) ask questions of participants.

Experimental designs. The use of control groups, longitudinal studies, and other scientific methods that carefully examine cause-and-effect relationships are less common in art program evaluations than in medical research, primarily due to higher personnel costs relative to other forms of evaluation. Experiments are worth considering as they do have the potential to be more rigorous and persuasive, but they must be built in during the early design stages of the program. The challenge is to design an experiment that controls the many variables of cause and effect. For example, how can you be sure that improved tolerance is the result of your theater program or another factor like parental influence?

Here are four experimental designs you might consider using.

Pre- and post-tests. You administer a test before and after your program that measures attitudes, knowledge, or skills related to your intended outcomes. If your tests are accurate, then measured improvements represent positive evidence that you are advancing on your outcomes. Because of its relative simplicity, this may be the most common experimental design for program evaluation.

Portfolio examination. Student visual artwork or writing is gathered and assessed by qualified persons, noting changes in student work throughout the program. The evaluator also may note differences between students participating in the studied program and those not participating. This is a fairly common evaluation method for visual arts programs. It also may be readily applied to writing projects or other programs that produce tangible products that can be observed.

Control group studies compare some aspect of an experimental group with the same aspect in a closely comparable group that does not participate in the program being evaluated. For example, if you were developing health-awareness theater programs for a group of at-risk teens, you would identify another group of teens. Control group arts evaluations are rare as this design requires that you find a control group and measure and compare indicators for both groups.

Control group evaluation designs are simpler if you have access to existing information that may serve as an indicator of outcome achievement. It is relatively simple to determine if your arts program improves school attendance in your experimental school compared to a similar school without your program. Each school will routinely track attendance, which is your indicator.

Longitudinal studies track an experimental group of participants over time. Because some arts program outcomes may only be realized over several years, a longitudinal study might provide the most effective evaluation. For this kind of experiment you would follow a specific group of individuals and measure one or more indicators at specific intervals over time. For arts program evaluations this may be most feasible with contained populations such as a class of school children or residents of a retirement home or correctional facility. Longitudinal studies are relatively rare in the arts because they take so much time and expense.

If you use existing data collected by your partner institution, this evaluation design becomes more feasible than if you must observe or interview your sample over many years.

Observation

It is quite common to employ observation in program evaluation. Most arts managers use observation to monitor whether their programs are working or not. Ironically, this method may be overlooked since it's so obvious. The risk, of course, is that evaluations based on simple observations may not be valid if care isn't taken to maintain rigor and avoid bias. Participants or an outside evaluator may conduct observation, or the program can be observed indirectly by studying its results.

Participant observation. Any knowledgeable program participant can be recruited to help evaluate as an observer. Teachers, artists, or program coordinators who are participating in your program are oriented to the task of systematically recording observations about the effects of the program.

An external funder may be skeptical of an evaluation based on observations by participants who have a stake in finding positive outcomes. To counter this risk and to be effective, you should develop a rubric or other measurement checklist along with a research protocol that prescribes when and how observations are to be recorded.

Outside observation. The observations and documentation of a professional evaluator who monitors the program may be more credible than a participant observer, but also may increase your program expenses.

Indirect observation. You may choose to observe indirectly to save costs, to protect privacy of participants, or to avoid any affects on the program caused by the presence of observers during the program. A portfolio review cited earlier is a kind of indirect observation. You might also employ photo, video, or audio documentation of the process or results of the program. (These can also be advocacy and fundraising tools if the program is successful.) Journal writing is another choice. In this, students or other program participants record their thoughts and observations in personal journals, which are reviewed to answer one or more evaluation questions by knowledgeable persons.

Figure 6: Sample Project Assessment Rubric

Students use a variety of art forms—such as dance, music, theater, and visual arts—to create projects that are appropriate in terms of the dimensions indicated in the left column.

	Not Yet	Almost	Meets Standard	Exceeds Standard
Skill Development	Little evidence of technique appropriate to the intent of the project	Exhibits technique appropriate to the intent of the project, with some weakness	Exhibits technique appropriate to the intent of the project	Meets standard, plus highly sophisticated technique
Making Connections	No commentary on relationship between arts and math	Minimal commentary	Thorough explanation of relationship between math and arts	Meets standard plus additional insight
Reflection and Critique	No evidence of reflection or critique	Some evidence of reflection or critique	Written evidence of reflection and critique	Thorough use of reflection and critique
Approach to Work	No evidence of working through problems or creatively generating ideas	Some evidence of working through problems and creatively generating ideas	Evidence of both working through problems and creatively generating ideas	Meets standard plus extraordinary effort.

Ask Questions

Asking questions and recording answers is another kind of indirect observation. Questioning is perhaps the single most common way to collect new information to evaluate a program. Choices range from oral interviews and group meetings to written evaluation forms and surveys. These can be as simple as a phone conversation with an audience member or as sophisticated as a stratified sample survey.

There are at least four ways you can ask questions. (See the Strategic Planning chapter for more information on asking questions. Many planning methods are useful in program evaluation as well.)

Interviews of individuals (in person or by phone). Interview leaders or other designated spokespeople for groups (president of the neighborhood association), or interview a representative sample of the group itself (a random group of neighbors).

Moderated group discussions. Group discussions—focus groups of participants and expert panels of observers—are more efficient in that one conversation taps the opinions of ten or so people. Group interactions may lead to richer information than single interviews.

Public meetings. Public agencies may be obliged by law to evaluate their programs or overall efforts using facilitated open public forums of parents, neighbors, or other constituents the program intends to impact.

Written questions and answers. Surveys and evaluation forms may be the most efficient way to sample opinions from large numbers of constituents.

For more thorough information on the methods of questioning, please see the Appendix for Methods of Asking Questions: Interviews, Focus Groups, Surveys, and Forms.

Step 2: Analyze Evaluation Data

Evaluation data comes mostly in numbers and words. If your data is primarily numeric, you are doing *quantitative research*. This has historically been considered the most

SAMPLING

We must digress a bit into statistical science. There is a risk when you talk to just a few people from your program that your evaluation may be biased if those people differ in some significant way from others in your program with whom you did not talk. You should understand the distinction between a population and a sample.

If you observe all events or interview everyone who participated in your program under evaluation, evaluation is easier because you are contacting the whole *population* for your program. This makes for a thorough evaluation with no risk for statistical error. But this can be too time consuming, expensive, or unfeasible.

POPULATION

SAMPLE

Most evaluation observes some of the programs or asks questions of some of the participants. The evaluators sample the population of activities and participants. If the sample looks very much like the whole population, conclusions drawn from the small, observed group will be true of the larger group: the evaluation will be free from sampling errors. Errors occur when the observed group differs in some significant way from the larger population. If you only interview people who volunteered to help with evaluation, you risk a sampling error by missing people who are less prone to participate. You minimize the risk of sampling bias by being deliberate about the people you question. This is called sampling. In essence, you pick a sample that is representative of the whole population of beneficiaries of your program.

Sampling methods. It is a highly recommended that you seek professional assistance in sampling.

Random sample. Pull names from a hat or obtain a list of random numbers from a statistics book or computer program and sample the corresponding numbers from your population.

Systematic sample. Select every tenth (or third or whatever) name or event.

Segmented or stratified sample. Group your population into similar clusters (e.g., by age, artists and teachers, etc.) and then select a random or regular-interval sample from each cluster.

Deliberate sample. Intentionally select individuals from the population so that the mix of your sample is representative of the whole population.

credible and is the domain of statistics. If your evaluation data are words or portfolios or anything other than numbers, you are doing *qualitative research*. These labels are misleading in that you can also quantify common elements within qualitative data.

This brief summary should prepare you to seek statistical analysis from your evaluation consultant or friendly college faculty member. As noted below, you can do some simple analysis without statistical training.

Making Sense of Numbers

Reduce the data. To analyze numeric data, you first have to reduce the information into summary form. If you have 150 surveys, evaluation forms, or test scores, you must summarize this information. The low-tech way is to manually count the number of respondents who checked possible boxes and record the results. Tick marks on a blank evaluation form are an easy way to keep track until you type up the summary.

Data entry is made easier, though, by setting up a table on an electronic spreadsheet (Excel, Quattro, Lotus, etc.) and entering the data from each completed form. These programs allow for summing, averages, and simple statistical analysis. For more sophisticated analysis, you may export the finished spreadsheet into a statistical analysis program (SYSTAT, SPSS, etc.). Some analyses, such as cross tabulations, are much simpler with statistical programs.

Display the data. There are many ways to reveal trends or results.

Count responses. (Twelve artists completed evaluation forms. Or 240 kids participated in the program.)

Factor mean or average. (The artists had, on average, 15 years experience. The average residency was ten days.)

Find the median. (While the average was 15 years experience, the median experience of participating artists was ten years.) When there are a few very large or very small numbers in a group, sometimes the median number represents that group better than does the mean. For example, if you have a couple of millionaires in a group, their high incomes will skew the average upward.

Look for patterns. (There were two groups of artists, those with significant teaching experience and those without.)

Note most frequent responses. (Most often, artists reported they learned more than they had expected.)

Do cross tabulations. (Of the six artists who had not previously taught in classrooms, all said they would readily do so again.) Select responses from one variable (new teaching artists) and compare to another variable (willingness to teach again.) This can be done slowly by manual sorting, and is simple with a statistics program.

Perform statistical significance tests. (While students preferred painting to sculpting by a slight margin, the difference was not statistically significant.) If you are asking questions of a sample rather than the whole population, be aware that some differences may be so small that they could be the result of chance. Pollsters describe such differences as within the *margin of error*. This is one area where you'll need the help of someone experienced in statistics. Informal evaluations probably don't need statistical significance testing. However, if you skip this step, be wary of making too much of small differences in your findings, especially if your sample is small. So if 20 percent of your sample said they learned a lot and 24 percent said they learned a little, you may not be able to say with confidence that more learned than didn't. You don't have to worry if you have asked questions of the whole population of program participants. Significance testing only applies to samples within larger populations.

Analyze content. Analyzing content is similar to analyzing numbers. You reduce textual data to summary form, analyze contents of the texts, and report results.

Much of arts program evaluation information is gathered in interviews, focus groups, and from written answers to open-ended questions. The results are expressed in words. Pages of notes may be intimidating, but it is possible to boil these down into a credible summary with content analysis. This analysis will still be subjective, but it is possible to analyze written data with nearly as much rigor as numbers. Just as in numerical analysis, the bulk of text must be reduced, analyzed, and reported to be useful for evaluation. Here is a summary of how to do "content analysis" of texts.

1. Gather the summarized interview or focus group notes or evaluation forms with narrative answers. (First summarize each interview or focus group meeting into a page or two.)
2. Read over the answers to one particular question in all of the evaluation forms or summary notes.
3. Look for patterns as you read and make notes of recurring answers or themes.
4. Make a short list of words or phrases that capture the sense of each recurring answer. Label each of these items with a word, number, or letter to create a code sheet. If several interviewees cited artistic quality as a problem, then "quality" becomes a category, and perhaps "Q" is its code.
5. Read back through the answers again and code similar statements (e.g., every mention of a concern for artistic quality is coded "Q"). Some people use numbers so that "quality" concerns are coded 1, and the next problem, say "funding," is coded 2.
6. Count coded items and note your results.
7. Select typical quotes to make your results more meaningful.
8. Write up your findings, citing numbers and quotes.

Example
Sixteen survey respondents, or 20 percent, noted artistic quality was a big concern. One teacher expressed a typical sentiment, "Even as we strive to improve standard test scores, we can't ignore the quality of the artistic experience. It is the high quality of the arts process that gives this program the power to help kids learn."

Step 3: How to Report Results

Evaluation results must be communicated if they are to do any good. Formal evaluations should be reported in writing.

Evaluations Answer These Questions

What did you intend to achieve with your program?

Were program activities consistent with your intentions?

If so, did you observe the intended outcomes?

What unintended outcomes did you also observe?

How do you account for the variations (observed outcomes from intended objectives)?

What changes should you make in your program based on evaluation?

How likely is it that observed outcomes were caused by your program activities?

How close were your actual outcomes to your intended outcomes?

What were the program's unintended outcomes? You may achieve some positive results or negative consequences that were not part of your plan.

What did you learn from your evaluation that will improve your program or plan new ones?

Questions for Policy Makers

Did this program serve the public interest?

Was this a good use of public funds?

Outline of an Evaluation Report

Cover page

Acknowledgements (funders, partners, program participants, evaluators)

Table of contents

Executive summary

Evaluation methods

Evaluation findings (results of statistical and/or content analysis)

Recommendations

Appendix

- Evaluation questions
- Interview and survey forms
- Copies of program descriptions and materials

It is useful to think of the audience, message, and format. Depending on your intended reader, you may need to organize versions of your report stressing different findings. Your board of directors or funders may want to see that you achieved your outcomes. A school board member may want to see findings about student learning. Your partners also may want to see if and how the program may need to change.

Use evaluation results. Evaluation results can be used to:

- improve programs;
- plan future programs;
- make decisions to cut or add programs;
- allocate resources among competing programs;
- be accountable to stakeholders and others about what was achieved and its impact;
- provide solid information for advocacy and fundraising; and
- improve program or organizational marketing.

CONCLUSION

Evaluation is becoming an expectation. You may have read this chapter because someone has required you to evaluate, you want the results to help you run better programs, or you want credible evidence for programs that are working well.

If evaluation shows that your programs are not having the impact you intended, the evidence gives information to help fix what is not working. You may either improve the programs or design new ones.

Evaluator David Karraker has said, "Evaluation can make you feel better about your work, in that you can be grounded and clear in what you intend to do and actually do.

Even when things don't work as you hoped, you know where you stand. Better find that out before you spend more time and energy doing more of what doesn't work. Then you can develop some strategies to improve it. Clarity is better than ambiguity."

REFERENCES

David Karraker contributed copy for this chapter.

Sikes, M. E. (2002, March). *Arts Education Managers Self-Assessment Final Report.* Arts Education Leadership Initiative. Washington, DC: National Assembly of State Arts Agencies.

U.S. Department of Education. (2003). *Evaluation Primer: Ensuring Evaluations Yield Valid and Reliable Findings.* Retrieved at www.ed.gov/offices/OUS/PES/primer6.html

United Way of America, (1996). *Measuring Program Outcomes: A Practical Approach.* Alexandria, VA: United Way of America.

United Way of America. (1996). *Measuring Program Outcomes: Training Kit.* Alexandria, VA: United Way of America.

W.K. Kellogg Foundation. (1998). *W.K. Kellogg Foundation Evaluation Handbook.* Retrieved at www.wkkf.org

W.K. Kellogg Foundation (2004). *Logic Model Development Guide.* Retrieved at www.wkkf.org

APPENDIX

METHODS OF ASKING QUESTIONS: INTERVIEWS, FOCUS GROUPS, SURVEY, AND FORMS

This section provides information relevant and referred to in the Strategic Planning, Marketing, and Community Organizing chapters.

Interviews

Most people have experience with interviews, so this is the easiest way to ask questions. Yet, for credible evaluation results, approach interviews with care. First, determine your sample. Who will you interview individually or in a focus group?

Next, determine the questions you will ask. Ordinarily you will ask simple, conversational questions at the outset and work toward more challenging questions. Start with factual questions to get the conversation going: Please tell me what the program looks like? Then ask tougher questions: What worked well? What could have been improved?

For consistency, set up an interview form that lists your questions. It may provide a space to summarize answers or just prompt you as you take notes on your note pad. If you take extensive notes, summarize key points on the interview form. This is particularly important if more than one person will be interviewing. You might add prompting questions that you can use if your interviewee is reticent. For example, given the question, What could be improved?, some interviewees will go on at length about problems with the program. Others may need prompting questions: Knowing what you know now, what might you have done differently? or Where were the problems?

For the most accuracy, tape or video record, transcribe, and then summarize. This is more time consuming and expensive than just taking notes during the interview, but it is more accurate. Research has documented that interviewers tend to hear what they expect and disregard contrary information. An alternative to recording is to have two notetakers who then compare for common understanding.

Set up interviews

1. Determine sample of participants to interview.
2. Schedule interviews.
3. Develop an interview guide of evaluation questions.
4. Ask your questions.
   a. Explain why you are asking questions and what will be done with the information.
   b. Promise anonymity (and keep that trust!).
   c. Ask for permission to take notes or record conversation.
   d. Ask and/or observe and record demographic questions (i.e., age, gender, race).

Interview Guide

PROGRAM

INTERVIEWEE

INTERVIEWER

DATE OF INTERVIEW

Hi, I'm [name] from [organization]. I understand you took part in the [program name].

I'm asking questions of a few participants to help us learn how well the program worked and how we can make it better. Would you have a few minutes to talk? Thanks. (If not, schedule a later time).

I'll report what you say but won't report who said it. OK?

Question 1: [list question]:

Question 2: [list question]:

Question 3: [list question]:

e. Start with simple descriptive inquiries (what did you make?) and move toward more subtle questions (how did you feel?).

f. Thank interviewee.

Listen carefully, and probe as needed to clarify answers or elicit more details. When the interview is over, summarize your notes.

Focus Groups and Other Moderated Discussions
Plan focus groups like group interviews, and have someone moderate. Focus groups may be more efficient than interviews and yield productive interactions among participants—one person's comments may stimulate others to contribute related ideas—in a way that can't happen with a single interviewee. In some settings, however, individuals may be more cautious and less candid in group discussions, particularly when people of differing rank or social status within a hierarchical organization meet together.

Set up focus groups

1. Select a representative sample.
2. Set a date and place, and allow from 60 to 90 minutes.
3. Invite enough people to have about eight to ten in the discussion.
4. Offer an incentive to participate (food is good).
5. Develop a short list of questions (could be your interview guide).
6. Moderate the discussion.
7. Take notes and/or record discussion.
8. Summarize results.

Public meetings. You can plan a public meeting much as you would a focus group. One critical difference is that you will have little idea how many people will show up. Unless the program being evaluated is very compelling, you may find your audience is small. It is helpful to invite some key people to be assured of a core group at the hearing.

One variation for strategic planning is a focus forum. This combines a focus group with a public meeting. A small group of panelists are invited and asked to respond to a set of evaluation or planning questions. The forum opens with a conversation among the prepared panelists and then the moderator invites the audience to participate in the latter half of the discussion. Any public meeting requires a skilled moderator and a recorder.

Asking Questions in Writing

Your evaluation questions should ask if your intentions have been realized. One way to do this is to state your intended objectives, the outcomes you seek to measure, and ask to what extent these have been realized. This is quite clear and direct and works with open-ended and fixed-response questions. This direct approach does risk that people will say what they think you want to hear. You may also miss some unintended consequences. A less directed approach is to ask people to simply describe what resulted from their experience with your program. This has less risk of bias, but requires open-ended questions and may generate lots of information unrelated to your intentions.

Evaluation forms. You can collect much data from evaluation forms. Think of these as written interviews. Unlike interviews, however, you cannot clarify questions or probe for deeper answers. The evaluation form must be short, simple, and clear.

An evaluation form can have two kinds of questions: open-ended questions that request a narrative answer, and fixed-response questions for which the respondent checks a box or circles their choice among a number of prepared answers. Please see the Strategic Planning chapter for examples of open-ended and fixed-response questions.

Open-ended questions allow for more discovery as answers are not predicted. Participant answers may be rich with emotion and nuance, and respond to questions you didn't think to answer. Remember as you write your questions to ask about outcomes that you hoped to achieve.

Example

How did this exhibition affect your knowledge and appreciation of local artists?

Fixed-response questions are much easier to analyze. Be very clear with the question and anticipate likely, unambiguous answers.

Example

Did this exhibition help you get to know and better appreciate our local artists?

☐ Yes, very much, ☐ Yes, a little, ☐ No, not very much, ☐ No, not at all

Fixed-response questions are not subtle. In the above example, visitors who already knew quite a bit about local artists may not find an answer that matches their experience. You might anticipate this by inviting comments. If you ask the wrong question, your answers may not be meaningful.

Fixed response questions should allow for a range of possible answers along a scale. A four-point scale is common. Avoid an odd number because it allows for a neutral middle choice. You want people to be decisive. An exception is questions about which a respondent might not have enough information to answer. Then add a "Don't know" response.

A good evaluation form includes both kinds of questions to combine the flexibility of narrative answers and the expedience and economy of fixed responses.

Evaluation forms are often handed out to participants at the conclusion of a program. Instructions can be repeated orally and the evaluator can answer questions about the evaluation form. Because they are often administered within the program itself, evaluation forms must be very concise, as time will be limited.

See the Online Companion for a sample Program Evaluation Form. (See the last page of this book for the Internet address.)

Surveys. Surveys are used to distribute evaluation forms to large groups of people, usually by mail, email, or on a website. (For more information, see the Appendix for the Strategic Planning chapter.)

Mailed surveys. Surveys are typically mailed to program participants. A survey package may include an outside envelope, a brief note explaining why the survey is important, the survey instrument itself, and a return addressed envelope. Some surveys are designed as self-mailers to reduce costs. Stamped or business reply envelopes will yield a higher rate of return. Alternatively, surveys can be inserted into newsletters or other correspondence.

Online surveys. You can reduce costs with electronic surveys. The obvious risk is that people without email or Internet access will be excluded. Electronic surveys can be a simple text document distributed by email to a group of program participants or to a listserv. As text emails have limited formatting options, you may rely on simple narrative questions rather than trying to devise a way for respondents to check boxes.

There are commercial and free versions of Web-based surveys. The best of these lead you through a process to design fixed-response, scaled answers, fill-in-the blank entries, and open-ended questions. Once designed, send the email announcement to your list. Recipients of your email message are asked to open a website where they can answer questions and submit answers online. You need not do any data entry. These e-survey applications also summarize responses and allow you to import raw data into a spreadsheet, word processor, or statistical program to do further analysis. Search an online browser for "online survey." At the time this is written, Americans for the Arts, WebMonkey, and Survey Suite offer good online survey tools.

Surveys are complicated enough that you should seek professional help. Evaluation consultants, marketing or social science faculty, graduate students, or planners could help with your survey.

Implementing a Survey

1. Select a sample that represents the population (random, systematic, or deliberate).
2. Design the questionnaire.
3. Test the questionnaire on a small sample and correct any ambiguous questions.
4. Print and distribute.
   a Keep survey to one page.
   b. Send with brief cover memo that explains why you need their involvement and requests response.
   c. Enclose self-addressed return envelope. (A stamp improves response.)
5. Send reminders (if you want a good return).
6. Collect surveys.
7. Code open-ended questions (see Analyze Content in this chapter).
8. Enter survey responses into a computer spreadsheet or statistical analysis program (or summarize responses by counting various responses with tick marks on a blank survey form).
9. Make sense of results (statistical analysis of numbers and content analysis of texts).
10. Summarize and write report of findings.

References

Chapter 2—Arts and the Economy: Fueling the Creative Engine

Borrup, T., & Partners for Livable Communities. (2005). *Creative Community Builder's Handbook.* St. Paul, MN: Fieldstone Alliance (formerly Wilder Publishing).

Dreeszen, C. (1997). *The Community Cultural Development Planning Handbook: A Guide for Community Leaders.* Washington, DC: Americans for the Arts.

Florida, R. (2002). *The Rise of the Creative Class.* New York: Basic Books.

Fukuyama, F. (1995). *Trust: The Social Virtues and the Creation of Prosperity.* New York: Free Press.

Grams, D., & Warr, M. (2003). *Leveraging Assets: How Small Budget Arts Activities Benefit Neighborhoods.* Chicago: Richard H. Driehaus Foundation and John D. and Catherine T. MacArthur Foundation.

Gratz, R. (1998). *Cities Back From the Edge.* New York: Preservation Press.

Gratz, R. (1994). *The Living City: How America's Cities are Being Revitalized by Thinking Small in a Big Way.* Washington, DC: Preservation Press.

Hawkes, J. (2004). *The Fourth Pillar of Sustainability: Culture's Essential Role in Public Planning.* Victoria, Australia: Humanities.com.

Huntington, S. P., & Harrison, L. E. (2000). *Culture Matters.* New York: Basic Books.

Jackson, M. (2003). *Investing in Creativity: A Study of the Support Structure for U.S. Artists.* Retrieved January 11, 2006, from http://www.usartistsreport.org/docs/ pdf/comprehensivereport.pdf

Jackson, M. & Herranz Jr., J. (2002). *Culture Counts in Community: A Framework for Measurement.* Washington, DC: Urban Institute.

Jacobs, J. (1984). *Cities and the Wealth of Nations.* New York: Vintage Books.

Jacobs, J. (1961). *The Death and Life of Great American Cities.* New York: Vintage Books.

Madden, K., & Kent, F. (2000). *How to Turn a Place Around.* New York: Project for Public Spaces.

Markusen, A., & King, D. (2003). *The Artistic Dividend.* Minneapolis, MN: University of Minnesota.

Plater-Zyberk, E., Duany, A., & Speck, J. (2000). *Suburban Nation.* New York: North Point Press.

Putnam, R. (2000). *Bowling Alone.* New York: Touchstone.

Putnam, R., & Feldstein, L. (2003). *Better Together.* New York: Simon and Schuster.

Rosenfeld, S. (2004). *Crafting a New Rural Development Strategy.* Economic Development America. Washington, DC: U.S. Department of Commerce Economic Development Administration.

Stern, M. J. (2003). *Performing Miracles.* New York: Center for an Urban Future.

Walker, C., Jackson, M., & Rosenstein, C. (2003). *Culture and Commerce, Traditional Arts in Economic Development.* Washington, DC: Urban Institute and the Fund for Folk Culture.

Whyte, W. H. (1980). *The Social Life of Small Urban Places.* Washington, DC: The Conservation Foundation.

Chapter 4—Strategic Planning

Allison, M., & Kaye, J. (2005). *Strategic Planning for Nonprofit Organizations* (2nd ed.). Hoboken, NJ: John Wiley & Sons.

Barry, B. W. (1997). *Strategic Planning Workbook for Nonprofit Organizations.* St. Paul, MN: Amherst Wilder Foundation.

Bryson, J. M. (2004). *Strategic Planning for Public and Nonprofit Organizations* (3rd ed.). San Francisco and Oxford: Jossey Bass.

Bryson, J. M., & Alston, F. K. (2004). *Creating and Implementing Your Strategic Plan: A Workbook for Public and Nonprofit Organizations* (2nd ed.). San Francisco: Jossey-Bass.

Dreeszen, C. (1998). *Community Cultural Planning Handbook: A Guide to Community Leaders.* Washington, DC: Americans for the Arts.

Dreeszen, C. (2001). *Learning Partnerships: Planning and Evaluation Workbooks and Online Help for Arts and Education Collaborations.* Amherst, MA: Arts Extension Service.

Dreeszen, C. (1999). *Who's On First? Resolving Problems of Implementation in Public-sector Planning.* Retrieved January 18, 2006, from http://www.nea.gov/resources/Lessons/ Dreeszen2.html

Dreeszen, C., Aprill, A., & Deasy, R. (1999). *Learning Partnerships: Improving Learning in Schools with Arts Partners in the Community.* Washington, DC: Arts Education Partnership.

Drucker, P. F. (1992). *Managing the Nonprofit Organization: Principles and Practices.* New York: Collins.

Mintzberg, H. (1987). *Crafting Strategy. The Harvard Business Review,* (July/August, 66).

Mintzberg, H. (1994). *The Rise and Fall of Strategic Planning.* New York: Free Press.

Mintzberg, H., Ahlstrand, B., & Lampel, J. (2005). *Strategy Bites Back: It is far more and less, than you ever imagined.* Upper Saddle River, NJ: Pearson Prentice Hall.

National Endowment for the Arts. (1985). *Surveying Your Arts Audience.* Washington, DC: Author.

Schwartz, P. (1991). *The Art of the Long View: Planning for the Future in an Uncertain World.* New York: Currency DoubleDay.

Senge, P. (1990). *The Fifth Discipline: The Art and Practice of the Learning Organization.* New York: Doubleday.

Stevens, L. K. (1987). *Community Cultural Planning Work Kit: Conducting a Community Cultural Assessment.* Amherst, MA: Arts Extension Service.

Stevens, L. K. (1990). *Community Cultural Planning Work Kit: Developing a Strategic Cultural Plan.* Amherst, MA: Arts Extension Service.

Stevens, L. K. (1990). In B. Schaffer Bacon, C. Dreeszen & K. Krieger (Eds.), *Developing a Strategic Cultural Plan: A Work Kit.* Amherst, MA: Arts Extension Service.

Warshawski, M., Barsdate, K. J., & Katz, J. (2000). *A State Arts Agency Strategic Planning Tool Kit.* Washington, DC: National Assembly of State Arts Agencies, National Endowment for the Arts, Arts Extension Service.

Wolf, T. (1999). *Managing a Nonprofit Organization in the Twenty-first Century.* New York: Free Press.

Chapter 5—Board Development

BoardSource. (2005). *The Source: Twelve Principles of Governance That Power Exceptional Boards.* Washington, DC: Author.

Bridges, W. (2003). *Managing Transitions: Making the Most of Change* (2nd ed.). Cambridge, MA: Da Capo Press.

Carver, J. (1997). *Boards That Make a Difference: A New Design for Leadership in Nonprofit and Public Organizations.* San Francisco: Jossey-Bass.

Chait, R. P., Ryan, W. P., & Taylor, B. E. (2005). *Governance as Leadership: Reframing the Work of Nonprofit Boards.* Hoboken, NJ: John Wiley & Sons.

Drucker, P. F. (1992). *Managing the Nonprofit Organization: Principles and Practices.* New York: Collins.

Fisher, R., & Ury, W. (1983). *Getting to Yes: Negotiating Agreement Without Giving In.* New York, NY: Penguin Books.

Huges, S. (1999). *To Go Forward, Retreat! The Board Retreat Handbook.* Washington, DC: BoardSource.

Wolf, T. (1999). *Managing a Nonprofit Organization in the Twenty-first Century.* New York: Free Press.

Chapter 6—The Art of Fundraising

Altman, M., & Caddy, J. (1994). *A Handbook for Rural Arts Collaborations.* St. Paul, MN: COMPAS.

Altman, M., & Caddy, J. (1994). *Rural Arts Collaborations: The Experience of Artists in Minnesota Schools and Communities.* St. Paul, MN: COMPAS.

American Association of Fundraising Counsel. (2002). *Giving USA.* Indianapolis, IN: AAFRC Trust for Philanthropy.

Art in Public Places, City of Minneapolis. (2001). *East Harriet Farmstead Neighborhood Criteria.* Minneapolis, MN: City of Minneapolis.

The Chronicle of Philanthropy: The Newspaper of the Nonprofit World. Retrieved January 19, 2006, from http://www.philanthropy.com/free/archive.htm.

COMPAS. (1999). *The Creative Current: Rural Arts as a Community Building Strategy* (1999). St. Paul, MN: Author.

Dove, K. E. (2000). *Conducting a Successful Capital Campaign.* San Francisco: Jossey-Bass.

Dove, K. E., Lindauer, J. A., & Madvig, C. P. (2001). *Conducting a Successful Annual Giving Program.* San Francisco: Jossey-Bass.

Dove, K. E., Spears, A. M., & Herbert, T. W. (2002). *Conducting a Successful Major Gifts and Planned Giving Program: A Comprehensive Guide and Resource.* San Francisco: Jossey-Bass.

Dreeszen, C. (1999). *Community Cultural Planning: Handbook for Community Leaders.* Washington, DC: Americans for the Arts.

Gingold, D. (1993). *Strategic Philanthropy in the 1990s: Handbook of Corporate Development Strategies for Nonprofit Managers.* Washington, DC: Diane Gingold and Associates.

Greenfield, J. M. (2002). *Fundraising Fundamentals: A Guide to Annual Giving for Professionals and Volunteers.* San Francisco: Jossey-Bass.

Hodiak, D., & Ryan, J. S. (2001). *Hidden Assets: Revolutionize Your Development Program with a Volunteer-driven Approach.* San Francisco: Jossey-Bass.

Jordan, R. R., & Quynn, K. L. (2002). *Planned Giving for Small Nonprofits.* San Francisco: Jossey-Bass.

Legon, R. D. (1997). *The Board's Role in Fund Raising.* Washington, DC: Association of Governing Boards of Colleges and Universities.

Minnesota Rural Arts Initiative. (1999). *Role of the Network Consultant.* St. Paul, MN: COMPAS.

Mixer, J. R. (1993). *Principles of Professional Fundraising: Useful Foundations for Successful Practice.* San Francisco: Jossey-Bass.

Prince, R. A., & Prince, K. M. (2001). *The Seven Faces of Philanthropy: A New Approach to Cultivating Major Donors.* San Francisco: Jossey-Bass.

Rosso, H. A. (1998). *Rosso on Fund Raising: Lessons From a Master's Lifetime Experience.* San Francisco: Jossey-Bass.

Schladweiler, K. (Ed.) (1999). *Foundation Fundamentals: A Guide to Grantseekers.* New York: Foundation Center.

Schoff, F. (Ed.) (2001). *The Foundation Center's Guide to Grantseeking on the Web.* New York: Foundation Center.

Seiler, T.L. (Ed.). (2003). *The Excellence in Fund Raising Workbook Series Set.* New York: Jossey-Bass.

Seltzer, M. (2001). *Securing Your Organization's Future: A Complete Guide to Fundraising Strategies.* New York: The Foundation Center.

Seymour, H. J. (1996). *Designs for Fund-Raising.* Columbus, OH: McGraw-Hill.

Winter, M., & Ray, K. L. (1992). *Collaboration Handbook: Creating, Sustaining, and Enjoying the Journey.* St. Paul, MN: Amherst H. Wilder Foundation.

Wolf, T. (1999). *Managing a Nonprofit Organization in the Twenty-first Century.* New York: Free Press.

Chapter 8—Personnel Management

Bridges, W. (2003). *Managing Transitions: Making the Most of Change* (2nd ed.). Cambridge, MA: Da Capo Press.

Cone Weaver, C. (1993). *Let's Get Personnel: A Handbook for Arts Organizations.* Raleigh, NC: North Carolina Arts Council.

Pierson, J., & Mintz, J. (1999). *Assessment of the Chief Executive: A Tool for Governing Boards and Chief Executives of Nonprofit Organizations.* Washington, DC: BoardSource.

Roosa, A. M., & Chin, P. L. (2002). *The AAM Guide to Writing an Employee Handbook.* Washington, DC: American Association of Museums.

Chapter 11—Program Development

American Association of Museums. (2002). *A Museums & Community Toolkit.* (2002). Washington, DC: Author.

American Composers Forum. *Continental Harmony Community Toolkit.* Retrieved May 15, 2006, from http://www.pbs.org/harmony/toolkit/index.html

Cleveland, W. (1992). *Art in Other Places: Artists at Work in America's Community and Social Institutions.* New York: Praeger.

Dreeszen, C. (1992). *Learning Partnerships Workshop and Planning Workbook.* Arts Extension Service. Retrieved May 15, 2006, from http://www.umass.edu/aes/ learningpartners/index.htm

Falk, J. H., & Dierking, J.D. (1992). *The Museum Experience.* Washington, DC: Whalesback Books.

Freeman, R., & Martinovich, P. (2001). *The Evolution of an Exhibit: Community Museums and Traveling Exhibits.* Toronto, Ontario: Ontario Museum Association.

Golden, J. (1980). *On the Dotted Line: The Anatomy of a Contract.* Syracuse, NY: Cultural Resources Council of Syracuse and Onondaga County.

Goldstein, B. (2005). *Public Art by the Book.* Washington, DC: Americans for the Arts in association with University of Washington Press.

Graves, J. B. (2005). *Cultural Democracy: The Arts, Community & the Public Purpose.* Chicago: University of Illinois Press.

Hillman, G. (1996). *Artists in the Community: Training Artists to Work in Alternative Settings.* Washington, DC: Americans for the Arts.

Katz, J., (Ed.). (1992). *Presenting, Touring and the State Arts Agencies.* Washington, DC: National Assembly of State Arts Agencies.

Klein, D. (2003). *Artists & Communities: America Creates for the Millennium.* Warshawski, M. (Ed.). Baltimore, MD: Mid Atlantic Arts Foundation and the National Endowment for the Arts.

Korza, P., & Atlas, C. (Eds.). (2005) *Critical Perspectives: Writings on Art and Civic Dialogue.* Washington, DC: Americans for the Arts.

Korza, P., Schaffer Bacon, B., & Assaf, A. (2005). *Civic Dialogue, Arts & Culture: Findings from Animating Democracy.* Washington, DC: Americans for the Arts.

Korza, P., & Schaffer Bacon, B. (Eds.). (2005) *Cultural Perspectives in Civic Dialogue: Case Studies from Animating Democracy.* Washington, DC: Americans for the Arts.

Leinhardt, G., Crowley, K., & Knutson, K. (2002). *Learning Conversations in Museums.* Mahwah, NJ: Lawrence Erlbaum Associates.

McCarthy, K., Brooks, A., Lowell, J., & Zakaras, L. (2001). *The Performing Arts in a New Era.* Santa Monica, CA: RAND Corporation.

McCarthy, K., & Jinnet, K. (2001). *A New Framework for Building Participation in the Arts.* Santa Monica, CA: RAND Corporation.

McCarthy, K., Ondaatje, E.H., Zakaras, L., & Brooks, A. (2005). *Gifts of the Muse: Reframing the Debate about the Benefits of the Arts.* Santa Monica, CA: RAND Corporation.

McDaniel, N., & Thorn, G. (1997). *Learning Audiences: Adult Arts Participation and the Learning Consciousness.* Washington, DC: The John F. Kennedy Center for the Performing Arts and the Association of Performing Arts Presenters.

Shagan, R. (1996). *Booking and Tour Management for the Performing Arts.* New York: Allworth Press.

Spitz, J. A., & Thom, M. (2003). *Urban Network : Museums Embracing Communities.* Chicago: Field Museum of Natural History.

Stoudt, C. (2005). *Stages of Transformation: Collaborations of the National Theatre Artist Residency Program.* New York: Theater Communications Group.

Talboys, G. K. (2006). *Museum Educator's Handbook.* Ashgate Publishing.

Wilson, J., & Udall, L. (1982). *Folk Festivals: A Handbook for Organization and Management.* Knoxville, TN: University of Tennessee Press.

Wolf, T. (2000). *Presenting Performances.* Washington, DC: Association of Performing Arts Presenters.

Chapter 12—Marketing

Andreasen, A. & Kotler P. (2002). *Strategic Marketing for Nonprofit Organizations* (6th ed.). Englewood Cliffs, NJ: Prentice-Hall.

Cady, P. C. & Hinand, M. (2001). *Increasing Cultural Participation: An Audience Development Planning Handbook for Presenters, Producers and Their Collaborators.* Retrieved from http://www.wallacefoundation.org/WF/KnowledgeCenter/KnowledgeTopics/ArtsParticipation/IncreasingCulturalParticipation.htm

Carr, E. (2004). *Sign-Up for Culture: The Arts Marketer's Guide to Building an Effective E-mail List.* New York: Patron Publishing.

Carr, E. (2003). *Wired for Culture: How E-mail is Revolutionizing Arts Marketing.* New York: Patron Publishing.

Gladwell, M. (2005). *Blink: The Power of Thinking Without Thinking* (1st ed.). New York: Little, Brown and Company.

Gladwell, M. (2002). *The Tipping Point: How Little Things Can Make A Big Difference* (2nd ed.). New York: Little, Brown and Company.

Grossnickle, J., & Raskin, O. (2001). *The Handbook of Online Marketing Research: Knowing Your Customer Using the Net.* New York: McGraw-Hill, Inc.

Kotler, P., & Scheff, J. (1997). *Standing Room Only: Strategies for Marketing the Performing Arts.* Boston: Harvard Buisiness School Press.

McCarthy, K., Brooks, A., Lowell, J., & Zakaras, L. (2001). *The Performing Arts in a New Era.* Retrieved from http://www.rand.org/pubs/monograph_reports/MR1367/

McCarthy, K., & Jinnett. K. (2001). *A New Framework for Building Participation in the Arts.* Retrieved from http://www.rand.org/pubs/monograph_reports/MR1323/ index.html

McCarthy, K., & Ondaatje, E. H. (2002). *From Celluloid to Cyberspace: The Media Arts and the Changing Arts World.* Retrieved from http://www.rand.org/pubs/ monograph_reports/MR1552/

McCarthy, K., Ondaatje, E. H., Brooks, A., & Szántó, A. (2005). *A Portrait of the Visual Arts: Meeting the Challenges of a New Era.* Retrieved from http://www.rand.org/pubs/ monographs/MG290/

McCarthy, K. F., Ondaatje, E. H., & Zakaras, L. (2001). *Guide to the Literature on Participation in the Arts.* Retrieved June 16, 2006 from http://www.rand.org/pubs/drafts/ DRU2308/index.html

Mohammed, R. (2005). *The Art of Pricing: How to Find the Hidden Profits to Grow Your Business.* New York: Random House.

Pue, L. M. (ed.). (2002). *Guide to Marketing the Arts in Your Non-Profit Organization.* Retrieved from http://www.nyfa.org/files_uploaded/NYFAMarketingGuide.pdf

Simone, K. (1997). *Building Audiences: Stories from America's Theaters—How Theaters Deal with Change in Building, Diversifying Audiences.* R. MacPherson & B. S. Trachtenberg (Eds.). Retrieved from http://www.wallacefoundation.org/WF/KnowledgeCenter/KnowledgeTopics/ArtsParticipation/ChangeinAudiences.htm

Sweeney, S. (2005). *101 Ways to Promote Your Web Site* (5th ed.). Gulf Breeze, FL: Maximum Press.

Urban Institue. (2002). *Subscriber Survey Training Manual and Procedures for Local Member Organizations.* Retrieved from http://www.operaamerica.org/about/parc/ PDFs/Manual.pdf

Walker, C. (2002). *Arts & Culture: Community Connections.* Retrieved from http://www.wallacefoundation.org/WF/KnowledgeCenter/KnowledgeTopics/ArtsParticipation/CommunityConnections.htm

Online Resources

Arts Marketing.org. http://www.artsmarketing.org/

Arts Marketing Institute. http://cac.ca.gov/ami/resources/resources.cfm

Increasing Cultural Participation Bibliography [Data file]. Available from Massachusetts Cultural Council website, http://www.massculturalcouncil.org/issues/ participation_biblio.html

Performing Arts Research Coalition. http://www.operaamerica.org/about/parc/ parc.html

Museums and the Web 2004. http://www.archimuse.com/mw2004/index.html

Vitality of Cultural Life Research Index. Available from John S. and James L. Knight Foundation website, http://www.knightfdn.org/default.asp?story=research/ cultural/index.asp

Chapter 13—Cultural Access

Design for Accessibility: An Arts Administrator's Guide. (1994). Washington, DC: National Assembly of State Arts Agencies and National Endowment for the Arts.

Everyone's Welcome: Universal Access in Museums. (1996). Washington, DC: American Association of Museums.

Hillman, G. (1996). *Artists in the Community: Training Artists to Work in Alternative Settings.* Washington, DC: Americans for the Arts.

Hillman, G. (1999). *Arts Programs for Juvenile Offenders in Detention and Corrections: A Guide to Promising Practices.* Washington, DC: National Endowment for the Arts.

Jenson, S. (2001). *Access, Activism and Art. American Theatre,* 18. New York: Theatre Communications Group.

Katz, E., & Ludins-Katz, F. (1987). *Freedom to Create.* Richmond, CA: National Institute of Art & Disabilities.

Katz, E., & Ludins-Katz, F. (1990). *Art and Disabilities.* Cambridge, MA: Brookline Books.

Lesser, A. (2001). *Beyond Access to Opportunity: A Guide to Planning a Universal Environment for the Arts.* New York: New York State Council on the Arts.

National Age Discrimination and National Bureau for Accessibility (2000). *Access for All Ages!* Utnect, Netherlands: Author.

Ostroff, E. (2002). *Beyond ADA to Universal Design.* St. Petersburg, FL: Arts Extension Service program.

Ostroff, E. (2002). *Designing for the 21st Century.* St. Petersburg, FL: VSA arts of Florida Universal Design Regional Workshop.

Palmer, J., & Nash, F. (1991). *The Hospital Arts Handbook.* Durham, NC: Duke University Medical Center.

Perlstein, S., & Bliss, J. (1994). *Generating Community: Intergenerational Partnerships Through the Expressive Arts.* Brooklyn, NY: Elders Share the Arts.

Proudhon, P.J. (1994). *What is Property: An Inquiry into the Principle of Right and Government.* Cambridge, MA: Cambridge University Press.

Sanoff, H. (1999). *Community Participation Methods in Design and Planning.* New York: Wiley, John & Sons, Inc.

Sarkissian, W. (1994). *The Community Participation Handbook: Resources for Public Involvement in the Planning Process.* Murdoch, WA: Institute for Science and Technology Policy, Murdoch University in association with Impacts Press.

Sherman, A., & Mill Street Loft. (1996). Arts Participation: A Greying America. *The Arts and Older Americans Monographs,* 5. New York: Americans for the Arts.

Story, M. F., Mueller, J. L., & Mace, R. (1998). *Universal Design File.* Raleigh, NC: The Center for Universal Design.

Sutton, S., & Kemp, S. (2002, March). Children as Partners in Neighborhood Placemakings: Lessons from International Design Charettes. *Journal of Environmental Psychology*, 22 (1-2), 171-189. Elsevier B.V.

Sutton, S., & FAIA, (2002). *Designing A Great Public Theatre Where All Can Perform Their Part.* Tallahassee, FL: Florida A & M University.

Thader, B., Chapple, J., & Osco, C.E. (1998). *Strategies for Inclusive Classroom Environments.* Washington, DC: VSA arts.

Chapter 14—Arts Education

Americans for the Arts. (1998). *YouthARTS Tool Kit.* Retrieved from http://www.americansforthearts.org/youtharts/about/

Arts Education Partnership. (2002). *Critical Links: Learning in the Arts and Student Academic and Social Development.* Retrieved from http://aep arts.org/PDF%20Files/ CriticalLinks.pdf

Arts Education Partnership (Producer). (1996). *The Arts and Children: A Success Story* [Video tape]. (Available from National Assembly of State Arts Agencies, 202-347-6352)

Consortium of National Arts Education Associations. (1994). *National Standards for Arts Education.* Retrieved from http://artsedge.kennedy-center.org/teach/standards/

Carr, J., & Silverstein, L. (n.d.). *Artists as Educators: Becoming Effective Workshop Leaders for Teachers.* Washington, DC: The John F. Kennedy Center for the Performing Arts Partners in Education.

Dreeszen C., Aprill A., & Deasy R. (1999). *Learning Partnerships: Improving Learning in Schools with Arts Partners in the Community.* Washington, DC: Arts Education Partnership.

Gaffney, K. (with Eaves, C., & Hulteen, C.). (2004). *Chrysalis: Professional Development for Artists in Education.* Black Bear Books and Artsgenesis, Inc.

The John F. Kennedy Center for the Performing Arts and the Kennedy Center Alliance for Arts Education Network. (2000). *A Community Audit for Arts Education: Better Schools, Better Skills, Better Communities.* Retrieved from http://www.kennedy-center.org/education/kcaaen/resources/CAudit6-9.pdf

The John F. Kennedy Center for the Performing Arts Partners in Education. (n.d.). *Giving Cues: Recommended Guidelines for Writing and Designing Performance Materials for Young People.* Washington, DC: Author.

Katz, J. (Ed.). (1988). *Arts and Education Handbook: A Guide to Productive Collaborations.* Washington, DC: National Assembly of State Arts Agencies.

Kennedy Center Alliance for Arts Education Network and Kennedy Center Partners in Education. (2000). *Arts Beyond the School Day: Extending the Power.* Retrieved from http://www.kennedy-center.org/education/kcaaen/resources/afterschool.pdf

Longley, L. (Ed.). (1999). *Gaining the Arts Advantage: Lessons from School Districts that Value Arts Education.* President's Committee on the Arts and Humanities and Arts Education Partnership, 1999. Retrieved from http://www.ecs.org/

Remer J. (1996). *Beyond Enrichment: Building Effective Arts Partnerships with Schools and Your Community.* Washington, DC: Americans for the Arts.

Remer J. (1990). *Changing Schools through the Arts: How to Build on the Power of an Idea.* Washington, DC: Americans for the Arts.

Spector H. (2001). *Arts Programs: Positive Alternatives for At-risk Youth.* Washington, DC: Americans for the Arts.

Welch, N., & Fisher, P. (1995). *Working Relationships: The Arts, Education and Community Development.* Washington, DC: Americans for the Arts and the Institute for Community Development and the Arts.

Wolf, T. (Ed.). (1983). *The Arts Go to School: An Arts-in-Education Handbook.* Washington, DC: Americans for the Arts.

Chapter 15—Program Evaluation

American Evaluation Association. See online resource section with links to evaluation how-to manuals. www.eval.org

Barsdate, K. (1996). *A State Arts Agency Performance Measurement Toolkit.* Washington, DC: National Assembly of State Arts Agencies.

Berk, R. A., & Ross, P. H. (1999). *Thinking about Program Evaluation 2.* Sage Publications.

Bond, S., Boyd, S., & Rapp, K. (1997). *Taking Stock: A Practical Guide to Evaluating Your Own Programs.* Chapel Hill, NC: Horizon Research.

Boulmetis, J., & Dutwin, P. (2000). *ABC's of Evaluation: Timeless Techniques for Program and Project Managers.* San Francisco: Jossey-Bass.

Cleveland, W. (2005). *Making Exact Change: How U.S. arts-based programs have made a significant and sustained impact on their communities.* Community Arts Network.

National Arts Stabilization. (2000, Fall). *Measuring Joy: Evaluation in the Arts* (No. 5).

Sikes, M. E. (2002, March). *Arts Education Managers Self-Assessment Final Report.* Arts Education Leadership Initiative. Washington, DC: National Assembly of State Arts Agencies.

Stecher, B.M., & Davis, W.A. (1987). *How to Focus an Evaluation.* Newbury Park, CA: Sage Publications.

U.S. Department of Education. (2003). *Evaluation Primer: Ensuring Evaluations Yield Valid and Reliable Findings.* Retrieved from www.ed.gov/offices/OUS/PES/primer6.html

United Way of America, (1996). *Measuring Program Outcomes: A Practical Approach.* Alexandria, VA: United Way of America.

United Way of America. (1996). *Measuring Program Outcomes: Training Kit.* Alexandria, VA: United Way of America.

W.K. Kellogg Foundation. (1998). *W.K. Kellogg Foundation Evaluation Handbook.* Retrieved at http://www.wkkf.org/

W.K. Kellogg Foundation (2004). *Logic Model Development Guide.* Retrieved at http://www.wkkf.org/

Contributors

Mary Altman has worked for over 20 years in the fields of public art, community art, and art education as an administrator, organizer, instructor, volunteer, and consultant. She has worked with arts groups across Minnesota and in several states on collaboration, cultural planning, artist training, rural arts development, budgeting, fundraising, and evaluation. Mary is currently the public arts administrator for the City of Minneapolis. Her publications include *A Handbook for Rural Arts Collaborations* (COMPAS 1993), as well as the chapter on community arts organizing for *Fundamentals of Arts Management* (Arts Extension Service 2006). Through a 1999 Leadership Initiatives in Neighborhoods fellowship from The St. Paul Companies, she studied cultural planning and community development models.

Barbara Schaffer Bacon codirects Animating Democracy at Americans for the Arts. Coauthor of *Civic Dialogue, Arts & Culture: Findings from Animating Democracy*, Barbara has written, edited, and contributed to several publications, including *The Cultural Planning Work Kit* and *Fundamentals of Local Arts Management.* She served for 13 years as executive director of the Arts Extension Service at the University of Massachusetts at Amherst. Consulting work includes program design and evaluation and arts management education for state and local arts agencies and private foundations nationally. Projects include a five-year plan for the New York State Council on the Arts, a twenty-year review of the North Carolina Arts Council's Grassroots Arts Program, and cultural plans for Northampton, Massachusetts and Rapid City, South Dakota. A University of Massachusetts graduate, Barbara is a board member of the Fund for Women Artists and the New WORLD Theater. She is also president of the Arts Extension Institute, Inc. and chairs her local school committee.

Tom Borrup has been a leader and innovator in nonprofit cultural and community development work for over 25 years. Based in Minneapolis, Tom consults with foundations, nonprofits, and public agencies across the United States. He has written many articles for publications in the arts, city planning, and philanthropy. His book, *The Creative Community Builders' Handbook*, was published in 2006 by Fieldstone Alliance. It tracks communities that have transformed themselves through the arts, and includes a how-to guide. In 2002, Tom was a Fellow in the Knight Program in Community Building at the University of Miami School of Architecture. As executive director of Intermedia Arts in Minneapolis from 1980 until 2002, he developed a nationally recognized cross-disciplinary, cross-cultural organization in a diverse urban community. Tom has served on many boards—including the Jerome Foundation, the National Alliance for Media Arts and Culture, and Appalshop— as well as funding and policy panels, for numerous funding institutions. He teaches for the Graduate Program in Arts Administration at Saint Mary's University of Minnesota, and for the Institute for Arts Management at the University of Massachusetts. He received his B.A. in Liberal Arts and M.A. in Communications and Public Policy from Goddard College.

Denise Boston-Moore, Ph.D., is an educator, consultant, and expressive arts specialist. She earned her Ph.D. in counseling psychology from Walden University, M.A. in psychology from Goddard College, and a B.F.A. in theater at the North Carolina School of the Arts. Boston-Moore specializes in play therapy, expressive movement, and mixed media. She has conducted numerous workshops and training programs for parents and professionals, as well as rites of passage adolescent training programs for urban youth.

Amy Brannock is a facilitator and consultant in the fields of arts management and nonprofit management. She specializes in facilitating meetings and retreats, guiding strategic planning, board and staff development, arts in education, and cultural tourism and community arts development. Her clients have included local arts agencies and schools in North Carolina, the National Endowment for the Arts, the Society for the Arts in Healthcare, ARTS North Carolina, and the North Carolina Theatre Conference. Formerly she was the director of Arts Carolina at the University of North Carolina at Chapel Hill (UNC-Chapel Hill). Amy was the North Carolina Arts Council's first arts and tourism director and served as the director of the Arts in Communities Program. In the late 1980's she was executive director of the Arts Council of the Lower Cape Fear following a stint as an arts in education program specialist and arts administration fellow at the National Endowment for the Arts. In her early career, Amy taught public school choral music. She holds a M.A. in Public Management from Carnegie Mellon University, a B.F.A. in Music Education from UNC-Chapel Hill, and is a candidate for a M.S.W. from UNC-Chapel Hill.

Maren Brown has over 20 years of experience in the field of arts management, primarily in museums (art, history, and science museums) and higher education. She received both her graduate (M.B.A.) and undergraduate degrees (B.A., arts management and women's studies) from the University of Massachusetts Amherst. She is a practicing egg tempera painter, and currently serves as the director of the Arts Extension Service (AES) at the University of Massachusetts at Amherst. During her career, Maren has directed an arts agency (funding organization) and a museum school, originated a family program series, developed school tours, curated an exhibition series of regional artists, and served a variety of other functions in museums. She is the founder of the Western Massachusetts Arts Alliance and serves on the Massachusetts Department of Education Arts Education Advisory Board and as a trustee on the Plan for Progress (a regional planning board).

Christine D. Burdett is an administrator, consultant, and educator in the nonprofit sector. She is development director at the Center for Children and Families in Norman, Oklahoma. Tina is also an instructor in the Master of Arts in Arts Administration program at Goucher College in Baltimore where she teaches the distance learning course Financial Management of the Arts. Tina's background in the arts includes community arts development with local arts agencies, statewide assemblies, and national service organizations.

Dorothy Chen-Courtin, Ph.D., is an independent marketing and management consultant for nonprofit organizations. With a background in both the for-profit and nonprofit sectors, she adapts best practices from the for-profit sector in her work with nonprofits. Her clients include national and regional foundations, state art commissions and art councils, as well as performing and visual arts organizations and museums. A frequent speaker on management and marketing issues nationwide, Dorothy is also a regular contributor of articles on the subject. She developed the arts marketing module for the distance learning course on arts management for the Arts Extension Service. She is a board member of the Arts Extension Institute, The Bostonian Society, Fruitlands Museums, and the Herald Tribune World Youth Forum Association. A Barnard College graduate, Dorothy earned a Ph.D. in oriental art history from Columbia and an M.B.A. from Northeastern.

Craig Dreeszen, Ph.D., directs Dreeszen & Associates, a consulting firm in Northampton, Massachusetts. Craig provides planning, evaluation, teaching, facilitation, and research for nonprofits, foundations, and public agencies. He is an educator, consultant, and writer who works nationally with arts and other community organizations on organizational development and strategic planning, collaborative planning, program evaluation, and community cultural planning. Craig earned his Ph.D. in planning and his M.ED. in organizational development at the University of Massachusetts Amherst. He is author of books, articles, and courses on planning, board development, arts education collaborations, and program evaluation. Craig directed the Arts Extension Service for 12 years.

Maryo Gard of Gunnison, Colorado, provides an array of services to the nonprofit world in general, and the community arts world in particular, through keynote speaking, writing, consulting, training, and teaching. Her specialty is community development and the arts—the linking of the arts to the furthering of broader community ends. She is especially interested in the history of community arts development, and increasingly her work focuses on this history and its implications for community arts workers today. Maryo began her 35-year community arts career working in The Arts and the Small Community project in rural Wisconsin—the first rural arts award ever made by the National Endowment for the Arts. She has worked for community arts councils in Connecticut, and for state arts agencies in Illinois and Colorado. She currently serves on her local arts center and community foundation boards, among others. Recent honors include the 2004 Arts Advocate of the Year award from the Gunnison Arts Center; the 2003 Arts Are the Heart award for service to the arts in Colorado; and, in 2001, an honorary doctor of humane letters degree from Goucher College. Maryo received the Selina Roberts Ottum Award from Americans for the Arts—its highest award for community arts development—in 1995.

Gay Powell Hanna, Ph.D., is the executive director of the Society for the Arts in Healthcare (SAH), an interdisciplinary membership organization dedicated to the integration of the arts into healthcare. Designated by the National Endowment for the Arts as a lead agency, SAH provides professional development, consultancies, grants, and awards to seed and sustain arts programs in various healthcare settings. Through faculty positions at Florida State University and University of South Florida from 1987 to 2002, Gay directed VSA arts of Florida, providing arts education programs for people with disabilities, including people with chronic illness. In 2001, she established the Florida Center for Creative Aging at the Florida Policy Exchange Center on Aging at the University of South Florida. A contributing author to numerous articles and books, Gay is noted for her expertise in accessibility and universal design. In addition, she is a practicing artist who maintains an active studio with work in private and corporate collections through the Southeastern United States. Gay holds a Ph. D. in arts education with a specialization in arts administration from Florida State University; a M.F.A. in sculpture from the University of Georgia; and a B.A. in studio art from Old Dominion University.

Dan Hunter is the executive director of the Massachusetts Advocates for the Arts, Sciences, and Humanities, a statewide advocacy and education group. An award-winning playwright, songwriter, and humorist, Dan also has 17 years' experience in politics and arts advocacy, serving as director of the Iowa Department of Cultural Affairs (a cabinet appointment requiring Senate confirmation) and running a successful advertising and political consultancy firm in Des Moines, Iowa. Dan is the author of two books, *Let's Keep Des Moines a Private Joke* and *The Search for Iowa (& We Don't Grow Potatoes).* He has written several plays, including *Un Tango en La Noche*, winner of a Kennedy Center Short Play Award, and *The Monkey King*, a finalist for the 2004 Heideman Award from the Actors Theatre of Louisville. He has performed a one-man show of topical humor in original song and has made numerous radio and television appearances (ABC's *Good Morning America*, National Public Radio, BBC, and CNN *Nightly News*). Dan earned his B.A. from Hampshire College, his M.A. in creative writing from Boston University, and an honorary doctor of humane letters from Goucher College.

Lisa Kammel is an arts consultant with an M.A. in arts administration from Florida State University. After completing her graduate degree, she spent four years working in North Carolina at the United Arts Council of Raleigh and Wake County and the Southeastern Center for Contemporary Art in Winston-Salem. Lisa returned to Florida where she worked with Arts for a Complete Education, with the VSA arts of Florida as a fundraising consultant and program coordinator for Putting Creativity to Work, and as a program specialist in the School Choice Office at the Florida Department of Education on research and public outreach with charter schools.

Norton J. Kiritz was the founder and president of the Grantsmanship Center. In 1971, he left his position as director of planning for Los Angeles County's anti-poverty agency to establish the Grantsmanship Center. His goal was to help community groups, nonprofit organizations, and public agencies that hoped to start programs or keep them alive, but lacked the know-how to make the potential benefits clear to donors. In the next three decades, Norton built the Center into the world's best-known training center for fund development and nonprofit program planning. In 2000, the California Community Foundation described his text, *Program Planning and Proposal Writing*, as "the proposal writer's bible." As president of the Grantsmanship Center and publisher of the organization's quarterly magazine—which has a circulation of more than 200,000 nonprofit and government agencies worldwide—Norton influenced the careers of nonprofit executives and the field at large. Norton passed away in 2006.

Pam Korza is codirector of Animating Democracy, a program of Americans for the Arts which fosters arts and humanities activity that encourages civic dialogue and engagement on contemporary issues. She is coauthor of *Civic Dialogue, Arts & Culture: Findings from Animating Democracy*, and coeditor of *Critical Perspectives: Writings on Art & Civic Dialogue*, and the five-book case study series, *Art & Civic Engagement.* Pam worked with the Arts Extension Service (AES) for 17 years. There she coordinated the National Public Art Policy Project in cooperation with the Visual Arts Program of the National Endowment for the Arts, which culminated in the book *Going Public: A field guide to developments in art in public places*, which she cowrote and edited. She directed the Boston-based New England Film and Video Festival, a regional independent film festival, and the New England Artists Festival and Showcase. As an independent consultant, her activities have included organizational assessment for a children's picture book museum initiated by internationally renowned book artist Eric Carle, evaluation of a citywide arts festival and published report commissioned by the Indianapolis Arts Council and the Lilly Endowment Inc., planning with the Maine Arts Commission for expanded artist services, and consultation with individual artists.

Halsey M. North and **Alice H. North** jointly head The North Group Inc. Since 1987, they have been assisting nonprofit arts agencies, theaters, performing arts centers, and arts service organizations with fundraising feasibility studies, capital and endowment campaigns, annual operating campaigns, solicitor training, strategic planning, board development and retreats, cultural planning, organizational assessments, business plans, and workshops on fundraising, board development, and planning. Halsey is the former executive director of the North Carolina Arts Council, the Charlotte Arts & Science Council, and New York City's Cultural Council Foundation. He has also been vice president of C.W. Shaver & Company and corporate contributions manager of Philip Morris Companies. Alice is a former investment banker. Halsey and Alice are both M.B.A.s and, between them, have received the Distinguished Service Award from the North Carolina Association of Arts Councils, the Chairman's Award from the National Assembly of Local Arts Agencies (now Americans for the Arts), and the Fan Taylor Award from the Association of Performing Arts Presenters.

David O'Fallon is president of MacPhail Center for Music in Minneapolis, Minnesota, one of the largest community music education centers in the nation. Previously, he served as executive director of the Perpich Center for Arts Education, a unique state agency in Minnesota housing the State Arts High School, the Professional Development Institute, and a research program. Prior to the Perpich Center, David served as the education director for the National Endowment for the Arts and as a senior staff member at The John F. Kennedy Center for the Performing Arts. He also helped initiate the Arts Education Partnership, consulted with educational and arts organizations across the United States (from small rural nonprofits to large national and multinational organizations), and consulted with the Leonard Bernstein family on the Bernstein Institute for Education through the Arts in Nashville, Tennessee. David serves on the boards of the American Composer's Forum and the Alliance of Young Artists & Writers, Scholastic Art Awards for Scholastic, Inc.

Stan Rosenberg is a 1977 graduate of the University of Massachusetts, Amherst, where he majored in arts management and community development. As a student, he founded the Arts Extension Service, an arts service organization dedicated to encouraging the use of the arts as a tool for social change and leadership development among artists and arts organizations. Stan has served in the Massachusetts legislature since 1987, first as a state representative and, since 1991, as a state senator. Among the Senate positions he has held are member, Committee on Education, Arts and Humanities, and leadership posts including assistant majority leader and president pro tempore of the State Senate. He has been the author and chief legislative strategist for a number of pieces of arts legislation, including an endowment incentive program, annual appropriations battles, and the recently approved cultural facilities program, a $500 million public private partnership to improve cultural facilities throughout the Commonwealth of Massachusetts. Stan has continued to serve as an arts consultant specializing in board retreats, strategic planning, and arts advocacy.

Shirley Sneve is director of radio and television at Native American Public Telecommunications (NAPT), where she directs the television production fund and the AIROS Radio Network. NAPT supports the creation, promotion, and distribution of Native public media. She moved to Nebraska from Amherst, Massachusetts, where she was director of the Arts Extension Service from 2001 to 2004. A member of the Rosebud Sioux Tribe in South Dakota, Shirley was a founder of Northern Plains Tribal Arts Juried Show and Market, the Oyate Trail cultural tourism byway, and the Alliance of Tribal Tourism Advocates. She has been the director of the Washington Pavilion of Arts and Science Visual Arts Center in Sioux Falls, assistant director of the South Dakota Arts Council, and minority affairs producer for South Dakota Public Broadcasting. Shirley has been adjunct professor in Native American Studies at Augustana College and the University of Sioux Falls, and a community cultural planning consultant. She is a graduate of South Dakota State University. Graduate work at the Universities of South Dakota and Massachusetts focused on management, community building, and the arts. Shirley serves on the boards of the Arts Extension Institute and The Association of American Cultures (TAAC).

Marete Wester, M.S., is director of arts policy information at Americans for the Arts. Previously, she was an arts management writer and consultant, and served as executive director of Dance New Jersey. While at Dance New Jersey, she instituted the first strategic planning and fundraising efforts aimed at building organizational capacity for web-based marketing and technical assistance services. She tripled the organization's membership by positioning Dance New Jersey as the state affiliate of the National Dance Education Organization, uniting dance educators with professional companies and artists under one umbrella. She serves as adjunct professor for arts administration in Seton Hall University's Graduate Department of Public and Healthcare Administration, and as an online instructor for the Arts Extension Service. In addition to authoring the chapter on arts education in *Fundamentals of Arts Management* (2006), she has written several monographs published by Americans for the Arts. Marete has been executive director of the Alliance for Arts Education/New Jersey, acting program specialist for presenting organizations at the National Endowment for the Arts, and associate director of program operations at the Staten Island Council on the Arts. She holds a B.A. of music performance degree from Wilkes University, Pennsylvania, and an M.A. in arts administration from Drexel University.

Sally Zinno was a consultant who worked with leaders of arts and cultural organizations and their funders to strengthen governance, management effectiveness, and financial results. She was a senior associate with National Arts Strategies (formerly National Arts Stabilization), where she directed the Columbus, Ohio, stabilization project. Before starting her consulting practice, she directed the administrative and financial operations at the Delaware Art Museum and the Harvard University Art Museums, and was the chief administrative officer at the Boston Museum of Science. She taught graduate courses in nonprofit administration and finance at Harvard, George Washington, and Tufts Universities. Sally passed away in 2005.

About the Arts Extension Service

The Arts Extension Service (AES) develops the arts in communities and community through the arts with professional education for arts managers, artists, and civic leaders.

AES achieves this through the following programs and services:

Courses

The Arts Extension Service's award-winning classes, workshops, and training programs are designed to meet the needs of artists, arts managers, and individuals interested in hands-on art experiences. A pioneer in online education, AES translated its *Fundamentals of Arts Management* text into a comprehensive series of Web-based courses that can be taken towards a Certificate in Arts Management. Training workshops for artists interested in learning business skills are also available from AES, as are noncredit courses in a variety of art forms.

Conferences

The Arts Extension Service annually presents its popular Summer Institute in Arts Management, an event held each June in Amherst, MA. Additional conferences are sponsored by regional and state agencies in other parts of the country. Each conference is designed to meet the varying needs of community arts professionals and volunteers, ranging from Fundamentals of Arts Management tracks for emerging leaders to *Beyond the Basics* sessions for those who have more experience in the field.

Consulting

Through a network of independent consultants, the Arts Extension Service offers an array of services for the field, including its Peer Advising Network Training Program. The program, offered throughout the United States in response to the increasing need for management assistance services of those with limited financial resources, trains members of the community arts field to provide management, program consulting, and training to their peers in community arts organizations.

Publications

AES publications provide practical information and tools for arts management and community cultural enhancement. AES has developed a variety of publications of value to arts administrators, educators, students, economic development specialists, artists, municipal officers, cultural advocates, regional and urban planners, civic leaders, tourism officials, and human service organizations. These highly practical books are written by working practitioners in the field who have a wealth of experience to share.

Special Projects

The field of community arts is in a state of constant flux and change, and the Arts Extension Service is constantly developing new programs that respond to the most urgent developments in the field. Its Peripheral Vision: A New Look at Communities program is aimed at developing curricula, training programs, and publications to help community leaders use the arts to revitalize their communities.

A

D

E

F

Q

T

U

V

To access the Online Companions to various *Fundamentals* chapters, please go to www.umass.edu/aes/fundamentals.